TRIBUTES FROM OUR PAST PROOFERS

It is incredible. It really needs to be published and circulated.

    Ted Shropshire
    Bixby, Oklahoma

Since reading this blending of the four Gospels and getting so much out of it, I would rather keep reading it in this format, than to read all four Gospels separately.

    David Willey
    Christian Attorney
    Toledo, Ohio

I am most impressed with the readability of the book. You have done an admirable job.

    Pastor Patrick J. Donadio
    Eagle River, Alaska

I am gaining quite a workable knowledge of the New Testament. Having all of Christ's words in bold print is an important addition. It calls us to the central figure of the Gospel—Christ Himself.

    Gary W. Eichhorn
    Christ Lutheran Church
    Charlotte, North Carolina

This book is going to touch a lot of people with a multitude of blessings, I have hoped for quite some time that a book like this would one day reach the marketplace. This volume seems perfect, especially since the quotes are chronologically arranged. I firmly believe you will bless many people with this book.

    George Francis Maida
    Christian Film Distributors
    New Hyde Park, New York

The influence of the Holy Spirit in this project is very obvious. It is being done as unto the Lord and will therefore be used by Him in many and good ways.

    Pastor Bob Swanger
    Columbus, Ohio

Truly this concept of gathering the four Gospels into a single narrative has made it come alive.

    Terry D. Worth
    Sister Bay, Wisconsin

I really like your format. I feel this is an excellent way to reach the unsaved, and the saved, with the Gospel.

    Bill Feltner
    Reno, Nevada

It helped to make "Easter" come alive quite vividly. I could actually feel my own presence at the various scenes.

> Josephine Whatley
> Toledo, Ohio

It was and is a labor of love—I have been disciplined by it and learned much. May He continue to bless you as you seek to bring His Word to all who will read it.

> Roy Schaetzel
> Attorney and Counselor
> Elmhurst, Illinois

It is a most worthwile project and may many people be benefited by it. May Christ be exalted and glorified, and many souls be won to the Kingdom of God through it all.

> Rev. Paul D. Plumb
> Birmingham, Alabama

I believe that God is going to richly bless your efforts because it is only seeking to glorify Him, and His Son, our Lord.

> Rev. Ralph C. Link
> St. Paul's United Church of Christ
> Butler, Pennsylvania

Since I am a believer, each time I read through the pages I felt the Spirit of the Lord. But I was also very aware that this will be great to give to the non-believer. The word of God is powerful. Your captions are a great help.

> Sharon Shock
> Defiance, Ohio

This book has helped me to spend more time with the Gospels, to analyze them and to gain a richer understanding of Christ's purpose on earth. I think it is good for both those who have not heard the Gospel message and those who have also been believers for a long time.

> Alida A. Raker
> Muskegon Heights, Michigan

I felt it to be very smooth and clear. Your headings and annotations were to the point and clarifying. I received a feeling of having covered everything that I do not get from reading the Gospels separately.

> Rusty Zeigler
> Midway, Kentucky

Once I get into it, I find it spiritually awakening.

> Connie Conlon
> Windsor, Ontario, Canada

DIRECT QUOTES
FROM JESUS

A MERGING OF THE FOUR GOSPELS OF
MATTHEW, MARK, LUKE AND JOHN
INTO AN ACCURATE CHRONOLOGICAL ORDER

THIS BOOK CAN ADD BILLIONS
OF YEARS TO YOUR LIFE

COMPILED, CLARIFIED AND AMPLIFIED
BY
Paul L. LaLiberté

…the word which ye hear is not Mine, but the Father's who sent Me.
Jn 14:24

Copyright © 2012 by Paul L. LaLiberté

DIRECT QUOTES FROM JESUS
by Paul L. LaLiberté

Printed in the United States of America

ISBN 9781622303045

All rights reserved solely by the author. The author guarantees all contents are original and do not infringe upon the legal rights of any other person or work. No part of this book may be reproduced in any form without the permission of the author. The views expressed in this book are not necessarily those of the publisher.

All Bible verses quoted herein are from the World English Bible, which is in the public domain. It is available on the internet and can be accessed by searching for the World English Bible.

This W.E.B. is a modern English translation based on the American Standard Version (ASV), which is also in the public domain, and is occasionally quoted herein.

At times the King James Version (KJV) has been used to more accurately state the message of the original Greek.

Any of the captions and commentaries in this book may be quoted in sermons, in written form, and in critical reviews. Also, it would be preferred that any of our commentaries not be shared on any radio, or television broadcast, so as not to pre-empt the preachers in the pulpit, nor Bible study leaders.

The picture of Jesus on the front cover is with compliments of Abingdon Press @ 1961, and is used by permission.

www.xulonpress.com

DEDICATED TO THE HONOR AND THE GLORY OF

GOD, THE FATHER,

GOD, THE SON, AND

GOD, THE HOLY SPIRIT

ACKNOWLEDGMENTS

I must give credit to my personal secretary of 44 years, Anna Phalen, who has been most faithful and dedicated.

To my very dear friend of sixty years, Patrick B. Conlon, whose persistence led me to keep myriad notes on 3x5 cards which proved most valuable in the assembling of this book.

To my brother, Gerard, who spent an entire year doing a yeoman's job of cutting and pasting from the various translations.

To my Amish-Mennonite friend, Lowell Yoder, who once told me that it is all right to read your Bible while on the potty. This "library time" has greatly advanced the completion of this book.

And to my wife and most loyal and devoted supporter, Barbara, who also proofed the manuscript in its entirety over and over again, upgrading it constantly.

TABLE OF CONTENTS

TRIBUTES FROM OUR PAST PROOFERS i

DEDICATION v

ACKNOWLEDGMENTS vii

A BRIEF INTRODUCTION xi

PREFACE xiv

PROLOGUE xv

CHAPTER I	THE BIRTH OF JESUS	17
CHAPTER II	JOHN THE BAPTIST IDENTIFIES THE MESSIAH	31
CHAPTER III	HIS FIRST MIRACLE AND HEALINGS	38
CHAPTER IV	THE DISCIPLES ARE CALLED	51
CHAPTER V	THE SERMON ON THE MOUNT	65
CHAPTER VI	HIS GROWING FAME	79
CHAPTER VII	TEACHING IN PARABLES	90
CHAPTER VIII	THE APOSTLES ARE SENT OUT	104
CHAPTER IX	JESUS CONFRONTS THE PHARISEES	119
CHAPTER X	HIS MAJESTY REVEALED	129
CHAPTER XI	JESUS IS GOD'S RIGHTFUL EMISSARY	139
CHAPTER XII	THE COMMITMENT TO THE CROSS	155
CHAPTER XIII	JESUS DENOUNCES THE PHARISEES	162
CHAPTER XIV	HIS SEARCH FOR THE LOST	177
CHAPTER XV	FIRST PREDICTIONS OF THE END	191
CHAPTER XVI	HIS ROYAL ENTRY INTO JERUSALEM	205
CHAPTER XVII	THE OLIVET DISCOURSE	221

THE POST-TRIBULATION RAPTURE CLARIFIED 241

ADDENDUM 242

A BRIEF END-TIMES SUMMARY 243

CHAPTER XVIII	CONTINUING CAUTIONARY ADVICE	244
CHAPTER XIX	THE LAST SUPPER	260
CHAPTER XX	HIS FAREWELL ADDRESS	272
CHAPTER XXI	HIS AGONY AND TRIALS	281
CHAPTER XXII	HIS CRUCIFIXION AND DEATH	297
CHAPTER XXIII	HIS RESURRECTION AND APPEARANCES	305

EPILOGUE 323

WHAT NOW? 324

PERSONAL OBSERVATIONS 325

OVERCOMERS 326

DIRECT WORDS OF PRAISE 327

ABOUT THE AUTHOR 328

TO ORDER MORE BOOKS 329

A BRIEF INTRODUCTION

What is offered in this book, is the entirety of the 3,767 verses from the four Gospels, leaving nothing out except an obvious duplication.

This is a treasury of the life of Jesus and His teachings, in some 23 chapters and numerous explanatory captions.

Every meaningful passage in this harmony of the gospels is preceded by a heading which paraphrases, and in an expository form, states what each segment is about.

This is intended to help a new Christian to better understand what each section is about, the first time he reads it.

Hopefully, this attempt at simplifying and magnifying the Word of the Lord will help even the very learned, to comprehend pertinent and insightful information, not previously perceived or caught.

All clarifying remarks in italics (and in parenthesis) are the author's own comments, which the reader is free to accept, or reject.

It may prove beneficial to have your own Bible handy to read alongside this book. There may be times when you will want to verify that what is written in this presentation is actually in your Bible—which is the inspired Word of God.

We pray that your reading and review of the life and teachings of Jesus will greatly increase your faith in Him—and in His wonderful promises to you.

THIS IS THE GOOD NEWS ABOUT

"<u>JESUS CHRIST</u>"

THE SON OF GOD (MARK 1:1)

PREFACE

By Luke, A Disciple of Paul

000   LUKE GIVES A REASON FOR CONTRIBUTING HIS GOSPEL FOR FUTURE POSTERITY.

Lk 1:1   Since many have undertaken to set in order a narrative concerning those matters which have been fulfilled among us,

Lk 1:2   even as those who from the beginning were eyewitnesses and servants of the Word delivered them to us,

Lk 1:3   it seemed good to me also, having traced the course of all things accurately from the beginning, to write to you in order, most excellent Theophilus,

Lk 1:4   that you might know the certainty concerning the things in which you were instructed.

PROLOGUE

By John, the Apostle

001   *BEFORE THE WORLD WAS CREATED, THE WORD (JESUS) ALREADY EXISTED (taken from Jn 1:1-18)*

Jn 1:1   In the beginning was the Word, and the Word was with God, and the Word was God.

Jn 1:2   The same was in the beginning with God.

Jn 1:3   All things were made through Him. Without Him was not anything made that has been made.

Jn 1:4   In Him was life, and the life was the Light of men.

Jn 1:5   The Light shines in the darkness, and the darkness has not overcome it.

002   *JOHN THE BAPTIST WAS SENT TO TESTIFY TO THE SON OF GOD (JN 1:6-8)*

Jn 1:6   There came a man, sent from God, whose name was John.

Jn 1:7   The same came as a witness, that he might testify about the Light, that all might believe through Him.

Jn 1:8   He was not the Light, but was sent that he might testify about the Light.

003   *JESUS' OWN PEOPLE RECEIVED HIM NOT (JN 1:9-11)*

Jn 1:9   The true Light that enlightens everyone was coming into the world.

Jn 1:10   He was in the world, and the world was made through Him, and the world did not recognize Him.

Jn 1:11   He came to His own, and those who were His own did not receive Him.

004   BUT THOSE WHO RECEIVE HIM BECOME CHILDREN OF GOD (JN 1:12,13)

Jn 1:12   But as many as received Him, to them He gave the right to become God's children, to those who believe in His Name;

Jn 1:13   Who were born not of blood, nor of the will of the flesh, nor of the will of man, but of God.

005   JESUS, THE "WORD OF GOD," BECAME A MAN FOR OUR BENEFIT (Jn 1:14-18)

Jn 1:14   The "Word" became flesh, and lived among us. We saw His glory, such glory as of the one and only Son of the Father, full of grace and truth.

Jn 1:15   John testified about Him. He cried out, saying, "This is He of whom I said, 'He who comes after me is greater than I, for He was before me.'"

Jn 1:16   From His fullness we all received grace upon grace.

Jn 1:17   For the law was given through Moses. But grace and truth were realized through Jesus Christ.

Jn 1:18   No one has seen God at any time. The One and only Son who is in the bosom of the Father, He has declared Him.

CHAPTER I

THE BIRTH OF JESUS

006   A VERY OLD COUPLE WINS GOD'S FAVOR (taken from Lk 1:5-14)

Lk 1:5   There was in the days of Herod, the king of Judea, a certain priest named Zacharias, of the priestly division of Abijah. He had a wife who was of the daughters of Aaron, and her name was Elizabeth.

Lk 1:6   They were both righteous before God, walking blamelessly in all the commandments and ordinances of the Lord.

Lk 1:7   But they had no child, because Elizabeth was barren, and they both were well advanced in years.

007   A SPECIAL MESSENGER FIRST APPEARS TO ZECHARIAS WHILE PERFORMING HIS RITUAL DUTIES IN KEEPING WITH JEWISH TRADITION (Lk 1:8-12)

Lk 1:8   Now it happened, while he executed the priest's office before God, when he took his turn,

Lk 1:9   according to the custom of the priest's office, his lot was to enter into the temple of the Lord and burn incense.

Lk 1:10   The whole multitude of the people were praying outside at that hour.

Lk 1:11   An angel of the Lord appeared to him, standing on the right side of the altar.

Lk 1:12   Zacharias was troubled when he saw him, and fear fell upon him.

008   THE ANGEL FORETELLS THE BIRTH OF ZECHARIAS'S SON AND OF THE REJOICING TO FOLLOW (Lk 1:13-14)

Lk 1:13   But the angel said to him, "Do not be afraid, Zacharias, because your request has been heard. Your wife, Elizabeth, will bear you a son, and you shall call his name, "John."

Lk 1:14   You will have joy and gladness, and many will rejoice at his birth."

009   THE MISSION OF JOHN THE BAPTIST IS EXPLAINED *(Lk 1:15-17)*

Lk 1:15   "For he will be great in the sight of the Lord. He will drink no wine nor strong drink. He will be filled with the Holy Spirit, even from his mother's womb. *(Num 6:3)*

Lk 1:16   He will turn many of the children of Israel to the Lord, their God.

Lk 1:17   He will go before Him in the spirit and power of Elijah, to turn the hearts of the fathers to their children, and the disobedient to the wisdom of the just, to prepare a people fit for the Lord."

010   ZECHARIAS QUESTIONS THE ANGEL'S MESSAGE AND IS GIVEN A TELL-TALE SIGN *(Lk 1:18-20)*

Lk 1:18   Zacharias said to the angel, "How can I be sure of this? For I am an old man, and my wife is well advanced in years."

Lk 1:19   The angel answered him, "I am Gabriel, who stands in the presence of God. I was sent to speak to you, and to bring you this Good News.

Lk 1:20   Behold, you will be silent and not able to speak until the day that these things will happen, because you did not believe my words, which will be fulfilled in their proper time."

011   THE ANGEL'S WORDS COME TRUE TO THE APPRECIATION OF THE OLD COUPLE *(Lk 1:21-25)*

Lk 1:21   The people were waiting for Zacharias, and they marveled that he delayed in the temple so long.

Lk 1:22   When he came out, he could not speak to them, and they perceived that he had seen a vision in the temple. He continued making signs to them, and remained mute.

Lk 1:23   It happened when the days of his service were fulfilled, he departed to his house.

Lk 1:24   After these days Elizabeth, his wife, conceived, and she hid herself five months, saying,

Lk 1:25   "Thus has the Lord done to me in the days in which He looked on me, to take away my shame among the people."

012 MATTHEW AND LUKE RECITE THE FOREFATHERS OF JESUS (Mt 1:1-17; Lk 3:32-38)

The legal ancestry of Jesus through Joseph, from Abraham to Jesus, is listed in Matthew 1:1-17. And Luke lists His biological ancestry through Mary, in reverse order from Jesus back to Adam, in Luke 3:23-38.

Mt 1:17 So all the generations from Abraham to David are fourteen generations, and from David to the exile into Babylon are fourteen generations, and from the carrying away to Babylon to the coming of Christ, are fourteen generations.

013 A YOUNG WOMAN FROM NAZARETH IS ALSO VISITED BY THE ANGEL GABRIEL (Mt 1:18; Lk 1:26-29)

Lk 1:26 Now in Elizabeth's sixth month, the angel Gabriel was sent from God to a city of Galilee, named Nazareth,

Lk 1:27 to a virgin pledged to be married to a man whose name was Joseph, of the house of David. The virgin's name was Mary.

Lk 1:28 Having come in, the angel said to her, "Rejoice, O highly favored one! The Lord is with you. Blessed are you among women!"

Lk 1:29 But when Mary saw him, she was greatly troubled at his saying, and wondered what kind of salutation this might be.

014 MARY WILL GIVE BIRTH TO A CHILD WHO WILL BE BORN TO BECOME A KING (Lk 1:30-38)

Lk 1:30 The angel said to her, "Do not be afraid, Mary, for you have found favor with God.

Lk 1:31 Behold, you will conceive in your womb and bring forth a Son, and you will name Him "Jesus."

Lk 1:32 He will be great, and will be called the "Son of the Most High." The Lord God will give Him the throne of His ancestor, David,

Lk 1:33 and He will reign over the house of Jacob forever. There will be no end to His Kingdom."

015 SHE HUMBLY ACCEPTS GOD'S WILL FOR HER LIFE (Lk 1:34-38)

Lk 1:34 Mary said to the angel, "How can this be since I am a virgin?"

Lk 1:35   The angel answered her, "The Holy Spirit will come upon you, and the power of the Most High will overshadow you. Therefore the "Holy One" who is born from you will be called the "Son of God."

Lk 1:36   Elizabeth, your relative, also has conceived a son in her old age, and this is the sixth month with her who was called barren.

Lk 1:37   For nothing is impossible with God." *(Gen 18:14)*

Lk 1:38   Mary said, "Behold the handmaid of the Lord. Be it done to me according to your word." *(Mary's "Fiat")* Then the angel departed from her.

016   MARY SHARES HER GREAT JOY WITH HER COUSIN ELIZABETH WHO PROPHESIES OVER MARY (Lk 1:39-42)

Lk 1:39   Mary arose in those days and went into the hill country with haste, into a city of Judah,

Lk 1:40   and entered into the house of Zacharias and greeted Elizabeth.

Lk 1:41   It happened, when Elizabeth heard Mary's greeting, that the baby leaped in her womb, and Elizabeth was filled with the Holy Spirit.

Lk 1:42   Elizabeth called out with a loud voice, saying, "Blessed are you among women, and blessed is the fruit of your womb!"

017   ELIZABETH RECOGNIZES THE LORD'S COMING (Lk 1:43-45)

Lk 1:43   "Why am I so favored, that the mother of my Lord should come to me?

Lk 1:44   For behold, when the voice of your greeting came into my ears, the baby leaped in my womb for joy!

Lk 1:45   Blessed is she who believes, for there will be a fulfillment of the things which have been spoken to her from the Lord!"

018   IN GIVING HER 'MAGNIFICAT' MARY IS LED TO EXALT THE LORD FOR HONORING HER, A HUMBLE SERVANT (LK 1:46-49)

Lk 1:46   Mary said, "My soul magnifies the Lord.

Lk 1:47   My spirit rejoices in God my Savior.

Lk 1:48 For He has looked at the humble state of His handmaid. From now on all generations will call me blessed.

Lk 1:49 For He who is mighty has done great things for me. Holy is His name."

019   AN ALL POWERFUL GOD BLESSES THE POOR AND GRATEFUL BUT HE REJECTS AND BRINGS DOWN THE PROUD (Lk 1:50-53)

Lk 1:50 "His mercy is from generation to generation on those who fear Him.

Lk 1:51 He has shown strength with His arm. He has scattered the proud in the imagination of their hearts.

Lk 1:52 He has put down princes from their thrones. And has exalted the lowly.

Lk 1:53 He has filled the hungry with good things. He has sent the rich away empty."

020   GOD FULFILLS HIS PROMISES TO HIS PEOPLE WHO HAD WAITED MANY CENTURIES FOR THEIR MESSIAH (Lk 1:54-56)

Lk 1:54 "He has given help to Israel, His servant, because He is merciful,

Lk 1:55 as He spoke to our fathers, to Abraham and his seed forever." *(Gen 17:7)*

Lk 1:56 Mary stayed with her about three months, and then returned to her house.

021   ELIZABETH DELIVERS HER BABY BUT THERE IS CONFUSION ABOUT NAMING HER CHILD (Lk 1:57-61)

Lk 1:57 Now the time that Elizabeth should give birth was fulfilled, and she brought forth a son.

Lk 1:58 Her neighbors and her relatives heard how the Lord had shown great mercy upon her, and they rejoiced with her.

Lk 1:59 It happened on the eighth day, that they came to circumcise the child, and they would have called him Zacharias, after the name of the father.

Lk 1:60 His mother answered, "Not so, but he will be called John."

Lk 1:61 They said to her, "There is no one among your relatives who is called by this name."

022   ZECHARIAS REGAINS HIS SPEECH AND THE EVENT CAUSES MUCH EXCITEMENT (Lk 1:62-66)

Lk 1:62   They made signs to his father, what he would have him called.

Lk 1:63   He asked for a writing tablet, and wrote, "His name is John." They all marveled.

Lk 1:64   His mouth was opened immediately, and his tongue freed, and he spoke, blessing God.

Lk 1:65   Awe came on all who lived around them, and all these sayings were talked about throughout all the hill country of Judea.

Lk 1:66   All who heard them held them up in their hearts, saying, "What then will this child be?" The hand of the Lord was with him.

023   JOHN'S FATHER IS LED TO PROPHESY GOD'S MESSAGE (Lk 1:67-80)

Lk 1:67   His father, Zacharias, was filled with the Holy Spirit, and prophesied, saying,

Lk 1:68   "Blessed be the Lord, the God of Israel, for He has visited and worked redemption for His people.

Lk 1:69   He has raised up a "Horn of Salvation" for us in the house of His servant David,

Lk 1:70   as He spoke by the mouth of His holy prophets who have been from of old,

Lk 1:71   salvation from our enemies, and from the hand of all who hate us."

024   PROTECTION IS ASSURED SO THEY COULD BECOME A HOLY NATION (Lk 1:72-75)

Lk 1:72   "To show mercy towards our fathers, to remember His holy covenant,

Lk 1:73   the oath which He spoke to Abraham, our father,

Lk 1:74   to grant to us that we, being delivered out of the hand of our enemies should serve Him without fear,

Lk 1:75   in holiness and righteousness before Him all the days of our lives."

025   ZECHARIAS PROCLAIMS THE WORK THAT HIS OWN SON WILL DO FOR THE LORD (Lk 1:76-80)

Lk 1:76   "And you, child, will be called a prophet of the Most High, for you will go before the face of the Lord to prepare His ways, *(Mal 3:1)*

Lk 1:77   to give knowledge of salvation to His people by the remission of their sins,

Lk 1:78   because of the tender mercy of our God, whereby the "Dawn from on High" will visit us,

Lk 1:79   to shine on those who sit in darkness and the shadow of death, to guide our feet into the way of peace."

Lk 1:80   The child grew, and became strong in spirit, and was in the desert until the day of his public appearance to Israel.

026   *MATTHEW TELLS US OF A TROUBLED JOSEPH WHO SEEKS TO BREAK HIS ENGAGEMENT TO MARY, BUT IS REASSURED BY THE HOLY SPIRIT (Mt 1:18-21)*

Mt 1:18   Now the birth of Jesus Christ was like this; after His mother Mary was engaged to Joseph, before they came together, she was found to be pregnant, by the Holy Spirit.

Mt 1:19   Joseph, her husband being a righteous man, and not willing to make her a public example, intended to put her away secretly.

Mt 1:20   And when he thought about these things, behold, an angel of the Lord appeared to him in a dream, saying, "Joseph, son of David, do not be afraid to take to yourself Mary as wife, for that which is conceived in her is of the Holy Spirit.

Mt 1:21   She shall bring forth a Son. You shall call His name Jesus, for it is He who shall save His people from their sins."

027   *MARY WEDS JOSEPH, WHO WILL BE THE GUARDIAN OF HER "VIRGIN-BORN" CHILD (Mt 1:22-25)*

Mt 1:22   Now all this has happened that it might be fulfilled which was spoken by the Lord through the prophet, saying,

Mt 1:23   "Behold, a virgin shall be with child, and shall bring forth a Son. They shall call His name "Immanuel," which is interpreted, "God with us." *(told to us some 700 years earlier in Isaiah 7:14)*

Mt 1:24   Joseph arose from his sleep and did as the angel of the Lord commanded him, and took Mary as wife unto himself,

Mt 1:25   and did not know her sexually until she had brought forth her "Firstborn Son." And would name Him Jesus.

028   THE ROMAN EMPIRE'S FIRST CENSUS SENDS JOSEPH AND MARY TO THE CITY OF DAVID (Lk 2:1-7)

Lk 2:1   Now it happened in those days that a decree went out from Caesar Augustus that all the world should be taxed.

Lk 2:2   This was the first enrollment made when Quirinius was governor of Syria.

Lk 2:3   All went to enroll themselves, everyone to his own city.

Lk 2:4   Joseph also went down from Galilee out of the city of Nazareth, into Judea, to the city of David, which is called Bethlehem, because he was of the house and family of David,

Lk 2:5   to register himself with Mary, being pregnant.

029   IN CROWDED BETHLEHEM, JESUS IS BORN IN A STABLE WITH ONLY A MANGER FOR A BASSINET (Lk 2:6,7)

Lk 2:6   It happened, while they were there, that the day had come that she should give birth.

Lk 2:7   She brought forth her firstborn Son and wrapped Him in bands of cloth, and laid Him in a feeding trough, because there was no room for them in the inn.

030   AN ANGEL ANNOUNCES TO LOWLY SHEPHERDS THE BIRTH OF THEIR SAVIOR (Lk 2:8-18)

Lk 2:8   There were shepherds in the same country staying in the field, keeping watch by night over their flock.

Lk 2:9   And lo, an angel of the Lord stood by them, and the glory of the Lord shone around them, and they were terrified.

Lk 2:10   The angel said to them, "Do not be afraid, I bring you Good News, of great joy, which will be to all the people.

Lk 2:11   For there is born to you, this day, in the city of David, a Savior, who is "Christ, the Lord." *(Isa 9:6)*

Lk 2:12 This is the sign unto you. You will find a baby wrapped in strips of cloth, lying in a manger."

031   A HOST OF ANGELS CONFIRM THE VERY SPECIAL EVENT (Lk 2:13-15)

Lk 2:13 Suddenly, there was with the angel a multitude of the heavenly host praising God, singing,

Lk 2:14 "Glory to God in the highest, and on earth peace, good will toward men."

Lk 2:15 It happened, when the angels went away from them into heaven, that the shepherds said one to another, "Let us go to Bethlehem now, and see this thing that has happened, which the Lord has made known to us."

032   GUARDIANS OF SHEEP, ARE THE FIRST ONES TO BEHOLD THE SACRIFICAL "LAMB OF GOD" (Lk 2:16-20)

Lk 2:16 They came with haste and found both Mary and Joseph. And the baby was lying in the feeding trough.

Lk 2:17 When they saw it, they told everyone the saying which was spoken to them about this child.

Lk 2:18 All who heard it wondered at the things which were spoken to them by the shepherds.

Lk 2:19 But Mary kept all these sayings, pondering them in her heart.

Lk 2:20 The shepherds returned, glorifying and praising God for all the things that they had heard and seen, just as it was told them.

033   JESUS IS PRESENTED IN THE TEMPLE TO BE CIRCUMCISED AND NAMED (Lk 2:21)

Lk 2:21 When eight days were fulfilled for the circumcision of the baby, His name was called Jesus, which was given by the angel before He was conceived in the womb.

034   FORTY DAYS AFTER THE BIRTH, JESUS IS PRESENTED AGAIN TO UPHOLD JEWISH TRADITION AND THE RULES OF MOSES (Lk 2:22-38)

Lk 2:22 When the days of her purification according to the Law of Moses were fulfilled, they brought Him up to Jerusalem to present Him to the Lord.

Lk 2:23 As it is written in the law of the Lord, "Every male who opens the womb shall be called holy to the Lord," *(Ex 13:12)*

Lk 2:24 and to offer a sacrifice according to that which is said in the law, "a pair of turtledoves, or two young pigeons."

035   A GOD-FEARING MAN IS HONORED TO SEE ISRAEL'S PROMISED SAVIOR BEFORE HE DIES (Lk 2:25-32)

Lk 2:25 Behold, there was a man in Jerusalem whose name was Simeon. This man was righteous and devout, looking for the Consolation of Israel, and the Holy Spirit was on him.

Lk 2:26 It had been revealed to him by the Holy Spirit that he should not see death before he had seen the "Lord's Messiah."

Lk 2:27 He came in the Spirit into the temple. The parents brought in the child, Jesus, that they might do concerning Him according to the custom of the law.

Lk 2:28 Simeon received Him into his arms, and blessed God.

036   SIMEON IS LED TO PROPHESY THAT JESUS WOULD BECOME A BLESSING FOR ALL PEOPLES (Lk 2:28-32)

Lk 2:29 "Now You may release Your servant in peace Lord, according to Your word.

Lk 2:30 For my eyes have seen Your "Salvation,"

Lk 2:31 which you have prepared before the face of all peoples,

Lk 2:32 a "Light of Revelation" to all nations, and the "Glory of Your people Israel."

037   HE REVEALS THE PURPOSE WHICH JESUS WILL FULFILL AND TELLS OF MARY'S SUFFERING TO COME (Lk 2:33-35)

Lk 2:33 Joseph and Mary were marveling at the things which were spoken concerning Him,

Lk 2:34 and Simeon blessed them, and said to Mary, His mother, "Behold, this child is set for the falling and the rising of many in Israel, and for a sign *(the cross?)* which will be spoken against.

Lk 2:35 Yes, a sword will pierce through your own soul, that the thoughts of many hearts may be revealed."

038   *THE PROPHETESS ANNA ALSO RECOGNIZES THE "SAVING LORD" (Lk 2:36-38)*

Lk 2:36   There was one Anna, a prophetess, the daughter of Phanuel of the tribe of Asher. She was of a great age, having lived with her husband seven years from her virginity.

Lk 2:37   She had been a widow for about eighty-four years, who did not depart from the temple, worshipping with fasting and petitioning night and day.

Lk 2:38   Coming up at that very hour, she gave thanks to the Lord, and spoke of Him to all those who were looking for redemption in Jerusalem.

039   *ORIENTAL PHILOSOPHERS ARE LED TO SEEK THEIR "STAR OF HOPE" (Mt 2:1-12)*

Mt 2:1   Now when Jesus was born in Bethlehem of Judea in the days of King Herod, <u>wise men</u> *(not kings or royalty)* from the east came to Jerusalem, saying,

Mt 2:2   "Where is He who is born "King of the Jews?" For we saw His star in the east, and have come to worship Him."

> *(Legend says that it took the three Magi two years travelling to reach Bethlehem. Could these possibly have been representing the very ancient Hindu, Buddhist and Confucian religions coming to pay tribute to the veritable Son of the Almighty Creator?)*

040   *JESUS IS BORN IN THE CITY OF DAVID IN FULFILLMENT OF ANOTHER PROPHECY (Mt 2:3-6)*

Mt 2:3   When King Herod heard it he was troubled, and all Jerusalem with him.

Mt 2:4   Gathering together all the chief priests and scribes of the people, he asked them where the Messiah would be born.

Mt 2:5   They said to him, "In Bethlehem of Judea, for this is written through the prophet,

Mt 2:6   'You Bethlehem, in the land of Judah, are in no way least among the princes of Judah. For out of you shall come forth a "Ruler," who shall shepherd My people, Israel.'"

041   *HEROD GIVES HIS REASON TO FIND THE WHEREABOUTS OF THE "ROYAL CHILD" (Mt 2:7,8)*

Mt 2:7   Then Herod privately called the wise men, and learned from them exactly what time the star appeared.

Mt 2:8   He sent them to Bethlehem and said, "Go and search diligently for the young child. When you have found Him, bring me word, so that I also may come and worship Him."

042   *THE GUIDING STAR LEADS THEM TO THE LITTLE INFANT (Mt 2:9-12)*

Mt 2:9   They, having heard the king went their way. And behold the star which they saw in the east, went before them, until it came and stood over where the young child was.

Mt 2:10   When they saw the star, they rejoiced with exceedingly great joy.

> *Jer 29:13 You shall seek Me, and find Me, when you shall search for Me with all your heart.*

Mt 2:11   They came into the house and saw the child with Mary, His mother, and they fell down and worshiped Him. Opening their treasures, they offered to Him gifts of gold *(for His royalty)*, frankincense *(for His divinity)*, and myrrh *(for His sufferings to come and later burial)*.

Mt 2:12   Being warned in a dream that they should not return to Herod, they went back to their own country another way.

043   *A CAUTION FROM THE LORD SENDS THE HOLY FAMILY TO SEEK REFUGE IN A STRANGE LAND (Mk 2:13-21)*

Mt 2:13   Now when they had departed, an angel of the Lord appeared to Joseph in a dream, saying, "Arise and take the small child and His mother, and flee into Egypt. Stay there until I tell you, for Herod will seek the young child to destroy Him."

Mt 2:14   He arose and took the child and His mother by night, and departed into Egypt,

Mt 2:15   and was there until the death of Herod, that it might be fulfilled which was spoken by the Lord through the prophet, saying, "Out of Egypt I have called My Son." (quoted in Hos 11:1)

044   *KING HEROD WANTS TO PROLONG HIS OWN REIGN BY KILLING INNOCENT BABY BOYS (Mt 2:16-18)*

Mt 2:16   Then Herod, when he saw that he was mocked by the wise men, was exceedingly angry. He sent out his soldiers, and killed all the male children who were in Bethlehem and in the surrounding countryside, two years old and under, according to the exact time which he had learned from the wise men.

Mt 2:17   Then that which was spoken by Jeremiah the prophet was fulfilled, saying,

Mt 2:18   "A voice was heard in Ramah, lamentation, weeping and great mourning, Rachel weeping for her children. She could not be comforted, because they are no more." (Jer 31:15)

045   *THE BETHEHEM MURDERER SOON DIES AND JOSEPH IS LED TO TAKE THE FAMILY BACK TO THE HOLY LAND (Mt 2:19-23)*

Mt 2:19   But when Herod was dead, behold, an angel of the Lord appeared again in a dream to Joseph in Egypt, saying,

Mt 2:20   "Arise and take the young child and His mother, and go back into the land of Israel, for those who sought the child's life are dead."

Mt 2:21   He arose and took the young child and His mother, and came into the land of Israel.

046   *JESUS GROWS UP IN NAZARETH, BLESSED OF GOD (Mt 2:22,23; Lk 2:39,40)*

Mt 2:22   But when Joseph heard that Archelaus was reigning over Judea in the place of his father, Herod, he was afraid to go there. Being warned in a dream, he withdrew into the region of Galilee,

Mt 2:23   and came and lived in a city called Nazareth, that it might be fulfilled which was spoken through the prophets, "He will be called a Nazarene."

Lk 2:40   The child was growing, and was becoming strong in spirit, being filled with wisdom, and the grace of God was upon Him.

047   *WHEN HE IS TWELVE, THEY MAKE THEIR ANNUAL PILGRIMAGE TO JERUSALEM FOR THE USUAL PASSOVER CELEBRATION (Lk 2:41-50)*

Lk 2:41   His parents went every year to Jerusalem at the feast of the Passover.

Lk 2:42   When He was twelve years old, they went up to Jerusalem according to the custom of the feast.

Lk 2:43   When they had fulfilled their days, as they were returning, the boy Jesus stayed behind in Jerusalem. Joseph and His mother did not know it,

Lk 2:44   but supposing Him to be among the travellers, they went a day's journey, then looked for Him among their relatives and acquaintances.

Lk 2:45   When they did not find Him, they returned to Jerusalem, looking for Him.

048   *THE BOY JESUS IS FOUND IN THE TEMPLE HOLDING HIS OWN IN A DISCUSSION WITH THE ELDERS (Lk 2:46-50)*

Lk 2:46   It happened after three days they found Him in the temple, sitting in the midst of the teachers, both listening to them, and asking them questions.

Lk 2:47   All who heard Him were amazed at His understanding and His answers.

Lk 2:48   When they saw Him they were astonished, and His mother said to Him, "Son, why have You treated us this way? Your father and I have been anxiously looking for You."

Lk 2:49   He said to them, **"WHY WERE YOU LOOKING FOR ME? DID YOU NOT KNOW THAT I MUST BE ABOUT MY FATHER'S BUSINESS?"**

Lk 2:50   They did not understand the saying which He spoke to them.

049   *HE GROWS PHYSICALLY AND MENTALLY TO THE AGE OF 30 BEFORE HE WOULD BEGIN HIS MINISTRY (Lk 2:51,52)*

Lk 2:51   He went with them, and came to Nazareth and He was subject to them. His mother kept all these sayings in her heart.

Lk 2:52   And Jesus increased in wisdom and stature, and in favor with God and men.

> *It would have been difficult to foretell who the Messiah would be from clues which the Bible gave us until after the fact. For example; He will be born in Bethlehem (Mic 5:2), out of Egypt have I called My Son (Hos 11:1), He will be called a Nazarene (Mt 2:23).*

CHAPTER II

JOHN THE BAPTIST IDENTIFIES THE MESSIAH

050   THOSE WHO WANT FORGIVENESS MUST REPENT AND BE BAPTIZED (taken from Mt 3:2; Lk 3:1-3)

Lk 3:1   Now in the fifteenth year of the reign of Tiberius Caesar, Pontius Pilate being governor of Judea, and Herod being tetrarch of Galilee, and his brother Philip tetrarch of the region of Ituraea and Trachonitis, and Lysanias tetrarch of Abilene,

Lk 3:2   during the high priesthood of Annas and Caiaphas, the word of God came to John, the son of Zacharias, in the wilderness.

Lk 3:3   John came into the entire region around the Jordan, preaching the baptism of repentance for the remission of sins.

Mt 3:2   "Repent, for the Kingdom of Heaven is at hand!"

051   MARK TELLS US HOW JOHN THE BAPTIST'S MINISTRY BEGINS JUST AS GOD HAD SPOKEN THROUGH THE PROPHETS (Mt 3:3; Mk 1:2-5; Lk 3:4-6)

Mk 1:2   As it is written in the prophets, "Behold, I send My messenger ahead of You, who will prepare the way before You. *(referred to in Mal 1:1)*

Mk 1:3   The voice of one crying in the wilderness, make ready the way of the Lord! Make His paths straight! (Isa 40:3)

Lk 3:5   Every valley will be filled. Every mountain and hill will be brought low. The crooked road will become straight, and the rough places made smooth.

Lk 3:6   All flesh will see God's salvation." (Isa 52:10)

052   MANY COME TO JOHN IN REPENTANCE (Mt 3:4; Mk 1:4,5)

Mt 3:4   Now John himself wore clothing made of camel's hair, with a leather belt around his waist. His food was locusts and wild honey.

Mk 1:4 John came baptizing in the wilderness and preaching the baptism of repentance for the forgiveness of sins.

Mk 1:5 All the country of Judea and all those of Jerusalem went out to see him. They were baptized by him in the Jordan River, confessing their sins.

053   JOHN SCOLDS THE HYPOCRITES AND NON-BELIEVERS WHO COME TO BE BAPTIZED (Mt 3:7-10; Lk 3:7-9)

Mt 3:7 But when he saw many of the Pharisees and Sadducees coming for his baptism, he said to them, "You offspring of vipers, who warned you to flee from the wrath to come?

Mt 3:8 Therefore bring forth proof of your repentance!

Mt 3:9 Do not say to yourselves, 'We have Abraham for our father,' for I tell you that God is able to raise up children to Abraham from these stones.

Mt 3:10 Even now the axe lies at the root of the trees. Therefore every tree that does not bring forth good fruit is cut down, and cast into the fire."

054   THE BAPTIZER GIVES SOME SUGGESTIONS AS TO WHAT IS EXPECTED OF THEM (Lk 3:10-14)

Lk 3:10 The multitudes asked him, "What then must we do?"

Lk 3:11 He answered them, "He who has two coats, let him give one to him who has none. He who has food, let him do likewise."

Lk 3:12 Tax collectors also came to be baptized, and they said to him, "Teacher, what must we do?"

Lk 3:13 He said to them, "Collect no more than that which is appointed to you."

Lk 3:14 Soldiers also asked him, saying, "What about us? What must we do?" He said to them, "Extort money from no one by violence, neither accuse anyone wrongfully. Be content with your wages."

055   JOHN TESTIFIES THAT HE IS NOT THE MESSIAH AND DESCRIBES THE "PURIFYING LORD" TO COME (Mt 3:11,12; Lk 3:15-18)

Lk 3:15 All the people were in expectation, and all men reasoned in their hearts concerning John, whether perhaps he was the Christ.

Mt 3:11 "I indeed baptize you in water for repentance, but He who comes after me is mightier than I. Whose shoes I am not worthy to carry. He will baptize you in the Holy Spirit—and with fire.

Mt 3:12 His winnowing fork is in His hand, and He will thoroughly cleanse His threshing floor. He will gather His wheat into the barn. But the chaff, He will burn up in a fire which will never be put out."

Lk 3:18 In many other ways he preached the Good News to the people.

056   *JESUS SUBMITS TO THE LAW OF GOD AND IS BAPTIZED BY HIS COUSIN, JOHN THE BAPTIST (Mt 3:13-17; Mk 1:9-11; Lk 3:21,22)*

Mt 3:13 Then Jesus came from Galilee to the Jordan, to John, to be baptized by him.

Mt 3:14 But John wanted to prevent Him, saying, "I need to be baptized by You, and yet You come to me?"

Mt 3:15 But Jesus, answering, said to him, **"ALLOW IT NOW, FOR THIS IS THE PROPER WAY FOR US TO FULFILL ALL THAT GOD REQUIRES."** Then he agreed and baptized Jesus.

057   *HEAVEN OPENS AND THE SPIRIT OF GOD COMES DOWN UPON THE "LIGHT OF LIFE" (Mt 3:16; Mk 1:10,11; Lk 3:21,22)*

Lk 3:21 Now it happened, when all the people were baptized, Jesus also had been baptized, and was praying...

Mt 3:16 He went up directly from the water. And behold, the heavens were opened to Him.

Lk 3:22 And the Holy Spirit descended in a bodily form, in the shape of a dove on Him. And a voice came out of heaven, saying, ***"YOU ARE MY BELOVED SON. IN YOU I AM WELL PLEASED."*** *(Isa 42:1)*

058   *JESUS IS COMPELLED TO GO INTO THE WILDERNESS TO FAST AND BE TEMPTED FOR FORTY DAYS (Mt 4:1-11; Mk 1:12,13; Lk 4:1-13)*

Mk 1:12 Immediately the Spirit drove Him out into the wilderness,

Lk 4:2 for forty days, being tempted by the devil. He ate nothing in those days. Afterward, when these days were completed He was hungry.

Lk 4:3   The devil said to Him, "If You are the Son of God, command this stone to become bread."

Mt 4:4   But Jesus answered, **"IT IS WRITTEN, 'MAN SHALL NOT LIVE BY BREAD ALONE, BUT BY EVERY WORD THAT PROCEEDS OUT OF THE MOUTH OF GOD.'"** *(Deut 8:3)*

059   *JESUS SHOWS US HOW TO FIGHT THE ENEMY BY QUOTING SCRIPTURES TO SATAN (Mt 4:5-11; Lk 4:9-12)*

Lk 4:9   Satan led Him to Jerusalem, and set Him on the pinnacle of the temple, and said to Him, "If You are the Son of God, cast Yourself down from here,

Lk 4:10   for it is written, 'He will put His angels in charge of You, to guard You,'

Lk 4:11   and, 'on their hands they will bear You up, lest perhaps You dash Your foot against a stone.'"

Lk 4:12   Jesus answering, said to him, **"IT HAS BEEN SAID, 'YOU SHALL NOT TEMPT THE LORD YOUR GOD.'"** (Deut 6:16)

060   *JESUS, OUR "EMANCIPATOR," PERSEVERES TO THE POINT OF EXHAUSTION (Mt 4:8-11; Lk 4:5-13)*

Mt 4:8   Again, the devil took Him to an exceedingly high mountain, and showed Him all the kingdoms of the world, and their glory.

Mt 4:9   He said to Him, "I will give You all of these things, if You will fall down and worship me."

Mt 4:10   Then Jesus said to him, **"GET BEHIND ME, SATAN! FOR IT IS WRITTEN, 'YOU SHALL WORSHIP THE LORD YOUR GOD, AND YOU SHALL SERVE HIM ONLY.'"** *(Deut 6:13)*

Lk 4:13   When the devil had tried every temptation, he departed from Him until another time.

Mt 4:11   ...and behold, angels came and ministered to Jesus.

061   *MESSENGERS ARE SENT BY THE JEWISH AUTHORITIES TO JOHN WHO STATES HIS PRIMARY PURPOSE (Jn 1:19-23)*

Jn 1:19   This is John's testimony. The Jews sent priests and Levites from Jerusalem to ask him, "Who are you?"

Jn 1:20   John declared, and did not deny, but said, "I am not the Christ."

Jn 1:21   They asked him, "Who then? Are you Elijah?" He said, "I am not." "Are you the prophet?" He answered, "No."

Jn 1:22   They said therefore to him, "Who are you? Give us an answer to take back to those who sent us. What do you say about yourself?"

Jn 1:23   He said, "I am the voice of one crying in the wilderness, 'Make straight the way of the Lord,' as Isaiah the prophet said." (Isa 40:3)

062   *THE BAPTIST TELLS THEM ABOUT JESUS WHO IS "HIGH AND EXALTED" (Jn 1:24-28)*

Jn 1:24   The ones who had been sent were from the Pharisees and they questioned him.

Jn 1:25   They asked him, "Why then do you baptize, if you are not the Christ, nor Elijah, nor the prophet?"

Jn 1:26   John answered them, "I baptize in water, but among you stands One whom you do not know.

Jn 1:27   He is the One who comes after me, who is higher than I, whose sandal straps I am not worthy to loosen."

Jn 1:28   These things were done in Bethany beyond the Jordan, where John was baptizing.

063   *JOHN PROCLAIMS JESUS AS SENT FROM GOD (Jn 1:29-31)*

Jn 1:29   The next day, he saw Jesus coming to him, and said, "Behold, the Lamb of God, who takes away the sin of the world!

Jn 1:30   This is He of whom I said, 'After me comes a Man who is preferred before me, for He existed before me.'

Jn 1:31   I did not know Him, but for this reason I came baptizing in water, that He would be revealed to all Israel."

064   *A REVELATION FROM THE BAPTIZER SINGLES JESUS OUT AS THE VERY "SON OF GOD" (Jn 1:32-34)*

Jn 1:32   John testified, saying, "I have seen the Spirit descending like a dove out of heaven, and it lingered over Him.

Jn 1:33   I did not recognize Him, but He who sent me to baptize in water said to me, 'On whomever you will see the Spirit descending and remaining on Him, the same is He who baptizes in the Holy Spirit.'

Jn 1:34   I have seen it, and do testify that this is the Son of God."

065   *JOHN THE BAPTIST DIRECTS HIS OWN DISCIPLES TO JESUS (Jn 1:35-39)*

Jn 1:35   Again, the next day, John was standing with two of his disciples *(learners)*,

Jn 1:36   and he looked at Jesus as He walked, and said, "Behold, the Lamb of God!"

Jn 1:37   The two disciples heard him speak this, they then followed Jesus.

> *Pr 3:5 Trust in the Lord with all thine heart; and lean not unto thine own understanding.*

Jn 1:38   Jesus turned, and saw them following, and said to them, **"WHAT ARE YOU LOOKING FOR?"** They said to Him, "Rabbi" *(Teacher)*, "where are You staying?"

Jn 1:39   He said to them, **"COME, AND SEE."** They came and saw where He was living, and they stayed with Him that day. It was about the tenth hour.

066   *ONE OF THE DISCIPLES BRINGS HIS BROTHER SIMON (Jn 1:40-42)*

Jn 1:40   One of the two who heard John, and followed Him, was Andrew, Simon Peter's brother.

Jn 1:41   He first found his own brother, Simon, and said to him, "We have found the Messiah!" which being interpreted is the Christ.

Jn 1:42   He brought him to Jesus. Jesus looked at him, and said, **"YOU ARE SIMON THE SON OF JONAH. YOU SHALL BE CALLED CEPHAS,"** which is by interpretation means Peter, or a stone.

067   *JESUS FINDS PHILIP, WHO BRINGS NATHANAEL (Jn 1:43-51)*

Jn 1:43   On the next day, He was determined to go into Galilee, and He found Philip. Jesus said to him, **"FOLLOW ME."**

Jn 1:44   Now Philip was from Bethsaida, of the city of Andrew and Peter.

Jn 1:45   Philip found Nathanael, and said to him, "We have found Him, of whom Moses in the law and the prophets wrote, Jesus of Nazareth, the son of Joseph." *(Deut 18:15)*

Jn 1:46   Nathanael said to him, "Can any good thing come out of Nazareth?" Philip said to him, "Come and see."

068   *NATHANAEL ACKNOWLEDGES THE "ALL SEEING JESUS" (Jn 1:47-51)*

Jn 1:47   Jesus saw Nathanael coming to Him, and said about him, **"BEHOLD, AN ISRAELITE INDEED, IN WHOM IS NO DECEIT."**

Jn 1:48   Nathanael said to Him, "How do You know me?" Jesus answered him, **"BEFORE PHILIP CALLED YOU, WHEN YOU WERE UNDER THE FIG TREE, I SAW YOU."**

Jn 1:49   Nathanael answered Him, "Rabbi, You are the Son of God! You are 'King of Israel!'"

Jn 1:50   Jesus answered him, **"BECAUSE I TOLD YOU, 'I SAW YOU UNDERNEATH THE FIG TREE,' DO YOU BELIEVE? YOU WILL SEE EVEN GREATER THINGS THAN THESE."**

Jn 1:51   He said to him, **"MOST CERTAINLY, I TELL YOU, HEREAFTER YOU WILL SEE HEAVEN OPEN, AND THE ANGELS OF GOD ASCENDING AND DESCENDING ON THE SON OF MAN."** *(Jesus)*

CHAPTER III

HIS FIRST MIRACLE AND HEALINGS

069   *JESUS ATTENDS A VILLAGE WEDDING WITH HIS DISCIPLES (taken from Jn 2:1-11)*

Jn 2:1   The third day, there was a marriage in Cana of Galilee. Jesus' mother was there.

Jn 2:2   Jesus also was invited, with His disciples, to the marriage.

Jn 2:3   When the wine ran out, Jesus' mother said to Him, "They have no wine."

Jn 2:4   Jesus said to her, **"WOMAN, WHAT DOES THAT HAVE TO DO WITH ME? MY HOUR HAS NOT YET COME."**

Jn 2:5   His mother said to the servants, "Whatever He says to you, do it!"

070   *VERY LARGE JARS ARE COMPLETELY FILLED WITH WATER (Jn 2:6-10)*

Jn 2:6   Now there were six water pots of stone set there for the Jewish ceremonial washings, containing twenty to thirty gallons each.

Jn 2:7   Jesus said to them, **"FILL THE WATER POTS WITH WATER."** They filled them up to the brim.

Jn 2:8   He said to them, **"NOW DRAW SOME OUT, AND TAKE IT TO THE MAN IN CHARGE OF THE FEAST."** So they took it.

Jn 2:9   When the ruler of the feast tasted the water now become wine, they did not know where it came from, but the servants who had drawn the water knew. The man in charge of the feast called the bridegroom,

Jn 2:10   and said to him, "Everyone serves the good wine first, and when the guests have drunk freely, then that which is cheaper. But you have kept the best wine until now!"

071   THIS MIRACLE OF THE WINE BUILDS CONFIDENCE WITH HIS FOLLOWERS (Jn 2:11,12)

Jn 2:11   This was the beginning of the miracles Jesus did, in Cana of Galilee. It revealed His glory, and His disciples believed in Him.

Jn 2:12   After this, He went down to Capernaum, with His mother, His brothers, and His apostles. And they stayed there a few days.

072   HE DRIVES OUT OF THE TEMPLE THOSE WHO SEEK FINANCIAL GAIN (Jn 2:13-17)

Jn 2:13   The Passover of the Jews was at hand, and Jesus went to Jerusalem.

Jn 2:14   He found in the temple those who sold oxen, sheep, and doves, and the changers of money, sitting.

Jn 2:15   He made a whip of cords, and threw all out of the temple, both the sheep and the oxen, and He poured out the changers' money, and overthrew their tables.

Jn 2:16   To those who sold the doves, He said, **"TAKE THESE THINGS OUT OF HERE DO NOT MAKE MY FATHER'S HOUSE A MARKETPLACE!"**

Jn 2:17   His disciples remembered that it was written, "Zeal for Your house will eat Me up."

073   JESUS, "OUR DELIVERER," MAKES AN EARLY PREDICTION OF HIS DEATH AND RESURRECTION (Jn 2:18-22)

Jn 2:18   The Jews therefore answered Him, "What sign will You show us, seeing that You do these things?"

Jn 2:19   Jesus answered them, **"DESTROY THIS TEMPLE, AND IN THREE DAYS I WILL RAISE IT UP."**

Jn 2:20   The Jews therefore said, "It took forty-six years to build this temple! Will You raise it up in three days?"

Jn 2:21   But He spoke of the temple of His body.

Jn 2:22   When therefore He was raised from the dead, His disciples remembered that He said this, and they believed the Scriptures, and the word, which Jesus had said.

074   *MANY BELIEVE WHEN THEY SEE HIS EARLY MIRACLES (Jn 2:23-25)*

Jn 2:23   Now when He was in Jerusalem during the feast of the Passover, many believed in His name, noticing the miracles which He did.

Jn 2:24   But Jesus did not trust them, because He knew all men.

Jn 2:25   He did not need for anyone to testify concerning another man, for He knew what was in man.

075   *IMPRESSED WITH JESUS, A CHURCH ELDER COMES SECRETLY TO SEEK THE "AUTHOR OF LIFE" AFTER DARK (Jn 3:1-21)*

Jn 3:1   Now there was a man of the Pharisees named Nicodemus, a ruler of the Jews. *(In his writings, John the evangelist, who was a Jew himself, often referred to the Hebrews as "the Jews.")*

Jn 3:2   The same came to Him by night, and said to Him, "Rabbi, we know that You are a teacher come from God, for no one can do these miracles that You do unless God is with Him."

Jn 3:3   Jesus answered him, **"MOST CERTAINLY, I TELL YOU, UNLESS ONE IS BORN AGAIN, HE CANNOT SEE THE KINGDOM OF GOD."**

076   *A PERSON MUST BE REBORN OF THE SPIRIT TO ENTER HEAVEN (Jn 3:4-8)*

Jn 3:4   Nicodemus said to Him, "How can a man be born when he is old? Can he enter a second time into his mother's womb, and be born?"

Jn 3:5   Jesus answered, **"MOST CERTAINLY I TELL YOU, UNLESS ONE IS BORN OF WATER, AND OF THE SPIRIT, HE CANNOT ENTER INTO THE KINGDOM OF GOD!**

Jn 3:6   **THAT WHICH IS BORN OF THE FLESH IS FLESH. THAT WHICH IS BORN OF THE SPIRIT IS SPIRIT.**

Jn 3:7   **DO NOT MARVEL THAT I SAID TO YOU, 'YOU MUST BE BORN AGAIN.'**

Jn 3:8   **THE WIND BLOWS WHERE IT WANTS TO, AND YOU HEAR ITS SOUND, BUT DO NOT KNOW WHERE IT COMES FROM AND WHERE IT IS GOING. SO IS EVERYONE WHO IS BORN OF THE SPIRIT."**

077   THERE IS SO MUCH MORE TO BE LEARNED ABOUT THE KINGDOM OF GOD (Jn 3:9-12)

Jn 3:9   Nicodemus answered Him, "How can these things be?"

Jn 3:10   Jesus answered him, "ARE YOU A TEACHER IN ISRAEL, AND DO NOT UNDERSTAND THESE THINGS?

Jn 3:11   MOST CERTAINLY I TELL YOU, WE SPEAK THAT WHICH WE KNOW, AND TESTIFY OF THAT WHICH WE HAVE SEEN, AND YOU DO NOT RECEIVE OUR TESTIMONY.

Jn 3:12   IF I TELL YOU EARTHLY THINGS AND YOU DO NOT BELIEVE THEM, HOW WILL YOU BELIEVE IF I TELL YOU OF HEAVENLY THINGS?"

078   JESUS, THE "GENTLE SAVIOR," TELLS OF HIS ORIGIN AND MISSION (Jn 3:13-18)

Jn 3:13   "NO ONE HAS ASCENDED INTO HEAVEN, BUT HE WHO DESCENDED OUT OF HEAVEN, THE SON OF MAN—WHO IS IN HEAVEN. *(even while here on earth)*

Jn 3:14   AS MOSES LIFTED UP THE SERPENT IN THE WILDERNESS *(Num 21:9)* EVEN SO MUST THE SON OF MAN BE LIFTED UP,

Jn 3:15   THAT WHOEVER BELIEVES IN HIM SHOULD NOT PERISH, BUT HAVE <u>ETERNAL LIFE</u>."

   (Know that you are saved. See 1 John 5:11-13)

079   NO GREATER GIFT HAS EVER BEEN GIVEN TO MANKIND (Jn 3:16-18)

Jn 3:16   "FOR GOD SO LOVED THE WORLD, THAT HE GAVE HIS ONE AND ONLY SON, THAT WHOEVER BELIEVES IN HIM SHOULD NOT PERISH, BUT HAVE ETERNAL LIFE.

Jn 3:17   FOR GOD DID NOT SEND HIS SON INTO THE WORLD TO JUDGE THE WORLD, BUT THAT THE WORLD SHOULD BE SAVED THROUGH HIM.

Jn 3:18   HE WHO BELIEVES IN HIM IS NOT JUDGED. HE WHO DOES NOT BELIEVE HAS BEEN JUDGED ALREADY, BECAUSE HE HAS NOT BELIEVED IN THE NAME OF THE ONE AND ONLY SON OF GOD."

080   *WHOEVER IS INCLINED TO DO GOOD WILL MOST LIKELY BE DRAWN TO JESUS, THE "ETERNAL LIGHT" (Jn 3:19-21)*

Jn 3:19   "THIS IS THE JUDGMENT, THAT THE LIGHT HAS COME INTO THE WORLD, AND MEN LOVED THE DARKNESS RATHER THAN THE LIGHT, FOR THEIR WORKS ARE EVIL.

Jn 3:20   FOR EVERYONE WHO DOES EVIL HATES THE LIGHT, AND DOES NOT COME TO THE LIGHT, LEST HIS WORKS WOULD BE EXPOSED.

Jn 3:21   BUT HE WHO LIVES BY THE TRUTH COMES TO THE LIGHT, THAT HIS WORKS MAY BE REVEALED, THAT THEY HAVE BEEN DONE THROUGH GOD."

081   *JOHN AND JESUS CONTINUE BAPTIZING WITH THEIR SEPARATE DISCIPLES (Jn 3:22-24)*

Jn 3:22   After these things, Jesus came with His disciples into the land of Judea. He stayed there with them, and baptized.

Jn 3:23   John also was baptizing in Enon near Salim, because there was <u>much water there</u>. Many came, and were baptized.

Jn 3:24   For John was not yet thrown into prison.

082   *THE BAPTIST GIVES HIS LAST TESTIMONY (Jn 3:25-29)*

Jn 3:25   There arose a question between some of John's disciples and the Jews about purification.

Jn 3:26   They came to John, and said to him, "Rabbi, He who was with you beyond the Jordan, to whom you have testified, behold, the same baptizes, and everyone is coming to Him."

Jn 3:27   John answered, "A man can receive nothing, unless it has been given him from heaven.

Jn 3:28   You yourselves verify that I said, 'I am not the Christ,' but, 'I have been sent before Him.'

Jn 3:29   He who has the bride is the bridegroom. But the friend of the bridegroom, who stands and hears Him, rejoices greatly because of the bridegroom's voice. By this, my joy is made full."

083   *JOHN DECLARES THE PRE-EMINENCE OF JESUS (Jn 3:30-33)*

Jn 3:30   "He must increase, but I must decrease!

Jn 3:31   He who comes from above is above all. He who is from the earth belongs to the earth, and speaks of earthly things. But He who comes from heaven is certainly above all.

Jn 3:32   What He has seen and heard, of that He testifies, and no one believes His witness.

Jn 3:33   He who has received His witness recognizes that God is true."

084   *WHOEVER BELIEVES IN JESUS, THE "SOURCE OF LOVE," ALREADY HAS ETERNAL LIFE (Jn 3:34-36)*

Jn 3:34   "For He whom God has sent speaks the words of God, for God gives His Spirit without limit.

Jn 3:35   The Father loves the Son, and has given all things into His hand.

Jn 3:36   One who believes in the Son has eternal life. But one who disobeys the Son will not see Life, for the wrath of God remains on him."

085   *HEROD ORDERS THAT JOHN THE BAPTIST BE ARRESTED (Mt 14:3; Lk 3:18-20)*

Lk 3:18   Then in many other ways John preached the Good News to the people,

Lk 3:19   but Herod the tetrarch, being condemned by John for taking Herodias, his brother's wife, and for all the evil things which Herod had done,

Lk 3:20   added to his crimes by locking John up in prison.

086   *UPON HEARING OF JOHN'S ARREST, JESUS IMMEDIATELY LEAVES FOR GALILEE (Mt 4:12; Mk 1:14; Jn 4:1-4)*

Jn 4:1   Therefore when the Lord knew that the Pharisees had heard that Jesus was making and baptizing more disciples than John,

Jn 4:2   (although Jesus Himself did not baptize, but His disciples did,)

Jn 4:3   He left Judea...

Mt 4:12   Now when Jesus heard that John was arrested, He withdrew into Galilee.

Jn 4:4   He needed to pass through Samaria.

087   ON HIS WAY HE MEETS A SAMARITAN WOMAN (Jn 4:5-42)

Jn 4:5   So He came to a city of Samaria, called Sychar, near the parcel of ground that the patriarch Jacob had given to his son, Joseph.

Jn 4:6   Jacob's well was there. Jesus therefore, being tired from His journey, sat down by the well. It was about the sixth hour. *(noon)*

Jn 4:7   A woman of Samaria came to draw water. Jesus said to her, **"GIVE ME A DRINK."**

Jn 4:8   His disciples had gone away into the city to buy food.

Jn 4:9   The Samaritan woman therefore said to Him, "How is it that You, being a Jew, ask for a drink from me, a Samaritan woman?" *(For Jews have no dealings with Samaritans who are considered to be only part Jewish.)*

088   *JESUS IS THAT "LIVING WATER" LEADING UP TO ETERNAL LIFE (Jn 4:10-14)*

Jn 4:10   Jesus answered her, **"IF YOU KNEW THE GIFT OF GOD, AND WHO IT IS WHO SAYS TO YOU, 'GIVE ME A DRINK,' YOU WOULD HAVE ASKED HIM, AND HE WOULD HAVE GIVEN YOU LIVING WATER."**

Jn 4:11   The woman said to Him, "Sir, You have nothing to draw with, and the well is deep. From where then have You that living water?

Jn 4:12   Are You greater than our father, Jacob, who gave us the well, and drank of it himself as did his children and his livestock?"

Jn 4:13   Jesus answered her, **"EVERYONE WHO DRINKS OF THIS WATER WILL THIRST AGAIN,**

Jn 4:14   **BUT WHOEVER DRINKS OF THE WATER THAT I WILL GIVE HIM WILL NEVER THIRST AGAIN. BUT THE WATER THAT I WILL GIVE HIM WILL BECOME IN HIM A WELL OF WATER SPRINGING UP TO ETERNAL LIFE."**

089   THE SAMARITAN WOMAN RECOGNIZES THAT JESUS IS A "HOLY MAN" *(Jn 4:15-19)*

Jn 4:15   The woman said to Him, "Sir, give me this water, so that I will not get thirsty, neither have to come all the way here to draw."

Jn 4:16   Jesus said to her, **"GO, CALL YOUR HUSBAND, AND COME BACK."**

Jn 4:17   The woman answered, "I have no husband." Jesus said to her, **"YOU SAID WELL, 'I HAVE NO HUSBAND,'**

Jn 4:18   FOR YOU HAVE HAD FIVE HUSBANDS, AND HE WHOM YOU NOW HAVE IS NOT YOUR HUSBAND. THIS YOU HAVE SAID TRULY."

Jn 4:19   The woman said to Him, "Sir, I perceive that You are a prophet."

090   JESUS, THE "MASTER TEACHER," SAYS THAT THE JEWS HAVE A BETTER UNDERSTANDING OF GOD *(Jn 4:20-22)*

Jn 4:20   "Our fathers worshiped in this mountain, and you Jews say that in Jerusalem is the place where people ought to worship."

Jn 4:21   Jesus said to her, **"WOMAN, BELIEVE ME, THE HOUR COMES WHEN NEITHER ON THIS MOUNTAIN NOR IN JERUSALEM, WILL YOU WORSHIP THE FATHER.**

Jn 4:22   YOU WORSHIP THAT WHICH YOU DO NOT KNOW. WE WORSHIP THAT WHICH WE KNOW. FOR SALVATION ORIGINATES WITH THE JEWS."

091   PEOPLE CAN PRAY MORE EFFECTIVELY WITH THE FATHER'S SPIRIT *(Jn 4:23,24)*

Jn 4:23   "BUT THE HOUR COMES, AND NOW IS, WHEN THE TRUE WORSHIPERS WILL WORSHIP THE FATHER IN SPIRIT, AND IN TRUTH. FOR THE FATHER SEEKS SUCH TO BE HIS WORSHIPERS.

Jn 4:24   GOD IS SPIRIT, AND THOSE WHO WORSHIP HIM MUST WORSHIP HIM IN SPIRIT AND IN TRUTH."

*092	JESUS REVEALS TO THE WOMAN THAT HE IS THE CHRIST, THE "ANOINTED ONE" (Jn 4:25-30)*

Jn 4:25	The woman said to Him, "I know that the Messiah is coming, who is called Christ. When He comes, He will declare to us all things."

Jn 4:26	Jesus said to her, **"I AM HE, THE ONE WHO IS SPEAKING TO YOU."**

*093	THE WOMAN GOES BACK TO SYCHAR AND BECOMES HIS FIRST MISSIONARY (Jn 4:27-30)*

Jn 4:27	At this, His disciples came. They marveled that He was speaking in public to a woman. Yet no one asked Him, "What are You looking for?" or, "Why do You speak with her?"

Jn 4:28	So the woman left her water pot, and rushed into the city, and said to the people,

Jn 4:29	"Come, see a man who told me everything that I ever did. Can this be the Christ?"

Jn 4:30	They went out of the city, and were coming to Him.

*094	JESUS, THE "OBEDIENT SAVIOR," TELLS THE DISCIPLES THAT HE HUNGERS TO DO FATHER GOD'S WILL (Jn 4:31-34)*

Jn 4:31	Meanwhile, the disciples urged Him, saying, "Rabbi *(teacher)*, eat."

Jn 4:32	But He said to them, **"I HAVE FOOD TO EAT THAT YOU DO NOT KNOW ABOUT."**

Jn 4:33	The disciples therefore said one to another, "Has anyone brought Him something to eat?"

Jn 4:34	Jesus said to them, **"MY FOOD IS TO DO THE WILL OF HIM WHO SENT ME—AND TO FINISH HIS WORK."**

*095	MANY CAN CONTRIBUTE TO REAP A HARVEST OF SOULS (Jn 4:35-38)*

Jn 4:35	**"DO YOU NOT SAY, 'THERE ARE YET FOUR MONTHS UNTIL THE HARVEST?' BEHOLD, I TELL YOU. LIFT UP YOUR EYES AND LOOK AT THE FIELDS, THAT THEY ARE WHITE FOR HARVEST ALREADY!**

Jn 4:36 HE WHO REAPS RECEIVES WAGES, AND GATHERS FRUIT TO ETERNAL LIFE. SO THAT BOTH HE WHO SOWS AND HE WHO REAPS MAY REJOICE TOGETHER.

Jn 4:37 FOR IN THIS THE SAYING IS TRUE, 'ONE SOWS, AND ANOTHER REAPS.'

Jn 4:38 I SENT YOU TO REAP WHERE YOU HAVE NOT LABORED. OTHERS HAVE LABORED THERE, BUT YOU SHARE IN THEIR LABOR."

096   HIS STAY AND TESTIMONY IN SAMARIA CAUSE MANY TO BELIEVE AND ACCEPT HIM (Jn 4:39-44)

Jn 4:39 From that city many of the Samaritans believed in Him because of the word of the woman, who testified, "He told me everything that I did."

Jn 4:40 So when the Samaritans came to Him, they begged Him to stay with them. He stayed there two days.

Jn 4:41 Many more believed because of His words.

Jn 4:42 They said to the woman, "Now we believe. Not because of your speaking, for we have heard for ourselves, and know that this is indeed the Christ, the "Savior of the World."

Jn 4:43 After the two days He went out from there and continued into Galilee.

Jn 4:44 For Jesus Himself testified that a prophet has no honor in his own country.

097   . . . JESUS AND HIS MESSAGE ARE ACCEPTED BY THE GALILEANS (Mt 4:17; Mk 1:15; Lk 4:14,15; Jn 4:45)

Jn 4:45 So when He came into Galilee the Galileans received Him, having seen all the things that He did in Jerusalem at the feast, for they also had gone to the feast.

Mt 4:17 From that time, Jesus began to preach and to say, **"REPENT! FOR THE KINGDOM OF GOD IS AT HAND."**

> *(The primary message John the Baptist taught was to repent. (Mt 3:2) Likewise Jesus now tells us in (Mt 4:17) to repent. And Peter will emphasize in his first sermon (Acts 2:38) that we have a need to repent—to turn our lives around.)*

Mk 1:15 and saying, **"THE TIME HAS COME, AND THE KINGDOM OF GOD IS AT HAND! REPENT, AND BELIEVE IN THE GOOD NEWS."** *(of forgiveness, love and acceptance)*

Lk 4:14 Jesus came in the power of the Spirit into Galilee, and news about Him spread through all the surrounding area.

Lk 4:15 He taught in their synagogues, being glorified by all.

098   *A GOVERNMENT OFFICIAL REQUESTS THE HELP OF JESUS, THE "GREAT PHYSICIAN," TO HEAL HIS SON (Jn 4:46-54)*

Jn 4:46 Jesus came therefore again to Cana of Galilee, where He changed the water into wine. There was a certain nobleman whose son was sick at Capernaum.

Jn 4:47 When he heard that Jesus had come out of Judea into Galilee, he went to Him, and begged Him that He would come down and heal his son, for he was at the point of death.

Jn 4:48 Jesus therefore said to him, **"<u>UNLESS</u> YOU SEE SIGNS AND WONDERS, YOU WILL IN NO WAY BELIEVE!"**

Jn 4:49 The nobleman said to Him, "Sir, come down before my child dies."

Jn 4:50 Jesus said to him, **"GO YOUR WAY. YOUR SON LIVES."** The man believed the word that Jesus spoke to him, and he went his way.

099   *THE OFFICIAL'S FAITH AND TRUST IS REWARDED WITH A TIMELY CURE (Jn 4:51-54)*

Jn 4:51 As he was now going down, his servants met him and reported, saying "Your child lives!"

Jn 4:52 So he inquired of them the hour when he began to get better. They said therefore to him, "Yesterday at the seventh hour, the fever left him."

Jn 4:53 So the father knew that it was at that hour in which Jesus said to him, **"YOUR SON LIVES."** He believed, as did his whole household.

Jn 4:54 This is again the second sign that Jesus did, having come out of Judea into Galilee.

100   *JESUS MAKES A PUBLIC STATEMENT IN HIS HOME TOWN OF NAZARETH (Lk 4:16-30)*

Lk 4:16 He came to Nazareth, where He had been brought up. He entered, <u>as was His custom</u>, into the synagogue <u>on the Sabbath day</u>, and stood up to read.

Heb 10:25 Let us not neglect our assembling together, as the custom of some is, but exhorting one another…

Lk 4:17 The book of the prophet Isaiah was handed to Him. He opened the book, and found the place where it was written,

Lk 4:18 "THE SPIRIT OF THE LORD IS ON ME, BECAUSE HE HAS ANOINTED ME TO PREACH THE GOOD NEWS TO THE POOR. HE HAS SENT ME TO HEAL THE BROKENHEARTED, TO PROCLAIM DELIVERANCE TO THE CAPTIVES, RECOVERING OF SIGHT TO THE BLIND, TO SET AT LIBERTY THOSE THAT ARE OPPRESSED, *(Isa 61:1-3)*

Lk 4:19 AND TO PROCLAIM THE ACCEPTABLE YEAR OF THE LORD."

101   JESUS IS FAVORABLY RECEIVED, BUT FAMILIARITY PREVENTS THEIR ACCEPTANCE OF HIM, THE HOLY "GIFT OF GOD" (Lk 4:20-24)

Lk 4:20 He closed the book, gave it back to the attendant, and sat down. The eyes of all in the synagogue were fixed on Him.

Lk 4:21 He began to tell them, **"TODAY, THIS SCRIPTURE HAS BEEN FULFILLED IN YOUR HEARING."**

Lk 4:22 All testified about Him, and wondered at the gracious words which proceeded out of His mouth, and they said, "Is this not Joseph's son?"

Lk 4:23 He said to them, **"DOUBTLESS YOU WILL TELL ME THIS PROVERB, 'PHYSICIAN, HEAL YOURSELF. WHATEVER WE HAVE HEARD DONE AT CAPERNAUM, DO ALSO HERE IN YOUR HOMETOWN.'"**

Lk 4:24 He said, **"MOST CERTAINLY I TELL YOU, NO PROPHET IS ACCEPTED IN HIS HOMETOWN."**

102   GOD'S BLESSING WAS LIMITED TO A WIDOW (Lk 4:25-27)

Lk 4:25 "BUT TRULY I TELL YOU, THERE WERE MANY WIDOWS IN ISRAEL IN THE DAYS OF ELIJAH, WHEN THE SKY WAS SHUT UP FOR THREE YEARS AND SIX MONTHS, AND A GREAT FAMINE CAME OVER ALL THE LAND.

Lk 4:26 ELIJAH WAS SENT TO NONE OF THEM, EXCEPT TO ZAREPHATH, IN THE LAND OF SIDON, TO A WOMAN WHO WAS A WIDOW."

103   THEY BECOME ANGRY WHEN JESUS INCLUDES GENTILES AS RECIPIENTS OF GOD'S BLESSINGS (Lk 4:28-30)

Lk 4:27   "**THERE WERE MANY LEPERS IN ISRAEL IN THE TIME OF ELISHA THE PROPHET, YET NOT ONE OF THEM WAS CLEANSED, EXCEPT NAAMAN, THE SYRIAN.**"

Lk 4:28   They were all filled with wrath in the synagogue, as they heard these things.

Lk 4:29   They rose up, threw Him out of the city, and led Him to the brow of the hill that their city was built on, that they might throw Him off the cliff.

Lk 4:30   But He, passing through their midst, went His way.

104   REJECTED IN HIS HOME TOWN, HE MOVES ON TO CAPERNAUM AS ISAIAH PROPHESIED (Mt 4:13-16; Lk 4:31)

Mt 4:13   Leaving Nazareth, He came and lived in Capernaum, which is by the sea, in the region of Zebulun and Naphtali,

Mt 4:14   that it might be fulfilled which was spoken through Isaiah the prophet, saying,

Mt 4:15   "The land of Zebulun and the land of Naphtali, toward the sea, beyond the Jordan, Galilee of the Gentiles.

Mt 4:16   The people who sat in darkness saw a great Light. And to those who sat in the shadow of death, Light has sprung up." *(referring to Isa 9:1,2)*

CHAPTER IV

THE DISCIPLES ARE CALLED

105 JESUS TEACHES TO A LARGE CROWD FROM PETER'S BOAT (taken from Mt 4:18; Mk 1:16; Lk 5:1-3)

Lk 5:1 Now it happened, while the multitude pressed on Him to hear the word of God that He was standing by the lake of Gennesaret.

Mk 1:16 He saw Simon, and Andrew the brother of Simon, casting a net into the sea, for they were fishermen.

Lk 5:2 He saw two boats standing by the lake, but the fishermen had left them, and were washing their nets.

Lk 5:3 He entered into one of the boats, which was Simon's, and asked him to put out a little from the land. He sat down and taught the multitudes from the boat.

106 THE DISCIPLE IS REWARDED WITH A HUGE CATCH OF FISH (Lk 5:4-11)

Lk 5:4 When He had finished speaking, He said to Simon, **"PUT OUT INTO THE DEEP,** *(further into the missionary fields)* **AND LET DOWN YOUR NETS FOR A CATCH."**

Lk 5:5 Simon answered Him, "Master, we worked all night, and took nothing, but at Your word I will let down the net."

Ps 55:22 Cast thy burden upon the Lord, and He shall sustain thee…

Lk 5:6 When they had done this, they caught such a great amount of fish, that their net was almost breaking.

107 PETER IS HUMBLED AND FEELS INADEQUATE TO BE IN THE PRESENCE OF JESUS (Lk 5:7-9)

Lk 5:7 They beckoned to their partners in the other boat, that they should come and help them. They came, and filled both boats, so that they were almost sinking.

Lk 5:8 But Simon Peter, when he saw it, fell down at Jesus' knees, saying, "Depart from me, for I am a sinful man Lord."

Lk 5:9 He was amazed and all who were with him, at the large catch of fish which they had caught.

108   JESUS CALLS SOME FISHERMEN TO FULL-TIME MIINISTRY (Mt 4:18-22; Mk 1:16-20; Lk 5:10,11)

Lk 5:10 Jesus said to Simon, **"DO NOT BE AFRAID. FROM NOW ON YOU WILL BE CATCHING MEN."**

Mk 1:19 Going on a little further from there, He saw James the son of Zebedee, and John, his brother, who were in the boat mending the nets.

Mt 4:19 He said to them, **"COME AFTER ME, AND I WILL MAKE YOU FISHERS OF MEN."**

Mk 1:20 They left their father, Zebedee, in the boat with the hired servants, and went with Jesus.

109   PEOPLE ARE IMPRESSED WITH HIS TEACHINGS AS HE COMMANDS RESPECT IN CAPERNAUM (Mk 1:21,22; Lk 4:31,32)

Mk 1:21 They went into Capernaum, and immediately on the Sabbath day He entered into the synagogue and taught.

Mk 1:22 They were impressed with His teaching, for He taught them as having authority, and not as the scribes.

110   JESUS, THE "DIVINE LIGHT," DRIVES OUT AN EVIL SPIRIT FROM A MAN WHO IS POSSESSED (Mk 1:23-28; Lk 4:33-37)

Lk 4:33 In the synagogue there was a man who had the spirit of an unclean demon, and he cried out with a loud voice,

Lk 4:34 saying, "Ah! What have we to do with You, Jesus of Nazareth? Have You come to destroy us? I know who You are. The "Holy One of God!""

Mk 1:25 Jesus rebuked him, saying, **"BE QUIET, AND COME OUT OF HIM!"**

Mk 1:26 The unclean spirit, convulsing him and crying with a loud voice, came out of him.

Mk 1:27   They were all amazed, so that they questioned among themselves, saying, "What is this? A new teaching? For with authority He commands even the evil spirits, and they obey Him!"

Lk 4:37   News about Him went out into every part of the surrounding region.

111   JESUS HEALS SIMON PETER'S MOTHER-IN-LAW (Mt 8:14,15; Mk 1:29-31; Lk 4:38,39)

Mk 1:29   Immediately, when they had come out of the synagogue, they came into the house of Simon and Andrew, with James and John.

Lk 4:38   Simon's mother-in-law was afflicted with a great fever, and they begged Him for her sake.

Mt 8:15   He touched her hand, and the fever left her. She got up and served them all.

112   JESUS, "OUR HEALER," CURES MANY OF DEMON POSSESSION (Mt 8:16,17; Mk 1:32-34; Lk 4:40,41)

Mt 8:16   When evening came, they brought to Him many possessed with demons. He cast out the spirits with a word, and healed all who were sick,

Mt 8:17   that it might be fulfilled which was spoken through Isaiah the prophet, saying, "He took our infirmities, and bore our diseases." *(Isa 53:4)*

Lk 4:41   Demons also came out from many, crying out, and saying, "You are the Christ, the Son of God!" Rebuking them, He did not allow them to speak, because they knew that He was the Messiah.

113   JESUS RISES BEFORE DAYLIGHT AND GOES TO A QUIET PLACE TO PRAY (Mt 8:1; Mk 1:35-38; Lk 4:42)

Mk 1:35   Early in the morning, while it was still dark, He rose up and went out, and departed into a deserted place, and prayed there.

Mk 1:36   Simon and those who were with Him searched for Him.

Mk 1:37   When they found Him they told Him, "Everyone is looking for You."

Lk 4:42   ...they held on to Him, so that He would not go away from them.

Mt 8:1   ...great multitudes followed Him.

114 JESUS GAINS POPULARITY AS HE HEALS AND PREACHES THROUGHOUT GALILEE (Mt 4:23-25; Mk 1:39; Lk 4:43,44)

Mt 4:23 Jesus went about in all Galilee, teaching in their synagogues, preaching the Good News of the Kingdom, and healing every disease and every sickness among the people.

Mt 4:24 The report about Him went out into all the surrounding countryside. They brought to Him all who were sick, afflicted with various diseases and torments, possessed with demons, epileptics, and paralytics, and He healed them.

Lk 4:44 He was preaching freely in the synagogues of Galilee.

115 A LEPER IS MADE WELL WHICH DRAWS MANY MORE TO JESUS (Mt 8:2-4; Mk 1:40-45; Lk 5:12,16)

Lk 5:12 It happened, while He was in one of the cities, behold, there was a man full of leprosy. When he saw Jesus, he fell on his face, and begged Him, saying, "Lord, if You want to, You can make me clean."

Mt 8:3 Jesus stretched out His hand, and touched him, saying, **"I DO WANT TO. BE MADE CLEAN."** Immediately his leprosy left him.

Mt 8:4 Jesus said to him, **"SEE THAT YOU TELL NOBODY, BUT GO, SHOW YOURSELF TO THE PRIEST, AND OFFER THE GIFT THAT MOSES COMMANDED, AS A TESTIMONY TO THEM."** *(Lev 13:49)*

Mk 1:45 But he went out, and began to proclaim it much, and to spread the matter, so that Jesus could no more openly enter into a city. And they came to Him from everywhere.

Lk 5:16 But He withdrew Himself into the desert, and prayed.

116 A CROWD GATHERS TO SEE JESUS, THE "MIRACLE WORKER" (Mt 9:1-8; Mk 2:1-12; Lk 5:17-26)

Mk 2:1 When He entered again into Capernaum after some days, it was heard that He was in a certain house.

Lk 5:17 It happened on one of those days, that He was teaching, and there were Pharisees and teachers of the law sitting by, who had come out of every village of Galilee, Judea, and Jerusalem. The power of the Lord was with Him to heal even them.

Mk 2:2 Immediately many were gathered together, so that there was no more room, not even around the door, and He preached the word to them.

117   JESUS NOTICES THE FAITH OF THOSE WANTING A MAN TO BE HEALED (Mt 9:1,2; Mk 2:3-5; Lk 5:21-26)

Lk 5:18   Behold, men brought a paralyzed man on a cot, and they sought to bring him in to lie before Jesus.

Lk 5:19   Not finding a way to bring him in because of the crowd, they went up to the housetop, and let him down through the tiles, on his cot in front of Jesus.

Mt 9:2   Jesus, <u>seeing their faith</u>, said to the paralytic, **"SON, CHEER UP! YOUR SINS ARE FORGIVEN YOU."**

118   THOSE IN CHARGE QUESTION HIS AUTHORITY TO FORGIVE SIN (Mt 9:3-5; Mk 2:6-9; Lk 5:21-23)

Lk 5:21   The scribes and the Pharisees began to reason, saying, "Who is this that speaks blasphemies? Who can forgive sins, but God alone?"

Mt 9:4   Jesus, knowing their thoughts, said, **"WHY DO YOU THINK EVIL IN YOUR HEARTS?**

Mk 2:9   **WHICH IS EASIER, TO TELL THE PARALYTIC, 'YOUR SINS ARE FORGIVEN,' OR TO SAY, 'ARISE, AND TAKE UP YOUR BED, AND WALK?' "**

119   JESUS, THE "GOD OF MERCY," DEMONSTRATES HIS ABILITY TO HEAL AND FORGIVE SINS (Mt 9:6-8; Mk 2:10-12; Lk 5:24-26)

Mk 2:10   **"BUT THAT YOU MAY KNOW THAT THE "SON OF MAN" HAS AUTHORITY ON EARTH TO FORGIVE SINS,"** then He said to the paralytic,

Mk 2:11   **"I TELL YOU, ARISE, TAKE UP YOUR MAT. AND GO TO YOUR HOME."**

Lk 5:25   Immediately he rose up before them, and took up that which he was laying on and departed to his house, glorifying God.

Mt 9:8   But when the multitudes saw it, they marveled and glorified God also, who had given such authority to men.

120   HE CALLS EVEN A TAX COLLECTOR TO BECOME A DISCIPLE (Mt 9:9; Mk 2:13,14; Lk 5:27,28)

Mk 2:13   He went out again by the seaside. Everyone came to Him, and He taught them.

Mk 2:14   As He passed by, He saw Levi, the son of Alphaeus, sitting at the tax office, and He said to him, **"FOLLOW ME."**

Lk 5:28   He left everything, and rose up and followed Him.

121   JESUS CORRECTS THEIR OBJECTIONS TO HIS ASSOCIATION WITH SINNERS (Mt 9:10-13; Mk 2:15-17; Lk 5:29-32)

Mk 2:15   It happened that He was reclining at a table in Levi's house. Many tax collectors and sinners sat down with Jesus and His disciples, for there were many, who had followed Him.

Mk 2:16   The scribes and the Pharisees, when they saw that He was eating with the sinners and tax collectors, said to His disciples, "Why is it that He eats and drinks with tax collectors and sinners?"

Mt 9:12   When Jesus heard it, He said to them, **"THOSE WHO ARE HEALTHY HAVE NO NEED FOR A PHYSICIAN, BUT THOSE WHO ARE SICK DO.**

Mt 9:13   BUT YOU GO AND LEARN WHAT THIS SAYING MEANS, 'I DESIRE MERCY, AND NOT SACRIFICE,' FOR I CAME NOT TO CALL THE RIGHTEOUS, BUT SINNERS TO REPENTANCE."

122   ALL TRUE FOLLOWERS OF JESUS WILL FAST WHEN THE TIME COMES (Mt 9:14,15; Mk 2:18-20; Lk 5:33-35)

Mk 2:18   John's disciples and the Pharisees were fasting, and they came and asked Him, "Why do John's disciples and the disciples of the Pharisees fast, but Your disciples do not fast?"

Mk 2:19   Jesus said to them, **"CAN THE GUESTS OF THE BRIDEGROOM** *(Jesus)* **FAST WHILE THE BRIDEGROOM IS WITH THEM? AS LONG AS THEY HAVE THE BRIDEGROOM WITH THEM, THEY SHOULD NOT FAST.**

Mk 2:20   BUT THE DAY WILL COME WHEN THE BRIDEGROOM WILL BE TAKEN AWAY FROM THEM, <u>AND THEN</u> MY DISCIPLES WILL FAST."

123   JESUS REFERS TO THE OLD ORDER AND SUGGESTS THE BEGINNING OF A NEW BELIEF SYSTEM (Mt 9:16,17; Mk 2:21,22; Lk 5:36-39)

Mk 2:21   "NO ONE SEWS A PIECE OF UNSHRUNK CLOTH ON AN OLD GARMENT. THE PATCH SHRINKS AND THE NEW TEARS AWAY FROM THE OLD, AND A WORSE HOLE IS MADE.

Mt 9:17 NEITHER DO PEOPLE PUT NEW WINE INTO OLD WINESKINS. THE SKINS WOULD BURST, AND THE WINE BE SPILLED, AND THE SKINS RUINED. NO, THEY PUT NEW WINE INTO FRESH WINESKINS, AND BOTH ARE PRESERVED.

Lk 5:39 NO MAN HAVING DRUNK OLD WINE IMMEDIATELY DESIRES ANY NEW. FOR HE SAYS, 'THE OLD IS BETTER.' "

124   HE GOES TO JERUSALEM AND COMES TO THE POOL AT BETHESDA (Jn 5:1-47)

Jn 5:1   After these things, there was a feast of the Jews, and Jesus went up to Jerusalem.

Jn 5:2   Now in Jerusalem by the sheep gate, there is a pool, which is called in Hebrew, Bethesda, having five porches.

Jn 5:3   Nearby lay a great many of those who were sick, blind, lame, or paralyzed, waiting for the moving of the water,

Jn 5:4   for an angel went down at certain times into the pool, and stirred up the water. Whoever stepped in first after the stirring of the water was made whole from whatever disease he had.

125   JESUS, THE "HEART OF MERCY," HAS PITY FOR A HOPELESS INVALID UNABLE TO HELP HIMSELF (Jn 5:5-9)

Jn 5:5   A certain man was there, who had been sick for thirty-eight years.

Jn 5:6   When Jesus saw him lying there, and knew that he had been sick for a long time, He asked him, **"DO YOU WANT TO BE MADE WELL?"**

Jn 5:7   The sick man answered Him, "Sir, I have no one to put me into the pool when the water is stirred up. While I am coming, another steps down ahead of me."

Jn 5:8   Jesus said to him, **"ARISE, TAKE UP YOUR MAT, AND WALK ."**

Jn 5:9   Immediately the man was made well and took up his mat and walked. Now that day was the Sabbath. *(their Saturday, a holy day)*

126   THE HEALING IRRITATES THE RELIGIOUS AUTHORITIES (Jn 5:10-16)

Jn 5:10   So the Jews said to him who was cured, "It is the Sabbath. It is not lawful for you to carry your mat."

Jn 5:11 He answered them, "He who made me well, the same said to me, 'Take up your mat, and walk.'"

Jn 5:12 Then they asked him, "Who is the man who said to you, 'Take up your mat, and walk?'"

Jn 5:13 But he who was healed did not know who it was, for Jesus had withdrawn, a crowd being in that place.

127   THE SABBATH HEALING WILL LEAD TO THE PERSECUTION OF JESUS (Jn 5:14-16)

Jn 5:14 Afterward Jesus found him in the temple, and said to him, **"BEHOLD, YOU ARE MADE WELL. SIN NO MORE, SO THAT NOTHING WORSE HAPPENS TO YOU."**

Jn 5:15 The man went away, and told the Jews that it was Jesus who had made him well.

Jn 5:16 For this cause the Jews began to persecute Jesus and sought to kill Him, because He did these things on a Sabbath.

128   HE TELLS THEM THAT HE IS THE "SON OF THE HIGHEST" WHICH MAKES THEM EVEN MORE ANGRY (Jn 5:17-19)

Jn 5:17 But Jesus answered them, **"MY FATHER IS ALWAYS WORKING. SO I TOO MUST WORK."**

Jn 5:18 For this cause therefore the Jews sought all the more to kill Him, because He not only broke the Sabbath, but now calls God His own father, making Himself equal with God.

Jn 5:19 Jesus therefore answered them, **"MOST CERTAINLY, I TELL YOU, THE SON CAN DO NOTHING OF HIMSELF, EXCEPT WHAT HE SEES THE FATHER DOING. FOR WHATEVER THINGS HE DOES, THESE THE SON ALSO DOES LIKEWISE."**

129   BEING A BLESSED SON GIVES HIM COMPLETE EQUALITY WITH THE FATHER (Jn 5:20-23)

Jn 5:20 **"FOR THE FATHER HAS AFFECTION FOR THE SON, AND SHOWS HIM ALL THINGS THAT HE HIMSELF DOES. HE WILL SHOW HIM EVEN GREATER WORKS THAN THESE THAT YOU MAY MARVEL.**

Jn 5:21 **THE FATHER RAISES THE DEAD AND GIVES THEM LIFE, EVEN SO THE SON ALSO GIVES LIFE TO WHOM HE DESIRES.**

Jn 5:22 FOR THE FATHER JUDGES NO ONE, BUT HE HAS GIVEN ALL JUDGMENT TO HIS SON,

Jn 5:23 THAT ALL MAY HONOR THE SON, EVEN AS THEY HONOR THE FATHER. HE WHO DOES NOT HONOR THE SON DOES NOT HONOR THE FATHER WHO SENT HIM."

130 JESUS, THE "DOOR TO HEAVEN," OFFERS US AN OPPORTUNITY TO GAIN ETERNAL LIFE (Jn 5:24-29)

Jn 5:24 "MOST CERTAINLY I TELL YOU, HE WHO HEARS MY WORD, AND BELIEVES HIM WHO SENT ME, HAS ETERNAL LIFE. HE DOES NOT COME INTO JUDGMENT, BUT PASSES FROM DEATH INTO LIFE. *(life after life)*

Jn 5:25 MOST CERTAINLY, I TELL YOU, THE HOUR COMES, AND NOW IS, WHEN THE DEAD WILL HEAR THE SON OF GOD'S VOICE, AND THOSE WHO HEAR WILL LIVE.

Jn 5:26 FOR AS THE FATHER IS SELF-EXISTENT (I AM THAT I AM) EVEN SO HE GAVE TO HIS SON ALSO TO HAVE LIFE IN HIMSELF."

131 EVERYONE WILL BE RESURRECTED, THEN REWARDED, OR PUNISHED, ACCORDING TO THEIR ACTIONS (Jn 5:27-29)

Jn 5:27 "GOD ALSO GAVE HIM AUTHORITY TO EXECUTE JUDGMENT, BECAUSE HE IS THE SON OF MAN.

Jn 5:28 DO NOT MARVEL AT THIS, FOR THE HOUR COMES, IN WHICH ALL THAT ARE IN THE TOMBS WILL HEAR HIS VOICE,

Jn 5:29 AND WILL COME OUT; THOSE WHO HAVE DONE GOOD, TO THE RESURRECTION AND LIFE, AND THOSE WHO HAVE DONE EVIL, TO THE RESURRECTION AND CONDEMNATION."

132 JESUS, THE "LOVER OF THE LOST," IS ALWAYS IN THE WILL OF THE FATHER (Jn 5:30-40)

Jn 5:30 "I CAN OF MYSELF DO NOTHING. AS I HEAR, I JUDGE. AND MY JUDGMENT IS RIGHTEOUS, BECAUSE I DO NOT SEEK MY OWN WILL—BUT ONLY THE WILL OF MY FATHER WHO SENT ME.

Jn 5:31 IF I TESTIFY ABOUT MYSELF, MY WITNESS IS NOT VALID.

Jn 5:32 IT IS ANOTHER WHO TESTIFIES ABOUT ME. I KNOW THAT THE TESTIMONY WHICH HE TESTIFIES ABOUT ME IS TRUE."

133   JOHN WAS A GOOD WITNESS TO JESUS, THE "MAJESTIC LIGHT" (Jn 5:33-35)

Jn 5:33 "YOU HAVE ENQUIRED OF JOHN, AND HE HAS TESTIFIED TO "THE TRUTH." *(Jesus)*

Jn 5:34 BUT THE TESTIMONY WHICH I RECEIVE IS NOT FROM MAN. HOWEVER, I SAY THESE THINGS THAT YOU MAY BE SAVED.

Jn 5:35 JOHN WAS A BURNING AND SHINING LIGHT, AND YOU WERE WILLING TO REJOICE FOR A WHILE IN HIS LIGHT."

134   THE MIRACLES OF JESUS ALSO ENDORSE HIS LORDSHIP (Jn 5:36-38)

Jn 5:36 "BUT THE TESTIMONY WHICH I HAVE IS GREATER THAN THAT OF JOHN. FOR THE WORKS WHICH THE FATHER GAVE ME TO ACCOMPLISH, THE VERY WORKS THAT I DO, TESTIFY ABOUT ME THAT THE FATHER HAS SENT ME.

Jn 5:37 THE FATHER HIMSELF, WHO SENT ME, HAS INDEED TESTIFIED ABOUT ME. YOU HAVE NEITHER HEARD HIS VOICE AT ANY TIME, NOR EVER SEEN HIM IN PERSON.

Jn 5:38 YOU DO NOT KEEP HIS WORD LIVING IN YOU, BECAUSE YOU DO NOT BELIEVE IN HIM WHOM HE SENT."

135   IGNORING THE PROPHECIES OF OLD WILL CAUSE THEM TO LOSE ETERNAL LIFE (Jn 5:39-41)

Jn 5:39 "YOU SEARCH THE SCRIPTURES, BECAUSE YOU THINK THAT IN THEM YOU HAVE ETERNAL LIFE. BUT THESE ARE THEY WHICH SPEAK ABOUT ME.

Jn 5:40 YET, YOU WILL NOT COME TO ME, THAT YOU MAY HAVE LIFE.

Jn 5:41 I DO NOT RECEIVE HONOR FROM MEN."

136   HE REBUKES THEM FOR THEIR COLDNESS AND DISBELIEF (Jn 5:42-44)

Jn 5:42   "BUT I KNOW YOU, THAT YOU DO NOT HAVE GOD'S LOVE IN YOURSELVES.

Jn 5:43   I HAVE COME IN MY FATHER'S NAME, AND YOU DO NOT RECEIVE ME. IF ANOTHER COMES IN HIS OWN NAME *(the prince of darkness)* **YOU WILL RECEIVE HIM.**

Jn 5:44   HOW CAN YOU BELIEVE, WHO RECEIVE HONOR FROM ONE ANOTHER, AND SEEK NOT THE HONOR THAT COMES FROM GOD ONLY?"

137   MOSES HIMSELF WILL ACCUSE THOSE AMONG THEM REFUSING TO ACCEPT THE FULFILLMENT OF SCRIPTURES (Jn 5:45-47)

Jn 5:45   "DO NOT THINK THAT I WILL ACCUSE YOU TO THE FATHER. THERE IS ONE WHO ACCUSES YOU, AND THAT IS MOSES, ON WHOM YOU HAVE SET YOUR HOPE.

Jn 5:46   FOR IF YOU BELIEVED MOSES, YOU WOULD BELIEVE ME, FOR HE WROTE ABOUT ME.

Jn 5:47   BUT IF YOU DO NOT BELIEVE HIS WRITINGS, HOW WILL YOU BELIEVE MY WORDS?"

138   THE DISCIPLES PLUCK GRAIN TO EAT ON THE SABBATH IN VIOLATION OF THE LAW (Mt 12:1-8; Mk 2:23-28; Lk 6:1-4)

Mt 12:1   At that time, Jesus walked on the Sabbath day through the grain fields. His disciples were hungry and began to pluck heads of grain to eat.

Mt 12:2   But the Pharisees, when they saw it, said to Him, "Look, Your disciples do what is not lawful to do on the Sabbath."

Mt 12:3   But He said to them, **"HAVE YOU NOT READ WHAT DAVID DID WHEN HE WAS HUNGRY, ALONG WITH THOSE WHO WERE WITH HIM,**

Mt 12:4   HOW HE ENTERED INTO GOD'S HOUSE, AND ATE THE SHOW BREAD, WHICH WAS NOT LAWFUL FOR HIM TO EAT, NEITHER FOR THOSE WHO WERE WITH HIM, BUT ONLY FOR THE PRIESTS?"

139   *THE AUTHORITY OF JESUS IS CLEARLY REVEALED (Mt 12:5-8; Mk 2:26-28; Lk 6:5)*

Mt 12:5   "OR HAVE YOU NOT READ IN THE LAW, THAT ON THE SABBATH DAY, THE PRIESTS IN THE TEMPLE DISHONOR THE SABBATH, AND ARE NOT GUILTY?

Mt 12:6   BUT I TELL YOU THAT ONE GREATER THAN THE TEMPLE IS HERE.

Mt 12:7   BUT IF YOU HAD KNOWN WHAT THIS MEANS, 'I DESIRE MERCY, AND NOT SACRIFICE,' YOU WOULD NOT HAVE CONDEMNED THE GUILTLESS." *(Hos 6:6)*

Mk 2:27   He said to them, "**THE SABBATH WAS MADE FOR MAN, NOT MAN FOR THE SABBATH.** *(Ex 23:12)*

Mk 2:28   THEREFORE THE SON OF MAN IS LORD EVEN OF THE SABBATH."

140   *THE QUESTION OF HEALING ON THE SABBATH COMES UP AGAIN (Mt 12:9-14; Mk 3:1-6; Lk 6:6-11)*

Mk 3:1   He entered again into the synagogue, and there was a man there whose hand was withered.

Lk 6:7   The scribes and the Pharisees watched Him, to see whether He would heal on the Sabbath, that they might find an accusation against Him.

Lk 6:8   But He knew their thoughts, and He said to the man who had the withered hand, "**RISE UP, AND STAND IN THE MIDDLE.**" He arose and stood.

Mk 3:4   He said to them, "**IS IT LAWFUL ON THE SABBATH DAY TO DO GOOD, OR TO DO HARM? TO SAVE A LIFE, OR TO KILL?**" But they were silent.

Mt 12:11 He said to them, "**WHAT MAN IS THERE AMONG YOU, WHO HAS ONE SHEEP, AND IF THIS ONE FALLS INTO A PIT ON THE SABBATH DAY, WILL HE NOT GRAB ON TO IT, AND LIFT IT OUT?**

Mt 12:12 OF HOW MUCH MORE VALUE THEN IS THIS MAN THAN A SHEEP? THEREFORE IT IS LAWFUL TO DO GOOD ON THE SABBATH DAY."

Mk 3:5   Then He looked around at them with anger, being grieved at the hardening of their hearts.

141   JESUS HEALS THE MAN WHICH LEADS TO THE LORD'S UNDOING (Mt 12: 13-15; Lk 6:9-11)

Mt 12:13   Then He told the man, **"STRETCH OUT YOUR HAND."** He stretched it out, and it was restored whole, just like the other.

Lk 6:11   But they were filled with rage, and talked with one another about what they might do to Jesus.

Mk 3:6   The Pharisees went out, and immediately conspired with Herod's people, how they might destroy Him.

Mt 12:15   Jesus, perceiving that, withdrew from there…

142   JESUS, THE "FORGIVER OF SINS," MOVES TOWARD THE SEA AND A LARGE CROWD FOLLOWS (Mk 3:7-12)

Mk 3:7   Jesus withdraws to the sea with His disciples, and a great multitude followed Him from Galilee and from Judea,

Mk 3:8   also from Jerusalem, from Idumaea, beyond the Jordan, and those from around Tyre and Sidon. A great crowd, who heard what great things He did, came to Him.

Mk 3:9   He spoke to His disciples that a little boat should stay near Him because of the crowd, so that they would not crush Him.

143   JESUS RESTORES ALL WHO COME TO HIM (Mt 12:15; Mk 3:10,11)

Mk 3:10   For He had healed many, so that as many as had diseases pressed on Him that they might touch Him.

Mk 3:11   The unclean spirits, whenever they saw Him, fell down before Him, and cried, "You are the Son of God!"

Mt 12:15   …Great multitudes followed Him, and He healed them all.

144   WHAT ISAIAH SAID ABOUT JESUS IS TO COME TRUE (Mt 12:16-21)

Mt 12:16   He commanded them that they should not make Him known,

Mt 12:17   that it might be fulfilled which was spoken through Isaiah the prophet, saying,

Mt 12:18 "Behold, My servant whom I have chosen, My beloved in whom My soul is well pleased. I will pour My Spirit on Him. He will proclaim justice to the nations."

145   THE PROPHECY CONTINUES WITH JESUS BEING A GENTLE MAN *(Mt 12:19-21)*

Mt 12:19 "He will not strive, nor shout; neither will anyone hear His voice in the streets.

Mt 12:20 He will not break a bruised reed. He will not quench a smoking flax, until He leads goodness to victory.

Mt 12:21 In His name, the nations will hope." *(Isa 42:1-4)*

146   JESUS, THE "PRAYER WARRIOR," SPENDS A WHOLE NIGHT PRAYING, THEN SELECTS HIS DISCIPLES *(Mt 10:1-4; Mk 3:13-19; Lk 6:12-16)*

Lk 6:12 It happened in these days, that He went out to the mountain to pray, and He continued all night in prayer to God.

Lk 6:13 When it was day, He called His disciples, and from them He chose twelve whom He also named apostles.

Mk 3:14 He appointed the twelve that they might be with Him, and that He might send them out to preach,

Mk 3:15 and to have authority to heal sicknesses and to cast out demons.

147   THE TWELVE APOSTLES ARE CHOSEN AND SINGLED OUT *(Mt 10:2-4; Mk 3:16-19; Lk 6:14-16)*

Lk 6:14 Simon, whom He also named Peter, Andrew, his brother, James, John, Philip, Bartholomew,

Lk 6:15 Matthew, Thomas, James, the son of Alphaeus, Simon, who was called the Zealot,

Lk 6:16 Judas the son of James, and Judas Iscariot, who became a traitor.

CHAPTER V

THE SERMON ON THE MOUNT

148   JESUS OUTLINES HIS PRIMARY MESSAGES IN THIS, HIS INAUGURAL ADDRESS (taken from Mt 5:1-7; Lk 6:17-49)

Lk 6:17   He came down with them and stood on a level place, with a company of His disciples, and a great number of the people from all Judea and Jerusalem, and from the sea coast of Tyre and Sidon, who came to hear Him and to be healed of their diseases,

Lk 6:18   as well as those who were troubled by unclean spirits, and they were being healed.

Lk 6:19   Everyone sought to touch Him, for power came out from Him and healed them all.

149   JESUS BEGINS BY TELLING WHO IS MOST FAVORED BY GOD (Mt 5:2-12; Lk 6:20-26)

Mt 5:2   He spoke out and began to teach them, saying,

Mt 5:3   "BLESSED ARE THE POOR IN SPIRIT, FOR THEIRS IS THE KINGDOM OF HEAVEN.

Mt 5:4   BLESSED ARE THOSE WHO MOURN, FOR THEY SHALL BE COMFORTED.

Mt 5:5   BLESSED ARE THE GENTLE IN SPIRIT, FOR THEY SHALL INHERIT THE EARTH.

Mt 5:6   BLESSED ARE THOSE WHO HUNGER AND THIRST AFTER RIGHTEOUSNESS, FOR THEY SHALL BE FILLED."

150   HE CONTINUES WITH BLESSINGS FOR THOSE WHO ARE GOD-CONSCIOUS AND WHO HAVE A CONSIDERATION FOR OTHERS (Mt 5:7-9)

Mt 5:7   "BLESSED ARE THE MERCIFUL, FOR THEY SHALL OBTAIN MERCY.

Mt 5:8   BLESSED ARE THE PURE IN HEART, FOR THEY SHALL SEE GOD.

Mt 5:9 BLESSED ARE THE PEACEMAKERS, FOR THEY SHALL BE CALLED CHILDREN OF GOD.

Lk 6:21 BLESSED ARE YOU WHO HUNGER NOW, FOR YOU WILL BE FILLED. BLESSED ARE YOU WHO WEEP NOW, FOR YOU WILL LAUGH."

151   EVEN PERSECUTION FOR THE KINGDOM SHOULD BE ACCEPTED AS A PRIVILEGE (Mt 5:10-12; Lk 6:22,23)

Mt 5:10 "BLESSED ARE THOSE WHO ARE PERSECUTED FOR RIGHTEOUSNESS' SAKE, FOR THEIRS IS THE KINGDOM OF HEAVEN.

Mt 5:11 BLESSED ARE YOU WHEN PEOPLE REPROACH YOU, PERSECUTE YOU, AND SAY ALL KINDS OF EVIL AGAINST YOU FALSELY, FOR MY SAKE.

Mt 5:12 REJOICE, AND BE EXCEEDINGLY GLAD, FOR GREAT IS YOUR REWARD IN HEAVEN. FOR THAT IS HOW THEY PERSECUTED THE PROPHETS WHO CAME BEFORE YOU. *(2 Chr 36:16)*

Lk 6:22 BLESSED ARE YOU WHEN MEN SHALL HATE YOU, AND WHEN THEY SHALL EXCLUDE AND MOCK YOU, AND CALL OUT YOUR NAME AS EVIL, FOR THE SON OF MAN'S SAKE.

Lk 6:23 REJOICE IN THAT DAY, AND LEAP FOR JOY, FOR BEHOLD, YOUR REWARD IS GREAT IN HEAVEN, FOR THEIR FATHERS DID THE SAME THING TO THE PROPHETS."

152   BUT JESUS WARNS THE SELFISH AND SELF-INDULGENT (Lk 6:24-29)

Lk 6:24 "BUT WOE TO YOU WHO ARE RICH! FOR YOU HAVE RECEIVED YOUR CONSOLATION.

Lk 6:25 WOE TO YOU, YOU WHO ARE FULL NOW, FOR YOU WILL BE HUNGRY. WOE TO YOU WHO LAUGH NOW, FOR YOU WILL MOURN AND WEEP.

Lk 6:26 WOE WHEN MEN SPEAK WELL OF YOU, FOR THEIR FATHERS DID THE SAME THING TO THE FALSE PROPHETS."

153   PEOPLE HAVE AN OCCASION TO BLESS OTHERS (Mt 5:13-16)

Mt 5:13 "YOU ARE THE SALT OF THE EARTH BUT IF THE SALT HAS LOST ITS FLAVOR, WITH WHAT WILL IT BE SALTED? IT IS THEN GOOD FOR NOTHING,

BUT TO BE CAST OUT AND TRODDEN UNDER THE FEET OF MEN.

Mt 5:14   YOU ARE THE LIGHT OF THE WORLD. A CITY LOCATED ON A HILL CANNOT BE HIDDEN.

Mt 5:15   NEITHER DO YOU LIGHT A LAMP, AND PUT IT UNDER A BASKET, BUT ON A STAND, AND IT SHINES TO ALL WHO ARE IN THE HOUSE.

Mt 5:16   EVEN SO, LET YOUR LIGHT SHINE BEFORE MEN, THAT THEY MAY SEE YOUR GOOD WORKS, AND GLORIFY YOUR FATHER WHO IS IN HEAVEN."

154   *JESUS ENDORSES AND STRESSES THE IMPORTANCE OF THE CODE OF MOSES (Mt 5:17-20)*

Mt 5:17   "DO NOT THINK THAT I CAME TO DESTROY THE LAW OR THE PROPHETS. I DID NOT COME TO DESTROY, BUT TO FULFILL IT.

Mt 5:18   FOR MOST CERTAINLY, I TELL YOU, UNTIL HEAVEN AND EARTH PASS AWAY, NOT EVEN THE SMALLEST LETTER, OR ONE TINY PEN STROKE SHALL IN ANY WAY PASS AWAY FROM THE LAW, UNTIL ALL THINGS ARE ACCOMPLISHED.

Mt 5:19 WHOEVER, THEREFORE, SHALL BREAK EVEN THE LEAST COMMANDMENT, AND TEACH OTHERS TO DO SO, SHALL BE CALLED LEAST IN THE KINGDOM OF HEAVEN. BUT WHOEVER SHALL DO AND TEACH THEM, SHALL BE CALLED GREAT IN THE KINGDOM OF HEAVEN.

Mt 5:20   FOR I TELL YOU THAT UNLESS YOUR RIGHTEOUSNESS EXCEEDS THAT OF THE SCRIBES AND PHARISEES, YOU SHALL IN NO WAY ENTER INTO THE KINGDOM OF HEAVEN."

155   *HE TEACHES ABOUT ANGER AND FEELINGS OF RESENTMENT (Mt 5:21-26)*

Mt 5:21   "YOU HAVE HEARD THAT IT WAS SAID TO THE ANCIENT ONES, 'YOU SHALL NOT MURDER,' AND 'WHOEVER SHALL MURDER SHALL BE IN DANGER OF THE JUDGMENT.'

Mt 5:22   BUT I TELL YOU, THAT EVERYONE WHO IS ANGRY WITH HIS BROTHER WITHOUT A CAUSE SHALL BE IN DANGER OF THE JUDGMENT, AND WHOEVER SHALL SAY TO HIS BROTHER, 'RACA!' *(idiot)* SHALL ANSWER TO THE COUNCIL, AND WHOEVER SHALL SAY, 'YOU FOOL!' SHALL BE IN DANGER OF THE FIRES OF HELL.

Mt 5:23 IF THEREFORE YOU ARE OFFERING YOUR GIFT AT THE ALTAR, AND THERE REMEMBER THAT YOUR BROTHER HAS ANYTHING AGAINST YOU,

Mt 5:24 LEAVE YOUR GIFT THERE BEFORE THE ALTAR, AND GO YOUR WAY. FIRST BE RECONCILED TO YOUR BROTHER, AND THEN COME BACK AND OFFER YOUR GIFT.

Mt 5:25 AGREE WITH YOUR ADVERSARY QUICKLY, WHILE YOU ARE WITH HIM IN THE WAY, LEST PERHAPS THE PROSECUTOR DELIVER YOU TO THE JUDGE, AND THE JUDGE DELIVER YOU TO THE OFFICER, AND YOU BE CAST INTO PRISON.

Mt 5:26 MOST CERTAINLY I TELL YOU, YOU SHALL BY NO MEANS GET OUT OF THERE, UNTIL YOU HAVE PAID THE LAST PENNY."

156   *ONE SHOULD ELIMINATE THE SOURCE OF SIN (Mt 5:27,28)*

Mt 5:27 "YOU HAVE HEARD THAT IT WAS SAID, 'YOU SHALL NOT COMMIT ADULTERY,

Mt 5:28 BUT I TELL YOU THAT EVERYONE WHO GAZES AT A WOMAN TO LUST AFTER HER HAS COMMITTED ADULTERY WITH HER ALREADY, IN HIS HEART." *(Prov 6:25)*

157   *EVERYONE SHOULD DO EVERYTHING TO AVOID DAMNATION (Mt 5:29,30)*

Mt 5:29 "IF YOUR RIGHT EYE CAUSES YOU TO SIN, PLUCK IT OUT AND THROW IT AWAY FROM YOU. FOR IT IS MORE PROFITABLE FOR YOU THAT ONE OF YOUR MEMBERS SHOULD PERISH, THAN FOR YOUR WHOLE BODY TO BE CAST INTO HELL.

Mt 5:30 IF YOUR RIGHT HAND CAUSES YOU TO COMMIT SIN, CUT IT OFF, AND THROW IT AWAY FROM YOU. FOR IT IS MORE PROFITABLE FOR YOU THAT ONE OF YOUR MEMBERS SHOULD PERISH, THAN FOR YOUR WHOLE BODY TO BE CAST INTO HELL."

158   *JESUS GIVES A PRELIMINARY TEACHING ABOUT DIVORCE (Mt 5:31,32)*

Mt 5:31 "IT WAS ALSO SAID, 'WHOEVER SHALL PUT AWAY HIS WIFE, LET HIM GIVE HER A WRITING OF DIVORCE,

Mt 5:32 BUT I TELL YOU THAT WHOEVER PUTS AWAY HIS WIFE EXCEPT FOR THE CAUSE OF SEXUAL IMMORALITY, MAKES HER AN ADULTERESS. AND

WHOEVER MARRIES HER WHEN SHE IS PUT AWAY COMMITS ADULTERY."

159   IT IS BEST TO REFRAIN FROM MAKING UNNECESSARY PROMISES (Mt 5:33-37)

Mt 5:33 "AGAIN YOU HAVE HEARD THAT IT WAS SAID TO THEM OF OLD, 'YOU SHALL NOT MAKE FALSE VOWS, BUT SHALL PERFORM YOUR VOWS TO THE LORD.'

Mt 5:34 BUT I TELL YOU, DO NOT SWEAR AT ALL, NEITHER BY HEAVEN, FOR IT IS THE THRONE OF GOD,

Mt 5:35 NOR BY THE EARTH, FOR IT IS THE FOOTSTOOL OF HIS FEET, NOR BY JERUSALEM, FOR IT IS THE CITY OF THE GREAT KING.

Mt 5:36 NEITHER SHALL YOU SWEAR BY YOUR HEAD, FOR YOU CANNOT MAKE ONE HAIR WHITE OR BLACK.

Mt 5:37 BUT LET YOUR 'YES' BE 'YES' AND YOUR 'NO' BE 'NO.' WHATEVER IS MORE THAN THESE IS OF THE EVIL ONE."

160   DO NOT RETALIATE OR TAKE REVENGE (Mt 5:38,39; Lk 6:27,28)

Mt 5:38 "YOU HAVE HEARD THAT IT WAS SAID, 'AN EYE FOR AN EYE, AND A TOOTH FOR A TOOTH.'

Mt 5:39 BUT I TELL YOU, DO NOT RESIST HIM WHO IS EVIL, BUT WHOEVER STRIKES YOU ON YOUR RIGHT CHEEK, TURN TO HIM THE OTHER ALSO."

Heb 10:30 ... Revenge is Mine, says the Lord...

161   JESUS, THE "MAN OF PEACE," TELLS US TO GREET OPPRESSION WITH KINDNESS (Mt 5:40-41; Lk 6:29)

Mt 5:40 "IF ANYONE SUES YOU TO TAKE AWAY YOUR COAT, LET HIM HAVE YOUR OUTER COAT ALSO.

Mt 5:41 WHOEVER COMPELS YOU TO GO ONE MILE, GO WITH HIM TWO.

Lk 6:29 TO HIM WHO STRIKES YOU ON THE CHEEK, OFFER HIM ALSO THE OTHER."

162   GIVE MATERIALLY TO GAIN SPIRITUALY (Mt 5:42; Lk 6:30,31)

Mt 5:42   "GIVE TO HIM WHO ASKS YOU, AND DO NOT TURN AWAY FROM HIM WHO DESIRES TO BORROW FROM YOU. *(Deut 15:8)*

Lk 6:30   AND DO NOT ASK HIM WHO TAKES AWAY YOUR GOODS TO GIVE THEM BACK AGAIN.

Lk 6:31   AS YOU WOULD LIKE PEOPLE TO DO TO YOU, DO EXACTLY SO TO THEM!"

163   CONQUER YOUR ENEMY WITH LOVE (Mt 5:43-45; Lk 6:27)

Mt 5:43   "YOU HAVE HEARD THAT IT WAS SAID, 'YOU SHALL LOVE YOUR NEIGHBOR, AND HATE YOUR ENEMY.'

Mt 5:44   BUT I TELL YOU, LOVE YOUR ENEMIES. BLESS THOSE WHO CURSE YOU. DO GOOD TO THOSE WHO HATE YOU. AND PRAY FOR THOSE WHO MISTREAT YOU, AND PERSECUTE YOU,

Mt 5:45   THAT YOU MAY BE CHILDREN OF YOUR FATHER WHO IS IN HEAVEN. FOR HE MAKES HIS SUN TO RISE ON THE EVIL AND THE GOOD, AND SENDS RAIN ON THE JUST AND THE UNJUST.

Lk 6:27   BUT I TELL YOU WHO HEAR ME, LOVE YOUR ENEMIES, DO GOOD TO THOSE WHO HATE YOU."

164   A CHRISTIAN MUST LIVE MORE HONORABLY THAN THE PAGANS (Mt 5:46-47; Lk 6:32-34)

Lk 6:32   "IF YOU LOVE ONLY THOSE WHO LOVE YOU, WHAT CREDIT IS THAT TO YOU? FOR EVEN SINNERS LOVE THOSE WHO LOVE THEM.

Lk 6:33   IF YOU DO GOOD TO THOSE WHO DO GOOD TO YOU, WHAT CREDIT IS THAT TO YOU? FOR EVEN SINNERS DO THE SAME.

Lk 6:34   IF YOU LEND TO THOSE FROM WHOM YOU HOPE TO RECEIVE BACK WHAT CREDIT IS THAT TO YOU? EVEN SINNERS LEND TO SINNERS TO RECEIVE BACK AS MUCH.

Mt 5:47   IF YOU GREET ONLY YOUR FRIENDS, WHAT MORE DO YOU DO THAN OTHERS? DO NOT EVEN THE TAX COLLECTORS DO THE SAME?"

165   THERE ARE MANY OCCASIONS TO DO GOOD TO WIN THOSE WHO ARE LOST
(Mt 5:48; Lk 6:35,36)

Lk 6:35 "BUT LOVE YOUR ENEMIES, AND DO GOOD. AND LEND, EXPECTING NOTHING BACK, AND YOUR REWARD WILL BE GREAT, AND YOU WILL BE CHILDREN OF THE MOST HIGH, FOR HE IS KIND TOWARD THE UNTHANKFUL AND EVIL.

Lk 6:36 THEREFORE BE MERCIFUL, EVEN AS YOUR FATHER IS ALSO MERCIFUL.

Mt 5:48 STRIVE TO BE PERFECT, JUST AS YOUR FATHER IN HEAVEN IS PERFECT."

166   CHARITY SHOULD BE DONE WITH MODESTY AND WITH THE RIGHT MOTIVES
(Mt 6:1-4)

Mt 6:1 "BE CAREFUL THAT YOU DO NOT DO YOUR CHARITABLE GIVING BEFORE MEN, TO BE SEEN BY THEM, OR ELSE YOU WILL HAVE NO REWARD FROM YOUR FATHER WHO IS IN HEAVEN.

Mt 6:2 THEREFORE WHEN YOU DO MERCIFUL DEEDS, DO NOT SOUND A TRUMPET BEFORE YOURSELF, AS THE HYPOCRITES DO IN THE SYNAGOGUES AND IN THE STREETS, THAT THEY MAY GET GLORY FROM MEN. MOST CERTAINLY I TELL YOU, THEY HAVE RECEIVED THEIR REWARD.

Mt 6:3 BUT WHEN YOU DO MERCIFUL DEEDS, DO NOT LET YOUR LEFT HAND KNOW WHAT YOUR RIGHT HAND DOES,

Mt 6:4 SO THAT YOUR MERCIFUL DEEDS MAY BE IN SECRET. THEN YOUR FATHER WHO SEES IN SECRET WILL REWARD YOU OPENLY."

167   JESUS, THE "TRUE WEALTH," INTRODUCES THE PRINCIPLE OF INCREASE
(Mt 7:2; Lk 6:37,38)

Lk 6:37 "DO NOT JUDGE, AND YOU WILL NOT BE JUDGED. DO NOT CONDEMN, AND YOU WILL NOT BE CONDEMNED. FORGIVE, AND YOU WILL BE FORGIVEN.

Mt 7:2 FOR BY WHATEVER JUDGMENT YOU JUDGE, YOU WILL BE JUDGED, AND WITH WHATEVER MEASURE YOU MEASURE, IT WILL BE MEASURED BACK TO YOU.

Lk 6:38 GIVE, AND IT WILL BE GIVEN TO YOU. GOOD MEASURE, PRESSED DOWN, SHAKEN TOGETHER, AND RUNNING OVER, WILL MEN GIVE UNTO YOUR BOSOM. FOR WITH THE SAME MEASURE *(percentage or volume)* YOU MEASURE *(you give out)* IT WILL BE MEASURED *(returned)* BACK TO YOU."

> *2 Cor 9:6,7...Remember this, he who sows sparingly will also reap sparingly. He who sows bountifully will also reap bountifully...for God loves a cheerful giver.*

168   *JESUS INSTRUCTS HIS FOLLOWERS ON HOW TO PRAY (Mt 6:5-13)*

Mt 6:5 "WHEN YOU PRAY, YOU SHOULD NOT BE SEEN AS THE HYPOCRITES. FOR THEY LOVE TO STAND AND PRAY IN THE SYNAGOGUES AND ON THE CORNERS OF THE STREETS, THAT THEY MAY BE SEEN BY MEN. MOST CERTAINLY, I TELL YOU, THEY HAVE RECEIVED THEIR REWARD.

Mt 6:6 BUT YOU, WHEN YOU PRAY, ENTER INTO YOUR PRIVATE ROOM. AND HAVING SHUT YOUR DOOR, PRAY TO YOUR FATHER WHO IS IN THE SECRET PLACE, AND YOUR FATHER WHO SEES YOU THERE WILL REWARD YOU OPENLY.

Mt 6:7 IN PRAYING, DO NOT USE VAIN REPETITIONS, AS THE HEATHENS DO, FOR THEY THINK THAT THEY WILL BE HEARD FOR THEIR MUCH SPEAKING.

Mt 6:8 THEREFORE, DO NOT BE LIKE THEM, FOR YOUR FATHER KNOWS WHAT THINGS YOU NEED, BEFORE YOU ASK HIM."

169   *HE GIVES US THE 'LORD'S PRAYER' AS A BEGINNING MODEL (Mt 6:9-13)*

Mt 6:9 "PRAY LIKE THIS, 'OUR FATHER WHO IS IN HEAVEN, MAY YOUR NAME BE KEPT HOLY.

Mt 6:10 LET YOUR KINGDOM COME. LET YOUR WILL BE DONE, AS IN HEAVEN, SO ON EARTH.

Mt 6:11 GIVE US TODAY OUR DAILY BREAD.

Mt 6:12 FORGIVE US OUR OFFENSES, AS WE ALSO FORGIVE THOSE WHO OFFEND US.

Mt 6:13 BRING US NOT INTO TEMPTATION. BUT DELIVER US FROM EVIL. FOR YOURS IS THE KINGDOM, THE POWER, AND THE GLORY, NOW AND FOREVER. AMEN.'"

170   JESUS OFFERS A CONDITION TO OBTAIN FORGIVENESS (Mt 6:14,15)

Mt 6:14 "FOR IF YOU FORGIVE MEN THEIR TRESPASSES, YOUR HEAVENLY FATHER WILL ALSO FORGIVE YOU.

Mt 6:15 BUT IF YOU DO NOT FORGIVE MEN THEIR OFFENSES, NEITHER WILL YOUR FATHER FORGIVE YOU YOUR OFFENSES."

171   HE INFORMS US ON HOW TO FAST MEANINGFULLY (Mt 6:16-18)

Mt 6:16 "MOREOVER WHEN YOU FAST *(to willingly go without food for a period of time)* DO NOT BE LIKE THE HYPOCRITES, WITH SAD FACES. FOR THEY NEGLECT THEIR FACES, THAT THEY MAY BE SEEN BY MEN TO BE FASTING. MOST CERTAINLY I TELL YOU, THEY HAVE RECEIVED THEIR REWARD.

Mt 6:17 BUT YOU, WHEN *(not if)* YOU FAST, ANOINT YOUR HEAD, AND WASH YOUR FACE,

Mt 6:18 SO THAT YOU ARE NOT SEEN BY MEN TO BE FASTING, BUT BY YOUR FATHER WHO IS IN SECRET. AND YOUR FATHER, WHO SEES IN SECRET, WILL REWARD YOU OPENLY."

172   YOU GIVE TO YOURSELF WHEN YOU GIVE TO OTHERS (Mt 6:19-21)

Mt 6:19 "DO NOT LAY UP TREASURE FOR YOURSELVES HERE ON THE EARTH; WHERE MOTHS DESTROY AND RUST CORRUPTS, AND THIEVES BREAK INTO AND STEAL.

Mt 6:20 BUT LAY UP FOR YOURSELVES TREASURES IN HEAVEN, WHERE NEITHER MOTH NOR RUST CONSUME, AND WHERE THIEVES DO NOT BREAK IN AND STEAL.

Mt 6:21 FOR WHERE YOUR TREASURE IS, THERE YOUR HEART WILL BE ALSO."

173   BE FILLED WITH GOD'S LIGHT AND SERVE HIM ONLY (Mt 6:22-24)

Mt 6:22 "THE LAMP OF THE BODY IS THE EYE. IF THEREFORE YOUR EYE IS SOUND, YOUR WHOLE BODY WILL BE FULL OF LIGHT.

Mt 6:23 BUT IF YOUR EYE IS BAD, YOUR WHOLE BODY WILL BE FULL OF DARKNESS. IF THEREFORE THE LIGHT THAT IS IN YOU IS DARKNESS, HOW TERRIBLY GREAT IS THAT DARKNESS!

Mt 6:24 NO ONE CAN SERVE TWO MASTERS, FOR EITHER HE WILL HATE THE ONE AND LOVE THE OTHER, OR ELSE HE WILL PREFER THE ONE AND NEGLECT THE OTHER. YOU CANNOT SERVE BOTH GOD AND MAMMON."

174   *YOU CAN TRUST GOD TO PROVIDE FOR YOUR NEEDS (Mt 6:25-34; Lk 12:22-31)*

Mt 6:25 "THEREFORE I TELL YOU, DO NOT BE ANXIOUS FOR YOUR LIFE, WHAT YOU WILL EAT, OR WHAT YOU WILL DRINK, NOR YET FOR YOUR BODY, WHAT YOU WILL WEAR. IS NOT LIFE MORE THAN FOOD, AND THE BODY MORE THAN CLOTHING?

Mt 6:26 SEE THE BIRDS OF THE SKY, THAT THEY DO NOT SOW, NEITHER DO THEY REAP, NOR GATHER INTO BARNS. YET YOUR HEAVENLY FATHER FEEDS THEM. ARE YOU NOT OF MUCH MORE VALUE THAN THEY?

Mt 6:27 WHICH OF YOU BY BEING ANXIOUS CAN ADD ONE MOMENT TO HIS LIFESPAN?"

175   *TRUST IN GOD'S DIVINE PROVIDENCE (Mt 6:28-30; Lk 12:26-28)*

Lk 12:26 "IF THEN YOU ARE NOT ABLE TO MANAGE EVEN THE SMALLEST THINGS, WHY DO YOU WORRY ABOUT THE REST?

Mt 6:28 WHY ARE YOU TROUBLED ABOUT CLOTHING? CONSIDER THE LILIES OF THE FIELD, HOW THEY GROW. THEY DO NOT TOIL, NEITHER DO THEY SPIN,

Mt 6:29 YET I TELL YOU THAT EVEN SOLOMON IN ALL HIS GLORY WAS NOT DRESSED LIKE ONE OF THESE.

Mt 6:30 BUT IF GOD SO CLOTHES THE GRASS OF THE FIELD, WHICH TODAY LIVES, AND TOMORROW IS THROWN INTO THE FIRE, WILL HE NOT MUCH MORE CLOTHE YOU? O YOU OF LITTLE FAITH!"

176   *LOOK AFTER THE THINGS OF GOD AND HE WILL PROVIDE FOR YOU (Mt 6:31-34; Lk 12:29-31)*

Lk 12:29 "DO NOT SEEK WHAT YOU WILL EAT OR WHAT YOU WILL DRINK. NEITHER BE ANXIOUS.

Lk 12:30 FOR THE PAGANS OF THE WORLD SEEK AFTER ALL OF THESE THINGS. AND YOUR FATHER KNOWS THAT YOU NEED THESE THINGS.

Mt 6:33 BUT SEEK FIRST GOD'S KINGDOM, AND HIS RIGHTEOUSNESS. AND ALL THESE THINGS WILL BE GIVEN TO YOU AS WELL. *(1 Chr 16:11)*

Mt 6:34 THEREFORE DO NOT BE CONCERNED ABOUT TOMORROW, FOR TOMORROW WILL HAVE ENOUGH WORRIES OF ITS OWN. EACH DAY HAS ITS OWN PROBLEMS."

177   DO NOT FIND FAULT IN ANOTHER WITHOUT JUDGING YOURSELF FIRST (Mt 7:3-5, Lk 6:41,42)

Mt 7:3 "WHY DO YOU SEE THE SPECK THAT IS IN YOUR BROTHER'S EYE, BUT DO NOT CONSIDER THE LOG THAT IS IN YOUR OWN EYE?

Mt 7:4 OR HOW WILL YOU TELL YOUR BROTHER, 'LET ME REMOVE THE SPECK FROM YOUR EYE,' AND BEHOLD, THE LOG IS IN YOUR OWN EYE?

Mt 7:5 YOU HYPOCRITE! FIRST REMOVE THE LOG OUT OF YOUR OWN EYE, AND THEN YOU CAN SEE CLEARLY TO REMOVE THE SPECK OUT OF YOUR BROTHER'S EYE."

178   AVOID WITNESSING TO THOSE WHO ARE TOO HARD AND DIFFICULT (Mt 7:6)

Mt 7:6 "DO NOT GIVE THAT WHICH IS HOLY TO DOGS, NEITHER THROW YOUR PEARLS BEFORE THE PIGS, LEST THEY TRAMPLE THEM UNDER THEIR FEET, THEN TURN AND TEAR YOU TO PIECES."

179   BE NOT AFRAID TO A. S. K. (Mt 7:7-11; Lk 11:9-13)

Mt 7:7 "ASK, AND IT WILL BE GIVEN YOU. SEEK, AND YOU WILL FIND. KNOCK, AND IT WILL BE OPENED FOR YOU.

Mt 7:8 FOR EVERYONE WHO ASKS RECEIVES. HE WHO SEEKS, FINDS. AND TO HIM WHO KNOCKS, IT WILL BE OPENED.

Mt 7:9 OR WHO IS THERE AMONG YOU, WHO, IF HIS SON ASKS HIM FOR BREAD, WILL GIVE HIM A STONE?

Mt 7:10 OR IF HE ASKS FOR A FISH, WILL GIVE HIM A SERPENT?

Lk 11:12 OR IF HE ASKS FOR AN EGG, HE WILL NOT GIVE HIM A SCORPION, WILL HE?

Lk 11:13 IF YOU THEN, BEING EVIL, KNOW HOW TO GIVE GOOD GIFTS TO YOUR CHILDREN, HOW MUCH MORE WILL YOUR HEAVENLY FATHER GIVE THE HOLY SPIRIT TO THOSE WHO ASK HIM?"

180   LEARN UNSELFISHNESS BY PRACTICING THE 'GOLDEN RULE' (Mt 7:12; Lk 6:31)

Mt 7:12 "THEREFORE, WHATEVER YOU DESIRE FOR MEN TO DO TO YOU, YOU SHOULD ALSO DO TO THEM, FOR THIS IS THE MEANING OF THE LAW AND THE PROPHETS."

181   THERE ARE TWO GATES LEADING INTO ETERNITY, SO CHOOSE THE RIGHT ONE (Mt 7:13,14)

Mt 7:13 "ENTER IN BY THE NARROW GATE. FOR WIDE IS THE GATE AND BROAD IS THE WAY THAT LEADS TO DESTRUCTION. AND MANY ARE THOSE WHO ENTER IN BY IT.

Mt 7:14 BUT STRAIGHT IS THE GATE, AND NARROW IS THE WAY THAT LEADS TO LIFE! BUT FEW ARE THOSE WHO FIND IT."

182   BE VERY SELECTIVE OF YOUR TEACHERS (Lk 6:39,40)

Lk 6:39 He spoke a parable to them. "CAN THE BLIND LEAD THE BLIND? WILL THEY NOT BOTH FALL INTO A DITCH?

Lk 6:40 A DISCIPLE IS NOT ABOVE HIS TEACHER, BUT EVERYONE WHEN HE IS FULLY TRAINED, WILL BE LIKE HIS TEACHER."

183   GUARD AGAINST FALSE AND SELF-SERVING LEADERS (Mt 7:15-20; Lk 6:41-44)

Mt 7:15 "BEWARE OF FALSE PROPHETS WHO COME TO YOU IN SHEEP'S CLOTHING, BUT INWARDLY ARE HUNGRY WOLVES.

Mt 7:16 BY THEIR FRUITS YOU WILL KNOW THEM.

Lk 6:43 FOR THERE IS NOT A GOOD TREE THAT BRINGS FORTH ROTTEN FRUIT, NOR AGAIN A BAD TREE THAT BRINGS FORTH GOOD FRUIT.

Lk 6:44 FOR EACH TREE IS KNOWN BY ITS OWN FRUIT. FOR PEOPLE DO NOT GATHER FIGS FROM THORNS, NOR DO THEY GATHER GRAPES FROM A BRAMBLE BUSH."

184   BE WATCHFUL OF THOSE WHO DRAW ATTENTION TO THEMSELVES AND NOT TO GOD (Mt 7:19,20; Lk 6:45)

Mt 7:19 "EVERY TREE THAT DOES NOT GROW GOOD FRUIT IS CUT DOWN, AND THROWN INTO THE FIRE.

Mt 7:20 THEREFORE BY THEIR FRUITS *(works)* YOU WILL KNOW THEM.

Lk 6:45 THE GOOD MAN OUT OF THE GOOD TREASURE OF HIS HEART BRINGS OUT THAT WHICH IS GOOD. AND THE EVIL MAN OUT OF THE EVIL TREASURE OF HIS HEART BRINGS OUT THAT WHICH IS EVIL. FOR OUT OF THE ABUNDANCE OF THE HEART, THE MOUTH SPEAKS."

185   SALVATION LIES IN LIVING ONE'S FAITH AND NOT IN MERELY PROFESSING IT (Mt 7:21-23; Lk 6:46)

Mt 7:21 "NOT EVERYONE WHO SAYS TO ME, 'LORD, LORD,' WILL ENTER INTO THE KINGDOM OF HEAVEN, BUT HE WHO DOES THE WILL OF MY FATHER WHO IS IN HEAVEN.

Mt 7:22 MANY WILL TELL ME IN THAT DAY, 'LORD, DID WE NOT PROPHESY IN YOUR NAME? AND IN YOUR NAME CAST OUT DEMONS? AND IN YOUR NAME DID MANY WONDERFUL WORKS?'

Mt 7:23 THEN I WILL TELL THEM, 'I NEVER KNEW YOU. DEPART FROM ME, YOU WHO WORK WICKEDNESS.'

Lk 6:46 WHY DO YOU CALL ME 'LORD, LORD,' AND DO NOT DO THE THINGS WHICH I SAY?"

186   HE CONCLUDES BY ADVISING THAT WE SHOULD BEGIN TO BUILD OUR FUTURE ON HIM, THE "SOLID ROCK" (Mt 7:24-27; Lk 6:47-49)

Mt 7:24 "EVERYONE THEREFORE WHO HEARS THESE WORDS OF MINE AND DOES THEM, I WILL COMPARE TO A WISE MAN, WHO BUILT HIS HOUSE ON A ROCK.

Mt 7:25   THE RAIN CAME DOWN, THE FLOODS CAME, AND THE WINDS BLEW, AND BEAT ON THAT HOUSE, AND IT DID NOT FALL, FOR IT WAS FOUNDED ON THE ROCK.

Lk 6:49   BUT HE WHO HEARS, AND DOES NOT DO, IS LIKE THE MAN WHO BUILT HIS HOUSE ON SAND, WITHOUT A FOUNDATION, AGAINST WHICH THE STREAMS DID FLOW...

Mt 7:27   THE RAIN CAME DOWN, THE FLOODS CAME, AND THE WINDS BLEW, AND BEAT ON THAT HOUSE, AND IT FELL—AND GREAT WAS ITS FALL."

187   THE HUGE CROWD REACTS FAVORABLY TO HIS COMPELLING TEACHINGS (Mt 7:28,29 & 8:1)

Mt 7:28   It happened, when Jesus had finished saying these things, that the people were astonished at His teaching,

Mt 7:29   for He taught them with authority, and not like the scribes.

Mt 8:1   When He came down from the mountain, great multitudes followed Him.

CHAPTER VI

HIS GROWING FAME

188   JESUS IS ASKED TO HEAL A ROMAN OFFICER'S SERVANT (taken from Lk 7:2-5)

Lk 7:2   A certain centurion's servant, who was dear to him, was sick and at the point of death.

Lk 7:3   When he heard about Jesus, he sent to Him elders of the Jews, asking Him to come and save his servant.

Lk 7:4   When they came to Jesus, they begged Him earnestly, saying, "He is worthy for you to do this for him,

Lk 7:5   for he loves our nation, and he built our synagogue for us."

189   THE MILITARY OFFICER EXPRESSES COMPLETE FAITH IN JESUS (Mt 8:5-8; Lk 7:6,7)

Mt 8:5   When He came into Capernaum, the centurion came to meet Him,

Mt 8:6   saying, "Lord, my servant lies in the house paralyzed, grievously tormented."

Mt 8:7   Jesus said to him, **"I WILL COME AND HEAL HIM."**

Mt 8:8   The centurion answered, "Lord, I am not worthy for You to come under my roof. Just say the word, and my servant will be healed."

190   JESUS BECOMES IMPRESSED WITH THE FOREIGNER'S FAITH AND HUMILITY (Mt 8:9-10; Lk 7:8,9)

Lk 7:8   "For I also am a man placed under authority, having under myself soldiers. I tell this one, 'Go!' and he goes, and to another, 'Come!' and he comes, and to my servant, 'Do this,' and he does it."

Mt 8:10 When Jesus heard it, He marveled, and said to those who followed, **"MOST CERTAINLY I TELL YOU, I HAVE NOT FOUND SO GREAT A FAITH, NO, NOT IN ALL ISRAEL."**

191   THE CENTURION'S CONFIDENCE IN CHRIST'S ABILITY TO HEAL THE SERVANT IS REWARDED (Mt 8:11-13; Lk 7:10)

Mt 8:11   "I TELL YOU THAT MANY WILL COME FROM THE EAST AND THE WEST, AND WILL SIT DOWN WITH ABRAHAM, ISAAC, AND JACOB IN THE KINGDOM OF HEAVEN.

Mt 8:12   BUT THE ACTUAL SONS OF THE KINGDOM WILL BE THROWN OUT INTO THE OUTER DARKNESS. THERE WILL BE WEEPING AND GNASHING OF TEETH."

Mt 8:13   Jesus said to the centurion, **"GO YOUR WAY. LET IT BE DONE FOR YOU AS YOU HAVE BELIEVED."** His servant was healed in that very hour.

192   JESUS, THE "FOUNTAIN OF LIFE," HAS PITY FOR A WIDOW'S LOSS OF HER SON (Lk 7:11-17)

Lk 7:11   It happened soon afterwards, that He went to a city called Nain. Many of His disciples, along with a great multitude, went with Him.

Lk 7:12   Now when He drew near to the gate of the city, behold, one who was dead was carried out, the only son of his mother, and she was a widow. Many people of the city were with her.

Lk 7:13   When the Lord saw her, He had compassion on her, and said to her, **"DO NOT CRY."**

193   THE SON BROUGHT BACK TO LIFE CAUSES EVEN MORE PUBLICITY (Lk 7:14-17)

Lk 7:14   He came near and touched the coffin, and the bearers stood still. He said, **"YOUNG MAN, I TELL YOU, ARISE!"**

Lk 7:15   He who was dead sat up, and began to speak. And He gave him to his mother.

Lk 7:16   Fear took hold of all, and they glorified God, saying, "A "Great Prophet" has arisen among us!" and, "God has visited His people!"

Lk 7:17   This report went out concerning Him in the whole of Judea, and in all the surrounding region.

194   *JOHN THE BAPTIZER SENDS ENQUIRING MESSENGERS TO JESUS (Mt 11:1-6; Lk 7:18-23)*

Lk 7:18   The disciples of John told him about all these things.

Lk 7:19   John, calling to himself two of his disciples, sent them to Jesus, saying, "Are You the One who is coming, or should we look for another?"

Lk 7:20   When the men had come to Jesus, they said, "John the Baptist has sent us to You, saying, 'Are You He who comes, or should we look for another?'"

Lk 7:21   In that hour He cured many of diseases and plagues and evil spirits, and to many who were blind He gave sight.

195   *JESUS PROCLAIMS THAT HIS TEACHINGS AND HEALINGS SPEAK FOR WHO HE IS (Mt 11:4-6; Lk 7:22,23)*

Mt 11:4   Jesus answered them, "GO AND TELL JOHN THE THINGS WHICH YOU HEAR AND SEE,

Mt 11:5   THE BLIND RECEIVE THEIR SIGHT, THE LAME WALK, THE LEPERS ARE CLEANSED, THE DEAF HEAR, THE DEAD ARE RAISED UP, AND THE POOR HAVE THE GOOD NEWS PREACHED TO THEM. *(Quoting from Isa 35:5)*

Mt 11:6   BLESSED IS HE WHO FINDS NO REASON TO BE DISPLEASED IN ME."

196   *HE SAYS THAT JOHN'S COMING WAS TO PRECEED THE MESSIAH (Mt 11:7-15; Lk 7:24-30)*

Mt 11:7   As these went their way, Jesus began to say concerning John, "WHAT DID YOU GO OUT INTO THE WILDERNESS TO SEE? A REED SHAKEN BY THE WIND?

Mt 11:8   BUT WHAT DID YOU GO OUT TO SEE? A MAN IN FINE CLOTHING? BEHOLD, THOSE WHO WEAR FINE CLOTHING ARE IN KING'S PALACES.

Mt 11:9   BUT WHY DID YOU GO OUT? TO SEE A PROPHET? YES, I TELL YOU, AND MUCH MORE THAN A PROPHET.

Mt 11:10 FOR THIS IS HE, OF WHOM IT IS WRITTEN, 'BEHOLD, I SEND MY MESSENGER AHEAD OF YOU, WHO WILL PREPARE THE WAY BEFORE YOU.'"

197   EVEN JOHN'S OWN COMING WAS FORETOLD *(Mt 11:11-15; Lk 7:28)*

Mt 11:11 "MOST CERTAINLY I TELL YOU, AMONG THOSE WHO ARE BORN OF WOMEN THERE HAS NOT ARISEN ANYONE GREATER THAN JOHN THE BAPTIZER, YET, HE WHO IS THE MOST HUMBLE IN THE KINGDOM OF HEAVEN IS GREATER THAN JOHN!

Mt 11:12 FROM THE DAYS OF JOHN THE BAPTIST UNTIL NOW, THE KINGDOM OF HEAVEN ENDURES VIOLENCE, AND THE VIOLENT *(eager Christians)* TRY TO TAKE IT BY FORCE *(not just drifters)*.

Mt 11:13 FOR ALL THE PROPHETS AND THE LAW PROPHESIED UP TO JOHN.

Mt 11:14 IF YOU ARE WILLING TO RECEIVE IT, JOHN IS ELIJAH, WHO WAS TO COME. *(Mal 4:5)*

Mt 11:15 HE WHO HAS EARS TO HEAR, LET HIM HEAR."

198   *THOSE IN AUTHORITY WILL NOT FOLLOW AND CO-OPERATE (Mt 11:16,17; Lk 7:29-32)*

Lk 7:29   When all the people and the tax collectors heard this, they declared God to be just, having been baptized with John's baptism.

Lk 7:30   But the Pharisees and the lawyers rejected the counsel of God, not being baptized by him themselves.

Lk 7:31   "TO WHAT THEN WILL I COMPARE THE PEOPLE OF THIS GENERATION? WHAT ARE THEY LIKE?

Lk 7:32   THEY ARE LIKE CHILDREN WHO SIT IN THE MARKETPLACE, AND CALL ONE TO ANOTHER, SAYING, 'WE PLAYED FOR YOU, AND YOU DID NOT DANCE. WE MOURNED, AND YOU DID NOT WEEP.'"

199   *THE PHARISEES AVOID BOTH THE STRICT TEACHINGS OF JOHN AND EVEN PERMISSIVENESS OF JESUS (Mt 11:18,19; Lk 7:33-35)*

Lk 7:33   "FOR JOHN THE BAPTIST CAME NEITHER EATING BREAD NOR DRINKING WINE, AND YOU SAY, 'HE HAS A DEMON.'

Lk 7:34   THE SON OF MAN HAS COME EATING AND DRINKING, AND YOU SAY, 'BEHOLD, A GLUTTONOUS MAN, AND A DRUNKARD, A FRIEND OF TAX COLLECTORS AND SINNERS!'

Mt 11:19 BUT WISDOM IS JUSTIFIED BY HER CHILDREN." *(by the results)*

200   JESUS, THE "BURDEN BEARER," INVITES ALL TO COME AND FIND REST IN HIM *(Mt 11:28-30)*

Mt 11:28 "COME TO ME, ALL YOU WHO LABOR AND ARE HEAVILY BURDENED, AND I WILL GIVE YOU REST.

Mt 11:29 TAKE MY YOKE UPON YOU, AND LEARN FROM ME, FOR I AM GENTLE AND LOWLY IN HEART, AND YOU WILL FIND REST FOR YOUR SOULS.

Mt 11:30 FOR MY YOKE IS EASY, AND MY BURDEN IS LIGHT."

> *1 Pet. 5:7 Casting all your cares upon Him, because He cares for thee (thee refers to one person. Ye refers to several people.)*

201   HE RECEIVES AN ANOINTING BY A SINFUL WOMAN AT THE HOME OF A PHARISEE *(Lk 7:36-50)*

Lk 7:36   One of the Pharisees invited Him to eat with him. He entered into the Pharisee's house, and sat at the table.

Lk 7:37   Behold, a woman in the city who was a sinner, when she knew that He was reclining in the Pharisee's house, she brought an alabaster jar of ointment.

Lk 7:38   She was at His feet weeping, she began to wet His feet with her tears, and she wiped them with the hair of her head, kissed His feet, and anointed them with the ointment.

Lk 7:39   Now when the Pharisee who had invited Him saw it, he said to himself, "This man, if He were a prophet, would have perceived who and what kind of woman this is who touches Him, that she is a sinner."

202   A GREAT PARDON PRODUCES GREAT LOVE IN RETURN *(Lk 7:40-43)*

Lk 7:40   Jesus answered him, "SIMON, I HAVE SOMETHING TO TELL YOU." He said, "Teacher, say on."

Lk 7:41   "A CERTAIN LENDER HAD TWO DEBTORS. THE ONE OWED FIVE HUNDRED SILVER COINS, AND THE OTHER FIFTY.

Lk 7:42   WHEN THEY COULD NOT PAY, HE FORGAVE THEM BOTH. WHICH OF THEM THEREFORE WILL LOVE HIM MOST?"

Lk 7:43 Simon answered, "He, I suppose, to whom he forgave the most." Jesus said to him, **"YOU HAVE JUDGED CORRECTLY."**

203   HER DEVOTION IS COMPARED TO THE LACK OF KINDNESS ON THE PART OF HIS HOST (Lk 7:44-50)

Lk 7:44 Turning to the woman, He said to Simon, **"DO YOU SEE THIS WOMAN? I ENTERED INTO YOUR HOUSE, AND YOU GAVE ME NO WATER FOR MY FEET. BUT SHE HAS WET MY FEET WITH HER TEARS, AND WIPED THEM WITH THE HAIR OF HER HEAD.**

Lk 7:45 YOU GAVE ME NO KISS, BUT SHE, SINCE THE TIME I CAME IN, HAS NOT CEASED TO KISS MY FEET.

Lk 7:46 YOU DID NOT ANOINT MY HEAD WITH OIL, BUT SHE HAS ANOINTED MY FEET WITH OINTMENT.

Lk 7:47 THEREFORE I TELL YOU, HER SINS, WHICH ARE MANY, ARE FORGIVEN, FOR SHE LOVED MUCH. BUT TO WHOM LITTLE IS FORGIVEN, THE SAME LOVES LITTLE."

204   BELIEF IN JESUS, THE "HOLY HEALER," BLESSES HER TO BE SET FREE (Lk 7:48-50)

Lk 7:48 He said to her, **"YOUR SINS ARE FORGIVEN."**

Lk 7:49 Those who sat at the table with Him began to say to themselves, "Who is this who even forgives sins?"

Lk 7:50 He said to the woman, **"YOUR FAITH HAS SAVED YOU. GO IN PEACE."**

205   SOME DEVOUT WOMEN USE THEIR MEANS TO SUPPORT THE FLEDGLING MINISTRY (Lk 8:1-3)

Lk 8:1 It happened soon afterwards, that He went about through cities and villages, preaching and bringing the Good News of the Kingdom of God. With Him were the twelve,

Lk 8:2 and certain women who had been healed of evil spirits and infirmities, Mary who was called Magdalene, from whom seven demons had gone out,

Lk 8:3 and Joanna the wife of Chuzas, Herod's steward, and Susanna and many others who gave to them from their possessions.

206   HIS OWN FRIENDS SET OUT TO RESTRAIN THE "MODEL OF VIRTUE" (Mk 3:20,21)

Mk 3:20   The multitude came together again, so that they could not so much as eat bread.

Mk 3:21   When His friends heard it, they went out to seize Him, for they said, "He is insane."

207   HE HEALS A POSSESSED PERSON WHICH DRAWS A BLASPHEMOUS ACCUSATION (Mt 12:22-28; Lk 11:14-20)

Mt 12:22   Then one possessed by a demon, blind and mute, was brought to Him and He healed him, so that the blind and mute man both spoke and saw.

Mt 12:23   All the people were amazed, and said, "Can this be the son of David?"

Lk 11:15   But some of them said, "He casts out demons by Beelzebul, (also spelled Beelzebub in some translations), the prince of the demons."

208   IT IS IMPOSSIBLE FOR JESUS TO COME FROM THE NETHERWORLD (Mt 12:24; Mk 3:22,23; Lk 11:16)

Mk 3:22   The scribes who came down from Jerusalem said, "He has Beelzebul," and, "By the prince of the demons He casts out the demons."

Lk 11:16   Others, testing Him, sought from Him a sign from heaven.

Mk 3:23   He summoned them, and said to them in parables, **"HOW CAN SATAN CAST OUT SATAN?"**

209   A HOUSE DIVIDED HAS NO INFLUENCE NOR POWER (Mt 12:25-27; Mk 3:24-26; Lk 11:14-19)

Mt 12:25   Knowing their thoughts, Jesus said to them, **"EVERY KINGDOM DIVIDED AGAINST ITSELF IS BROUGHT TO DESTRUCTION, AND EVERY CITY OR HOUSE DIVIDED AGAINST ITSELF WILL NOT STAND.**

Mt 12:26   IF SATAN CASTS OUT SATAN, HE IS DIVIDED AGAINST HIMSELF. HOW THEN WILL HIS KINGDOM STAND?

Mt 12:27   IF I, BY BEELZEBUL CAST OUT DEMONS, BY WHOM DO YOUR SONS CAST THEM OUT? THEREFORE THEY WILL BE YOUR JUDGES."

210   *JESUS, THE "EVER FAITHFUL," HAS STRENGTH IN THE FATHER'S SPIRIT TO PERFORM WHAT NEEDS TO BE DONE (Mt 12:28,29; Mk 3:27; Lk 11:20-25)*

Mt 12:28 "HOWEVER IF I, BY THE SPIRIT OF GOD, CAST OUT DEMONS, THEN THE KINGDOM OF GOD HAS COME UPON YOU.

Mk 3:27 BUT NO ONE CAN ENTER INTO THE HOUSE OF THE STRONG MAN TO PLUNDER UNLESS HE FIRST BINDS THE STRONG MAN. AND THEN HE WILL PLUNDER HIS HOUSE.

Lk 11:21 WHEN THE STRONG MAN, FULLY ARMED, GUARDS HIS OWN DWELLING, HIS GOODS ARE SAFE.

Lk 11:22 BUT WHEN SOMEONE STRONGER ATTACKS HIM AND OVERCOMES HIM, HE TAKES FROM HIM HIS WHOLE ARMOR IN WHICH HE TRUSTED, AND DIVIDES HIS SPOILS."

211   *ONCE HEALED, DO NOT ALLOW A SPIRITUAL VACUUM (Mt 12:43-45; Lk 11:24-26)*

Lk 11:24 "THE UNCLEAN SPIRIT, WHEN HE HAS GONE OUT OF A MAN, PASSES THROUGH DRY PLACES, SEEKING REST, AND FINDING NONE, HE SAYS, 'I WILL TURN BACK TO MY HOUSE FROM WHICH I CAME OUT.'

Lk 11:25 WHEN HE RETURNS, HE FINDS IT SWEPT AND PUT IN ORDER.

Mt 12:45 THEN HE GOES, AND TAKES WITH HIMSELF SEVEN OTHER SPIRITS MORE EVIL THAN HE IS. AND THEY ENTER IN AND DWELL THERE. THE LAST STATE OF THAT MAN BECOMES WORSE THAN THE FIRST. EVEN SO WILL IT BE ALSO TO THIS EVIL GENERATION."

212   *AVOID THE UNPARDONABLE OFFENSE AGAINST THE HOLY SPIRIT (Mt 12:30-32; Mk 3:28-30; Lk 11:23)*

Mt 12:30 "HE WHO IS NOT WITH ME IS AGAINST ME, AND HE WHO DOES NOT GATHER WITH ME, SCATTERS.

Mt 12:31 THEREFORE I TELL YOU, EVERY SIN AND PROFANITY WILL BE FORGIVEN MEN, BUT THE BLASPHEMY AGAINST THE HOLY SPIRIT WILL NOT BE FORGIVEN MEN.

Mt 12:32 WHOEVER SPEAKS A WORD AGAINST THE SON OF MAN, IT WILL BE FORGIVEN HIM, BUT WHOEVER SPEAKS AGAINST THE HOLY SPIRIT, IT WILL

NOT BE FORGIVEN HIM, NEITHER IN THIS AGE, NOR IN THAT WHICH IS TO COME,

Mk 3:29 ...BUT IS GUILTY OF AN ETERNAL SIN."

213   A PERSON'S WORDS AND WORKS REVEAL WHAT IS IN HIS HEART (Mt 12:33-37)

Mt 12:33 "EITHER MAKE THE TREE GOOD AND ITS FRUIT GOOD, OR MAKE THE TREE CORRUPT AND ITS FRUIT CORRUPT, FOR THE TREE IS KNOWN BY ITS FRUIT.

Mt 12:34 YOU OFFSPRING OF VIPERS, HOW CAN YOU, BEING EVIL, SPEAK GOOD THINGS? FOR OUT OF THE ABUNDANCE OF THE HEART THE MOUTH SPEAKS.

Mt 12:35 THE GOOD MAN OUT OF HIS GOOD TREASURE BRINGS OUT GOOD THINGS, AND THE EVIL MAN OUT OF HIS EVIL TREASURE BRINGS OUT EVIL THINGS.

Mt 12:36 I TELL YOU THAT EVERY IDLE WORD THAT MEN SPEAK, THEY WILL GIVE AN ACCOUNT OF IT IN THE DAY OF JUDGMENT.

Mt 12:37 FOR BY YOUR OWN WORDS YOU WILL BE JUSTIFIED, AND BY YOUR OWN WORDS YOU WILL BE CONDEMNED."

214   JESUS REDUCES SENTIMENTALITY TO REALITY (Lk 11:27-28)

Lk 11:27 It came to pass, as He said these things, a certain woman out of the crowd lifted up her voice, and said to Him, "Blessed is the womb that bore You, and the breasts which nursed You!"

Lk 11:28 But He said, "ON THE CONTRARY, BLESSED ARE THOSE WHO HEAR THE WORD OF GOD, AND WHO KEEP IT."

215   HE PROMISES THAT ALL WILL SEE AN EVEN GREATER MIRACLE LATER (Mt 12:38-42; Lk 11:29-32)

Mt 12:38 Then certain of the scribes and Pharisees answered, "Teacher, we want to see a sign from You."

Lk 11:29 When the many were gathering together to Him, He began to say, "THIS IS AN

EVIL GENERATION. IT SEEKS AFTER A SIGN. NO SIGN WILL BE GIVEN TO IT BUT THE SIGN OF JONAH, THE PROPHET.

Mt 12:40 FOR AS JONAH WAS THREE DAYS AND THREE NIGHTS IN THE BELLY OF THE WHALE, SO WILL THE SON OF MAN BE THREE DAYS AND THREE NIGHTS IN THE HEART OF THE EARTH." *(Jon 1:17)*

216   JESUS, THE "EVERLASTING LIGHT," PROCLAIMS THAT HIS PRESENCE IS GREATER THAN THAT OF JONAH OR SOLOMON (Mt 12:41,42; Lk 11:30-32)

Lk 11:30 "FOR EVEN AS JONAH BECAME A SIGN TO THE NINEVITES, SO WILL ALSO THE SON OF MAN BE TO THIS GENERATION.

Mt 12:41 THE MEN OF NINEVEH WILL STAND UP IN THE JUDGMENT WITH THIS GENERATION AND WILL CONDEMN IT. FOR THEY REPENTED AT THE PREACHING OF JONAH, AND BEHOLD, SOMEONE GREATER THAN JONAH IS HERE.

Mt 12:42 THE QUEEN OF THE SOUTH WILL RISE UP IN THE JUDGMENT AGAINST THIS GENERATION, AND WILL CONDEMN IT. FOR SHE CAME FROM THE FAR ENDS OF THE EARTH TO HEAR THE WISDOM OF SOLOMON. AND BEHOLD, SOMEONE GREATER THAN SOLOMON IS HERE." *(1 Kgs 10:1)*

217   HIS MOTHER AND BROTHERS TRY TO REACH HIM (Mt 12:46,47; Mk 3:31,32; Lk 8:19,20)

Lk 8:19   His mother and brothers came to Him, and they could not come near Him for the crowd.

Mk 3:31   ...and standing outside, they sent to Him, calling Him.

Mt 12:47 One said to Him, "Your mother and Your brothers stand outside, seeking to speak to You."

218   JESUS POINTS TO HIS NEW AND LARGER FAMILY (Mt 12:48-50; Mk 3:33-35; Lk 8:21)

Mt 12:48 But He answered him who spoke to Him, **"WHO IS MY MOTHER? WHO ARE MY BROTHERS?"**

Mk 3:34   Looking around at those who sat around Him, He said, **"BEHOLD, MY MOTHER AND MY BROTHERS.**

Lk 8:21 MY MOTHER AND MY BROTHERS ARE THESE WHO HEAR THE WORD OF GOD, AND DO IT.

Mt 12:50 FOR WHOEVER DOES THE WILL OF MY FATHER WHO IS IN HEAVEN, HE IS MY BROTHER, AND SISTER, AND MOTHER."

CHAPTER VII

TEACHING IN PARABLES

219   JESUS USES AN UNUSUAL WAY TO PREACH TO A LARGE AUDIENCE (taken from Mt 13:1-3; Mk 4:1,2; Lk 8:4)

Mt 13:1   On that day Jesus went out of the house, and sat by the seaside.

Mk 4:1   A great number was gathered to Him, so that He entered into a boat on the sea, and sat down. All the people were on the land by the sea.

Lk 8:4   When a great many came together, and people from every city were coming to Him, He spoke by a parable. *(A story told to give a spiritual message.)*

220   HE TELLS THE PARABLE OF THE SOWER (Mt 13:4-9; Mk 4:3-9; Lk 8:5-8)

Lk 8:5   "THE FARMER WENT OUT TO SOW HIS SEED. AS HE SOWED, SOME FELL ALONG THE ROAD AND IT WAS TRAMPLED UNDER FOOT, AND THE BIRDS OF THE SKY DEVOURED IT.

Mt 13:5   OTHERS FELL ON ROCKY GROUND WHERE THEY DID NOT HAVE MUCH SOIL. AND IMMEDIATELY THEY SPRANG UP, BECAUSE THEY HAD NO DEPTH OF EARTH.

Mt 13:6   WHEN THE SUN HAD RISEN, THEY WERE SCORCHED. BECAUSE THEY HAD NO ROOT, THEY WITHERED AWAY.

Lk 8:7   SOME FELL AMID THE THORNS, AND THE THORNS GREW WITH IT, AND CHOKED IT.

Mt 13:8   SOME FELL INTO THE GOOD GROUND, AND GREW, AND BROUGHT FORTH FRUIT, SOME HUNDRED TIMES AS MUCH, SOME SIXTYFOLD, SOME THIRTY."

Mt 13:9   As He said these things, He called out, "HE WHO HAS EARS TO HEAR, LET HIM HEAR!"

221   JESUS, THE, "ETERNAL TRUTH," GIVES HIS REASON FOR USING PARABLES (Mt 13:10-17; Mk 4:10-12; Lk 8:10)

Mt 13:10   The disciples came, and said to Him, "Why do You speak to them in parables?"

Mt 13:11   He answered them, **"TO YOU IT IS GIVEN TO KNOW THE MYSTERIES OF THE KINGDOM OF HEAVEN. BUT IT IS NOT GIVEN TO THEM.**

Mt 13:12 FOR WHOEVER HAS, TO HIM WILL BE GIVEN, AND HE WILL HAVE ABUNDANCE. BUT WHOEVER DOES NOT HAVE MUCH, FROM HIM WILL BE TAKEN AWAY EVEN THAT WHICH HE HAS.

Mt 13:13 THEREFORE I SPEAK TO THEM IN PARABLES, BECAUSE SEEING THEY DO NOT SEE, AND HEARING, THEY DO NOT HEAR, NEITHER DO THEY UNDERSTAND." *(Jer 5:21)*

222   WE MUST HEAR INTENTLY TO GET THE MESSAGE (Mt 13:14,15)

Mt 13:14 "AND IN THEM THE PROPHECY OF ISAIAH IS FULFILLED, WHICH SAYS, 'BY HEARING YOU WILL HEAR, AND WILL IN NO WAY UNDERSTAND. SEEING YOU WILL SEE, AND WILL IN NO WAY PERCEIVE, *(Isa 6:10)*

Mt 13:15 FOR THIS PEOPLE'S HEART HAS GROWN CALLOUS. THEIR EARS ARE DULL OF HEARING. THEY HAVE CLOSED THEIR EYES, OR ELSE PERHAPS THEY MIGHT PERCEIVE WITH THEIR EYES, HEAR WITH THEIR EARS, UNDERSTAND WITH THEIR HEART, AND SHOULD TURN AGAIN, AND I WOULD HEAL THEM.' "

223   HEARERS THEN, AND READERS NOW, ARE PRIVILEDGED OVER THOSE WHO CAME EARLIER (Mt 13:16,17)

Mt 13:16   **"BUT BLESSED ARE YOUR EYES, FOR THEY SEE, AND YOUR EARS, FOR THEY HEAR.**

Mt 13:17 FOR MOST CERTAINLY I TELL YOU THAT MANY PROPHETS AND RIGHTEOUS MEN DESIRED TO SEE THE THINGS WHICH YOU SEE, AND DID NOT SEE THEM, AND TO HEAR THE THINGS WHICH YOU HEAR, AND DID NOT HEAR THEM."

224   JESUS, THE "ENCOURAGING LEADER," EXPLAINS THE PARABLE OF THE SOWER (Mt 13:18-23; Mk 4:13,14; Lk 8:9,11)

Lk 8:9   Then His disciples asked Him, "What does this parable mean?"

Mk 4:13 He said to them, "DO YOU NOT UNDERSTAND THIS PARABLE? HOW WILL YOU UNDERSTAND ALL OF THE PARABLES?

Lk 8:11 NOW THE PARABLE IS THIS, THE SEED IS THE WORD OF GOD.

Mk 4:14 THE FARMER SOWS THE WORD."

225 *THE VARIOUS REACTIONS TO THE GOSPEL ARE SIMILAR TO THE DIFFERENT TYPES OF SOIL (Mt 13:19-22; Mk 4:15-19; Lk 8:12-14)*

Lk 8:12 "THOSE ALONG THE ROAD ARE THOSE WHO HEAR, THEN THE DEVIL COMES, AND TAKES AWAY THE WORD FROM THEIR HEART, THAT THEY MAY NOT BELIEVE AND BE SAVED.

Lk 8:13 THOSE ON THE ROCKY GROUND ARE THEY WHO, WHEN THEY HEAR, RECEIVE THE WORD WITH JOY, BUT THESE HAVE NO ROOT, WHO BELIEVE FOR A WHILE, THEN FALL AWAY IN TIME OF TEMPTATION.

Lk 8:14 THAT WHICH FELL AMONG THE THORNS, THESE ARE THOSE WHO HAVE HEARD, AND AS THEY GO ON THEIR WAY THEY ARE CHOKED WITH CARES, RICHES, AND PLEASURES OF THIS LIFE, AND BRING NO FRUIT TO MATURITY."

226 *BUT SOME GRASP THE MEANING AND THEN WIN OTHERS TO GOD (Mt 13:23; Mk 4:20; Lk 8:15)*

Lk 8:15 "THAT IN THE GOOD GROUND, THESE ARE SUCH AS HAVE AN HONEST AND GOOD HEART, HAVING HEARD THE WORD, HOLD IT TIGHTLY, AND BRING FORTH FRUIT WITH PATIENCE.

Mt 13:23 ...SUCH IS HE WHO HEARS THE WORD, AND UNDERSTANDS IT, WHO MOST CERTAINLY BEARS FRUIT, AND BRINGS FORTH, SOME ONE HUNDRED TIMES AS MUCH, SOME SIXTY, AND SOME THIRTY."

227 *PASSING ON CHRIST'S LOVE WILL LEAD TO ONE'S EVEN GREATER UNDERSTANDING (Mk 4:21-25; Lk 8:16-18)*

Lk 8:16 "NO ONE, WHEN HE HAS LIT A LAMP, COVERS IT WITH A CONTAINER, OR PUTS IT UNDER A BED, BUT PUTS IT ON A STAND, THAT THOSE WHO ENTER IN MAY SEE THE LIGHT.

Lk 8:17 FOR NOTHING IS HIDDEN, THAT WILL NOT BE REVEALED, NOR ANYTHING SECRET, THAT WILL NOT BE MADE KNOWN AND COME TO LIGHT.

Mk 4:24 WITH WHATEVER MEASURE YOU MEASURE, IT WILL BE MEASURED BACK TO YOU, AND MORE WILL BE GIVEN TO YOU WHO HEAR.

Lk 8:18 BE CAREFUL THEREFORE HOW YOU HEAR. FOR WHOEVER HAS, TO HIM WILL BE GIVEN, AND WHOEVER DOES NOT HAVE, FROM HIM WILL BE TAKEN AWAY EVEN THAT WHICH HE THINKS HE HAS."

228   *BECOMING SPIRITUAL IS A CONSTANT MATURING PROCESS (Mk 4:26-29)*

Mk 4:26 He said, "THE KINGDOM OF GOD IS AS IF A MAN SHOULD CAST SEED ON THE EARTH,

Mk 4:27 AND SHOULD SLEEP AND RISE NIGHT AND DAY, AND THE SEED SHOULD SPRING UP AND GROW, HE DOES NOT KNOW HOW.

Mk 4:28 FOR THE EARTH BEARS FRUIT, FIRST THE BLADE, THEN THE EAR, THEN THE FULL GRAIN IN THE EAR.

Mk 4:29 BUT WHEN THE FRUIT IS RIPE, IMMEDIATELY HE PUTS FORTH THE SICKLE, BECAUSE THE HARVEST HAS COME."

229   *JESUS, OUR "PATIENT LORD," THEN TELLS THE PARABLE OF THE WEEDS AMONG THE WHEAT (Mt 13:24-30)*

Mt 13:24 He told another parable to them, saying, "THE KINGDOM OF HEAVEN IS LIKE A MAN WHO SOWED GOOD SEED IN HIS FIELD,

Mt 13:25 BUT WHILE PEOPLE SLEPT, HIS ENEMY CAME AND SOWED WEEDS ALSO AMONG THE WHEAT, AND WENT AWAY.

Mt 13:26 BUT WHEN THE BLADE SPRANG UP AND BROUGHT FORTH FRUIT, THEN THE WEEDS APPEARED ALSO."

230   *GOOD AND EVIL WILL GROW SIDE BY SIDE UNTIL JUDGMENT DAY (Mt 13:28-29)*

Mt 13:28 "HE SAID TO THEM, 'AN ENEMY HAS DONE THIS.' THE SERVANTS THEN ASKED HIM, 'DO YOU WANT US TO GO AND GATHER THEM UP?'

Mt 13:29 BUT HE SAID, 'NO, LEST PERHAPS WHILE YOU GATHER UP THE WEEDS, YOU ROOT UP SOME WHEAT WITH THEM.

Mt 13:30 LET BOTH GROW TOGETHER UNTIL THE HARVEST, AND IN THE HARVEST TIME I WILL TELL THE REAPERS,' 'FIRST, GATHER UP THE WEEDS, AND BIND THEM IN BUNDLES TO BURN THEM, BUT GATHER THE WHEAT INTO MY BARN.'"

> *(Jesus is telling us that good and evil must live side by side. The wicked people may be among us to perfect us. They are not to be removed, because some could be saved before they die. After all, that is where some of us were some years ago.)*

231   *EVEN THE SMALLEST OF FAITH WILL GROW IF EXERCISED (Mt 13:31-33; Mk 4:30-32; Lk 13:18-21)*

Mk 4:30 "HOW WILL WE LIKEN THE KINGDOM OF GOD? OR WITH WHAT PARABLE WILL WE ILLUSTRATE IT?

Mk 4:31 IT IS LIKE A GRAIN OF MUSTARD SEED, WHICH, WHEN IT IS SOWN IN THE EARTH, THOUGH IT IS SMALLER THAN ALL THE SEEDS THAT ARE ON THE EARTH,

Mk 4:32 YET WHEN IT IS SOWN, GROWS UP, AND BECOMES GREATER THAN ALL THE HERBS, AND PUTS OUT GREAT BRANCHES, SO THAT THE BIRDS OF THE SKY CAN LODGE UNDER ITS SHADOW."

Mt 13:33 He spoke another parable to them. **"THE KINGDOM OF HEAVEN IS LIKE YEAST, WHICH A WOMAN TOOK, AND HID IN THREE MEASURES OF MEAL, UNTIL IT WAS ALL LEAVENED."**

232   *JESUS, THE "IMAGE OF GOD," FULFILLS PROPHECY AS WAS FORETOLD (Mt 13:34,35; Mk 4:33,34)*

Mk 4:33 With many such parables He spoke the word to them, as they were able to hear them.

Mk 4:34 Without a parable He did not speak to them, but privately to His own disciples He explained everything.

Mt 13:35 It was so that it might be fulfilled which was spoken through the prophet, saying, "I will open my mouth in parables, I will utter things hidden from the foundation of the world."

233   *GOING INDOORS, JESUS EXPLAINS THE PARABLE OF THE WEEDS AND THE WHEAT (Mt 13:36-43)*

Mt 13:36 Then Jesus sent the people away, and went into the house. His disciples came to Him, saying, "Explain to us the parable of the weeds in the field."

Mt 13:37 He answered them, "HE WHO SOWS THE GOOD SEED IS THE SON OF MAN.

Mt 13:38 THE FIELD IS THE WORLD, AND THE GOOD SEED, THESE ARE THE CHILDREN OF THE KINGDOM, AND THE WEEDS ARE THE CHILDREN OF THE EVIL ONE.

Mt 13:39 THE ENEMY WHO SOWED THEM IS THE DEVIL. THE HARVEST IS THE END OF THE AGE, AND THE REAPERS ARE ANGELS."

234   HE DISCLOSES THE REWARD OR PUNISHMENT WHICH AWAITS EACH ONE OF THEM (Mt 13:40-42)

Mt 13:40 "AS THEREFORE THE WEEDS ARE GATHERED UP AND BURNED WITH FIRE, SO WILL IT BE AT THE END OF THIS AGE.

Mt 13:41 THE SON OF MAN WILL SEND OUT HIS ANGELS, AND THEY WILL GATHER OUT OF HIS KINGDOM ALL THOSE WHO CAUSE SIN, AND THOSE WHO LIVE IN SIN,

Mt 13:42 AND WILL CAST THEM INTO THE FURNACE OF FIRE. THERE WILL BE WEEPING AND THE GNASHING OF TEETH."

235   JESUS, THE "GIVING LORD," TELLS OF THE EXTRAORDINARY REWARD WHICH HIS SAINTS WILL RECEIVE (Mt 13:43)

Mt 13:43 "THEN THE RIGHTEOUS WILL SHINE FORTH <u>LIKE THE SUN</u> IN THE KINGDOM OF THEIR FATHER. HE WHO HAS EARS TO HEAR, LET HIM HEAR."

> *Rev 2:28 And I will give him the morning star.*

> *Dan 12:3 Those who are wise shall shine as the brightness of the firmament, and those who turn many to righteousness <u>as the stars</u> forever and ever.*

> *Ps 19:1 The heavens declare the glory of God. The firmament (the cosmos) reveals His (God's) handiwork.*

236   EACH PERSON MUST PRIZE HIS ETERNAL LIFE OVER ALL WORDLY POSSESSIONS (Mt 13:44-46)

Mt 13:44 "AGAIN, THE KINGDOM OF HEAVEN IS LIKE A TREASURE HIDDEN IN THE FIELD, WHICH A MAN FOUND, AND HID. IN HIS JOY, HE GOES AND SELLS ALL

THAT HE HAS, AND BUYS THAT FIELD.

Mt 13:45 AGAIN, THE KINGDOM OF HEAVEN IS LIKE A MAN WHO IS A MERCHANT SEEKING FINE PEARLS,

Mt 13:46 WHO HAVING FOUND ONE PEARL OF GREAT PRICE, HE WENT AND SOLD ALL THAT HE HAD, AND BOUGHT IT."

(Nothing should exceed our desire to possess Jesus, the "Pearl of Great Price.")

237   *JESUS GIVES A BRIEF PREVIEW OF THE LAST JUDGMENT (Mt 13:47-51)*

Mt 13:47 "AGAIN, THE KINGDOM OF HEAVEN IS LIKE A DRAGNET, THAT WAS CAST INTO THE SEA, AND GATHERED SOME FISH OF EVERY KIND,

Mt 13:48 WHICH, WHEN IT WAS FILLED, THEY DREW UP ON THE BEACH. THEY SAT DOWN, AND GATHERED THE GOOD ONES INTO CONTAINERS, BUT THE BAD THEY THREW AWAY.

Mt 13:49 SO WILL IT BE IN THE END OF THE WORLD. THE ANGELS WILL COME FORTH, AND SEPARATE THE WICKED FROM AMONG THE RIGHTEOUS,

Mt 13:50 AND WILL CAST THEM INTO THE FURNACE OF FIRE. THERE WILL BE WEEPING AND THE GNASHING OF TEETH."

Mt 13:51 Jesus said to them, "**HAVE YOU UNDERSTOOD ALL THESE THINGS?**" They answered Him, "Yes, Lord."

238   *TREASURES ARE TO BE FOUND IN BOTH THE OLD AND NEW TESTAMENTS (Mt 13:52-53)*

Mt 13:52 He said to them, "**THEREFORE EVERY SCRIBE WHO HAS BEEN MADE A DISCIPLE IN THE KINGDOM OF HEAVEN IS LIKE A MAN WHO IS A HOUSEHOLDER, WHO BRINGS OUT OF HIS TREASURE NEW AND OLD THINGS.**"

Mt 13:53 It happened that when Jesus had finished these parables, He departed from there.

239   *DURING A DANGEROUS STORM, THE FRIGHTENED APOSTLES WAKE UP JESUS FROM HIS AFTERNOON NAP (Mt 8:18,23-27; Mk 4:35-41; Lk 8:22-25)*

Mk 4:35 On that day, when evening had come, He said to them, "**LET US GO OVER TO THE OTHER SIDE.**"

Mk 4:36 Leaving the crowd they took Him with them, since He was in the boat. Other small boats were also with Him.

Mk 4:37 A big wind storm arose, and the waves beat into the boat, so much that the boat was already filled.

Mk 4:38 He himself was in the stern, asleep on a cushion *(see Mk 1:35)*, and they woke Him up, and told Him, "Teacher, do You not care that we are dying?"

Mt 8:26 He said to them, **"WHY ARE YOU FEARFUL, O YOU OF LITTLE FAITH?"** Then He got up, rebuked the wind and the sea…

240   THE DISCIPLES RECOGNIZE THE POWER OF JESUS, THEIR "SAFE HAVEN" BEYOND JUST HEALING (Mt 8:26,27; Mk 4:39-41; Lk 8:24,25)

Mk 4:39 …and said to the sea, **"PEACE! BE STILL!"** The wind ceased, and there was a great calm.

Mk 4:40 He said to them, **"WHY ARE YOU SO AFRAID? HOW IS IT THAT YOU HAVE NO FAITH?"** *(confidence in God)*

Mt 8:27 The men marveled, saying, "What kind of Man is this, that even the wind and the sea obey Him?"

> *2 Tim 1:7 For God hath not given us the spirit of fear; but of power, and of love, and of a sound mind.*

241   THEY CROSS THE LAKE AND COME UPON A MAN POSSESSED (Mt 8:28-34; Mk 5:1-20; Lk 8:26-39)

Lk 8:26 They arrived at the country of the Gadarenes, which is opposite Galilee.

Lk 8:27 When Jesus stepped ashore, a certain man out of the city who had demons for a long time met Him. He wore no clothes, and did not live in a house, but in the tombs.

Mk 5:3 Nobody could bind him any more, not even with chains,

Mk 5:4 because he had been often bound with fetters and chains, and the chains had been torn apart by him, and the fetters broken in pieces. Nobody had the strength to control him.

Mk 5:5 Always, night and day, in the tombs and in the mountains, he was crying out, and cutting himself with stones.

242 THE DEMONIAC IS POSSESSED BY MANY EVIL SPIRITS (Mt 8:29; Mk 5:6-9; Lk 8:28-30)

Mk 5:6 When he saw Jesus from afar, he ran and bowed down to Him,

Mk 5:7 and crying out with a loud voice, he said, "What have I to do with You, Jesus? You "Son of the Most High God," I adjure You by God, do not torment me."

Lk 8:30 Jesus asked him, **"WHAT IS YOUR NAME?"** He said, "Legion," for many demons had entered into him.

Mk 5:8 He said to him, **"COME OUT OF THE MAN, YOU UNCLEAN SPIRIT!"**

243 JESUS RIDS HIM OF THE DEMONS, WHO ARE CAST INTO A HERD OF SWINE (Mt 8:30-32; Mk 5:10-13; Lk 8:31-33)

Lk 8:31 The demons begged Him that He would not command them to go into the abyss.

Mt 8:30 Now there was a herd of many pigs feeding far away from them.

Mt 8:31 The demons begged Him, saying, "If You cast us out, permit us to go away into that herd of pigs."

Mt 8:32 He said to them, **"GO!"**

Mk 5:13 The unclean spirits came out and entered into the pigs. The herd of about two thousand rushed down the steep bank into the sea, and they were drowned in the sea.

244 THE TOWNSPEOPLE SHOW THEIR PRIORITIES BY SENDING JESUS AWAY, THEIR "ONLY HOPE" (Mt 8:33,34; Mk 5:14-17; Lk 8:34-37)

Lk 8:34 When those who fed them saw what had happened, they fled, and told it in the city and in the country.

Lk 8:35 People went out to see what had happened. They came to Jesus, and found the man from whom the demons had gone out, sitting at Jesus' feet, clothed and in his right mind, and they were afraid.

Mk 5:16 Those who saw it declared to them how it happened to him who was possessed by demons, and about the pigs.

Lk 8:37 All the people of the surrounding country of the Gadarenes asked Jesus to depart from them, for they were very much afraid. So Jesus entered the boat, and returned.

245 *THE VICTIM, NOW FREED, GOES FORTH TO PRAISE GOD'S GLORY (Mk 5:18-20; Lk 8:38,39)*

Mk 5:18 As Jesus was entering into the boat, he who had been possessed by demons begged Him that he might be with Him.

Mk 5:19 He did not allow him, but said to him, **"GO TO YOUR HOUSE, TO YOUR FRIENDS, AND TELL THEM WHAT GREAT THINGS THE LORD HAS DONE FOR YOU, AND HOW HE HAD MERCY ON YOU."**

Mk 5:20 He went his way, and began to proclaim in Decapolis *(the area east of the Jordan containing ten cities)* how Jesus had done great things for him, and everyone marveled.

  Ps 145:8 The Lord is gracious, and full of compassion; slow to anger, and of great mercy.

246 *AN OFFICIAL OF THE LOCAL SYNAGOGUE BEGS JESUS, THE "RESCUER," TO SAVE HIS DAUGHTER (Mt 8:18-26; Mk 5:21-43; Lk 8:40-56)*

Mk 5:21 When Jesus had crossed back over in the boat to the other side, a great crowd was gathered to Him, and He was by the sea.

Lk 8:40 The large group welcomed Him, for they were all waiting for Him.

Lk 8:41 Behold, there came a man named Jairus, and he was a ruler of the synagogue. He fell down at Jesus' feet, and begged Him to come into his house,

Lk 8:42 for he had an only daughter, about twelve years of age, and she was dying. But as He went, the people pressed against Him.

Mk 5:23 Jairus begged Him much, saying, "My little daughter is at the point of death. Please come and lay Your hands on her, that she may be made healthy, and live."

Mt 9:19 Jesus got up and followed him, as did His disciples.

247 *AS A LARGE CROWD FOLLOWS JESUS, A WOMAN TOUCHES HIM WITH GREAT FAITH TO GET HER OWN HEALING (Mt 9:20,21; Mk 5:24-29; Lk 8:42-44)*

Mk 5:24 A great multitude followed Him, and they pressed upon Him on all sides.

Mk 5:25 But a certain woman, who had an issue of blood for twelve years,

Mk 5:26 and had suffered many things in spite of many physicians, and who had spent all that she had, and was no better, but only grew worse,

Mk 5:27 having heard the things which Jesus did, came up behind Him in the crowd, and touched His clothes.

Mk 5:28 For she said, "If I just touch His clothes, I will be made well."

Mk 5:29 Immediately the flow of her blood was dried up, and she felt in her body that she was healed of her affliction.

248   ALTHOUGH SURROUNDED BY PEOPLE, JESUS KNEW SOMEONE REACHED HIM IN A MEANINGFULL WAY (Mt 9:22; Mk 5:30-32; Lk 8:45)

Mk 5:30 Immediately Jesus, perceiving in Himself that the power had gone out from Him, turned around in the crowd, and asked, **"WHO TOUCHED MY CLOTHES?"**

Mk 5:31 His disciples said to him, "You see the multitude pressing against You, and You say, 'Who touched Me?'"

Mk 5:32 He looked around to see her who had done this thing.

249   JESUS' LIFE OF SACRIFICE STORES ENERGY TO BENEFIT ANOTHER (Mt 9:22; Mk 5:33,34; Lk 8:46-48)

Lk 8:46 But Jesus said, **"SOMEONE DID TOUCH ME, FOR I PERCEIVED THAT POWER HAS GONE OUT OF ME."**

Lk 8:47 When the woman saw that she could not hide, she came trembling, and falling down before Him declared to Him in the presence of all the people the reason why she had touched Him, and how she was healed immediately.

Mk 5:34 He said to her, **"DAUGHTER, YOUR FAITH HAS MADE YOU WELL. GO IN PEACE, AND BE CURED OF YOUR DISEASE."**

> *Heb 11:6 Without faith it is impossible to please God...*

250   HE HEARS JAIRUS' DAUGHTER HAS DIED, BUT PROCEEDS WITH ASSURANCE (Mk 5:35-38; Lk 8:49,50)

Mk 5:35 While He was still speaking, people came from the synagogue ruler's house saying, "Your daughter is dead. Why bother the Teacher anymore?"

Lk 8:50 But Jesus hearing it, answered him, **"DO NOT BE AFRAID. ONLY BELIEVE, AND SHE WILL BE MADE WELL."**

(There are 365 "Fear Nots" in the Bible, one for every day of the year.)

Mk 5:38 He came to the synagogue ruler's house, and He saw a commotion, weeping, and great wailing.

2 Cor 5:7 For we walk by faith and not by sight.

251   *JESUS IS LAUGHED AT BY THE MOURNERS, BUT HE SHUTS OUT ALL THEIR UNBELIEF (Mt 9:24,25; Mk 5:39,40; Lk 8:51-53)*

Lk 8:51 When He came to the house, He did not allow anyone to enter in, except Peter, John, James...

Mk 5:39 When He had entered in, He said to them, **"WHY DO YOU MAKE ALL THIS FUSS AND WEEP? THE CHILD IS NOT DEAD, BUT IS ASLEEP."**

Lk 8:53 They were ridiculing Him, knowing that she was dead.

Mk 5:40 But He, having put them all out, took the father of the child, her mother, and those who were with Him, and went in where the child was lying.

252   *JESUS, THE "TENDER PHYSICIAN," BRINGS THE GIRL BACK TO LIFE AND EXPRESSES CONCERN FOR HER OTHER NEEDS (Mt 9:25,26; Mk 5:41-43; Lk 8:54-56)*

Mk 5:41 Taking the child by the hand, He said to her, **"TALITHA CUMI!"** which means, **"LITTLE GIRL, I TELL YOU, GET UP!"**

Lk 8:55 Her spirit returned, and she rose up immediately. He commanded that something be given to her to eat.

Lk 8:56 Her parents were amazed, but He charged them to tell no one what had been done.

Mt 9:26 The report of this went out into all that land.

253   *JESUS RESTORES SIGHT TO TWO BLIND MEN (Mt 9:27-31)*

Mt 9:27 As Jesus passed by from there, two blind men followed Him, calling out and saying, "Have mercy on us, "Son of David!" "

Mt 9:28 When He had come into the house, the blind men came to Him. Jesus said to them, **"DO YOU BELIEVE THAT I AM ABLE TO DO THIS?"** They told Him, "Yes, Lord."

Mt 9:29   Then He touched their eyes, saying, **"ACCORDING TO YOUR FAITH BE IT DONE TO YOU."**

Mt 9:30   Their eyes were opened. Jesus strictly tells them, saying, **"SEE THAT NO ONE KNOWS ABOUT THIS."**

Mt 9:31   But they went out and spread abroad His fame in all the land.

254   JESUS' SUPREMACY OVER DEVILS CAUSES FURTHER AMAZEMENT AND CRITICISM (Mt 9:32-34)

Mt 9:32   As they went out, behold, a mute man who was demon possessed was brought to Him.

Mt 9:33   When the demon was cast out by Jesus, the mute man spoke. The multitudes marveled, saying, "Nothing like this has ever been seen in Israel!"

Mt 9:34   But the Pharisees said, "By the prince of the demons, He casts out demons."

255   ON HIS LAST VISIT TO HIS HOME TOWN OF NAZARETH JESUS THE "LOVE OF GOD," REJECTED AGAIN (Mt 13:54-58; Mk 6:1-6)

Mk 6:1   He went out from there. He came into His own country, and His disciples followed Him.

Mk 6:2   When the Sabbath had come, He began to teach in the synagogue, and many hearing Him were astonished, saying, "Where did this man get these things?" and, "What is the wisdom that is given to this man, that such mighty works come about by His hands?

Mk 6:3   Is this not the carpenter, the son of Mary, and brother of James, Joses, Judah, and Simon? Are not His sisters here with us?" They were offended with Him.

256   THE "SACRED SON" IS IGNORED BY THOSE WHO SHOULD ACCEPT HIM THE MOST (Mt 13:57,58; Mk 6:4-6)

Mk 6:4   Jesus said to them, **"A PROPHET WILL BE TREATED WITH HONOR, EXCEPT IN HIS HOMETOWN, AND AMONG HIS OWN RELATIVES, AND IN HIS OWN HOME."** *(1 Sam 10:11)*

Mk 6:5   He could do no mighty work there, except that He laid His hands on a few sick people, and healed them.

Mk 6:6   He marveled because of their unbelief. Then He went to other villages teaching.

257 JESUS, THE "COMPASSIONATE ONE," TELLS US HOW WE CAN HELP SAVE THE MANY WHO ARE LOST (Mt 9:35-38)

Mt 9:35 Jesus went about all the cities and the villages, teaching in their synagogues, and preaching the Good News of the Kingdom, and healing every disease and every sickness among the people.

Mt 9:36 But when He saw the many people, He was moved with compassion for them, because they were confused and scattered, like sheep without a shepherd.

Mt 9:37 Then He said to His disciples, **"THE HARVEST INDEED IS PLENTIFUL, BUT THE LABORERS ARE FEW.**

Mt 9:38 PRAY THEREFORE THAT THE LORD OF THE HARVEST WILL SEND OUT LABORERS INTO HIS HARVEST."

(If you cannot go to the mission field on your feet, you can go on your knees.)

CHAPTER VIII

THE APOSTLES ARE SENT OUT

258 *THE APOSTLES ARE DELEGATED IN PAIRS WITH "DIVINE POWER" FROM JESUS (taken from Mt 10:1-42; Mk 6:7-13; Lk 9:1-6)*

Lk 9:1 He called the twelve together, and gave them power and authority over all demons, and to cure diseases.

Lk 9:2 He sent them forth to preach the Kingdom of God, and to heal the sick.

Mk 6:7 …and began to send them out two by two, and He gave them charge over unclean spirits.

259 *THEY ARE TO GO WITH VERY SPECIFIC INSTRUCTIONS TO HELP OTHERS (Mt 10:5-7)*

Mt 10:5 Jesus sent these twelve out, and commanded them, saying, **"DO NOT GO AMONG THE GENTILES, AND DO NOT ENTER INTO ANY CITY OF THE SAMARITANS.**

Mt 10:6 RATHER, GO TO THE LOST SHEEP OF THE HOUSE OF ISRAEL.

Mt 10:7 AS YOU GO PREACH, SAY, 'THE KINGDOM OF HEAVEN IS AT HAND!' "

260 *CHRIST'S REPRESENTATIVES SHOULD BE EAGER TO SHARE THE GOOD NEWS FREELY (Mt 10:8-10; Mk 6:8,9; Lk 10:4)*

Mt 10:8 "HEAL THE SICK, CLEANSE THE LEPERS, AND CAST OUT DEMONS. FREELY YOU HAVE RECEIVED, SO FREELY GIVE!

(Jesus is stressing service here, ahead of preaching. The very humble Saint Francis of Assisi is quoted as saying, "Preach the Gospel at all times. And occasionally use words.")

Mt 10:9 DO NOT TAKE ANY GOLD, NOR SILVER, NOR BRASS IN YOUR MONEY BELTS.

Mt 10:10 TAKE NO BAG FOR YOUR JOURNEY, NEITHER TWO COATS, NOR SHOES, NOR STAFF, FOR THE LABORER IS WORTHY OF HIS HIRE."

261   *HE INSTRUCTS HIS APOSTLES ON HOW TO CONDUCT THEMSELVES (Mt 10:11-13; Mk 6:10,11; Lk 10:5-7)*

Mt 10:11 "INTO WHATEVER CITY OR VILLAGE YOU ENTER, FIND OUT WHO IN IT IS TRUSTWORTHY, AND STAY THERE UNTIL YOU MOVE ON.

Mt 10:12 AS YOU ENTER INTO THE HOUSEHOLD, GREET THEM.

Lk 10:6 IF A SON OF PEACE IS THERE, YOUR PEACE WILL REST ON HIM, BUT IF NOT, IT WILL RETURN TO YOU.

Lk 10:7 REMAIN IN THAT SAME HOUSE EATING AND DRINKING THE THINGS THEY GIVE YOU. FOR THE LABORER IS WORTHY OF HIS WAGES. DO NOT GO FROM HOUSE TO HOUSE."

262   *A DISCIPLE SHOULD EXPECT ACCEPTANCE, OR REJECTION (Mt 10:14,15; Mk 6:11; Lk 10:8-12)*

Lk 10:8 "INTO WHATEVER CITY YOU ENTER, AND THEY RECEIVE YOU, EAT THE THINGS THAT ARE SET BEFORE YOU.

Lk 10:9 HEAL THE SICK WHO ARE THEREIN, AND TELL THEM, 'THE KINGDOM OF GOD HAS COME UPON YOU.'

Mk 6:11 WHOEVER WILL NOT RECEIVE YOU NOR HEAR YOU, AS YOU DEPART FROM THERE, SHAKE OFF THE DUST THAT IS UNDER YOUR SHOES FOR A TESTIMONY AGAINST THEM. ASSUREDLY, I TELL YOU, IT WILL BE MORE TOLERABLE FOR SODOM AND GOMORRAH IN THE DAY OF JUDGMENT THAN FOR THAT CITY!"

263   *JESUS, THE "WORD MADE FLESH," ADVISES THEM TO BE CAUTIOUS AND SELECTIVE IN THEIR EVANGELIZING (Mt 10:16; Mt 7:6)*

Mt 10:16 "BEHOLD, I SEND YOU OUT AS SHEEP AMONG WOLVES. THEREFORE BE WISE AS SERPENTS, AND HARMLESS AS DOVES.

Mt 7:6 "DO NOT GIVE THAT WHICH IS HOLY TO DOGS, NEITHER THROW YOUR PEARLS BEFORE PIGS, LEST PERHAPS THEY TRAMPLE THEM UNDER THEIR FEET, AND TURN AND TEAR YOU TO PIECES."

(This verse is repeated here to keep you from attempting to reach someone who is too arrogant, or too difficult. There are a great many others out there who are hungry for "The Word.")

264   HE FORETELLS OF SUFFERING TO COME AND THAT THEY WILL BE AIDED IN THEIR WITNESSING *(Mt 10:17-20)*

Mt 10:17 "BUT BEWARE OF MEN, FOR THEY WILL DELIVER YOU UP TO COUNCILS, AND IN THEIR SYNAGOGUES THEY WILL FLOG YOU.

Mt 10:18 YES, AND YOU WILL BE BROUGHT BEFORE GOVERNORS AND KINGS FOR MY SAKE, FOR A TESTIMONY AGAINST THEM AND THE GENTILES.

Mt 10:19 BUT WHEN THEY DELIVER YOU UP, DO NOT BE ANXIOUS HOW OR WHAT YOU WILL SAY, FOR IT WILL BE GIVEN YOU IN THAT HOUR WHAT YOU WILL SAY.

Mt 10:20 FOR IT IS NOT YOU WHO SPEAK, BUT THE SPIRIT OF YOUR FATHER WHO SPEAKS THROUGH YOU."

265   PERSECUTION WILL INTENSIFY BUT PERSEVERE TO THE VERY END *(Mt 10:21-23)*

Mt 10:21 "BROTHER WILL DELIVER UP BROTHER TO DEATH, AND THE FATHER HIS CHILD. CHILDREN WILL RISE UP AGAINST PARENTS, AND CAUSE THEM TO BE PUT TO DEATH.

Mt 10:22 YOU WILL BE HATED BY ALL MEN FOR MY NAME'S SAKE, BUT HE WHO HOLDS OUT TO THE END WILL BE SAVED.

Mt 10:23 BUT WHEN THEY PERSECUTE YOU IN ONE CITY, FLEE INTO THE NEXT *(but keep on telling the Good News).* **FOR MOST CERTAINLY I TELL YOU, YOU WILL NOT HAVE GONE THROUGH THE CITIES OF ISRAEL, UNTIL THE SON OF MAN HAS COME."**

266   FOLLOW THE MASTER'S PERFECT EXAMPLE AND BOLDLY SPREAD HIS WORD IN SPITE OF ABUSES *(Mt 10:24-27)*

Mt 10:24 "A DISCIPLE IS NOT ABOVE HIS TEACHER, NOR A SERVANT ABOVE HIS LORD.

Mt 10:25 IT IS ENOUGH FOR THE DISCIPLE THAT HE BE LIKE HIS TEACHER, AND THE SERVANT LIKE HIS LORD. IF THEY HAVE CALLED THE MASTER OF THE HOUSE BEELZEBUL, HOW MUCH MORE THOSE OF HIS HOUSEHOLD.

Mt 10:26 THEREFORE DO NOT BE AFRAID OF THEM, FOR THERE IS NOTHING COVERED THAT WILL NOT BE REVEALED, NOR HIDDEN THAT WILL NOT BE MADE KNOWN.

Mt 10:27 WHAT I TELL YOU IN THE DARK, SPEAK IN THE LIGHT, AND WHAT YOU HEAR WHISPERED IN YOUR EAR, PROCLAIM FROM THE HOUSETOPS."

267   *DENYING JESUS WILL HAVE ITS CONSEQUENCES (Mt 10:32,33)*

Mt 10:32 "EVERYONE THEREFORE WHO CONFESSES ME BEFORE MEN, HIM I WILL ALSO CONFESS BEFORE MY FATHER WHO IS IN HEAVEN.

> *Rom 10:9 ...if you will confess with your mouth that Jesus is Lord, and believe in your heart that God raised him from the dead, you will be saved.*

Mt 10:33 BUT WHOEVER DENIES ME BEFORE MEN, HIM I WILL ALSO DENY BEFORE MY FATHER WHO IS IN HEAVEN."

268   *TAKING A STAND FOR YOUR SAVIOR WILL CAUSE DIVISION (Mt 10:34-36)*

Mt 10:34 "DO NOT THINK THAT I CAME TO BRING PEACE ON THE EARTH. I DID NOT COME TO BRING PEACE, BUT A SWORD.

Mt 10:35 FOR I CAME TO SET A MAN AT ODDS AGAINST HIS FATHER, AND A DAUGHTER AGAINST HER MOTHER, AND A DAUGHTER-IN-LAW AGAINST HER MOTHER-IN-LAW.

Mt 10:36 A MAN'S FOES WILL BE THOSE OF HIS OWN HOUSEHOLD."

269   *JESUS, THE "ROCK OF AGES," CALLS EVERYONE TO TOTAL COMMITMENT (Mt 10:37-39)*

Mt 10:37 "HE WHO LOVES FATHER OR MOTHER MORE THAN ME IS NOT WORTHY OF ME. AND HE WHO LOVES SON OR DAUGHTER MORE THAN ME IS NOT WORTHY OF ME.

Mt 10:38 HE WHO DOES NOT TAKE UP HIS CROSS AND FOLLOW AFTER ME, IS NOT FIT TO BE MY DISCIPLE.

Mt 10:39 HE WHO SEEKS HIS LIFE WILL LOSE IT, AND HE WHO LOSES HIS LIFE FOR MY SAKE WILL FIND IT."

270   *RECEIVING AND HELPING GOD'S PEOPLE CARRIES SPECIAL BLESSINGS (Mt 10:40-42 & 11:1)*

Mt 10:40 "HE WHO RECEIVES YOU RECEIVES ME, AND HE WHO RECEIVES ME RECEIVES HIM WHO SENT ME.

Mt 10:41 HE WHO RECEIVES A PROPHET IN THE NAME OF A PROPHET WILL RECEIVE A PROPHET'S REWARD. HE WHO RECEIVES A RIGHTEOUS MAN IN THE NAME OF A RIGHTEOUS MAN WILL RECEIVE A RIGHTEOUS MAN'S REWARD.

Mt 10:42 WHOEVER GIVES A HUMBLE MAN A MERE CUP OF COLD WATER TO DRINK, BECAUSE HE IS MY DISCIPLE, MOST CERTAINLY I TELL YOU, HE WILL IN NO WAY LOSE HIS REWARD."

Mt 11:1   It happened that when Jesus had finished directing His twelve disciples, He departed from there to teach and preach in their cities.

> *Pr 11:24,25 There is one who scatters, and increases yet more. There is one who withholds more than is appropriate, but receives poverty…The liberal soul shall be made fat. He who waters shall be watered also himself.*

271   *JESUS SENDS HIS DISCIPLES TO PREACH AND TO HEAL (Mk 6:12,13: Lk 9:6)*

Lk 9:6   They departed, and went throughout the villages, preaching the Good News, and healing everywhere.

Mk 6:12   They went out and preached that people should repent. *(Repentance means to turn away from your sinful past, and turn to God.)*

Mk 6:13   They cast out many demons, and anointed many with oil who were sick, and they healed them.

272   *WITH DIFFICULTY, HEROD HEARS THE LAST WORDS OF JOHN THE BAPTIST (Mt 14:3-12; Mk 6:17-20)*

Mk 6:17   Herod had ordered and arrested John, and bound him in prison for the sake of Herodias, for he had married her, his brother Philip's wife.

Mt 14:4   John said to him, "It is not lawful for you to have her."

Mk 6:19 Herodias set herself against him, and desired to kill him, but she could not,

Mk 6:20 Herod feared John, knowing that he was a righteous and holy man, Herod protected him. When he heard him, he was bothered, and yet he heard him gladly.

273   SALOME DANCES FOR HEROD WHO OFFERS TO REWARD HER *(Mt 14:6-8; Mk 6:21-24)*

Mk 6:21 Then a convenient day came, that Herod on his birthday made a supper for his nobles, the high officers, and the chief men of Galilee.

Mk 6:22 When the daughter of Herodias herself came in and danced, she pleased Herod and those sitting with him. The king said to the young woman, "Ask me whatever you want, and I will give it to you."

Mk 6:23 He swore to her, "Whatever you shall ask of me, I will give you, even up to half my kingdom."

Mk 6:24 She went out, and said to her mother, "What shall I ask?" She answered, "The head of John the Baptizer."

274   A GUARD EXECUTES THE BAPTIST AND DELIVERS JOHN'S HEAD *(Mt 14:8-12; Mk 6:25-29)*

Mk 6:25 She came in immediately with haste to the king, and asked, "I want you to give me right now, the head of John the Baptist, on a platter."

Mk 6:26 The king was exceedingly sorry, but for the sake of his oaths, and of his dinner guests, he could not refuse her.

Mk 6:27 Immediately the king sent out a soldier of his guard, and commanded to bring John's head, and he went and beheaded him in the prison,

Mk 6:28 and brought his head on a platter, and gave it to the young woman, and the young woman gave it to her mother.

Mt 14:12 His disciples came, and took the body, and buried it, then went and told Jesus.

275   HEROD'S CONSCIENCE BECOMES TROUBLED OVER THE MURDER OF JOHN *(Mt 14:1,2; Mk 6:14-16; Lk 9:7-9)*

Lk 9:7 Now Herod the Tetrarch heard of all that was being done by Jesus. He was very perplexed, because it was said by some that John had risen from the dead,

Lk 9:8 and by some that Elijah had appeared, and by others that one of the old prophets had risen again.

Mk 6:16 Herod, when he heard this, said, "This is John, whom I beheaded. He has risen from the dead.

Lk 9:9 But who is this, about whom I hear such things?" And he sought to see Him.

276 THE DISCIPLES RETURN TO GIVE AN ACCOUNT OF THEIR MINISTERING, THEN ARE CALLED AWAY TO A SPIRITUAL RETREAT (Mt 14:12; Mk 6:30-33; Lk 9:10, 11; Jn 6:1-27)

Mk 6:30 The apostles gathered themselves together with Jesus, and they told Him all things, whatever they had done, and all they had taught.

Mk 6:31 He said to them, **"COME AWAY INTO A DESERTED PLACE, AND REST A WHILE."** For there were many coming and going, and they had no leisure so much as to eat.

Mk 6:32 They went away in a boat…

277 CROWDS FOLLOW AROUND THE LAKE TO HEAR JESUS, THE "WORD OF LIFE" (Mt 14:13; Mk 6:33,34; Jn 6:2)

Mt 14:13 …When the people heard it, they followed Him on foot from the cities.

Jn 6:2 …because they saw His signs which He did on those who were sick.

Mk 6:34 Jesus came out, saw a great multitude, and He felt sorry for them, because they were like sheep without a shepherd, and He began to teach them many things.

278 JESUS INSTRUCTS AND HEALS THOSE WHO PURSUE HIM (Mt 13:14; Lk 9:11; Jn 6:3-6)

Lk 9:11 …He welcomed them, and spoke to them of the Kingdom of God, and He cured those who needed healing.

Jn 6:3 Jesus went up into the mountain, and He sat there with His disciples.

Jn 6:4 Now the Passover, the feast of the Jews, was at hand.

Jn 6:5 Jesus therefore lifting up His eyes, and seeing that a large crowd was coming to Him, said to Philip, **"WHERE ARE WE TO BUY BREAD, THAT ALL THESE MAY EAT?"**

Jn 6:6   This He said to test him, for He himself knew what He would do.

279   THE DISCIPLES ARE UNCERTAIN ABOUT FEEDING SUCH A LARGE NUMBER (Mt 14:15,16; Mk 6:35-38; Lk 9:12,13; Jn 6:7)

Jn 6:7   Philip answered Him, "Two hundred silver coins worth of bread is not sufficient for all these people to receive even a little."

Mk 6:35   When it was late in the day, His disciples came to Him, and said, "This place is deserted, and it is late in the day.

Mk 6:36   Send them away, that they may go into the surrounding country and villages, and buy themselves bread, for they have nothing to eat."

Mt 14:16   But Jesus said to them, **"THEY DO NOT NEED TO GO AWAY. YOU GIVE THEM SOMETHING TO EAT."**

Mk 6:37   They asked Him, "Shall we go and buy two hundred silver coins worth of bread, and give them something to eat?"

Mk 6:38   He said to them, **"HOW MANY LOAVES DO YOU HAVE? GO SEE."**

280   JESUS, WHO HAD FASTED FORTY DAYS, WILL NOW FEED MORE THAN 5,000 MEN (Mt 14:17-19; Mk 6:39-41; Lk 9:14-16; Jn 6:8-11)

Jn 6:8   One of His disciples, Andrew, Simon Peter's brother, said to Him,

Jn 6:9   "There is a boy here who has five barley loaves and two fish, but what are these among so many?"

Mt 14:18   He said, **"BRING THEM HERE TO ME."** *(bring whatever little you have to Jesus, He will multiply)*

Lk 9:14   ...He said to His disciples, **"MAKE THEM SIT DOWN IN GROUPS OF ABOUT FIFTY EACH."**

Mk 6:40   They sat down in groups, by hundreds, and by fifties.

Lk 9:16   He took the five loaves and the two fish, and looking up to heaven; He blessed them, and broke them, and gave them to the disciples to set before the multitude.

281   *JESUS, THE "GREAT PROVIDER," DEMONSTRATES HIS ABUNDANT PROVISION FOR ALL (Mt 14:20,21; Mk 6:42-44; Lk 9:17; Jn 6:12,13)*

Jn 6:12   When they were filled, He said to His disciples, **"GATHER UP THE BROKEN PIECES WHICH ARE LEFT OVER, THAT NOTHING BE LOST."**

Lk 9:17   They ate, and were all filled. They gathered up twelve baskets of broken pieces that were left uneaten.

Mt 14:21   Those who ate were about five thousand men, besides women and children.

282   HE BY-PASSES THE SPOTLIGHT AND REFUSES TO BE MADE THEIR KING (Mt 14:22,23; Mk 6:45,46; Jn 6:14,15)

Jn 6:14   When therefore the people saw the miracle which Jesus did, they said, "This is truly the Prophet who comes into the world." *(Deut 18:18)*

Mk 6:45   Immediately He made His disciples get into the boat, and to go ahead to the other side, to Bethsaida…

Jn 6:15   Jesus therefore, perceiving that the crowd was about to come and take Him bodily, to make Him King, withdrew again by Himself.

Mt 14:23   After He had sent them away, He went up into the mountain by Himself to pray.

283   ON A DANGEROUS SEA HIS DISCIPLES SEE HIM WALK ON WATER (Mt 14:24-33; Mk 6:47-52; Jn 6:16-20)

Mk 6:47   When evening had come, the boat was in the midst of the sea, and He was alone on the land.

Mk 6:48   Seeing them distressed in rowing, for the wind was contrary to them, about the fourth watch of the night He came to them, walking on the sea, and He would have passed by them.

Mt 14:26   When the disciples saw Him walking on water, they were troubled, saying, "It is a ghost!" and they cried out for fear.

Mt 14:27   But Jesus spoke to them, saying **"IT'S ALLRIGHT! IT IS I! DO NOT BE AFRAID."**

284   PETER TAKES HIS EYES OFF JESUS, AND BEGINS TO PERISH (Mt 14:28-31)

Mt 14:28   Peter answered Him and said, "Lord, if it is You, command me to come to You on the waters."

Mt 14:29 He said, "**COME!**" Peter stepped out from the boat, and walked on the waters to come to Jesus.

Mt 14:30 But when he saw that the wind was strong he was afraid, and beginning to sink he cried out, saying, "Lord, save me!"

Mt 14:31 Jesus stretched out His hand, took hold of him, and said to him, "**YOU OF LITTLE FAITH, WHY DID YOU DOUBT?**"

> *Ps 145:8 The Lord is near unto all them that call upon Him…*

285   CALM RETURNS AS THEIR FAITH INCREASES AND THEIR DESTINATION IS REACHED *(Mt 14:32,33; Mk 6:51,52; Jn 6:21)*

Mt 14:32 When they got up into the boat, the wind ceased.

Mt 14:33 Those who were in the boat worshiped Him, saying, "You are truly the Son of God!"

Mk 6:51 They were very amazed among themselves, and marveled.

Jn 6:21 Immediately the boat was at the land where they were going.

286   HIS REPUTATION CAUSES MANY TO BRING OTHERS TO BE MADE WELL *(Mt 14:34-36; Mk 6:53-56)*

Mk 6:53 When they had crossed over, they came to land at Gennesaret, and anchored near the shore.

Mk 6:54 When they had come out of the boat, the people recognized Him,

Mk 6:55 and ran around that whole region, and began to bring those who were sick, on their mats, to where they heard He was.

Mk 6:56 Wherever He entered, into villages, or into cities, or into the country, they laid the sick in the marketplaces, and begged Him that they might touch just the fringe of His garment, and as many as touched Him were made well.

287   THOSE WHO WERE FED ARE TOLD TO SEEK JESUS, "THE GIVER," AND NOT THE GIFTS *(Jn 6:22-26)*

Jn 6:22 On the next day, the multitude that stood on the other side of the sea saw that there was no other boat there, except the one in which His disciples had embarked, and that Jesus had not entered with His disciples into the boat, but His disciples had gone across by themselves.

Jn 6:23   However boats from Tiberias came near to the place where they ate the bread after the Lord had given thanks.

Jn 6:24   When the crowd therefore saw that Jesus was not there, nor His disciples, they themselves got into boats, and came to Capernaum, seeking Jesus.

Jn 6:25   When they found Him on the other side of the sea, they asked Him, "Rabbi, when did You come here?"

Jn 6:26   Jesus answered them, **"MOST CERTAINLY I TELL YOU, YOU SEEK ME, NOT BECAUSE YOU SAW MIRACLES, BUT BECAUSE YOU ATE OF THE LOAVES, AND WERE FILLED."**

288   *JESUS IS OUR LIVING FOOD FROM HEAVEN IN WHOM WE MUST BELIEVE (Jn 6:27-29)*

Jn 6:27   **"DO NOT WORK FOR FOOD WHICH PERISHES, BUT FOR FOOD WHICH LIVES ON TO ETERNAL LIFE, WHICH THE SON OF MAN WILL GIVE TO YOU. FOR GOD THE FATHER HAS CONFIRMED HIM."**

Jn 6:28   They said therefore to Him, "What must we do, that we may work the works of God?"

Jn 6:29   Jesus answered them, **"THIS IS THE WILL OF GOD, THAT YOU BELIEVE IN HIM WHOM HE HAS SENT."**

289   *JESUS ANSWERS THEIR REQUEST FOR A SIGN BY SUGGESTING THEY TURN TO HIM, THE "SOURCE OF LIFE" (Jn 6:30-33)*

Jn 6:30   They said therefore to Him, "What then will You do for a sign, that we may see, and believe You? What work will You do?

Jn 6:31   Our fathers ate the manna in the wilderness. As it is written, 'He gave them bread out of heaven to eat.' "

Jn 6:32   Jesus therefore said to them, **"MOST CERTAINLY I TELL YOU, IT WAS NOT MOSES WHO GAVE YOU THE BREAD OUT OF HEAVEN. IT IS MY FATHER WHO GIVES YOU THE REAL BREAD OUT OF HEAVEN.**

Jn 6:33   **FOR THE "BREAD OF GOD"** *(Jesus)* **IS THAT WHICH COMES DOWN OUT OF HEAVEN, AND GIVES LIFE TO THE WORLD."**

290   *HE REVEALS SPIRITUAL FOOD THAT ALWAYS SATISFIES (Jn 6:34-36)*

Jn 6:34   They said therefore to Him, "Lord, give us this bread."

Jn 6:35   Jesus said to them, **"I AM THE "BREAD OF LIFE." HE WHO COMES TO ME WILL NOT BE HUNGRY, AND HE WHO BELIEVES IN ME WILL NEVER BE THIRSTY.**

Jn 6:36   I TOLD YOU THAT YOU HAVE SEEN ME. BUT STILL YOU DO NOT BELIEVE."

291   *THOSE DRAWN TO JESUS WILL FIND HIM AND WILL LIVE ETERNALLY (Jn 6:37-40)*

Jn 6:37   "ALL THOSE WHOM THE FATHER GIVES ME WILL COME TO ME. HE WHO COMES TO ME I WILL IN NO WAY TURN AWAY.

Jn 6:38   FOR I HAVE COME DOWN FROM HEAVEN NOT TO DO MY OWN WILL, BUT THE WILL OF HIM WHO SENT ME.

Jn 6:39   THIS IS THE WILL OF MY FATHER WHO SENT ME, THAT OF ALL HE HAS GIVEN TO ME I SHOULD LOSE NO ONE, BUT SHOULD RAISE THEM UP AT THE LAST DAY.

Jn 6:40   THIS IS THE WILL OF THE ONE WHO SENT ME, THAT EVERYONE WHO SEES THE SON, AND BELIEVES IN HIM, SHOULD HAVE ETERNAL LIFE. AND I WILL RAISE HIM UP ON THE LAST DAY!"

292   *AS THEY BEGIN TO DISAGREE, JESUS, THE "BEACON OF HOPE," AFFIRMS THAT THOSE TO BE SAVED ARE ALREADY CHOSEN BY GOD (Jn 6:41-44)*

Jn 6:41   The Jews therefore murmured concerning Him, because He said, **"I AM THE BREAD WHICH CAME DOWN OUT OF HEAVEN."**

Jn 6:42   They said, "Is this not Jesus, the son of Joseph, whose father and mother we know? How then does He say, **"I HAVE COME DOWN OUT OF HEAVEN?"**

Jn 6:43   Therefore Jesus answered them, **"DO NOT MURMUR AMONG YOURSELVES.**

Jn 6:44   NO ONE CAN COME TO ME UNLESS THE FATHER WHO SENT ME DRAWS HIM. AND I WILL RAISE HIM UP ON THE LAST DAY."

293   ANYONE WHO BELIEVES IN JESUS WILL HAVE AN EVERLASTING REWARD (Jn 6:45-47)

Jn 6:45 "IT IS WRITTEN BY THE PROPHETS, 'THEY WILL ALL BE TAUGHT BY GOD.' THEREFORE EVERYONE WHO HEARS FROM THE FATHER, AND HAS LEARNED, COMES TO ME. *(Isa 54:13)*

Jn 6:46 NOT THAT ANYONE HAS SEEN THE FATHER, EXCEPT HE WHO IS FROM GOD. HE HAS SEEN THE FATHER.

Jn 6:47 MOST CERTAINLY, I TELL YOU, HE WHO BELIEVES IN ME HAS ETERNAL *(never-ending)* LIFE."

> *1 Jn 5:12 He that hath the Son hath life; and he that hath not the Son of God hath not life.*

294   JESUS IS THE "NEW MANNA" FROM HEAVEN WHICH OFFERS LASTING SUSTENANCE (Jn 6:48-51)

Jn 6:48 "I AM THE BREAD OF LIFE.

Jn 6:49 YOUR FATHERS ATE THE MANNA IN THE WILDERNESS, AND THEY DIED.

Jn 6:50 THIS IS THE BREAD WHICH COMES DOWN OUT OF HEAVEN, THAT ANYONE MAY EAT OF IT AND NOT DIE.

Jn 6:51 I AM THE "LIVING BREAD" WHICH CAME DOWN OUT OF HEAVEN. IF ANYONE EATS OF THIS BREAD, HE WILL LIVE FOREVER. YES, THE BREAD WHICH I WILL GIVE IS MY FLESH, WHICH I WILL GIVE FOR THE LIFE OF THE WORLD."

295   HE OFFERS A GLORIOUS ASSURANCE TO ALL WHO PARTAKE IN FULL COMMUNION (Jn 6:52-56)

Jn 6:52 The Jews therefore contended with one another, saying, "How can this Man give us His flesh to eat?"

Jn 6:53 Jesus therefore said to them, "MOST CERTAINLY I TELL YOU, UNLESS YOU EAT THE FLESH OF THE SON OF MAN AND DRINK HIS BLOOD, YOU WILL NOT HAVE LIFE IN YOURSELVES.

Jn 6:54 HE WHO EATS MY FLESH **AND** DRINKS MY BLOOD HAS ETERNAL LIFE. AND I WILL RAISE HIM UP ON THE LAST DAY.

Jn 6:55 FOR MY FLESH IS REAL FOOD INDEED, AND MY BLOOD IS DRINK INDEED.

Jn 6:56 HE WHO EATS MY FLESH AND DRINKS MY BLOOD LIVES IN ME, AND I IN HIM!"

296   JESUS, THE "VERY GOD OF HEAVEN," REPEATS HIS MESSAGE FOR ALL TO UNDERSTAND (Jn 6:57-59)

Jn 6:57 "AS THE "LIVING FATHER" SENT ME, I LIVE BY THE FATHER. SO HE WHO FEEDS ON ME EVEN HE WILL ALSO LIVE THROUGH ME.

Jn 6:58 THIS IS THE BREAD WHICH CAME DOWN OUT OF HEAVEN. BUT NOT AS OUR FATHERS ATE THE MANNA, AND DIED. HE WHO EATS THIS BREAD WILL LIVE FOREVER."

Jn 6:59 He said these things in the synagogue, as He taught in Capernaum.

297   JESUS, THE "WISDOM OF GOD," GIVES ANOTHER REASON FOR SEEKING THE HOLY SPIRIT (Jn 6:60-63)

Jn 6:60 Therefore many of His disciples, when they heard this, said, "This is a difficult teaching! Who can listen to this?"

Jn 6:61 But Jesus knowing in Himself that His disciples grumbled at this said to them, **"DOES THIS CAUSE YOU TO WAVER?**

Jn 6:62 THEN WHAT IF YOU WOULD SEE THE SON OF MAN ASCENDING TO WHERE HE WAS BEFORE?

Jn 6:63 IT IS THE SPIRIT WHO GIVES LIFE. THE FLESH PROFITS NOTHING. THE WORDS THAT I SPEAK TO YOU THEY ARE SPIRIT, AND THEY ARE LIFE."

298   THIS DIFFICULT TEACHING CAUSES MANY WHO WERE FOLLOWING HIM TO DEFECT (Jn 6:64-66)

Jn 6:64 "BUT THERE ARE SOME OF YOU WHO DO NOT BELIEVE." For Jesus knew from the beginning who they were who did not believe, and who it was who would betray Him.

Jn 6:65 He said, **"FOR THIS CAUSE HAVE I SAID TO YOU THAT NO ONE CAN COME TO ME, UNLESS HE IS CALLED BY MY FATHER."**

Jn 6:66 Because of this, many of His disciples turned away, and walked no more with Him.

299   *BUT THE WORD OF GOD CANNOT BE COMPROMISED (Jn 6:67-69)*

Jn 6:67   Jesus said therefore to the twelve, **"DO YOU ALSO WANT TO GO AWAY?"**

Jn 6:68   Simon Peter answered Him, "Lord, to whom would we go? You have the words of eternal life.

Jn 6:69   We have come to believe and know that You are the Christ, the "Son of the Living God." "

300   *JESUS KNOWINGLY ALLOWS A DEMON TO BE AMONG THE TWELVE, TO FULFILL SCRIPTURE (Jn 6:70,71 & 7:1)*

Jn 6:70   Jesus answered them, **"DID I NOT CHOOSE YOU TWELVE, YET ONE OF YOU IS A DEVIL?"**

Jn 6:71   Now He spoke of Judas, the son of Simon Iscariot, for it was he who would betray Him, being one of the twelve.

Jn 7:1   After these things, Jesus walked in Galilee, for He would not walk in Judea, because the Jews sought to kill Him.

CHAPTER IX

JESUS CONFRONTS THE PHARISEES

301 A JERUSALEM DELEGATION COMES TO QUESTION JESUS, THE "LORD OF OUR SALVATION" (taken from Mt 15:1-20; Mk 7:1-23)

Mt 15:1 Then Pharisees and scribes came to Jesus from Jerusalem.

Mk 7:2 Now when they saw some of His disciples eating bread with defiled hands, that is, unwashed hands, they found fault.

Mk 7:3 For the Pharisees and all the Jews do not eat unless they wash their hands and forearms, holding to the tradition of the elders.

Mk 7:4 They do not eat when they come from the marketplace, unless they bathe themselves, and there are many other things, which they hold to; the washings of cups, pitchers, bronze vessels, and tables.

302 JESUS IS CRITICAL OF THEIR OUTWARD APPEARANCE WHILE DISOBEYING GOD'S COMMANDS (Mt 15:7-9; Mk 7:6-8)

Mk 7:5 The Pharisees and the scribes asked Him, "Why do Your disciples not walk according to the tradition of the elders, but eat their bread with unwashed hands?"

Mt 15:7 "YOU HYPOCRITES! WELL DID ISAIAH PROPHESY OF YOU, SAYING,

Mt 15:8 'THESE PEOPLE DRAW NEAR TO ME WITH THEIR MOUTH, AND HONOR ME WITH THEIR LIPS, BUT THEIR HEART IS FAR FROM ME. *(Isa 29:13)*

Mt 15:9 AND IN VAIN DO THEY WORSHIP ME, TEACHING AS DOCTRINE RULES MADE BY MEN.'

Mk 7:8 FOR YOU SET ASIDE THE COMMANDMENT OF GOD, AND HOLD TIGHTLY TO THE TRADITION OF MEN, THE WASHING OF PITCHERS AND CUPS, AND YOU DO MANY OTHER SUCH THINGS."

303   JESUS, THE "PERFECT MODEL," QUESTIONS THE CONDUCT OF THE RELIGIOUS LEADERS (Mt 15:3-7; Mk 7:9-13)

Mt 15:3 "...WHY DO YOU DISOBEY THE COMMANDMENT OF GOD BY YOUR TRADITIONS?

Mk 7:10 FOR MOSES SAID, 'HONOR YOUR FATHER AND YOUR MOTHER' AND, 'HE WHO SPEAKS EVIL OF FATHER OR MOTHER, LET HIM BE PUT TO DEATH.'
(Ex 20:12; Ex 21:17)

Mt 15:5 BUT YOU SAY, 'WHOEVER MAY TELL HIS FATHER OR HIS MOTHER, THAT WHATEVER HELP YOU HAVE GOTTEN FROM ME, IS A GIFT DEVOTED TO GOD,

Mt 15:6 AND SHALL NOT HONOR HIS FATHER OR MOTHER SHALL BE FREE.' THUS YOU HAVE MADE THE COMMANDMENT OF GOD VOID BECAUSE OF YOUR TRADITION,

Mk 7:13 ...WHICH YOU HAVE HANDED DOWN. YOU DO MANY THINGS LIKE THIS."

304   OUT OF THE FULLNESS OF THE HEART THE MOUTH SPEAKS (Mt 15:10,11; Mk 7:14-16)

Mk 7:14 He called all the people to Himself, and said to them, "HEAR ME, ALL OF YOU, AND UNDERSTAND.

Mk 7:15 THERE IS NOTHING FROM OUTSIDE OF THE MAN, THAT GOING INTO HIM CAN DEFILE HIM, BUT THE THINGS WHICH PROCEED OUT OF THE MAN ARE THOSE THAT DEFILE THE MAN.

Mk 7:16 IF ANYONE HAS EARS TO HEAR, LET HIM HEAR!"

305   FOLLOWERS OF THOSE WHO ARE SPIRITUALLY BLIND WILL PERISH WITH THEM (Mt 15:12-14)

Mt 15:12 Then the disciples came, and said to Him, "Do You know that the Pharisees were offended, when they heard this saying?"

Mt 15:13 But He answered, "EVERY PLANT WHICH MY HEAVENLY FATHER DID NOT PLANT WILL BE UPROOTED.

Mt 15:14 LEAVE THEM ALONE. THEY ARE BLIND GUIDES OF THE BLIND. IF THE BLIND LEAD THE BLIND, BOTH WILL FALL INTO A DITCH."

306 JESUS, THE "ABLE EDUCATOR," CLARIFIES HIS MESSAGE FOR HIS INQUISITIVE DISCIPLES (Mt 15:15-17; Mk 7:17-19)

Mk 7:17 When He had entered into a house away from the multitude, His disciples asked Him what He meant.

Mk 7:18 He said to them, **"ARE YOU THUS WITHOUT UNDERSTANDING ALSO? DO YOU NOT PERCEIVE THAT WHATEVER GOES INTO THE MAN FROM OUTSIDE CANNOT DEFILE HIM,**

Mk 7:19 BECAUSE IT DOES NOT GO INTO HIS HEART, BUT INTO HIS STOMACH, THEN IS EXPELLED, THUS PURIFYING ALL FOODS?"

307 EVIL GENERATED IN A PERSON'S HEART CAN LEAD TO IMMORAL ACTS (Mt 15:18-20; Mk 7:20-23)

Mt 15:18 "BUT THE THINGS WHICH PROCEED OUT OF THE MOUTH COME OUT OF THE HEART, AND THEY DEFILE THE MAN.

Mk 7:21 FOR FROM WITHIN, OUT OF THE HEARTS OF MEN, PROCEED EVIL THOUGHTS, ADULTERIES, SEXUAL SINS, MURDERS,

Mk 7:22 THEFTS, COVETINGS, WICKEDNESS, DECEIT, LUSTFUL DESIRES, JEALOUSY, BLASPHEMY, PRIDE, AND FOOLISHNESS.

Mk 7:23 ALL THESE EVIL THINGS COME FROM WITHIN.

Mt 15:20 THESE ARE THE THINGS WHICH CORRUPT THE MAN, BUT TO EAT WITH UNWASHED HANDS DOES NOT DEFILE THE MAN."

308 A GENTILE WOMAN CRIES OUT TO JESUS, THE "HELPING HAND," FOR HIS ASSISTANCE (Mt 15:21-28; Mk 7:24-30)

Mk 7:24 From there He arose, and went away into the borders of Tyre and Sidon. He entered into a house, and did not want anyone to know it, but He could not escape notice.

Mk 7:25 For a woman, whose little daughter had an unclean spirit, having heard of Him, came and fell down at His feet.

Mk 7:26 Now the woman was a Greek, a Syrophoenician by race. She begged Him that He would cast the demon out of her daughter.

309   HE ATTEMPTS TO IGNORE HER BUT SHE PERSISTS (Mt 15:22-27; Mk 7:27,28)

Mt 15:22 "Have mercy on me, Lord, You "Son of David," my daughter is severely demonized!"

Mt 15:23 But He answered her not a word. His disciples came and begged Him, saying, "Send her away, for she cries after us."

Mt 15:24 But He answered, **"I WAS NOT SENT TO ANYONE BUT TO THE LOST SHEEP OF THE HOUSE OF ISRAEL.**

Mk 7:27 **LET THE CHILDREN BE FILLED FIRST, FOR IT IS NOT APPROPRIATE TO TAKE THE CHILDREN'S BREAD AND THROW IT TO DOGS."**

Mk 7:28 But she answered Him, "Yes, Lord. Yet even the dogs under the table eat the children's crumbs."

310   A GOOD ANSWER LEADS TO HER DAUGHTER'S HEALING (Mt 15:28; Mk 7:29-31)

Mk 7:29 He said to her, **"FOR THIS SAYING, GO YOUR WAY. THE DEMON HAS GONE OUT OF YOUR DAUGHTER.**

Mt 15:28 **WOMAN, GREAT IS YOUR FAITH! BE IT DONE TO YOU EVEN AS YOU DESIRE."** And her daughter was healed from that hour.

Mk 7:30 She went away to her house, and found the child resting on the bed, with the demon gone out.

>   *Gal 3:11 ...the just shall live by faith.*

Mk 7:31 Again He departed from the borders of Tyre and Sidon, and came to the sea of Galilee, through the region of Decapolis.

311   JESUS, THE "RESTORER," DOES THE UNUSUAL TO CLEAR A MAN'S SPEECH AND HEARING (Mt 15:29; Mk 7:32-37)

Mt 15:29 He went up into the mountain, and sat there.

Mk 7:32 They brought to Him one who was deaf and had an impediment in his speech. They begged Him to lay His hand on him.

Mk 7:33 He took him aside from the people, privately, and put His fingers into his ears, and He spat, and touched his tongue.

Mk 7:34 Looking up to heaven, He sighed, and said to him, **"EPHPHATHA!"** that is, **"BE OPENED!"**

312   THIS HEALING LEADS TO EVEN MORE UNWANTED PUBLICITY (Mk 7:35-37)

Mk 7:35 Immediately his ears were opened, and the difficulty of his tongue was released, and he spoke clearly.

Mk 7:36 He commanded them that they should tell no one, but the more He commanded them, so much the more widely they proclaimed it.

Mk 7:37 They were astonished beyond measure, saying, "He has done all things well. He makes even the deaf to hear, and the mute to speak!"

313   HE RESPONDS TO THE NEEDS OF ALL WHO ARE SICK (Mt 15:30,31)

Mt 15:30 A great many came to Him, having with them the lame, blind, mute, maimed, and many others, and they put them down at His feet. He healed them,

Mt 15:31 so that the crowd wondered when they saw the mute speaking, the injured made whole, the lame walking, and blind seeing—and they glorified the "God of Israel."

314   JESUS, THE "CARING LEADER," ADDRESSES THE PROBLEM OF FEEDING ANOTHER LARGE FOLLOWING (Mt 15:32-39; Mk 8:1-10)

Mk 8:1 In those days, when there was a great many people following, and they had nothing to eat, Jesus called His disciples to Himself, and said to them,

Mk 8:2 **"I FEEL SORRY FOR THESE PEOPLE, BECAUSE THEY HAVE STAYED WITH ME NOW THREE DAYS, AND HAVE NOTHING TO EAT.**

Mk 8:3 **IF I SEND THEM AWAY HUNGRY TO THEIR HOME, THEY WILL FAINT ON THE WAY, FOR SOME OF THEM HAVE COME A LONG WAY."**

Mk 8:4 His disciples answered Him, "How could one satisfy these people with bread here in a deserted place?"

315   THANKFUL PRAISE TO DIVINE PROVIDENCE BRINGS A SECOND MIRACULOUS FEEDING (Mt 15:34-39; Mk 8:5-10)

Mt 15:34 Jesus said to them, **"HOW MANY LOAVES DO YOU HAVE?"** They said, "Seven, and a few small fish."

Mt 15:35 He commanded the people to sit down on the ground.

Mt 15:36 He took the seven loaves and the fish. He gave thanks and broke them, and gave them to the disciples, and the disciples to the people.

Mt 15:37 They all ate, and were filled. They took up seven baskets full of the broken pieces that were left over.

Mt 15:38 Those who ate were four thousand men, besides women and children.

Mt 15:39 Then He sent away the crowd, got into the boat, and came into the borders of Magdala.

316   OFFICIALS AGAIN DESIRE A MIRACLE TO PROVE JESUS *(Mt 16:1-4; Mk 8:11,12)*

Mk 8:11 The Pharisees came out and began to question Him, seeking from Him a sign from heaven, and testing Him.

Mk 8:12 He sighed deeply in His spirit, and said, **"WHY DOES THIS GENERATION SEEK A SIGN? MOST CERTAINLY I TELL YOU, NO SIGN WILL BE GIVEN TO THIS GENERATION."**

317   INDICATIONS ARE GIVEN TO EXPECT WHAT IS COMING *(Mt 16:2-4; Lk 12:54-56)*

Lk 12:54 He said to the crowd also, **"WHEN YOU SEE A CLOUD RISING FROM THE WEST, IMMEDIATELY YOU SAY, 'A SHOWER IS COMING,' AND SO IT HAPPENS.**

Mt 16:2 **WHEN IT IS EVENING, YOU SAY, 'IT WILL BE FAIR WEATHER, FOR THE SKY IS RED.'**

Lk 12:55 **WHEN A SOUTH WIND BLOWS, YOU SAY, 'THERE WILL BE A SCORCHING HEAT,' AND IT HAPPENS.**

Mt 16:3 **IN THE MORNING, 'IT WILL BE FOUL WEATHER TODAY, FOR THE SKY IS RED AND THREATENING.' HYPOCRITES! YOU KNOW HOW TO INTERPRET THE APPEARANCE OF THE SKY, BUT YOU CANNOT TELL THE SIGNS OF THESE TIMES."**

318   *JESUS, THE "DIVINE VOICE," EXPLAINS THAT THEIR UNGODLINESS PREVENTS THEM FROM PERCEIVING THE OBVIOUS (Mt 16:4; Mk 8:12,13; Lk 12:56)*

Mt 16:4 **"AN EVIL AND ADULTEROUS GENERATION SEEKS AFTER A SIGN. THERE WILL BE NO SIGN GIVEN TO IT, EXCEPT THE SIGN OF THE PROPHET JONAH."**

Mk 8:13 He left them, and again entering into the boat, departed to the other side.

319   ANOTHER OF HIS TEACHINGS IS NOT IMMEDIATELY UNDERSTOOD (Mt 16:5-12; Mk 8:14-16)

Mk 8:14 They forgot to take bread, and they did not have more than one loaf in the boat with them.

Mk 8:15 He warned them, saying, **"TAKE HEED, BEWARE OF THE YEAST** *(teachings)* **OF THE PHARISEES, AND THE YEAST** *(worldliness)* **OF HEROD."**

Mt 16:7 They reasoned among themselves, saying, "We brought no bread."

Mt 16:8 Jesus, perceiving it, said, **"WHY DO YOU DISCUSS AMONG YOURSELVES, YOU OF LITTLE FAITH, BECAUSE YOU HAVE BROUGHT NO BREAD?"**

320   BY INSTRUCTING AND GIVING UNTO OTHERS, ONE ALSO RECEIVES AND GRASPS EVEN MORE (Mt 16:9,10; Mk 8:19-21)

Mk 8:17 **"...DO YOU NOT SEE IT YET, NEITHER UNDERSTAND? IS YOUR HEART STILL HARDENED?**

Mk 8:18 **HAVING EYES, DO YOU NOT SEE? HAVING EARS, DO YOU NOT HEAR? DO YOU NOT REMEMBER?**

Mk 8:19 **WHEN I BROKE THE FIVE LOAVES AMONG THE FIVE THOUSAND, HOW MANY BASKETS FULL OF BROKEN PIECES DID YOU TAKE UP?"** They told Him, "Twelve."

Mk 8:20 **"WHEN THE SEVEN LOAVES FED THE FOUR THOUSAND, HOW MANY BASKETS FULL OF BROKEN PIECES DID YOU TAKE UP?"** They told him, "Seven."

Mk 8:21 He asked them, **"DO YOU NOT UNDERSTAND, YET?"**

321   HIS FOLLOWERS ONES ARE TO BE WARY OF MISLEADING SHEPHERDS (Mt 16:11,12)

Mt 16:11 **"HOW IS IT THAT YOU DO NOT PERCEIVE THAT I DID NOT SPEAK TO YOU CONCERNING BREAD? BUT BEWARE OF THE YEAST OF THE PHARISEES AND SADDUCEES."**

Mt 16:12 Then they understood that He did not tell them to beware of the yeast of bread, but of the teachings of the Pharisees and Sadducees.

322   THE "GUIDING LIGHT" RESTORES A BLIND MAN'S SIGHT NEAR BETHESDA (Mk 8:22-26)

Mk 8:22   Jesus comes to Bethsaida. They brought a blind man to Him, and begged Him to touch him.

Mk 8:23   He took hold of the blind man by the hand, and brought him out of the village. When He had spit on his eyes, and laid His hands on him, He asked him if he saw anything.

Mk 8:24   He looked up, and said, "I see men, for I see them like trees walking."

323   A SECOND HEALING IS NECESSARY TO STRENGTHEN THE MAN'S EYESIGHT (Mk 8:25,26)

Mk 8:25   Then again He laid His hands on his eyes. He looked intently, and was restored, and saw everyone clearly.

   Rom 1:17 ...from faith to faith

Mk 8:26   He sent him away to his house, saying, **"DO NOT ENTER INTO THE VILLAGE, NOR TELL ANYONE IN THE VILLAGE."**

324   THE DISCIPLES ARE ASKED TO IDENTIFY WHO JESUS THEIR "BENEFACTOR" IS (Mt 16:13-17; Mk 8:27-29; Lk 9:18-20)

Mt 16:13   Now when Jesus came into the parts of Caesarea Philippi…

Lk 9:18   It happened, as He was praying alone, that the disciples were with Him, and He asked them, **"WHO DO PEOPLE SAY THAT I AM?"**

Mt 16:14   They said, "Some say, John the Baptist, some say, Elijah, and others, Jeremiah, or one of the prophets."

325   PETER'S REVELATION THAT JESUS IS THE MESSIAH IS DIVINELY INSPIRED (Mt 16:15-17; Mk 8:27-29; Lk 9:20)

Mt 16:15   He said to them, **"BUT WHO DO YOU SAY THAT I AM?"**

Mt 16:16   Simon Peter answered, "You are the Christ, the Son of the Living God."

Mt 16:17 Jesus answered him, "BLESSED ARE YOU, SIMON SON OF JONAH, FOR FLESH AND BLOOD HAS NOT REVEALED THIS TO YOU, BUT MY FATHER WHO IS IN HEAVEN."

326   *GOD WILL ESTABLISH HIS CHURCH ON FAITH, SUCH AS PETER'S Mt 16:18-20; Mk 8:30; Lk 9:21)*

Mt 16:18 "I ALSO TELL YOU THAT YOU ARE PETER, AND ON THIS ROCK I WILL BUILD MY CHURCH, AND THE GATES OF HELL WILL NOT PREVAIL AGAINST IT.

Mt 16:19 I WILL GIVE TO YOU THE KEYS OF THE KINGDOM OF HEAVEN, AND WHATEVER YOU BIND ON EARTH WILL HAVE BEEN BOUND IN HEAVEN, AND WHATEVER YOU ALLOW ON EARTH WILL BE ALLOWED IN HEAVEN."

Mt 16:20 Then He commanded the disciples that they should tell no one that He was the Christ.

327   *JESUS ADMONISHES PETER FOR BEING USED BY SATAN (Mt 16:21-23; Mk 8:31-33; Lk 9:22)*

Lk 9:22 "THE SON OF MAN MUST SUFFER MANY THINGS, AND BE REJECTED BY THE ELDERS, CHIEF PRIESTS, AND SCRIBES, AND BE KILLED. AND ON THE THIRD DAY BE RAISED UP."

Mt 16:22 Peter took Him aside, and began to rebuke Him, saying, "Far be it for You, Lord! This will never be done to You."

Mk 8:33 But He, turning around, and seeing His disciples, scolded Peter, and said, "GET THEE BEHIND ME, SATAN...

Mt 16:23 ...YOU ARE A HINDRANCE TO ME. FOR YOU ARE NOT SETTING YOUR MIND ON THE THINGS OF GOD, BUT ON THE THINGS OF MEN."

Isa 43:11 "I, even I, AM the Lord: and beside Me there is no savior."

328   *JESUS, OUR "TRUE DESTINY," URGES HIS WOULD-BE FOLLOWERS TO FORSAKE THE WORLD TO GAIN PERPETUAL LIFE (Mt 16:24-28; Mk 8:34-38; Lk 9:23-27)*

Mk 8:34 He called the multitude to Himself with His disciples, and said to them, "WHOEVER WANTS TO COME AFTER ME, LET HIM DENY HIMSELF, TAKE UP HIS CROSS EVERY DAY, AND FOLLOW ME. *(imitate Me)*

Lk 9:24 FOR WHOEVER DESIRES TO SAVE HIS LIFE WILL LOSE IT, BUT

WHOEVER WILL LOSE HIS LIFE FOR MY SAKE, THE SAME WILL SAVE IT.

Mt 16:26 FOR WHAT WILL IT PROFIT A MAN, IF HE GAINS THE WHOLE WORLD, AND LOSES HIS SOUL? OR WHAT WILL A MAN GIVE IN EXCHANGE FOR HIS SOUL?"

329   *THE EXTENT OF OUR GLORY AND HONOR IS UP TO EACH INDIVIDUAL (Mt 16:27,28; Mk 8:38 & 9:1; Lk 9:26,27)*

Mk 8:38 "FOR WHOEVER WILL BE ASHAMED OF ME AND OF MY MESSAGE IN THIS WICKED AND SINFUL GENERATION, THE SON OF MAN ALSO WILL BE ASHAMED OF HIM, WHEN HE COMES IN THE GLORY OF HIS FATHER... *(Do not be a closet Christian)*

Mt 16:27 FOR THE SON OF MAN WILL COME IN THE GLORY OF HIS FATHER, WITH HIS ANGELS, AND THEN HE WILL RENDER TO EVERYONE ACCORDING TO HIS DEEDS."

> *(We are saved by grace, lest we should boast. Eph 2:8,9 But we are rewarded for our good works, as stated here in Mt 16:27 and in Ps 62:12; Pr 24:12; Isa 59:18; Jer 17:10; Rom 2:6; 1 Cor 3:8; Rev 14:13; 20:12,13; and 22:12.)*

Mk 9:1 He said to them, "MOST CERTAINLY I TELL YOU, THERE ARE SOME STANDING HERE WHO WILL IN NO WAY TASTE DEATH UNTIL THEY SEE THE KINGDOM OF GOD COME WITH POWER."

CHAPTER X

HIS MAJESTY REVEALED

330   AT THE 'TRANSFIGURATION' THREE DISCIPLES SEE A PREVIEW OF HIS "SOVEREIGNTY" (taken from Mt 17:1-13; Mk 9:2-13; Lk 9:28-36)

Mt 17:1   After six days, Jesus took with Him Peter, James, and John his brother, and brought them up into a high mountain by themselves.

Lk 9:29   As He was praying, the appearance of His face was altered…

Mt 17:2   He was transfigured before them. His face shone like the Sun, and His garments became as white as the Light.

> *Rev 1:16 …and His countenance was as the sun shineth in His strength.*

> *Ps 84:11 For the Lord is a sun…*

> *(Also see Jn 8:12 & 9:5; Rev 22:16)*

331   TWO MEN REPRESENTING THE LAW AND THE PROPHETS GIVE WITNESS TO THE SPECIAL MISSION OF JESUS (Mt 17:3; Mk 9:4; Lk 9:30-32)

Lk 9:30   Behold, two men were talking with Him, who were Moses and Elijah,

Lk 9:31   who appeared in glory, and spoke of His coming departure, which He was about to accomplish at Jerusalem.

Lk 9:32   Now Peter and those who were with Him were heavy with sleep, but when they were fully awake, they saw His glory, and the two men who stood with Him.

332   A SUDDEN CLOUD COVER ALARMS THE THREE DISCIPLES (Mt 17:4; Mk 9:5,6; Lk 9:33,34)

Lk 9:33   It happened, as they were parting from them, that Peter said to Jesus, "Master, it is good for us to be here. Let us make three tents; one for You, and one for Moses, and one for Elijah," not knowing what he said.

Lk 9:34   While he said these things, a cloud came and overshadowed them, and they were afraid as they entered into the cloud.

333   GOD THE FATHER AGAIN ACKNOWLEDGES AND HONORS HIS "DEARLY BELOVED SON" (Mt 17:5-8; Mk 9:7,8; Lk 9:35,36)

Mt 17:5   Behold, a voice came out of the cloud, saying, *"THIS IS MY BELOVED SON, IN WHOM I AM WELL PLEASED... (Ps 2:7)*

Lk 9:35   *...MY "CHOSEN ONE." LISTEN TO HIM."*

Mt 17:6   When the disciples heard it, they fell on their faces, and were very afraid.

Mt 17:7   Jesus came and touched them and said, **"GET UP, AND DO NOT BE AFRAID."**

Mt 17:8   Lifting up their eyes, they saw no one, except Jesus alone.

334   PETER, JAMES AND JOHN ARE UNCERTAIN ABOUT THE NEW CONCEPT OF A RESURRECTION AFTER DEATH (Mt 17:9; Mk 9:9,10; Lk 9:36)

Mt 17:9   As they were coming down from the mountain, Jesus commanded them, saying, **"DO NOT TELL ANYONE WHAT YOU SAW, UNTIL THE SON OF MAN HAS RISEN FROM THE DEAD."**

Mk 9:10   They kept this saying to themselves, questioning what the "rising from the dead" meant.

Lk 9:36   They were silent, and told no one in those days any of the things which they had seen.

335   ELIJAH'S COMING HAS BEEN FULFILLED BY JOHN THE BAPTIST (Mt 17:10-13; Mk 9:11-13)

Mt 17:10   His disciples asked Him, saying, "Then why do the scribes say that Elijah must come first?"

Mk 9:12   He said to them, **"ELIJAH INDEED COMES FIRST, AND RESTORES ALL THINGS. HOW IS IT WRITTEN ABOUT THE SON OF MAN, THAT HE SHOULD SUFFER MANY THINGS AND BE DESPISED?**

Mt 17:12   **BUT I TELL YOU THAT ELIJAH HAS COME ALREADY, AND THEY DID NOT RECOGNIZE HIM, BUT DID TO HIM WHATEVER THEY WANTED TO. EVEN SO THE SON OF MAN WILL ALSO SUFFER BY MEN."**

Mt 17:13 Then the disciples understood that He spoke to them of John the Baptist.

336 JESUS, THE "JOY BRINGER," IS SOUGHT TO HEAL AN EPILEPTIC WHICH THE DISCIPLES COULD NOT (Mt 17:14-21; Mk 9:14-29; Lk 9:37-40)

Lk 9:37 It happened on the next day, when they had come down from the mountain, that a great many met Jesus.

Mk 9:14 Coming to the disciples, He saw many around them as well, and scribes questioning them.

Mk 9:15 Immediately all the people, when they saw Him, were greatly amazed, and running to Him, greeted Him.

Mk 9:16 He asked the scribes, **"WHAT ARE YOU DISCUSSING WITH THEM?"**

Mk 9:17 One of them answered, "Teacher, I brought to You my son, who has a mute spirit,

Mk 9:18 and whenever it seizes him, it throws him down, and he foams at the mouth, and grinds his teeth, and wears him out. I asked Your disciples to cast it out, and they were not able."

337 HEALING ALSO REQUIRES BELIEVING ON THE PART OF THE RECIPIENT (Mt 17:17; Mk 9:19-24; Lk 9:41,42)

Mk 9:19 He answered him, **"UNBELIEVING GENERATION, HOW LONG SHALL I BE WITH YOU? HOW LONG SHALL I BEAR YOUR LACK OF FAITH? BRING HIM TO ME."**

Mk 9:20 They brought him to Him, and when Jesus saw him, immediately the spirit convulsed him, and he fell on the ground, rolling and foaming at the mouth.

Mk 9:21 He asked his father, **"HOW LONG HAS IT BEEN SINCE HE HAS BEEN THIS WAY?"** He said, "From childhood.

Mk 9:22 Often it has cast him both into the fire and into the water, to destroy him. But if you can do anything, have compassion on us, and help us."

Mk 9:23 Jesus said to him, **"IF YOU CAN BELIEVE, ALL THINGS ARE POSSIBLE TO HIM WHO BELIEVES."**

Mk 9:24 Immediately the father of the child cried out with tears, "I do believe. Help thou my unbelief!"

338 JESUS EXPELS THE DIFFICULT SPIRIT TO THE SURPRISE OF THE PEOPLE (Mt 17:18; Mk 9:25-27; Lk 9:42)

Mk 9:25 When Jesus saw that many came running towards them, He rebuked the unclean spirit, saying to him, **"YOU MUTE AND DEAF SPIRIT, I COMMAND YOU, COME OUT OF HIM, AND NEVER ENTER HIM AGAIN!"**

Mk 9:26 Having cried out, and convulsed greatly, it came out of him. The boy became like one dead, so much that many said, "He is dead."

Mk 9:27 But Jesus took him by the hand, and raised him up, and he arose.

339 SOME BENEFITS COME ONLY THROUGH DISCIPLINE AND PRAYER (Mt 17:19-21; Mk 9:28,29)

Mk 9:28 When He had come into the house, His disciples asked Him privately, "Why could we not cast it out?"

Mt 17:20 He said to them, **"BECAUSE OF YOUR UNBELIEF. FOR MOST CERTAINLY I TELL YOU, IF YOU HAVE FAITH AS A GRAIN OF MUSTARD SEED, YOU WILL TELL THIS MOUNTAIN, 'MOVE FROM HERE TO THERE,' AND IT WILL MOVE, AND NOTHING WILL BE IMPOSSIBLE FOR YOU.**

Mt 17:21 BUT THIS KIND DOES NOT GO OUT EXCEPT BY PRAYER AND FASTING."

340 JESUS, OUR "LIFE-GIVER," AGAIN PREDICTS HIS DEATH AND RISING FROM THE DEAD (Mt 17:22,23; Mk 9:30-32; Lk 9:43-45)

Lk 9:43 They were all astonished at the majesty of God. But while all were marveling at all the things which Jesus did, He said to His disciples,

Lk 9:44 **"LET THESE WORDS SINK INTO YOUR EARS, FOR THE SON OF MAN WILL BE DELIVERED UP INTO THE HANDS OF MEN.**

Mk 9:31 ...AND THEY WILL KILL HIM, AND AFTER HE IS KILLED, ON THE THIRD DAY HE WILL RISE AGAIN."

Lk 9:45 But they did not understand this saying. It was concealed from them, that they should not perceive it, and they were hesitant to ask Him about this saying.

341   *HE OBEYS AN ORDINANCE TO AVOID CAUSING OFFENSE (Mt 17:24-27)*

Mt 17:24   When they had come to Capernaum, those who collected the coins came to Peter, and said, "Does your teacher not pay the tribute?"

Mt 17:25   He said, "Yes." When he came into the house, Jesus anticipated him, saying, **"WHAT DO YOU THINK, SIMON? FROM WHOM DO THE KINGS OF THE EARTH RECEIVE TAXES OR TRIBUTE? FROM THEIR CHILDREN, OR FROM STRANGERS?"**

Mt 17:26   Peter said to Him, "From strangers." Jesus said to him, **"THEREFORE THE CHILDREN ARE EXEMPT.**

Mt 17:27   BUT, SO AS NOT TO OFFEND THEM, GO TO THE SEA, CAST A HOOK, AND TAKE UP THE FIRST FISH THAT COMES UP. WHEN YOU HAVE OPENED ITS MOUTH, YOU WILL FIND A COIN. TAKE THAT, AND GIVE IT TO THEM FOR ME AND YOU."

342   *JESUS DISCUSSES WITH HIS DISCIPLES THEIR AMBITIOUS PURSUIT (Mt 18:1-5; Mk 9:33-37; Lk 9:46-48)*

Mk 9:33   He came to Capernaum, and when He was in the house He asked them, **"WHAT WERE YOU ARGUING AMONG YOURSELVES ON THE WAY?"**

Mk 9:34   But they were silent, for they had discussed with one another on the way about who was the greatest.

Lk 9:47   Jesus, perceiving the reasoning of their hearts...

Mk 9:35   He sat down, and called the twelve, and He said to them, **"IF ANY MAN WANTS TO BE FIRST, HE MUST MAKE HIMSELF LAST OF ALL, AND SERVANT OF ALL."**

343   *JESUS, THE "THRONE OF GRACE," ASSOCIATES HIMSELF WITH THE YOUNG AND UNDERPRIVILEDGED (Mt 18:1-5; Mk 9:36,37; Lk 9:47,48)*

Mt 18:1   At the same time, came the disciples unto Jesus, saying, "Who is the greatest in the kingdom of heaven?"

Mk 9:36   He took a little child, and set him in their midst. Taking him in His arms, He said to them,

Mt 18:3   "MOST CERTAINLY I TELL YOU, UNLESS YOU CHANGE, AND BECOME AS LITTLE CHILDREN, YOU WILL IN NO WAY ENTER INTO THE KINGDOM OF HEAVEN.

Mt 18:4 WHOEVER THEREFORE HUMBLES HIMSELF AS THIS LITTLE CHILD, *(totally believing, relying on, and trusting his Heavenly Father)*, **THE SAME IS THE GREATEST IN THE KINGDOM OF HEAVEN."**

Lk 9:48 "WHOEVER RECEIVES THIS LITTLE CHILD IN MY NAME RECEIVES ME. WHOEVER RECEIVES ME RECEIVES HIM WHO SENT ME. FOR WHOEVER IS LEAST AMONG YOU, THIS ONE WILL BE GREAT."

344   *OUR "KIND LEADER" TEACHES CHRISTIAN TOLERANCE FOR ONE ANOTHER (Mk 9:38-41; Lk 9:49,50)*

Mk 9:38 John said to Him, "Teacher, we saw someone who does not follow us, casting out demons in Your name, and we forbade him, because he does not follow us."

Mk 9:39 But Jesus said, **"DO NOT FORBID HIM, FOR THERE IS NO ONE WHO WILL DO A MIGHTY WORK IN MY NAME, AND SOON AFTER SPEAK EVIL OF ME.**

Mk 9:40 **FOR WHOEVER IS NOT AGAINST US IS ON OUR SIDE.**

Mk 9:41 **FOR WHOEVER WILL GIVE YOU A CUP OF WATER TO DRINK IN MY NAME, BECAUSE YOU BELONG TO CHRIST, MOST CERTAINLY I TELL YOU, HE WILL IN NO WAY LOSE HIS REWARD."**

345   *JESUS, THE "ALL KNOWING," WARNS THOSE WHOSE EXAMPLE LEAD OTHERS ASTRAY (Mt 18:6,7; Mk 9:42; Lk 17:1-3)*

Lk 17:1 He said to the disciples, **"IT IS POSSIBLE THAT OCCASIONS OF SIN COULD COME, BUT WOE TO HIM THROUGH WHOM THEY COME**

Lk 17:2 **IT WOULD BE BETTER FOR HIM IF A LARGE MILLSTONE WERE HUNG AROUND HIS NECK, AND HE WERE THROWN INTO THE SEA, RATHER THAN HE SHOULD CAUSE ONE OF THESE LITTLE ONES TO STUMBLE.**

Lk 17:3 **SO BE CAREFUL..."**

346   *AVOID THE SOURCE OF TEMPTATION OR FACE THE REALITY OF HELL (Mt 18:8,9; Mk 9:43-48)*

Mk 9:43 **"IF YOUR HAND CAUSES YOU TO SIN, CUT IT OFF. IT IS BETTER FOR YOU TO ENTER INTO LIFE MAIMED, RATHER THAN HAVING YOUR TWO HANDS TO GO INTO HELL, INTO THE UNQUENCHABLE FIRE,**

Mk 9:44 'WHERE THEIR WORMS DO NOT DIE, AND THE FIRE IS NOT PUT OUT.

Mk 9:45 IF YOUR FOOT CAUSES YOU TO SIN, CUT IT OFF. IT IS BETTER FOR YOU TO ENTER INTO LIFE WITHOUT ONE FOOT, RATHER THAN HAVING YOUR TWO FEET AND BE CAST INTO GEHENNA *(hell)*, INTO THE FIRE THAT WILL NEVER BE QUENCHED

Mk 9:46 'WHERE THEIR WORMS DO NOT DIE, AND THE FIRE IS NOT PUT OUT.

Mk 9:47 IF YOUR EYE CAUSES YOU TO FALL, CAST IT OUT. IT IS BETTER FOR YOU TO ENTER INTO THE KINGDOM OF GOD WITH ONE EYE, RATHER THAN HAVING TWO EYES TO BE CAST INTO THE FIRE,

Mk 9:48 'WHERE THE WORMS DO NOT DIE, AND THE FIRE IS NOT QUENCHED."

347 JESUS TELLS OF GOD'S CONCERN FOR CHILDREN AND FOR THOSE WHO ARE LOST (Mt 18:10-14)

Mt 18:10 "SEE THAT YOU DO NOT DESPISE ONE OF THESE LITTLE ONES, FOR I TELL YOU THAT IN HEAVEN THEIR ANGELS ALWAYS SEE THE FACE OF MY FATHER WHO IS IN HEAVEN.

Mt 18:11 FOR THE SON OF MAN CAME TO SEEK AND TO SAVE THAT WHICH WAS LOST.

Mt 18:12 WHAT DO YOU THINK? IF A MAN HAS ONE HUNDRED SHEEP, AND ONE OF THEM GOES ASTRAY, DOES HE NOT LEAVE THE NINETY-NINE, GO TO THE MOUNTAINS, AND SEEK THAT WHICH HAS GONE ASTRAY?

Mt 18:13 IF HE FINDS IT, MOST CERTAINLY I TELL YOU, HE REJOICES OVER IT MORE THAN OVER THE NINETY-NINE WHICH HAVE NOT GONE ASTRAY.

Mt 18:14 EVEN SO, IT IS NOT THE WILL OF YOUR FATHER WHO IS IN HEAVEN THAT EVEN ONE OF THESE LITTLE ONES SHOULD PERISH."

348 ALWAYS ATTEMPT TO MAKE UP WITH SOMEONE WHO SINS AGAINST YOU (Mt 18:15-17)

Mt 18:15 "IF YOUR BROTHER SINS AGAINST YOU, GO, SHOW HIM HIS FAULT BETWEEN YOU AND HIM ALONE. IF HE LISTENS TO YOU, YOU HAVE GAINED YOUR BROTHER BACK. *(A brother usually refers to a fellow believer; a neighbor, to one who is not yet a believer.)*

Mt 18:16 BUT IF HE DOES NOT LISTEN, TAKE ONE OR TWO MORE WITH YOU, THAT BY THE MOUTH OF TWO OR THREE WITNESSES EVERY WORD MAY BE CONFIRMED.

Mt 18:17 IF HE REFUSES TO LISTEN TO THEM, TELL IT TO THE ASSEMBLY. IF HE REFUSES TO HEAR THE ASSEMBLY ALSO, LET HIM BE TO YOU AS A PAGAN AND A PUBLICAN."

349   *ANY FOLLOWER OF JESUS, OUR "SAVING LORD," HAS THE CAPACITY TO FORGIVE ANOTHER PERSON (Mt 18:18; Lk 17:3,4)*

Mt 18:18 "MOST CERTAINLY I TELL YOU, WHATEVER THINGS YOU BIND ON EARTH WILL HAVE BEEN BOUND IN HEAVEN, AND WHATEVER THINGS YOU RELEASE ON EARTH WILL HAVE BEEN RELEASED IN HEAVEN.

Lk 17:3 BE CAREFUL, IF YOUR BROTHER SINS AGAINST YOU, REBUKE HIM. IF HE REPENTS, FORGIVE HIM.

Lk 17:4 IF HE SINS AGAINST YOU SEVEN TIMES IN ONE DAY, AND SEVEN TIMES RETURNS, SAYING, 'I REPENT,' YOU MUST FORGIVE HIM."

350   *COMING TOGETHER IN A PRAYER OF AGREEMENT GETS ANSWERED (Mt 18:19,20)*

Mt 18:19 "AGAIN, ASSUREDLY I TELL YOU, THAT IF TWO OF YOU WILL AGREE ON EARTH CONCERNING ANYTHING THAT THEY WILL ASK, IT WILL BE DONE FOR THEM BY MY FATHER WHO IS IN HEAVEN.

Mt 18:20 FOR WHERE TWO OR THREE ARE GATHERED TOGETHER IN MY NAME, THERE I AM IN THEIR MIDST."

351   *WE MUST FORGIVE WITHOUT RESERVATION (Mt 18:21,22)*

Mt 18:21 Then Peter came and said to Him, "Lord, how often shall my brother sin against me, and I forgive him? Until seven times?"

Mt 18:22 Jesus said to him, "I DO NOT TELL YOU UNTIL SEVEN TIMES. BUT, UNTIL SEVENTY TIMES SEVEN."

352   A KING GRANTS TOTAL FORGIVENESS TO A SERVANT SEEKING MERCY (Mt 18:23-27)

Mt 18:23 "THEREFORE THE KINGDOM OF HEAVEN IS LIKE A CERTAIN KING, WHO WANTED TO SETTLE ACCOUNTS WITH HIS SERVANTS.

Mt 18:24 WHEN HE HAD BEGUN TO RECONCILE, ONE WAS BROUGHT TO HIM WHO OWED HIM TEN THOUSAND TALENTS.

Mt 18:25 BUT BECAUSE HE COULD NOT PAY, HIS LORD COMMANDED HIM TO BE SOLD, WITH HIS WIFE, HIS CHILDREN, AND ALL THAT HE HAD SO PAYMENT CAN BE MADE.

Mt 18:26 THE SERVANT THEREFORE FELL DOWN AND KNELT BEFORE HIM, SAYING, 'LORD, HAVE PATIENCE WITH ME, AND I WILL REPAY YOU ALL!'

Mt 18:27 THE LORD OF THAT SERVANT, BEING MOVED WITH COMPASSION, RELEASED HIM, AND FORGAVE HIM THE DEBT."

353   BUT THE FORGIVEN SERVANT REFUSES TO PARDON ANOTHER (Mt 18:28-30)

Mt 18:28 "BUT THAT SERVANT WENT OUT, AND FOUND ONE OF HIS FELLOW SERVANTS, WHO OWED HIM ONLY ONE HUNDRED SILVER COINS, AND HE GRABBED HIM, AND TOOK HIM BY THE THROAT, SAYING, 'PAY ME WHAT YOU OWE!'

Mt 18:29 SO HIS FELLOW SERVANT FELL DOWN AT HIS FEET AND BEGGED HIM, SAYING, 'HAVE PATIENCE WITH ME, AND I WILL REPAY YOU!'

Mt 18:30 HE WOULD NOT, BUT WENT AND CAST HIM INTO PRISON, UNTIL HE SHOULD PAY BACK THAT WHICH WAS DUE."

354   A MERCIFUL FATHER DEALS HARSHLY WITH THOSE WHO ARE UNFORGIVING (Mt 18:31-35)

Mt 18:31 "SO WHEN HIS FELLOW SERVANTS SAW WHAT WAS DONE, THEY WERE EXCEEDINGLY UPSET AND CAME AND TOLD THEIR LORD WHAT HAPPENED.

Mt 18:32 THEN HIS LORD CALLED HIM IN, AND SAID TO HIM, 'YOU WICKED SERVANT I FORGAVE YOU THAT LARGE DEBT, BECAUSE YOU BEGGED ME.

Mt 18:33 SHOULD YOU NOT ALSO HAVE HAD MERCY ON YOUR FELLOW SERVANT, EVEN AS I HAD MERCY ON YOU?'

Mt 18:34 HIS LORD WAS ANGRY, AND DELIVERED HIM TO THE JAILERS, UNTIL HE SHOULD PAY ALL THAT WAS DUE TO HIM.

Mt 18:35 SO WILL MY HEAVENLY FATHER ALSO DO TO YOU, IF YOU DO NOT FORGIVE YOUR BROTHER—FROM YOUR HEARTS."

CHAPTER XI

JESUS IS GOD'S RIGHTFUL EMISSARY

355   *HIS OWN BROTHERS ARE WITNESSES TO HIS DEEDS, BUT HAVE DIFFICULTY BELIEVING (taken from Jn 7:2-5)*

Jn 7:2   Now a feast of the Jews, the Feast of Booths, was at hand.

Jn 7:3   His brothers therefore said to Him, "Depart from here, and go into Judea, that Your disciples also may see the works which You do.

Jn 7:4   For no one does anything in secret, if he seeks to be known openly. Since You do these things, reveal Yourself to the world."

Jn 7:5   Yet even His own brothers did not believe in Him.

356   *JESUS SENDS HIS BROTHERS ON AHEAD TO THE FESTIVAL BY THEMSELVES (Jn 7:6-9)*

Jn 7:6   Jesus therefore said to them, **"MY TIME HAS NOT YET COME, BUT ANY TIME IS GOOD FOR YOU.**

Jn 7:7   **THE WORLD CANNOT HATE YOU, BUT IT HATES ME, BECAUSE I BRING TO THEIR ATTENTION THAT ITS WORKS ARE EVIL.**

Jn 7:8   **YOU GO UP TO THE FEAST. I AM NOT GOING UP TO THIS FEAST JUST NOW, BECAUSE MY TIME HAS NOT YET COME."**

Jn 7:9   Having said these things to them, He stayed in Galilee.

357   *THE SANHEDRIN WANTS TO ARREST HIM, BUT THERE IS A MIXED REACTION AMONG THE PEOPLE (Jn 7:10-13)*

Jn 7:10   But when His brothers had gone up to the feast, then He also went up, not publicly, but as it were in secret.

Jn 7:11   The Jews therefore sought Him at the feast, and said, "Where is He?"

Jn 7:12   There was much murmuring among the people concerning Him. Some said, "He is a good man." Others said, "Not so, He leads the people astray."

Jn 7:13   Yet no one spoke openly of Him for fear of the Jews.

358   OUR "COURAGEOUS LORD" BRAVELY BEGINS TO TEACH OPENLY IN THE LARGE JERUSALEM TEMPLE (Jn 7:14-16)

Jn 7:14   But when it was now the middle of the feast, Jesus went up into the temple and taught.

Jn 7:15   The Jews therefore marveled, saying, "How does this Man know so much, having never been educated?"

Jn 7:16   Jesus therefore answered them, **"MY TEACHING IS NOT MINE, BUT HIS WHO SENT ME."**

359   HE DECLARES THE DIVINE ORIGIN OF HIS TEACHINGS (Jn 7:17-20)

Jn 7:17   **"IF ANYONE DESIRES TO DO GOD'S WILL, HE WILL KNOW ABOUT MY TEACHING, WHETHER IT IS FROM GOD, OR IF I AM SPEAKING ON MY OWN.**

Jn 7:18   **HE WHO SPEAKS FOR HIMSELF SEEKS HIS OWN GLORY, BUT HE WHO SEEKS THE GLORY OF HIM WHO SENT HIM IS TRUE, AND NO EVIL INTENT IS IN HIM.**

Jn 7:19   **DID NOT MOSES GIVE YOU THE LAW, AND YET NONE OF YOU KEEPS THE LAW? WHY DO YOU SEEK TO KILL ME?"** *(See Jn 5:18)*

Jn 7:20   The multitude answered, "You have a demon! Who seeks to kill You?"

360   JESUS DRAWS ATTENTION TO THEIR INCONSISTENT PRACTICES WHILE THEY IGNORE HIS GOOD WILL (Jn 7:21-24)

Jn 7:21   Jesus answered them, **"I DID ONE DEED, AND YOU ALL MARVEL BECAUSE OF IT.**

Jn 7:22   **MOSES HAS GIVEN YOU CIRCUMCISION (NOT THAT IT CAME FROM MOSES, BUT FROM YOUR FATHERS), AND ON THE SABBATH YOU CIRCUMCISE A BOY.**

Jn 7:23 **IF A BOY RECEIVES CIRCUMCISION ON THE SABBATH, THAT THE LAW OF MOSES IS NOT BROKEN, ARE YOU ANGRY WITH ME, BECAUSE I MADE A MAN COMPLETELY HEALTHY ON THE SABBATH?**

Jn 7:24 **DO NOT JUDGE ACCORDING TO APPEARANCE, BUT JUDGE PROPERLY."**

361   CAN THIS JESUS (the man) BE THE CHRIST (the Messiah)? (Jn 7:25-27)

Jn 7:25 Therefore some of them of Jerusalem said, "Is not this He whom they seek to kill?

Jn 7:26 Behold, He speaks openly, and they say nothing to Him. Can it be that the rulers indeed know that this is truly the Christ?

Jn 7:27 However we know where this Man comes from, but when the Christ comes, no one will know where He comes from."

362   HIS BOLD CLAIM DRIVES SOME TO ANGER BUT CAUSES OTHERS TO WONDER (Jn 7:28-31)

Jn 7:28 Jesus therefore cried out in the temple, teaching and saying, **"YOU BOTH KNOW ME, AND KNOW WHERE I AM FROM. I HAVE NOT COME OF MYSELF, BUT HE WHO SENT ME IS TRUE; WHOM YOU DO NOT KNOW.**

Jn 7:29 **I KNOW HIM, BECAUSE I AM FROM HIM, AND HE SENT ME."**

Jn 7:30 They sought therefore to take Him, but no one laid a hand on Him, because His hour had not yet come.

Jn 7:31 But many believed in Him. They said, "When the Christ comes, He will not do more signs than those which this Man has done, will He?"

363   JESUS' COMMENT ABOUT RETURNING TO THE FATHER LEADS TO MORE CONFUSION (Jn 7:32-36)

Jn 7:32 The Pharisees heard the people murmuring these things concerning Him. The chief priests and the Pharisees sent officers to arrest Him.

Jn 7:33 Then Jesus said, **"I WILL BE WITH YOU A LITTLE WHILE LONGER, THEN I WLL GO TO HIM WHO SENT ME.**

Jn 7:34 **YOU WILL SEEK ME, AND WILL NOT FIND ME. WHERE I AM GOING, YOU CANNOT COME."**

Jn 7:35 The Jews therefore said among themselves, "Where will this Man go that we will not find Him? Will He go to the dispersion of our people among the Greeks, and teach the Greeks?"

Jn 7:36 What is this word that He said, 'You will seek me, and will not find me, and where I am going, you cannot come' "

364 *JESUS, "THE BELOVED," INVITES ALL WHO THIRST FOR RIGHTEOUSNESS TO COME TO HIM TO RECEIVE THE HOLY SPIRIT (Jn 7:37-39)*

Jn 7:37 Now on the last and greatest day of the feast, Jesus stood and cried out, **"IF ANYONE IS THIRSTY, LET HIM COME TO ME AND DRINK.**

Jn 7:38 **HE WHO BELIEVES IN ME, AS THE SCRIPTURE HAS SAID, FROM WITHIN HIM WILL FLOW RIVERS OF LIVING WATER."** *(Isa 44:3)*

Jn 7:39 But He said this about the Spirit, which those believing in Him were to receive. For the Holy Spirit was not yet given, because Jesus was not yet glorified.

365 *HIS REMARKS CAUSE A DISCUSSION AND EVEN DIVISION AMONG THE PEOPLE (Jn 7:40-44)*

Jn 7:40 Many of the people therefore, when they heard these words, said, "This is truly the prophet."

Jn 7:41 Others said, "This is the Christ." But some said, "What? Does the Christ come out of Galilee?

Jn 7:42 Has not the Scripture said that the Christ comes of the seed of David, and from Bethlehem, the village where David was?" *(Mic 5:2)*

Jn 7:43 So there arose a division because of Him.

Jn 7:44 Some of them would have arrested Him, but no one laid hands on Him.

366 *THE GUARDS SENT TO MAKE AN ARREST ARE IMPRESSED WITH JESUS AND RETURN EMPTY HANDED (Jn 7:45-49)*

Jn 7:45 The officers therefore came to the chief priests and Pharisees, and they said to them, "Why did you not bring Him?"

Jn 7:46 The officers answered, "No man ever spoke like this Man!"

Jn 7:47   The Pharisees therefore answered them, "You are not also led astray, are you?

Jn 7:48   Have any of the rulers or of the Pharisees believed in Him?

Jn 7:49   But this multitude that does not know the law is accursed."

367   *A SIMPLE REMARK BY AN HONEST MAN REVEALS THE UNBELIEF OF THOSE IN AUTHORITY (Jn 7:50-52 & 8:1)*

Jn 7:50   Nicodemus (he who came to Him by night, being one of them) said to them,

Jn 7:51   "Does our law judge a man, unless it first hears from him personally and knows what he does?"

Jn 7:52   They answered him, "Are you also from Galilee? Search and see that no prophet has arisen out of Galilee."

Jn 8:1   Jesus then went to the Mount of Olives.

368   *A WOMAN CAUGHT IN ADULTERY IS BROUGHT TO HIM FOR JUDGMENT BY HARSH LEADERS (Jn 8:2-5)*

Jn 8:2   Now very early in the morning, He came again into the temple, and all the people came to Him. He sat down, and taught them.

Jn 8:3   The scribes and the Pharisees brought a woman taken in adultery. Having set her in the middle,

Jn 8:4   they told Him, "Teacher, we found this woman in adultery, in the very act.

Jn 8:5   Now in our law, Moses commanded us to stone such to death. What then do You say about this?"

369   *A VERY "HUMAN JESUS" (perhaps struck by her beauty?) WRITES HER NAME DOWN TO GET HER OUT OF HIS MIND (Jn 8:6)*

Jn 8:6   They said this testing Him, that they might have something to accuse Him of. But Jesus stooped down, and wrote on the ground with his finger.

> *Heb 4:15 For we have not an high priest which cannot be touched with the feeling of our infirmities, but was <u>in all points tempted</u> like as we are, yet without sin.*

(If Jesus was also tempted sexually, as Heb 4:15 suggest, it is possible that this Jn 8:6 reference may be the only place in the Gospels where this might have occurred. But what is your guess? Where in the Gospels might Jesus have been tempted sexually? And why would He stoop this first time, then a second time coming up?)

370   JESUS, A "GENEROUS FORGIVER," STOOPS A SECOND TIME TO WRITE HER SIN ON SAND SOON TO BE FORGOTTEN *(Jn 8:7,8)*

Jn 8:7   But when they continued asking Him, He looked up and said to them, **"HE WHO IS WITHOUT SIN AMONG YOU, LET HIM THROW THE FIRST STONE AT HER."**

Jn 8:8   <u>He stooped down again</u>, and with His finger wrote on the ground.

371   THE SELF-CONDEMNED LEAVE, AND THE FORGIVEN WOMAN IS GIVEN A NEW LEASE ON LIFE *(Jn 8:9-11)*

Jn 8:9   They, when they heard it, being convicted by their conscience, went out one by one, beginning from the oldest even to the last. Jesus was left alone with the woman where she was, standing in front of Him..

Jn 8:10   Jesus, stood up, saw her and said, **"WOMAN, WHERE ARE YOUR ACCUSERS? DID NO ONE CONDEMN YOU?"**

Jn 8:11   She said, "No one, Lord." Jesus said, **"NEITHER DO I CONDEMN YOU. GO YOUR WAY. FROM NOW ON, SIN NO MORE."**

372   IN AN OPEN DEBATE WITH THE PHARISEES, JESUS MAKES A BOLD CLAIM TO BE THE "LIGHT OF THE WORLD" *(Jn 8:12-16)*

Jn 8:12   Again, therefore, Jesus spoke to them, saying, **"I AM THE LIGHT OF THE WORLD. HE WHO FOLLOWS ME WILL NOT WALK IN DARKNESS, BUT WILL HAVE THE LIGHT OF LIFE."**

>   *1 Jn 1:5 …God is light…*

Jn 8:13   The Pharisees therefore said to Him, "You testify about Yourself. Your testimony is not valid."

Jn 8:14   Jesus answered them, **"EVEN IF I TESTIFY ABOUT MYSELF, MY TESTIMONY IS TRUE, FOR I KNOW WHERE I CAME FROM, AND WHERE I AM GOING. BUT YOU DO NOT KNOW WHERE I CAME FROM, OR WHERE I AM GOING.**

Jn 8:15 YOU JUDGE ACCORDING TO THE FLESH. I JUDGE NO ONE.

Jn 8:16 EVEN IF I DO JUDGE, MY JUDGMENT IS TRUE, FOR I AM NOT ALONE. BUT I AM WITH THE FATHER WHO SENT ME."

373   STILL TEACHING IN THE TEMPLE, JESUS DECLARES THAT HE HAS GOD AS HIS WITNESS (Jn 8:17-20)

Jn 8:17 "IT IS ALSO WRITTEN IN YOUR LAW THAT THE TESTIMONY OF TWO PEOPLE IS VALID.

Jn 8:18 I AM ONE WHO TESTIFIES ABOUT MYSELF, AND THE FATHER WHO SENT ME ALSO TESTIFIES ABOUT ME."

Jn 8:19 They said therefore to Him, "Where is your Father?" Jesus answered, **"YOU KNOW NEITHER ME, NOR MY FATHER. IF YOU KNEW ME, YOU WOULD KNOW MY FATHER ALSO."**

Jn 8:20 Jesus spoke these words in the treasury, as He taught in the temple. Yet no one arrested Him, because His hour had not yet come.

374   JESUS, THE "SEEKER OF THE LOST," WARNS UNBELIEVERS THEY CANNOT BE SAVED WITHOUT BELIEVING IN HIM (Jn 8:21-24)

Jn 8:21 Jesus said therefore again to them, **"I AM GOING AWAY, AND YOU WILL SEEK ME, AND YOU WILL DIE IN YOUR SINS. WHERE I GO, YOU CANNOT COME."**

Jn 8:22 The Jews therefore said, "Will He kill himself, because He says, 'Where I am going, you cannot come?'"

Jn 8:23 He said to them, **"YOU ARE FROM BENEATH. I AM FROM ABOVE. YOU ARE OF THIS WORLD. I AM NOT OF THIS WORLD.**

Jn 8:24 **I SAID THEREFORE TO YOU THAT YOU WILL DIE IN YOUR SINS, FOR UNLESS YOU BELIEVE THAT I AM WHO I AM, YOU WILL INDEED DIE IN YOUR SINS."**

375   JESUS EXPLAINS THAT HE RELAYS ONLY WHAT HE HEARS FROM GOD (Jn 8:25-27)

Jn 8:25 They said therefore to Him, "Who are you?" Jesus said to them, **"JUST WHAT I HAVE BEEN SAYING TO YOU FROM THE BEGINNING.**

Jn 8:26 I HAVE MANY THINGS TO SAY AND TO JUDGE ABOUT YOU. HOWEVER, HE WHO SENT ME IS TRUE. AND THE THINGS WHICH I HEARD FROM HIM, THESE I SAY TO THE WORLD."

Jn 8:27 They did not understand that He spoke to them about the Father.

376   *THE "DUTIFUL SON" ALWAYS HAS GOD THE FATHER WITH HIM (Jn 8:28-30)*

Jn 8:28 Jesus therefore said to them, **"WHEN YOU HAVE LIFTED UP THE SON OF MAN** *(on the cross)* **THEN YOU WILL KNOW THAT I AM HE. I DO NOTHING OF MYSELF, BUT AS MY FATHER TAUGHT ME, I SAY THESE THINGS.**

Jn 8:29 **HE WHO SENT ME IS WITH ME. THE FATHER HAS NOT LEFT ME ALONE. FOR I ALWAYS DO THE THINGS THAT ARE PLEASING TO HIM."**

Jn 8:30 As He spoke these things, many believed in Him.

377   *BE A CITIZEN IN GOD'S KINGDOM, OR A SLAVE TO SATAN (Jn 8:31-33)*

Jn 8:31 Jesus therefore said to those Jews who believed him, **"IF YOU REMAIN IN MY WORD, THEN YOU ARE TRULY MY DISCIPLES.**

Jn 8:32 **YOU WILL KNOW THE TRUTH, AND THE TRUTH WILL MAKE YOU FREE."**

Jn 8:33 They answered Him, "We are Abraham's seed, and have never been in bondage to anyone. How do You say, 'We will be made free?'"

378   *JESUS OFFERS FREEDOM FROM BONDAGE TO OUR SENSES (Jn 8:34-36)*

Jn 8:34 Jesus answered them, **"MOST CERTAINLY I TELL YOU, EVERYONE WHO COMMITS SIN IS THE SLAVE OF SIN.**

Jn 8:35 **A SERVANT DOES NOT LIVE IN THE HOUSE FOREVER. BUT A SON REMAINS FOREVER.**

Jn 8:36 **IF THEREFORE THE SON MAKES YOU FREE, YOU WILL BE FREE INDEED."**

379   JEWISH DESCENDANTS WHO DO NOT BELIEVE IN THE FULFILLMENT OF SCRIPTURE ARE NOT TRUE SONS OF ABRAHAM (Jn 8:37-39)

Jn 8:37 **"I KNOW THAT YOU ARE ABRAHAM'S SEED, YET YOU SEEK TO KILL ME, BECAUSE MY WORD FINDS NO PLACE IN YOU.**

Jn 8:38 **I SAY THE THINGS WHICH I HAVE LEARNED FROM MY FATHER. AND YOU DO THE THINGS WHICH YOU HAVE LEARNED FROM YOUR FATHER."**

Jn 8:39   They answered Him, "Our father is Abraham." Jesus said to them, **"IF YOU WERE ABRAHAM'S CHILDREN, YOU WOULD DO THE WORKS OF ABRAHAM."**

380   JESUS RELATES THAT HIS PRESENCE AND TEACHINGS ARE THE WILL OF THE FATHER (Jn 8:40-42)

Jn 8:40 **"BUT NOW YOU SEEK TO KILL ME, A MAN WHO HAS TOLD YOU THE TRUTH, WHICH I HEARD FROM GOD. ABRAHAM DID NOT DO THIS.**

Jn 8:41 **YOU DO THE WORKS OF YOUR FATHER."** They said to Him, "We were not born of sexual immorality. We have one Father, God."

Jn 8:42   Therefore Jesus said to them, **"IF GOD WERE YOUR FATHER, YOU WOULD LOVE ME, FOR I PROCEEDED AND HAVE COME FROM GOD. FOR I HAVE NOT COME OF MYSELF, BUT HE SENT ME."**

381   JESUS, THE "VENERABLE LORD," CONTINUES TO OPPOSE THE JEWISH AUTHORITIES (Jn 8:43,44)

Jn 8:43 **"WHY DO YOU NOT UNDERSTAND MY SPEECH? BECAUSE YOU CANNOT HEAR MY MESSAGE.**

Jn 8:44 **YOU ARE OF YOUR FATHER, THE DEVIL, AND YOU WANT TO DO THE DESIRES OF YOUR FATHER. HE WAS A MURDERER FROM THE BEGINNING, AND DOES NOT STAND IN THE TRUTH, BECAUSE THERE IS NO TRUTH IN HIM. WHEN HE SPEAKS A LIE, HE SPEAKS ON HIS OWN, FOR HE IS A LIAR, AND THE FATHER OF LIES."**

382   GOD'S CHILDREN WILL ALWAYS BE SENSITIVE TO HIS VOICE (Jn 8:45-47)

Jn 8:45 **"BUT BECAUSE I TELL THE TRUTH, YOU DO NOT BELIEVE ME.**

Jn 8:46 **WHICH OF YOU CONVICTS ME OF SIN? IF I TELL THE TRUTH, WHY DO YOU NOT BELIEVE ME?**

Jn 8:47 HE WHO IS OF GOD HEARS THE WORDS OF GOD. FOR THIS CAUSE YOU DO NOT HEAR, BECAUSE YOU ARE NOT OF GOD."

383   GOD, THE FATHER, APPROVES OF JESUS' EFFORTS (Jn 8:48-50)

Jn 8:48   Then the Jews answered Him, "Do we not say well that You are a Samaritan, and have a demon?"

Jn 8:49   Jesus answered, **"I DO NOT HAVE A DEMON, BUT I HONOR MY FATHER, WHILE YOU DISHONOR ME.**

Jn 8:50   **I DO NOT SEEK MY OWN GLORY. THERE IS ONE WHO SEEKS IT AND JUDGES."**

384   THE PROMISE OF ETERNAL LIFE BRINGS A NEGATIVE REACTION FROM THE CROWD (Jn 8:51-53)

Jn 8:51   **"MOST CERTAINLY, I TELL YOU, IF A PERSON KEEPS MY WORD, HE WILL NEVER SEE DEATH."**

Jn 8:52   Then the Jews said to Him, "Now we know that You have a demon. Abraham died, and the prophets, and You say, 'If a man keeps My word, he will never taste of death.'

Jn 8:53   Are You greater than our father, Abraham, who died? The prophets also died. Who do You make Yourself out to be?"

385   THE FATHER AND THE SON TOTALLY ACCEPT EACH OTHER (Jn 8:54-56)

Jn 8:54   Jesus answered, **"IF I GLORIFY MYSELF, MY GLORY IS NOTHING. IT IS MY FATHER WHO GLORIFIES ME, OF WHOM YOU SAY THAT HE IS YOUR GOD.**

Jn 8:55   **YOU HAVE NOT KNOWN HIM, BUT I KNOW HIM. IF I SAY, 'I DO NOT KNOW HIM,' I WOULD BE LIKE YOU, A LIAR. BUT I KNOW HIM, AND KEEP HIS WORD.**

Jn 8:56   **YOUR FATHER ABRAHAM REJOICED TO SEE MY DAY. HE SAW IT, AND WAS GLAD."**

386   JESUS, THE "CO-CREATOR," WITH THE FATHER DECLARES HIS PRIOR EXISTENCE (Jn 8:57-59)

Jn 8:57   The Jews therefore said to Him, "You are not yet fifty years old, and have You seen Abraham?"

Jn 8:58 Jesus said to them, **"MOST CERTAINLY, I TELL YOU, BEFORE ABRAHAM CAME INTO EXISTENCE, I AM."**

Jn 8:59 Therefore they took up stones to throw at Him, but Jesus hid Himself, and went out of the temple, having gone through their midst, and so passed by.

(It seems Jesus was determined to be crucified as He went out of His way to anger even those Jews who believed in Him at the beginning of this discussion, in Jn 8:31.)

387   *A PERSON'S INFIRMITY IS AN OCCASION FOR GOD TO WORK A MIRACLE (Jn 9:1-5)*

Jn 9:1   As He was walking, He saw a man blind from birth.

Jn 9:2   His disciples asked Him, "Rabbi, who sinned, this man or his parents, that he was born blind?"

Jn 9:3   Jesus answered, **"NEITHER DID THIS MAN SIN, NOR HIS PARENTS, BUT THAT THE WORKS OF GOD MIGHT BE REVEALED IN HIM."**

388   *AS LONG AS JESUS' GLORY SHINES, ALL THINGS ARE POSSIBLE (Jn 9:4-7)*

Jn 9:4   **"I MUST WORK THE WORKS OF HIM WHO SENT ME, WHILE IT IS DAY. THE NIGHT IS COMING, WHEN NO ONE CAN WORK.**

Jn 9:5   **WHILE I AM IN THE WORLD, I AM THE "LIGHT OF THE WORLD!"**

Rev 22:16 …I AM…the "Bright and Morning Star."

Jn 9:6   When He had said this, He spat on the ground, made mud with his saliva, and touched the blind man's eyes with the mud,

Jn 9:7   and said to him, **"GO, WASH IN THE POOL OF SILOAM."** So he went away, washed, and came back seeing.

389   *NOW ABLE TO SEE, THE MAN IS QUESTIONED BY SOME WHO KNEW HIM (Jn 9:8-13)*

Jn 9:8   The neighbors therefore, and those who knew that he was blind before, said, "Is this not he who sat and begged?"

Jn 9:9   Others were saying, "It is he." Still others were saying, "He looks like him." The man said, "I am he."

Jn 9:10   They therefore were asking him, "How were your eyes opened?"

Jn 9:11   He answered, "A man called Jesus made mud, anointed my eyes, and said to me, 'Go to the pool of Siloam, and wash.' So I went away and washed, and I received my sight."

Jn 9:12   Then they asked him, "Where is He?" He said, "I do not know."

Jn 9:13   They brought him who had been blind to the Pharisees.

390   THE HEALING CAUSES THE PHARISEES TO ARGUE AMONG THEMSELVES *(Jn 9:14-16)*

Jn 9:14   It was a Sabbath when Jesus made the mud and opened his eyes.

Jn 9:15   Again therefore the Pharisees asked him how he received his sight. He said to them, "He put mud on my eyes, I washed, and now I see."

Jn 9:16   Some therefore of the Pharisees said, "This man is not from God, because He does not keep the Sabbath." Others said, "How can a man who is a sinner do such signs?" There was a division among them.

391   THEY CARRY ON THEIR QUESTIONING BY INTERROGATING THE MAN'S PARENTS *(Jn 9:17-23)*

Jn 9:17   Therefore they asked the blind man again, "What do you say about Him, the one who opened your eyes?" He said, "He is a prophet."

Jn 9:18   The Jews did not believe concerning him, that he had been blind, and had received his sight, until they called the parents of him who had received his sight,

Jn 9:19   and asked them, "Is this your son, whom you say was born blind? How then does he now see?"

392   THE PARENTS CONFIRM HIS BLINDNESS SINCE BIRTH *(Jn 9:20-23)*

Jn 9:20   His parents answered them, "We know that this is our son, and that he was born blind,

Jn 9:21   but how he now sees, we do not know, or who opened his eyes, we do not know. He is of age. Ask him. He can speak for himself."

Jn 9:22   His parents said these things because they feared the Jews, for the Jews had already agreed that if any man would confess Jesus as Christ, he would be put out of the synagogue.

Jn 9:23   Therefore his parents said, "He is of age. Ask him."

393   THEIR CONTINUED QUESTIONING OF HIS TESTIMONY BRINGS ON A CLASSIC ANSWER (Jn 9:24-25)

Jn 9:24   So they again called the man who was blind, and said to him, "Give glory to God. We know that this man is a sinner."

Jn 9:25   He therefore answered, "I do not know if He is a sinner. One thing I do know, I was blind, and now I see."

394   THE MAN'S OWN WITNESSING TO AN OBVIOUS HEALING IS DENIED BY THOSE WHO WILL NOT SEE (Jn 9:26-30)

Jn 9:26   They said to him again, "What did He do to you? How did He open your eyes?"

Jn 9:27   He answered them, "I told you already, and you did not listen. Why do you want to hear it again? You do not also want to become His disciples, do you?"

Jn 9:28   They insulted him and said, "You are His disciple, but we are disciples of Moses.

Jn 9:29   We know that God has spoken to Moses. But as for this Man, we do not know where He comes from."

Jn 9:30   The man answered them, "How amazing! You do not know where He comes from, yet He opened my eyes.

395   STILL OBSTINATE, THEY EX-COMMUNICATE THE MAN FROM THE TEMPLE (Jn 9:31-34)

Jn 9:31   "We know that God does not listen to sinners, but if anyone is a worshipper of God and does His will, He listens to him.

Jn 9:32   Since the world began it has never been heard of, that anyone opened the eyes of someone who was born blind.

Jn 9:33   If this Man were not from God, He could do nothing."

Jn 9:34   They answered him, "You were altogether born in sin, and do you teach us?" They threw him out.

396 *OUR "HEALING JESUS" SEEKS OUT THE PERSON WHO WAS MADE WELL AND THE MAN COMES TO BELIEVE (Jn 9:35-38)*

Jn 9:35 Jesus heard that they had thrown him out, and finding him, He said, **"DO YOU BELIEVE IN THE SON OF GOD?"**

> *(Pr 30: 4 ...Who has established all the ends of the earth? What is His name, and the name of His Son? Tell me if you know.)*

Jn 9:36 He answered, "Who is he, Lord, that I may believe in Him?"

Jn 9:37 Jesus said to him, **"YOU HAVE SEEN HIM, AND IT IS HE WHO SPEAKS WITH YOU."**

Jn 9:38 He said, "Lord, I believe!" and he worshiped Him.

397 *SEEING, BUT NOT BELIEVING, THE PHARISEES EXPOSE THEIR OWN SPIRITUAL BLINDNESS (Jn 9:39-41)*

Jn 9:39 Jesus said, **"I CAME INTO THIS WORLD FOR JUDGMENT, THAT THOSE WHO DO NOT SEE, MAY SEE; AND THAT THOSE WHO SEE MAY BECOME BLIND."**

Jn 9:40 Those of the Pharisees who were near Him heard these things, and said to Him, "Are we also blind?"

Jn 9:41 Jesus said to them, **"IF YOU WERE BLIND, YOU WOULD HAVE NO SIN, BUT NOW YOU SAY, 'WE SEE.' THEREFORE YOUR SIN REMAINS."**

398 *THE LORD'S SHEEP HEAR AND OBEY THEIR SHEPHERD (Jn 10:1-10)*

Jn 10:1 **"MOST CERTAINLY, I TELL YOU, ONE WHO DOES NOT ENTER BY THE DOOR INTO THE SHEEP FOLD, BUT CLIMBS UP SOME OTHER WAY, THE SAME IS A THIEF AND A ROBBER.**

Jn 10:2 **BUT ONE WHO ENTERS IN BY THE DOOR IS THE SHEPHERD OF THE SHEEP.**

Jn 10:3 **THE GATEKEEPER OPENS THE GATE FOR HIM, AND THE SHEEP LISTEN TO HIS VOICE. HE CALLS HIS OWN SHEEP BY NAME, AND LEADS THEM OUT."**

399   *THOSE WHO ACKNOWLEDGE JESUS, THE "EVERLASTING LIFE," WILL FOLLOW HIM (Jn 10:4-6)*

Jn 10:4 "WHENEVER HE BRINGS OUT HIS OWN SHEEP, HE GOES BEFORE THEM, AND THE SHEEP FOLLOW HIM, FOR THEY KNOW HIS VOICE.

Jn 10:5 THEY WILL BY NO MEANS FOLLOW A STRANGER, BUT WILL FLEE FROM HIM, FOR THEY DO NOT KNOW THE VOICE OF A STRANGER."

Jn 10:6 Jesus spoke this parable to them, but they did not understand what He was telling them.

400   *JESUS IS THE DOOR TO THAT ETERNAL AND ABUNDANT LIFE (Jn 10:7-10)*

Jn 10:7 Jesus therefore said to them again, "MOST CERTAINLY, I TELL YOU, I AM THE SHEEP'S DOOR.

Jn 10:8 ALL WHO CAME BEFORE ME ARE THIEVES AND ROBBERS, BUT THE SHEEP DID NOT LISTEN TO THEM.

Jn 10:9 I AM "THE DOOR." IF ANYONE ENTERS IN BY ME, HE WILL BE SAVED, AND WILL GO IN AND OUT, AND WILL FIND PASTURE.

Jn 10:10 THE THIEF ONLY COMES TO STEAL, KILL, AND DESTROY. I HAVE COME THAT THEY MAY HAVE LIFE, AND WOULD HAVE IT MORE ABUNDANTLY."

401   *HE REVEALS HOW HE WILL PROVE HIMSELF TO BE THE "TRUE SHEPHERD" (Jn 10:11-13)*

Jn 10:11 "I AM THE "GOOD SHEPHERD." THE GOOD SHEPHERD LAYS DOWN HIS LIFE FOR THE SHEEP.

Jn 10:12 HE WHO IS A HIRED HAND AND NOT A SHEPHERD, WHO DOES NOT OWN THE SHEEP, SEES THE WOLF COMING, LEAVES THE SHEEP, AND FLEES. THE WOLF SNATCHES THE SHEEP, AND SCATTERS THEM.

Jn 10:13 THE HIRED HAND FLEES BECAUSE HE IS A HIRED HAND, AND DOES NOT CARE FOR THE SHEEP."

   Zec 11:17 Woe to the idle shepherd that leaveth the flock…

402   *JESUS HAS MANY GROUPS WHO WILL FOLLOW HIS LEAD (Jn 10:14-16)*

Jn 10:14 "I AM THE GOOD SHEPHERD. I KNOW MY OWN AND MY SHEEP

KNOW ME.

Jn 10:15   EVEN AS THE FATHER KNOWS ME, AND I KNOW THE FATHER. I LAY DOWN MY LIFE FOR THE SHEEP.

Jn 10:16   I HAVE OTHER SHEEP, WHICH ARE NOT OF THIS FOLD. I MUST BRING THEM ALSO, AND THEY WILL HEAR MY VOICE. THEY WILL BECOME ONE FLOCK WITH ONE SHEPHERD."

> *Eph 4:5 One Lord, one faith, one baptism.*

403   *JESUS, THE "ALL CAPABLE," HAS THE ABILITY TO GIVE UP HIS LIFE AND THE POWER TO TAKE IT BACK AGAIN (Jn 10:17,18)*

Jn 10:17   "THEREFORE THE FATHER LOVES ME, BECAUSE I LAY DOWN MY LIFE, THAT I MAY TAKE IT UP AGAIN.

Jn 10:18   NO ONE TAKES IT AWAY FROM ME, BUT I LAY IT DOWN BY MYSELF. I HAVE POWER TO LAY IT DOWN, AND I HAVE POWER TO TAKE IT UP AGAIN. I RECEIVED THIS ABILITY FROM MY FATHER."

404   *ACCEPTING OR REJECTING JESUS WILL CAUSE DIVISION (Jn 10:19-21)*

Jn 10:19   Therefore an argument arose again among the Jews because of these words.

Jn 10:20   Many of them said, "He has a demon, and is insane! Why do you listen to Him?"

Jn 10:21   Others said, "These are not the sayings of one possessed by a demon. It is not possible for a demon to open the eyes of the blind, is it?"

CHAPTER XII

THE COMMITMENT TO THE CROSS

405   IN HIS FINAL DEPARTURE FROM GALILEE, JESUS IS DETERMINED TO MARCH TOWARD JERUSALEM AND ON TO CALVARY (taken from Lk 9:51-53)

Lk 9:51   It came to pass, when the days were near that He should be taken up, He intently set His face to go to Jerusalem,

Lk 9:52   and sent messengers before Him. They went, and entered into a village of the Samaritans, so as to prepare for Him.

Lk 9:53   They did not receive Him, because He was traveling with His face set towards Jerusalem.

406   JESUS, THE "LORD OF THE HARVEST," CAME TO SAVE MEN AND NOT TO SLAY THEM (Lk 9:54-56)

Lk 9:54   When His disciples, James and John, saw this, they said, "Lord, do You want us to command fire to come down from the sky, and destroy them, just as Elijah did?"

Lk 9:55   But He turned and rebuked them, **"YOU DO NOT KNOW OF WHAT KIND OF SPIRIT YOU ARE MADE OF.**

Lk 9:56   **FOR THE SON OF MAN DID NOT COME TO DESTROY MEN'S LIVES, BUT TO SAVE THEM."** They then went to another village.

407   THE APOSTLES CONTINUE THEIR WANDERING SEMINARY TRAINING (Mt 8:19,20; Lk 9:57,58)

Lk 9:57   As they went on the way, a certain man said to Him, "I want to follow You wherever You go, Lord."

Lk 9:58   Jesus said to him, **"FOXES HAVE HOLES, AND THE BIRDS OF THE SKY HAVE NESTS, BUT THE SON OF MAN HAS NO PLACE TO LAY HIS HEAD."**

408   *DO NOT HESITATE OR STRAY IF YOU WISH TO BECOME CHRIST'S DISCIPLE*
(Mt 8:21,22; Lk 9:59-62)

Lk 9:59   He said to another, **"FOLLOW ME!"** But he said, "Lord, allow me first to go and bury my father."

Lk 9:60   But Jesus said to him, **"LEAVE THE DEAD TO BURY THEIR OWN DEAD.** *(Let non-believers take care of other non-believers, material things, the past, etc.)* **BUT YOU GO AND PREACH THE KINGDOM OF GOD."**

Lk 9:61   Another also said, "I want to follow You, Lord, but first allow me to say good-bye to my family."

Lk 9:62   But Jesus said to him, **"NO ONE, HAVING PUT HIS HANDS TO THE PLOW AND LOOKING BACK, IS FIT FOR THE KINGDOM OF GOD."**

(The Lord is calling you into His all-volunteer army.)

409   *THERE IS MORE THAN ONE WAY TO PARTICIPATE IN THE SAVING OF SOULS*
(Lk 10:1-3)

Lk 10:1   Now after these things, the Lord also appointed seventy others, and sent them <u>two by two</u>, ahead of Him into every city and place, where He was about to travel.

Lk 10:2   Then He said to them, **"THE HARVEST IS INDEED PLENTIFUL, BUT THE LABORERS ARE FEW. PRAY THEREFORE TO THE LORD OF THE HARVEST, THAT HE MAY SEND OUT LABORERS INTO HIS HARVEST.**

Lk 10:3   GO YOUR WAYS. BEHOLD, I SEND YOU OUT AS LAMBS AMONG WOLVES."

410   *OUR "STEADFAST LORD" PREDICTS BITTER JUDGMENT ON THOSE WHO HAVE NEED TO REFORM THEIR LIFE-STYLE (Mt 11:20-24; Lk 10:13-16)*

Mt 11:20   Then He began to condemn the cities in which most of His mighty works had been done, because they did not repent.

Lk 10:13 "WOE TO YOU, CHORAZIN! WOE TO YOU, BETHSAIDA! FOR IF THE MIGHTY WORKS HAD BEEN DONE IN TYRE AND SIDON WHICH WERE DONE IN YOU, THEY WOULD HAVE REPENTED LONG AGO, SITTING IN SACKCLOTH AND ASHES.

Lk 10:14 BUT IT WILL BE MORE TOLERABLE FOR TYRE AND SIDON IN THE JUDGMENT THAN FOR YOU."

411   TO REJECT A BEARER OF THE GOOD NEWS IS TO REJECT JESUS, THEIR "CREATOR AND SAVIOR" (Mt 11:23,24; Lk 10:15,16)

Mt 11:23 "YOU, CAPERNAUM, WHO ARE EXALTED TO HEAVEN, YOU WILL GO DOWN TO HADES. FOR IF THE MIGHTY WORKS HAD BEEN DONE IN SODOM WHICH WERE DONE IN YOU, IT WOULD HAVE SURVIVED UNTIL THIS DAY.

Mt 11:24 BUT I TELL YOU THAT IT WILL BE MORE TOLERABLE FOR THE LAND OF SODOM ON THE DAY OF JUDGMENT, THAN FOR YOU.

Lk 10:16 WHOEVER LISTENS TO YOU LISTENS TO ME, AND WHOEVER REJECTS YOU REJECTS ME. WHOEVER REJECTS ME REJECTS HIM WHO SENT ME."

412   FOLLOWING THEIR SUCCESSFUL MISSION, HE GIVES THEM FURTHER REASONS TO REJOICE (Lk 10:17-20)

Lk 10:17 The seventy later returned with joy, saying, "Lord, even the demons are subject to us in Your name!"

Lk 10:18 He said to them, **"I SAW SATAN FALLING LIKE LIGHTNING FROM HEAVEN.**

Lk 10:19 BEHOLD, I GIVE YOU AUTHORITY TO TREAD ON SERPENTS AND SCORPIONS, AND OVER ALL THE POWER OF THE ENEMY. NOTHING WILL IN ANY WAY HURT YOU.

Lk 10:20 NEVERTHELESS, DO NOT REJOICE IN THIS, THAT THE SPIRITS ARE SUBJECT TO YOU, BUT REJOICE THAT YOUR NAMES ARE WRITTEN IN HEAVEN."

413   JESUS IS FILLED WITH JOY AS HE THANKS HIS HEAVENLY FATHER AND SHARES HIM WITH US (Lk 10:21,22)

Lk 10:21 In that same hour Jesus rejoiced in the Holy Spirit, and said, **"I THANK YOU, O FATHER, LORD OF HEAVEN AND EARTH, THAT YOU HAVE HIDDEN THESE THINGS FROM THE WISE AND INTELLIGENT, AND REVEALED THEM TO YOUNG CHILDREN. YES, FATHER, FOR SO IT WAS PLEASING IN YOUR SIGHT."**

Lk 10:22 Turning to the disciples, He said, **"ALL THINGS HAVE BEEN DELIVERED TO ME BY MY FATHER. NO ONE KNOWS WHO THE SON IS, EXCEPT THE FATHER; AND WHO THE FATHER IS, EXCEPT THE SON; AND HE TO WHOM THE SON DESIRES TO REVEAL HIM."**

414   THE APOSTLES ARE PRIVILEGED TO BE AN EYE-WITNESS TO HIS FIRST COMING (Mt 13:16,17; Lk 10:23,24)

Lk 10:23 Turning to the disciples, He said privately, **"BLESSED ARE THE EYES WHICH SEE THE THINGS THAT YOU SEE.**

Mt 13:17 FOR MOST CERTAINLY I TELL YOU THAT MANY PROPHETS AND RIGHTEOUS MEN DESIRED TO SEE THE THINGS WHICH YOU SEE, AND DID NOT SEE THEM, AND TO HEAR THE THINGS WHICH YOU HEAR, AND DID NOT HEAR THEM."

415   JESUS, THE "GOD OF WISDOM," TELLS US OF THE TWO GREATEST COMMANDMENTS (Lk 10:25-28)

Lk 10:25 A certain lawyer stood up and tested Him, saying, "Teacher, what shall I do to inherit eternal life?"

Lk 10:26 He said to him, **"WHAT IS WRITTEN IN THE SCRIPTURES? HOW DO YOU READ IT?"** *(Deut 6:5)*

Lk 10:27 He answered, "You shall love the Lord your God with all your heart, with all your soul, with all your strength, and with all your mind—and your neighbor as yourself."

> *1 Jn 4:20 If a man says, "I love God," and hates his brother, he is a liar. For he who does not love his brother whom he has seen, how can he love God whom he has not seen?*

Lk 10:28 He said to him, **"YOU HAVE ANSWERED CORRECTLY. DO THIS AND YOU WILL LIVE."**

416   TWO CHURCH WORKERS IGNORE A MAN IN NEED (Lk 10:29-37)

Lk 10:29 But he, desiring to justify himself, asked Jesus, "Who is my neighbor?"

Lk 10:30 Jesus answered, **"A CERTAIN MAN WAS GOING DOWN FROM JERUSALEM TO JERICHO, AND HE FELL AMONG ROBBERS, WHO STRIPPED HIM AND BEAT HIM, AND DEPARTED, LEAVING HIM HALF DEAD.**

Lk 10:31 BY CHANCE A CERTAIN PRIEST WAS GOING DOWN THAT WAY. WHEN HE SAW HIM, HE PASSED BY ON THE OTHER SIDE.

> *Pr 28:27 He that giveth unto the poor shall not lack; but he that hideth his eyes shall have many a curse.*

Lk 10:32 IN THE SAME WAY A LEVITE ALSO, WHEN HE CAME TO THE PLACE, AND SAW HIM, PASSED BY ON THE OTHER SIDE."

1 Cor 13:1,2 If I speak with the languages of men and of angels, but do not have love, I have become sounding brass, or a clanging cymbal...If I have the gift of prophecy, and know all mysteries and all knowledge, and if I have all faith, so as to remove mountains, but do not have love, I am nothing.

417   BUT A GENTILE HELPS THE MAN IN MANY WAYS (Lk 10:33-35)

Lk 10:33 "BUT A CERTAIN SAMARITAN, AS HE TRAVELED, CAME WHERE HE WAS. WHEN HE SAW HIM, HE WAS MOVED WITH COMPASSION;

(Be kind to all strangers and look upon them as potential believers.)

Lk 10:34 1) CAME TO HIM, AND 2) BOUND UP HIS WOUNDS, 3) POURING ON OIL AND WINE, 4) HE SET HIM ON HIS OWN ANIMAL, AND 5) BROUGHT HIM TO AN INN, AND 6) TOOK CARE OF HIM.

Ps 41:1 Blessed is he who considers the helpless: the Lord will deliver him in time of trouble...

Lk 10:35 ON THE NEXT DAY, WHEN HE DEPARTED, 7) HE TOOK OUT TWO SILVER COINS, AND GAVE THEM TO THE INNKEEPER, AND SAID TO HIM, 'TAKE CARE OF HIM. WHATEVER YOU SPEND BEYOND THAT, 8) I WILL REPAY YOU WHEN I RETURN.' "

1 Cor 13:13 And now faith, hope, and love remain, these three. But the greatest of these is love.

418   JESUS, THE "BISHOP OF OUR SOULS," ALSO ANSWERS THAT EARLIER QUESTION ABOUT HOW TO FIND ETERNAL LIFE (Lk 10:36,37)

Lk 10:36 "NOW WHICH OF THESE THREE DO YOU THINK SEEMED TO BE A NEIGHBOR TO HIM WHO FELL AMONG THE ROBBERS?"

Lk 10:37 He said, "He who showed mercy on him." Then Jesus said to him, **"GO AND DO LIKEWISE."**

Pr. 19:17 He who has pity on the poor lends to the Lord. He will repay him.

419 MARTHA IS CONCERNED ABOUT ALL SHE HAS TO DO WHILE MARY TAKES TIME TO BE IN THE PRESENCE OF JESUS, HER "QUIET SANCTUARY" s (Lk 10:38-42)

Lk 10:38 It happened as they went on their way, He entered into a certain village, and a certain woman named Martha received Him into her house.

Lk 10:39 She had a sister called Mary, who also sat at Jesus' feet, and heard His words.

Lk 10:40 But Martha was distracted with much serving, and she came to Him, and said, "Lord, do You not care that my sister left me to serve alone? Ask her to help me."

Lk 10:41 Jesus answered her, **"MARTHA, MARTHA, YOU ARE ANXIOUS AND TROUBLED ABOUT MANY THINGS,**

Lk 10:42 BUT ONE THING IS NEEDED. MARY HAS CHOSEN THE GOOD PART, WHICH WILL NOT BE TAKEN AWAY FROM HER."

420 JESUS, "OUR ENCOURAGER," REPEATS THAT WE CAN COME DAILY BEFORE OUR HEAVENLY FATHER (Lk 11:1-4)

Lk 11:1 It happened, that when He finished praying in a certain place, one of His disciples said to Him, "Lord, teach us to pray, just as John also taught his disciples."

Lk 11:2 He said to them, **"WHEN YOU PRAY, SAY, 'OUR FATHER IN HEAVEN, MAY YOUR NAME BE KEPT HOLY. MAY YOUR KINGDOM COME. MAY YOUR WILL BE DONE ON EARTH, AS IT IS IN HEAVEN.**

Lk 11:3 GIVE US DAY BY DAY OUR DAILY BREAD.

Lk 11:4 FORGIVE US OUR SINS, AS WE OURSELVES ALSO FORGIVE EVERYONE WHO WRONGS US. BRING US NOT INTO TEMPTATION, BUT DELIVER US FROM THE EVIL ONE.' "

421 GOD WILL ANSWER BOLD AND PERSISTENT PRAYER (Lk 11:5-13)

Lk 11:5 He said to them, **"WHICH OF YOU, IF YOU GO TO A NEIGHBOR AT MIDNIGHT, AND TELL HIM, 'FRIEND, LEND ME THREE LOAVES OF BREAD,**

Lk 11:6 FOR A FRIEND OF MINE HAS COME TO ME FROM A JOURNEY, AND I HAVE NOTHING TO SET BEFORE HIM,'

Lk 11:7 AND HE FROM WITHIN WILL ANSWER AND SAY, 'DO NOT BOTHER ME. THE DOOR IS NOW SHUT, AND MY CHILDREN ARE ALSO IN BED. I CANNOT GET UP AND GIVE IT TO YOU.'

Lk 11:8 I TELL YOU, ALTHOUGH HE WILL NOT RISE AND GIVE IT TO HIM BECAUSE HE IS HIS FRIEND, YET BECAUSE OF HIS PERSISTENCE, HE WILL GET UP AND GIVE HIM AS MANY AS HE NEEDS."

422   *YOU CAN BE HIS LIGHT TO SPREAD GOD'S LOVE INTO THE WORLD (Mt 6:22,23; Lk 11:34-36)*

Mt 6:22 "THE LAMP OF THE BODY IS THE EYE. IF THEREFORE YOUR EYE IS SOUND, YOUR WHOLE BODY WILL BE FULL OF LIGHT.

Mt 6:23 BUT IF YOUR EYE IS EVIL, YOUR WHOLE BODY WILL BE FULL OF DARKNESS. IF THEREFORE THE LIGHT THAT IS IN YOU IS DARKNESS, HOW GREAT IS THAT DARKNESS!

Lk 11:35 SEE THAT THE LIGHT THAT IS IN YOU IS NOT DARKNESS.

Lk 11:36 IF THEREFORE YOUR WHOLE BODY IS FULL OF LIGHT, HAVING NO PART DARK, IT WILL BE FULL OF LIGHT, AS WHEN A LAMP WITH ITS BRIGHT SHINING GIVES YOU LIGHT."

CHAPTER XIII

JESUS DENOUNCES THE PHARISEES

423   *WHILE EATING WITH A PHARISEE, JESUS STRONGLY COMES AGAINST THEM (taken from Mt 23:13-36; Lk 11:37-54)*

Lk 11:37 Now as He spoke, a certain Pharisee asked Him to dine with him. He went in and sat at the table.

Lk 11:38 When the Pharisee saw it, he marveled that He had not first washed before dinner.

Lk 11:39 The Lord said to him…

Mt 23:25 "WOE TO YOU, SCRIBES AND PHARISEES, HYPOCRITES! FOR YOU CLEAN THE OUTSIDE OF THE CUP AND OF THE PLATTER, BUT WITHIN ARE FULL OF CORRUPTION AND GREED."

424   *JESUS, THE "SURE FOUNDATION," GIVES RELIGIOUS LEADERS A SIMPLE FORMULA TO ACHIEVE HOLINESS (Mt 23:24-26; Lk 11:40,41)*

Mt 23:24 "YOU BLIND GUIDES, WHO STRAIN OUT A GNAT, BUT SWALLOW A CAMEL.

Lk 11:40 YOU FOOLISH ONES, DID NOT HE WHO MADE THE OUTSIDE MAKE THE INSIDE ALSO?

Mt 23:26 YOU BLIND PHARISEE, FIRST CLEAN THE INSIDE OF THE CUP AND OF THE PLATTER, THAT ITS OUTSIDE MAY BECOME CLEAN ALSO.

Lk 11:41 …GIVE TO THE NEEDY SUCH THINGS AS YOU HAVE, AND BEHOLD, ALL THINGS WILL BE CLEAN TO YOU."

425   *JESUS CONDEMNS THEIR VISIBLE SHOWMANSHIP WHILE NEGLECTING IMPORTANT DUTIES TO GOD AND FELLOW MAN (Mt 23:23; Lk 11:42-44)*

Mt 23:23 "WOE TO YOU, SCRIBES AND PHARISEES, HYPOCRITES! FOR YOU <u>TITHE</u> MINT, DILL, AND CUMIN, AND HAVE LEFT UNDONE THE MORE IMPORTANT

MATTERS OF THE LAW; JUSTICE, MERCY, AND FAITH. BUT YOU <u>OUGHT TO HAVE DONE THESE</u> *(by these words Jesus was endorsing tithing—the giving of 10% of one's income to Christian causes)* **AND NOT TO HAVE LEFT THE OTHER UNDONE.**

Lk 11:42 ...BUT YOU BYPASS JUSTICE AND THE LOVE OF GOD...

Lk 11:43 WOE TO YOU PHARISEES! FOR YOU LOVE THE BEST SEATS IN THE SYNAGOGUES, AND GREETINGS IN THE MARKETPLACES.

Lk 11:44 WOE TO YOU, SCRIBES AND PHARISEES, HYPOCRITES! FOR YOU ARE LIKE HIDDEN GRAVES, AND MEN WHO WALK OVER THEM DO NOT SEE THEM."

426 JESUS, THE "HOLY RABBI," DISCREDITS LEADERS WHO PREACH RELIGION WITHOUT ANY CONCERN OF THEIR OWN (Mt 23:14,15; Lk 11:45,46)

Lk 11:45 One of the lawyers answered Him, "Teacher, in saying this You insult us also."

Lk 11:46 He said, **"WOE TO YOU LAWYERS ALSO! FOR YOU LOAD MEN WITH BURDENS THAT ARE DIFFICULT TO CARRY. AND YOU YOURSELVES WILL NOT EVEN LIFT ONE FINGER TO HELP CARRY THOSE BURDENS."**

427 JESUS PLACES THE BLAME FOR LOST SOULS SQUARELY ON THOSE WHO REFUSE TO READ THEIR BIBLE (Mt 23:13; Lk 11:52)

Mt 23:13 "BUT WOE TO YOU, SCRIBES AND PHARISEES, HYPOCRITES! BECAUSE YOU SHUT UP THE KINGDOM OF HEAVEN AGAINST MEN, FOR YOU DO NOT ENTER IN YOURSELVES, NEITHER DO YOU ALLOW THOSE WHO ARE WANTING TO ENTER IN."

428 CONVERTING OTHERS TO THE WRONG THEOLOGY WILL NOT HELP (Mt 23:15)

Mt 23:15 "WOE TO YOU, SCRIBES AND PHARISEES, HYPOCRITES! FOR YOU TRAVEL AROUND BY SEA AND LAND TO MAKE ONE CONVERT, AND WHEN HE BECOMES ONE, YOU MAKE HIM TWICE AS MUCH A SON OF GEHENNA AS YOURSELVES."

429 THEY OBSERVE MINOR RULES WHICH ARE NOT COMMANDED, BUT OVERLOOK CONDITIONS OF THE HEART (Mt 23:16-19)

Mt 23:16 "WOE TO YOU, YOU BLIND GUIDES, WHO SAY, 'WHOEVER SWEARS BY THE TEMPLE, IT IS NOTHING. BUT WHOEVER SWEARS BY THE GOLD OF THE

TEMPLE, HE IS OBLIGATED.'

Mt 23:17 YOU BLIND FOOLS! FOR WHICH IS GREATER, THE GOLD, OR THE TEMPLE THAT SANCTIFIES THE GOLD?

Mt 23:18 YOU ALSO SAY 'WHOEVER SWEARS BY THE ALTAR, IT IS NOTHING. BUT WHOEVER SWEARS BY THE GIFT THAT IS ON IT, HE IS OBLIGATED BY HIS OATH'

Mt 23:19 YOU BLIND FOOLS! FOR WHICH IS GREATER, THE GIFT, OR THE ALTAR THAT SANCTIFIES THE GIFT?"

430 ANY OATH IS MEANINGLESS IF MOTIVATED BY EXTERNAL APPEARANCE AND NOT BY INTERNAL SANCTIFICATION (Mt 23:20-22)

Mt 23:20 "HE THEREFORE WHO SWEARS BY THE ALTAR, SWEARS BY IT, AND BY EVERYTHING ON IT.

Mt 23:21 HE WHO SWEARS BY THE TEMPLE, SWEARS BY IT, AND BY HIM WHO IS LIVING IN IT.

Mt 23:22 HE WHO SWEARS BY HEAVEN, SWEARS BY THE THRONE OF GOD, AND BY HIM WHO SITS ON IT."

431 HE CONDEMNS THEM FOR THEIR PRETENDED HOLINESS TO COVER UP MORAL FAILINGS (Mt 23:27,28)

Mt 23:27 "WOE TO YOU, SCRIBES AND PHARISEES, HYPOCRITES! FOR YOU ARE LIKE WHITENED TOMBS, WHICH OUTWARDLY APPEAR BEAUTIFUL, BUT INWARDLY ARE FULL OF DEAD MEN'S BONES, AND OF ALL UNCLEANNESS.

Mt 23:28 EVEN SO, YOU ALSO OUTWARDLY APPEAR RIGHTEOUS TO MEN, BUT ON THE INSIDE YOU ARE FULL OF HYPOCRISY AND WICKEDNESS."

432 JESUS ANALYZES THEIR BOASTING AND SEEMING INTEREST IN THE PROPHETS (Mt 23:29-33; Lk 11:47,48)

Mt 23:29 "WOE TO YOU, SCRIBES AND PHARISEES, HYPOCRITES! FOR YOU BUILD THE TOMBS OF THE PROPHETS, AND DECORATE THE TOMBS OF THE RIGHTEOUS,

Mt 23:30 AND SAY, 'IF WE HAD LIVED IN THE DAYS OF OUR FATHERS, WE WOULD

NOT HAVE BEEN PARTAKERS WITH THEM IN THE BLOOD OF THE PROPHETS.'

Lk 11:48 SO YOU TESTIFY AND CONSENT TO THE WORKS OF YOUR FATHERS. FOR THEY KILLED THEM, AND YOU BUILD THEIR TOMBS.

Mt 23:32 COMPLETE, THEN, THE CRIMES OF YOUR FATHERS.

Mt 23:33 YOU SERPENTS, YOU OFFSPRING OF VIPERS, HOW WILL YOU ESCAPE THE JUDGMENT OF HELL." *(If the punishment is extreme and eternal, so are the rewards exceedingly great and ever-lasting.)*

433   *AND SO GOD WILL PUNISH THEM FOR PERSECUTING PAST SAINTS AND FUTURE FOLLOWERS (Mt 23:34-36; Lk 11:49-51)*

Mt 23:34 "THEREFORE BEHOLD, I SEND TO YOU PROPHETS, WISE MEN, AND SCRIBES. SOME OF THEM YOU WILL KILL AND CRUCIFY, AND SOME OF THEM YOU WILL FLOG IN YOUR SYNAGOGUES, AND PERSECUTE FROM CITY TO CITY.

Lk 11:50 THE BLOOD OF ALL THE PROPHETS, WHICH WAS SHED FROM THE BEGINNING OF THE WORLD, WILL BE REQUIRED OF THIS GENERATION,

Lk 11:51 FROM THE BLOOD OF ABEL TO THE BLOOD OF ZACHARIAH, WHO PERISHED BETWEEN THE ALTAR AND THE SANCTUARY. YES, I TELL YOU, IT WILL BE REQUIRED OF THIS GENERATION."

434   *SEVERE PUNISHMENT AWAITS THOSE WHO TAKE ADVANTAGE OF THE SIMPLE (Mt 23:14; Lk 11:53,54)*

Mt 23:14 "WOE TO YOU, SCRIBES AND PHARISEES, HYPOCRITES! FOR YOU DEVOUR WIDOWS' HOUSES, AND AS A PRETENSE YOU MAKE LONG PRAYERS. THEREFORE YOU WILL RECEIVE THE GREATER CONDEMNATION."

Lk 11:53 As He said these things to them, the scribes and the Pharisees began to be terribly angry, and attempt to draw many things out of Him,

Lk 11:54 lying in wait for Him, and seeking to catch Him in something He might say, that they might accuse Him.

435   *BECAUSE THEY REJECT JESUS, THEIR "MESSIAH," THEIR WORSHIP CENTER WILL BE DESTROYED (Mt 23:37-39; Lk 13:34,35)*

Mt 23:37 "JERUSALEM, JERUSALEM, WHO KILLS THE PROPHETS, AND STONES THOSE WHO ARE SENT TO HER! HOW OFTEN I WOULD HAVE GATHERED YOUR

CHILDREN TOGETHER, EVEN AS A HEN GATHERS HER CHICKS UNDER HER WINGS, AND YOU WOULD NOT!

Mt 23:38 BEHOLD, YOUR TEMPLE IS LEFT TO YOU FORSAKEN.

Mt 23:39 FOR I TELL YOU, YOU WILL NOT SEE ME FROM NOW ON, UNTIL YOU SAY, 'BLESSED IS HE WHO COMES IN THE NAME OF THE LORD!' "

436   *EVERY SECRET AND EVERY MOTIVE SHALL BE MADE KNOWN (Mt 10:26,27; Lk 12:1-3)*

Lk 12:1 Meanwhile, when a multitude of many thousands had gathered together, so much so that they trampled on each other, He began to tell His disciples first of all, **"BEWARE OF THE YEAST OF THE PHARISEES, WHICH IS HYPOCRISY.**

Lk 12:2 THERE IS NOTHING COVERED UP, THAT WILL NOT BE REVEALED, NOR HIDDEN, THAT WILL NOT BE MADE KNOWN.

Lk 12:3 THEREFORE WHATEVER YOU HAVE SAID IN THE DARKNESS WILL BE HEARD IN THE LIGHT. WHAT YOU HAVE WHISPERED IN THE EAR, IN PRIVATE ROOMS, WILL BE SHOUTED OUT."

437   *THOSE WHO KNOW NOT OUR HEAVENLY FATHER'S MERCY AND LOVE HAVE REASON TO FEAR (Mt 10:28; Lk 12:4,5)*

Lk 12:4 "I TELL YOU MY FRIENDS, DO NOT BE AFRAID OF THOSE WHO KILL THE BODY, AND AFTER THAT HAVE NO MORE THAT THEY CAN DO.

Lk 12:5 BUT I WILL FOREWARN YOU WHOM YOU SHOULD FEAR. FEAR HIM, WHO AFTER HE HAS KILLED THE BODY, HAS POWER TO CAST YOU INTO HELL. YES, I TELL YOU, HE IS THE ONE YOU SHOULD FEAR."

438   *GOD APPRECIATES EACH ONE OF US AS A SPECIAL INDIVIDUAL (Mt 10:29,31; Lk 12:6,7)*

Mt 10:29 "ARE NOT TWO SPARROWS SOLD FOR A PENNY? YET NOT ONE OF THEM FALLS TO THE GROUND APART FROM YOUR FATHER'S WILL,

Mt 10:30 BUT THE VERY HAIRS OF YOUR HEAD ARE ALL NUMBERED.

Mt 10:31 THEREFORE DO NOT BE AFRAID. YOU ARE OF MORE VALUE THAN MANY SPARROWS."

439 *PROFESS YOUR FAITH COURAGEOUSLY AND AVOID THE UNPARDONABLE SIN (Mt 10:32,33; Lk 12:8-10)*

Lk 12:8 "I TELL YOU, EVERYONE WHO CONFESSES ME BEFORE MEN, HIM WILL THE SON OF MAN ALSO CONFESS BEFORE THE ANGELS OF GOD.

Lk 12:9 BUT HE WHO DENIES ME BEFORE MEN WILL BE DENIED IN THE PRESENCE OF THE ANGELS OF GOD.

Lk 12:10 EVERYONE WHO SPEAKS A WORD AGAINST THE SON OF MAN WILL BE FORGIVEN, BUT WHOEVER BLASPHEMES AGAINST THE HOLY SPIRIT WILL NOT BE FORGIVEN."

440 *JESUS WARNS AGAIN ABOUT THE LOVE OF MATERIAL POSSESSIONS (Lk 12:13-15)*

Lk 12:13 One of the group said to Him, "Teacher, tell my brother to divide the inheritance with me."

Lk 12:14 But He said to him, "SIR, WHO MADE ME A JUDGE OR AN ARBITRATOR OVER YOU?"

Lk 12:15 He said to them, "BEWARE! KEEP YOURSELVES FROM GREED, FOR A MAN'S LIFE DOES NOT CONSIST OF THE ABUNDANCE OF THE THINGS WHICH HE POSSESSES."

441 *JESUS, THE "GIVER OF ALL THINGS," TELLS A STORY ABOUT A SELFISH RICH MAN (Lk 12:16-21)*

Lk 12:16 He spoke a parable to them, saying, "THE LAND OF A CERTAIN RICH MAN BROUGHT FORTH ABUNDANTLY.

Lk 12:17 HE REASONED WITHIN HIMSELF, SAYING, 'WHAT WILL I DO, BECAUSE I DO NOT HAVE ROOM TO STORE MY CROPS?'

> *Deut 8:18 But thou shall remember the Lord thy God: for it is He that giveth thee power to get wealth…*

Lk 12:18 HE SAID, 'THIS IS WHAT I WILL DO. I WILL TEAR DOWN MY BARNS, AND BUILD BIGGER ONES, AND THERE I WILL STORE ALL MY GRAIN AND MY GOODS.

> *Jas 4:4 …know ye not that friendship of the world is enmity with God. Whosoever therefore will be a friend of the world is the enemy of God.*

Lk 12:19 I WILL TELL MY SOUL, 'SOUL, YOU HAVE MANY GOODS LAID UP FOR MANY YEARS. TAKE YOUR EASE, EAT, DRINK, BE MERRY.' "

442   *EVERYONE IS BUT A HEARTBEAT AWAY FROM A VAST ETERNITY (Lk 12:20,21)*

Lk 12:20 "BUT GOD SAID TO HIM, 'YOU FOOL, TONIGHT YOUR SOUL IS REQUIRED OF YOU. THE THINGS WHICH YOU HAVE PREPARED, WHOSE WILL THEY BE?'

(Many people fail to see that they will spend much more time in eternity than on planet earth.)

Lk 12:21 SO IS HE WHO LAYS UP TREASURE FOR HIMSELF, AND IS NOT RICH AS FAR AS GOD IS CONCERNED."

Heb 9:27 ...it is appointed unto men once to die, but after this the judgment.

443   *SEEK FIRST THE KINGDOM OF GOD TO FIND LASTING TREASURE (Lk 12:32-34)*

Lk 12:32 "DO NOT BE AFRAID, LITTLE FLOCK, FOR IT IS YOUR FATHER'S GOOD PLEASURE TO GIVE YOU THE KINGDOM.

(If you can believe your Heavenly Father loves you, you could already be on your way to eternal life.)

Lk 12:33 SELL THAT WHICH YOU HAVE, AND GIVE TO THE NEEDY. MAKE FOR YOURSELVES PURSES WHICH DO NOT WEAR OUT, A TREASURE IN HEAVEN THAT DOES NOT FAIL, WHERE NO THIEF CAN GET TO, NEITHER MOTH DESTROY.

Lk 12:34 FOR WHERE YOUR TREASURE IS, THERE WILL YOUR HEART BE ALSO."

(We cannot give anything to God. We can only return a portion of all He has given us.)

444   *HIS PRESENCE IN THE WORLD WILL PRODUCE CONFLICT BETWEEN BELIEVER AND NON-BELIEVER (Lk 12:49-53)*

Lk 12:49 "I CAME TO SET THE WORLD ON FIRE. AND I WISH IT WERE ALREADY STARTED.

Lk 12:50 BUT I HAVE A BAPTISM TO SUFFER, AND HOW DISTRESSED I AM UNTIL IT IS OVER.

Lk 12:51 DO YOU THINK THAT I HAVE COME TO BRING PEACE IN THE EARTH? I TELL YOU, NO, BUT RATHER DIVISION.

Lk 12:52 FROM NOW ON, THERE WILL BE FIVE IN ONE HOUSE DIVIDED, THREE AGAINST TWO, AND TWO AGAINST THREE.

Lk 12:53 THEY WILL BE DIVIDED, FATHER AGAINST SON, AND SON AGAINST FATHER, MOTHER AGAINST DAUGHTER, AND DAUGHTER AGAINST HER MOTHER, MOTHER-IN-LAW AGAINST HER DAUGHTER-IN-LAW, AND DAUGHTER-IN-LAW AGAINST HER MOTHER-IN-LAW."

445   *ANY FOLLOWER OF JESUS, THE "HOLY LORD," MUST REFORM HIS LIFE OR FIND HIMSELF AMONG THE LOST (Lk 13:1-5)*

Lk 13:1   Now there were some present at the same time who told Him about the Galileans, whose blood Pilate had mixed with their animal sacrifices.

Lk 13:2   Jesus answered them, "DO YOU THINK THAT THESE GALILEANS WERE WORSE SINNERS THAN ALL THE OTHER GALILEANS, BECAUSE THEY SUFFERED SUCH THINGS?

Lk 13:3   I TELL YOU, NO, BUT UNLESS YOU REPENT, YOU WILL ALL PERISH IN THE SAME WAY.

Lk 13:4   OR THOSE EIGHTEEN ON WHOM THE TOWER IN SILOAM FELL AND KILLED THEM. DO YOU THINK THAT THEY WERE WORSE OFFENDERS THAN ALL THE MEN WHO DWELL IN JERUSALEM?

Lk 13:5   I TELL YOU, NO, BUT, UNLESS YOU REPENT, YOU WILL ALL LIKEWISE PERISH."

446   *ALL BELIEVERS MUST BECOME FRUITFUL FOR THE KINGDOM, OR BE CUT DOWN (Lk 13:6-9)*

Lk 13:6   He spoke this parable. "A CERTAIN MAN HAD A FIG TREE PLANTED IN HIS VINEYARD, AND HE CAME SEEKING FRUIT ON IT, AND FOUND NONE.

Lk 13:7   HE SAID TO THE VINE DRESSER, 'BEHOLD, THESE THREE YEARS I HAVE COME LOOKING FOR FRUIT ON THIS FIG TREE, AND FOUND NONE. CUT IT DOWN. WHY DOES IT TAKE UP SPACE?'

Lk 13:8   HE ANSWERED, 'LORD, LEAVE IT ALONE THIS YEAR ALSO, UNTIL I DIG AROUND IT, AND FERTILIZE IT.

Lk 13:9 IF IT BEARS FRUIT, FINE. BUT IF NOT, AFTER THAT, YOU CAN CUT IT DOWN.' "

447   *JESUS HEALS A CRIPPLED WOMAN THUS IGNORING A STRICT OBSERVANCE OF THE SABBATH (Lk 13:10-17)*

Lk 13:10 He was teaching in one of the synagogues on the Sabbath day.

Lk 13:11 Behold, there was a woman who had a spirit of infirmity eighteen years, and she was bent over, and could in no way straighten herself up.

Lk 13:12 When Jesus saw her He called her and said to her, **"WOMAN, YOU ARE FREED FROM YOUR INFIRMITY."**

Lk 13:13 He laid His hands on her, and immediately she stood up straight, and glorified God.

448   *THERE IS NO LIMITATION IN TIME AND PLACE TO PHYSICALLY HEAL OR SPIRITUALLY SAVE ANOTHER (Lk 13:14-17)*

Lk 13:14 The ruler of the synagogue, being indignant because Jesus had healed on the Sabbath, said to the crowd, "There are six days in which men ought to work. Therefore come on those days and be healed, and not on the Sabbath day!"

Lk 13:15 Therefore the Lord answered him, **"YOU HYPOCRITES! DO YOU NOT FREE YOUR OX OR YOUR DONKEY FROM THE STALL ON THE SABBATH, AND LEAD HIM AWAY TO WATER?**

Lk 13:16 OUGHT NOT THIS WOMAN, BEING A DAUGHTER OF ABRAHAM, WHOM SATAN HAD BOUND EIGHTEEN LONG YEARS, BE FREED FROM HER BONDAGE ON THE SABBATH DAY?"

Lk 13:17 As He said these things, all His adversaries were disappointed. But all the people rejoiced for all the glorious things that were done by Him.

449   *IN HIS FOURTH TEMPLE DISCOURSE, THE CROWD DEMANDS A DEFINITE STATEMENT ABOUT HIS DIVINITY (Jn 10:22-39)*

Jn 10:22 It was the Feast of the Dedication at Jerusalem, and it was winter.

Jn 10:23 And Jesus was walking in the temple, in Solomon's porch.

Jn 10:24 The Jews therefore encircled Him and said to Him, "How long will you hold us in suspense? If you are the Christ, tell us plainly."

450   JESUS, THE "EMINENT TEACHER," GIVES A REASON WHY ANSWERING THEM WOULD BE WORTHLESS (Jn 10:25,26)

Jn 10:25   Jesus answered them, **"I TOLD YOU, AND YOU DO NOT BELIEVE. THE WORKS THAT I DO IN MY FATHER'S NAME, THESE TESTIFY ABOUT ME.**

Jn 10:26   BUT YOU DO NOT BELIEVE, BECAUSE YOU ARE NOT OF MY SHEEP, AS I TOLD YOU."

451   HIS FOLLOWERS HAVE PROTECTION AS WELL AS ETERNAL LIFE (Jn 10:27-30)

Jn 10:27   "MY SHEEP HEAR MY VOICE, AND I KNOW THEM, AND THEY FOLLOW ME. *(Are you a follower of Jesus, or just a fan of Jesus?)*

Jn 10:28   I GIVE ETERNAL LIFE TO THEM. THEY WILL NEVER PERISH. AND NO ONE WILL SNATCH THEM OUT OF MY HAND.

Jn 10:29   MY FATHER, WHO HAS GIVEN THEM TO ME, IS GREATER THAN ALL. NO ONE IS ABLE TO SNATCH THEM OUT OF MY FATHER'S HAND."

452   THEY WISH TO STONE JESUS, THE "HOPE OF GLORY" WHEN HE PROCLAIMS HIS UNITY WITH THE FATHER (Jn 10:30-32)

Jn 10:30   "I AND THE FATHER ARE ONE."

Jn 10:31   Therefore the Jews took up stones again to stone Him.

Jn 10:32   Jesus answered them, **"I HAVE SHOWN YOU MANY GOOD WORKS FROM MY FATHER. FOR WHICH OF THOSE WORKS DO YOU STONE ME?"**

453   MANY HAVE THE POTENTIAL TO RISE ABOVE THEIR CIRCUMSTANCES (Jn 10:33-36)

Jn 10:33   The Jews answered Him, "We do not stone you for your good work, but for blasphemy, because you, being a man, make Yourself out to be God."

Jn 10:34   Jesus answered them, **"IS IT NOT WRITTEN IN YOUR LAW, 'I SAID, YOU ARE GODS?'**

Ps 82:6 *"You are gods, all of you are sons of the Most High."*

Jn 10:35 IF HE CALLED THEM GODS, TO WHOM THE WORD OF GOD CAME, AND THE SCRIPTURE CANNOT BE IGNORED,

Jn 10:36 WHY DO YOU SAY OF HIM WHOM THE FATHER SANCTIFIED AND SENT INTO THE WORLD? 'YOU BLASPHEME,' BECAUSE I SAID, 'I AM THE SON OF GOD?'"

454   *JESUS' DIVINE STATUS IS PROVEN BY HIS ACTIONS (Jn 10:37-39)*

Jn 10:37 "IF I DO NOT DO THE WORKS OF MY FATHER, DO NOT BELIEVE ME.

Jn 10:38 BUT IF I DO THEM, THOUGH YOU DO NOT BELIEVE ME, BELIEVE MY WORKS *(miracles and healings)* **THAT YOU MAY KNOW AND BELIEVE THAT THE FATHER IS IN ME, AND I IN THE FATHER."**

Jn 10:39 They sought again to seize Him, and He slipped out of their hands.

455   *JESUS, THE "SHINING LIGHT," TRAVELS EAST OF THE JORDAN WHERE HE MINISTERS TO MANY WHO BELIEVE IN HIM (Lk 13:22; Jn 10:40-42)*

Jn 10:40 He went away again beyond the Jordan into the place where John was first baptizing, and there He stayed.

Jn 10:41 Many came to Him. They said, "John indeed did no sign, but everything that John said about this man is true."

Jn 10:42 Many believed in Him there.

Lk 13:22 He went on His way through cities and villages, teaching, and traveling on to Jerusalem.

456   *JESUS WARNS THOSE WHO MERELY KNOW OF HIM BUT ARE NOT RIGHT WITH HIM (Lk 13:23-27)*

Lk 13:23 One said to Him, "Lord, are there few who will be saved?" He said to them,

Lk 13:24 "STRIVE TO ENTER IN BY THE NARROW DOOR. FOR MANY I TELL YOU WILL SEEK TO ENTER IN, AND WILL NOT BE ABLE.

Lk 13:25 WHEN ONCE THE MASTER OF THE HOUSE HAS RISEN UP, AND HAS LOCKED THE DOOR, AND YOU BEGIN TO STAND OUTSIDE, AND TO KNOCK AT

THE DOOR, SAYING, 'LORD, LORD, OPEN TO US!' THEN HE WILL ANSWER AND TELL YOU, 'I DO NOT KNOW YOU, OR WHERE YOU COME FROM.'

Lk 13:26 THEN YOU WILL BEGIN TO SAY, 'WE ATE AND DRANK IN YOUR PRESENCE, AND YOU TAUGHT IN OUR STREETS.'

Lk 13:27 HE WILL SAY, 'I TELL YOU, I DO NOT KNOW WHERE YOU COME FROM. DEPART FROM ME, YOU AND YOUR EVILDOINGS.' "

457   YOUR RELATIONSHIP WITH GOD IS MORE IMPORTANT THAN ANY RELIGIOUS OR SOCIAL STATUS (Lk 13:28-30)

Lk 13:28 "THERE WILL BE WEEPING AND GNASHING OF TEETH, WHEN YOU SEE ABRAHAM, ISAAC, JACOB AND ALL THE PROPHETS, IN THE KINGDOM OF GOD, AND YOURSELVES BEING THROWN OUT.

Lk 13:29 THEY WILL COME FROM THE EAST, WEST, NORTH, AND SOUTH, AND WILL SIT DOWN IN THE KINGDOM OF GOD.

Lk 13:30 BEHOLD, THERE ARE SOME WHO ARE LAST WHO WILL BE FIRST, AND THERE ARE SOME WHO ARE FIRST WHO WILL BE LAST."

458   JESUS, THE "PRINCE OF LIFE," CONTINUES ON HIS MARCH TOWARD JERUSALEM TO BE CRUCIFIED (Lk 13:31-33)

Lk 13:31 On that same day, some Pharisees came, saying to Him, "Get out of here, and go away, for Herod wants to kill you."

Lk 13:32 He said to them, "GO AND TELL THAT FOX, THAT I CAST OUT DEMONS AND PERFORM HEALINGS TODAY AND TOMORROW, AND THE THIRD DAY I'LL COMPLETE MY MISSION.

Lk 13:33 NEVERTHELESS I MUST GO ON MY WAY TODAY AND TOMORROW AND THE NEXT DAY, FOR IT CANOT BE THAT A PROPHET BE KILLED OUTSIDE OF JERUSALEM."

459   WHILE DINING WITH A CHIEF PHARISEE, JESUS QUESTIONS THEM ABOUT HEALING ON THE SABBATH (Lk 14:1-6)

Lk 14:1 It happened, when He went into the house of one of the rulers of the Pharisees on a Sabbath to eat bread, that they were watching Him.

Lk 14:2 Behold, a certain man who had dropsy was in front of Him.

Lk 14:3 Jesus, answering, spoke to the lawyers and Pharisees, saying, **"IS IT LAWFUL TO HEAL ON THE SABBATH?"**

460   JESUS, THE "EXCELLENT STANDARD," DRAWS ATTENTION TO THEIR PRIORITIES AND WARPED SENSE OF VALUES (Lk 14:4-6)

Lk 14:4 But they were silent. He took the man with the dropsy, and healed him, and let him go.

Lk 14:5 He answered them, **"WHICH OF YOU, IF YOUR SON OR AN OX FELL INTO A WELL, WOULD NOT IMMEDIATELY PULL HIM OUT ON A SABBATH DAY?"**

Lk 14:6 They could not answer Him regarding these things.

461   DO YOUR BEST TO AVOID AMBITION AND SELF-EXALTATION (Lk 14:7-9)

Lk 14:7 He spoke a parable to those who were invited, when He noticed how they chose the best seats, and said to them,

Lk 14:8 **"WHEN YOU ARE INVITED BY ANYONE TO A MARRIAGE FEAST, DO NOT SIT IN THE BEST SEAT, SINCE PERHAPS SOMEONE MORE HONORABLE THAN YOU MIGHT BE INVITED.**

Lk 14:9 **AND HE WHO INVITED BOTH OF YOU WOULD COME AND TELL YOU, 'MAKE ROOM FOR THIS PERSON.' THEN YOU WOULD BEGIN, WITH SHAME, TO TAKE THE LOWEST SEAT."**

462   OBTAIN SPECIAL RECOGNITION IN THE KINGDOM BY OBSERVING TRUE HUMILITY (Lk 14:10,11)

Lk 14:10 **"BUT WHEN YOU ARE INVITED, GO AND SIT IN THE LOWEST PLACE, SO THAT WHEN HE WHO INVITED YOU COMES, HE MAY TELL YOU, 'FRIEND, MOVE UP HIGHER.' THEN YOU WILL BE HONORED IN THE PRESENCE OF ALL WHO SIT AT THE TABLE WITH YOU.**

Lk 14:11 **FOR EVERYONE WHO EXALTS HIMSELF WILL BE HUMBLED, AND WHOEVER HUMBLES HIMSELF WILL BE EXALTED."**

463   SEEK HEAVENLY RATHER THAN EARTHLY REWARDS BY OFFERING GENUINE HOSPITALITY TO THOSE LESS FORTUNATE (Lk 14:12-14)

Lk 14:12 He also said to the one who had invited Him, **"WHEN YOU MAKE A DINNER OR**

A SUPPER, DO NOT CALL YOUR FRIENDS, NOR YOUR BROTHERS, NOR YOUR KINSMEN, NOR RICH NEIGHBORS. FOR PERHAPS THEY MIGHT RETURN THE FAVOR, AND PAY YOU BACK.

Lk 14:13 BUT WHEN YOU MAKE A FEAST, INVITE THE POOR, THE CRIPPLED, THE LAME, AND THE BLIND,

Lk 14:14 AND YOU WILL BE BLESSED, BECAUSE THEY DO NOT HAVE A WAY TO REPAY YOU. FOR YOU WILL BE REPAID IN THE RESURRECTION OF THE RIGHTEOUS."

464   NO LOVE ON EARTH SHOULD EXCEED THAT WHICH YOU HAVE FOR YOUR CREATOR AND SAVIOR (Lk 14:25-33)

Lk 14:25 Now a great many were going with Him. He turned and said to them,

Lk 14:26 "IF ANYONE COMES TO ME, AND DOES NOT DISREGARD HIS OWN FATHER, MOTHER, WIFE, CHILDREN, BROTHERS, AND SISTERS, YES, AND HIS OWN LIFE ALSO, HE CANNOT BE MY DISCIPLE.

Lk 14:27 WHOEVER DOES NOT CARRY HIS OWN CROSS, AND FOLLOW AFTER ME, CANNOT BE MY DISCIPLE."

465   EACH FOLLOWER SHOULD COUNT THE COST OF DISCIPLESHIP AS JESUS WILL NOT ACCEPT A PARTIAL COMMITMENT (Lk 14:28-30)

Lk 14:28 "WHICH OF YOU, DESIRING TO BUILD A BUILDING, DOES NOT FIRST SIT DOWN AND COUNT THE COST, TO SEE IF HE HAS ENOUGH TO COMPLETE IT?

Lk 14:29 IT MAY BE WHEN HE HAS LAID A FOUNDATION AND IS NOT ABLE TO FINISH, EVERYONE WHO SEES HIM WILL BEGIN TO MOCK HIM,

Lk 14:30 SAYING, 'THIS MAN BEGAN TO BUILD, AND WAS NOT ABLE TO FINISH.'"

466   AN APOSTLE MUST BE WILLING TO SURRENDER ALL TO FOLLOW THE LORD (Lk 14:31-33)

Lk 14:31 "OR WHAT KING, AS HE GOES TO ENCOUNTER ANOTHER KING IN WAR, WILL NOT SIT DOWN FIRST AND CONSIDER WHETHER HE IS ABLE WITH TEN THOUSAND TO COMBAT HIM WHO COMES AGAINST HIM WITH TWENTY THOUSAND?

Lk 14:32 AND, WHILE THE OTHER IS YET A GREAT WAY OFF, HE SENDS AN ENVOY, AND ASKS FOR CONDITIONS OF PEACE.

Lk 14:33 SO THEREFORE WHOEVER OF YOU DOES NOT GIVE UP ALL THAT HE HAS, HE CAN NOT BE MY DISCIPLE."

467   *DO NOT LOSE YOUR ZEAL FOR THE LORD (Mt 5:13; Mk 9:50; Lk 14:34,35)*

Mt 5:13 "YOU ARE THE SALT OF THE EARTH, BUT IF THE SALT HAS LOST ITS FLAVOR, WITH WHAT WILL IT BE SALTED? IT IS THEN GOOD FOR NOTHING, BUT TO BE CAST OUT AND TRODDEN UNDER THE FEET OF MEN.

Lk 14:35 IT IS FIT NEITHER FOR THE SOIL NOR FOR THE MANURE PILE. IT IS THROWN OUT. HE WHO HAS EARS TO HEAR, LET HIM HEAR.

Mk 9:50 SALT IS GOOD, BUT IF THE SALT HAS LOST ITS SALTINESS, WITH WHAT WILL YOU SEASON IT? HAVE SALT IN YOURSELVES, AND BE AT PEACE WITH ONE ANOTHER."

> *(Salt can "purify" our culture, salt can "add flavor" to Christian living, salt can "preserve" the Word of God.)*

468   *CHRISTIANS ARE TO ENLIGHTEN THE WORLD BY RADIATING HIS LIGHT AND LOVE TO OTHERS (Mt 5:14-16; Lk 11:33)*

Mt 5:14 "YOU ARE THE LIGHT OF THE WORLD. A CITY LOCATED ON A HILL CANNOT BE HIDDEN.

Lk 11:33 NO ONE, WHEN HE HAS LIT A LAMP PUTS IT IN A SECRET PLACE OR UNDER A BASKET, BUT ON A STAND, THAT THOSE WHO COME IN MAY SEE THE LIGHT.

Mt 5:15 ...AND IT SHINES TO ALL WHO ARE IN THE HOUSE.

Mt 5:16 EVEN SO, LET YOUR LIGHT SO SHINE BEFORE MEN, THAT THEY MAY SEE YOUR GOOD WORKS, AND THEREBY GLORIFY YOUR FATHER WHO IS IN HEAVEN."

CHAPTER XIV

HIS SEARCH FOR THE LOST

469   JESUS TELLS OUTCASTS AND PROFESSIONALS ALIKE ABOUT GOD'S FORGIVENESS AND MERCY (taken from Lk 15:1-32)

Lk 15:1 Now all the tax collectors and sinners were coming close to Him to hear Him.

Lk 15:2 The Pharisees and the scribes murmured, saying, "This man welcomes sinners, and eats with them."

Lk 15:3 He told them this parable,

470   JESUS, THE "LOVER OF OUR SOULS," REVEALS HIS CONCERN FOR EACH ONE US (Lk 15:4-7)

Lk 15:4 "WHICH OF YOU MEN, IF YOU HAD ONE HUNDRED SHEEP, AND LOST ONE OF THEM, WOULD NOT LEAVE THE NINETY-NINE IN THE PASTURE, AND GO AFTER THE ONE THAT WAS LOST, UNTIL HE FOUND IT?

Lk 15:5 WHEN HE HAS FOUND IT, HE CARRIES IT ON HIS SHOULDERS, REJOICING.

Lk 15:6 WHEN HE COMES HOME, HE CALLS TOGETHER HIS FRIENDS AND HIS NEIGHBORS, SAYING TO THEM, 'REJOICE WITH ME, FOR I HAVE FOUND MY SHEEP WHICH WAS LOST!'

Lk 15:7 I TELL YOU THAT LIKEWISE THERE WILL BE MORE JOY IN HEAVEN OVER ONE SINNER WHO REPENTS, THAN OVER NINETY-NINE RIGHTEOUS PEOPLE WHO NEED NO REPENTANCE."

471   THERE IS ECSTASY IN HEAVEN OVER ANY SINNER WHO COMES TO THE LORD (Lk 15:8-10)

Lk 15:8 "OR WHAT WOMAN, IF SHE HAD TEN DRACHMA COINS, IF SHE LOST ONE DRACHMA COIN, WOULD NOT LIGHT A LAMP, SWEEP THE HOUSE, AND SEEK DILIGENTLY UNTIL SHE FOUND IT?

Lk 15:9 WHEN SHE HAS FOUND IT, SHE CALLS TOGETHER HER FRIENDS AND NEIGHBORS, SAYING, 'REJOICE WITH ME, FOR I HAVE FOUND THE DRACHMA WHICH I HAD LOST.'

Lk 15:10 EVEN SO, I TELL YOU, THERE IS JOY IN THE PRESENCE OF THE ANGELS OF GOD OVER ONE SINNER REPENTING."

472   *A HEAVENLY FATHER IS GENEROUS TO A CARELESS SON WHO BECOMES WASTEFUL WITH HIS TIME AND INHERITANCE (Lk 15:11-32)*

Lk 15:11 He said, "A CERTAIN MAN HAD TWO SONS.

Lk 15:12 THE YOUNGER OF THEM SAID TO HIS FATHER, 'FATHER, GIVE ME MY SHARE OF YOUR PROPERTY.' SO, HE DIVIDED HIS LIVELIHOOD BETWEEN THEM.

Lk 15:13 NOT MANY DAYS AFTER, THE YOUNGER SON GATHERED ALL HE HAD TOGETHER AND TRAVELED INTO A FAR COUNTRY. THERE HE WASTED HIS PROPERTY WITH EXPENSIVE LIVING."

473   *THE WAYWARD SON COMES TO KNOW THE EMPTINESS OF PURSUING A LIFE OF SENSUOUS PLEASURES (Lk 15:14-16)*

Lk 15:14 "WHEN HE HAD SPENT ALL OF IT, THERE AROSE A SEVERE FAMINE, AND HE BEGAN TO BE IN NEED.

Lk 15:15 HE WENT AND JOINED HIMSELF TO ONE OF THE CITIZENS OF THAT COUNTRY, WHO SENT HIM INTO HIS FIELDS TO FEED PIGS.

Lk 15:16 HE WANTED TO FILL HIS BELLY WITH THE HUSKS THAT THE PIGS ATE, BUT NO ONE GAVE HIM ANY."

> *Rom 6:23 For the wages of sin is death; but the gift of God is eternal life through Jesus Christ our Lord.*

474   *HE WAKES UP TO CONSIDER THE SECURITY HE HAD LEFT BEHIND (Lk 15:17-19)*

Lk 15:17 "BUT WHEN HE CAME TO HIS SENSES HE SAID, 'HOW MANY HIRED SERVANTS OF MY FATHER HAVE BREAD ENOUGH TO SPARE, AND I AM HERE DYING OF HUNGER!

Lk 15:18   I WILL GET UP AND GO TO MY FATHER, AND WILL TELL HIM, "FATHER, I HAVE SINNED AGAINST HEAVEN, AND AGAINST YOU.

> *(Was it Mother Theresa? who said, "There is no saint without a past. There is no sinner without a future.")*

Lk 15:19   I AM NO LONGER WORTHY TO BE CALLED YOUR SON. TREAT ME AS ONE OF YOUR HIRED SERVANTS.'"

475   *AN EVER-PATIENT, EVER-LOVING FATHER REACHES OUT TO HIS PRODIGAL SON (Lk 15:20-24)*

Lk 15:20   "HE AROSE, AND CAME TO HIS FATHER. BUT WHILE HE WAS STILL FAR OFF, HIS FATHER SAW HIM, AND WAS MOVED WITH COMPASSION, AND RAN, AND FELL ON HIS NECK, AND KISSED HIM.

Lk 15:21   THE SON SAID TO HIM, 'FATHER, I HAVE SINNED AGAINST HEAVEN, AND IN YOUR SIGHT. I AM NO LONGER WORTHY TO BE CALLED YOUR SON.'"

476   *UPON HEARING HIS REPENTENT SON'S CONFESSION, THE FATHER REJOICES OVER THEIR RECONCILIATION (Lk 15:22-24)*

Lk 15:22   "BUT THE FATHER SAID TO HIS SERVANTS, 'BRING OUT THE BEST ROBE, AND PUT IT ON HIM. PUT A RING ON HIS HAND, AND SHOES ON HIS FEET.

Lk 15:23   GET THE FATTED CALF, KILL IT, AND LET US EAT, AND CELEBRATE,

Lk 15:24   FOR THIS, MY SON, WAS DEAD, AND IS ALIVE AGAIN. HE WAS LOST, AND IS FOUND.' AND THEY BEGAN TO CELEBRATE. "

> *Jer 29:11   For I know the thoughts that I think toward you, says Yahweh, thoughts of peace, and not of evil, to give you hope and a future.*

> *(If you would take one step in God's direction, He would run a million miles to walk alongside with you and lead you into His Kingdom.)*

477   *A SINCERE, HARD WORKING CHRISTIAN LEARNS OF HIS FATHER'S FORGIVENESS OF THE LOST BROTHER (Lk 15:25-27)*

Lk 15:25   "NOW HIS ELDER SON WAS IN THE FIELD. AS HE CAME NEAR TO THE HOUSE, HE HEARD MUSIC AND DANCING.

Lk 15:26 HE CALLED ONE OF THE SERVANTS TO HIM, AND ASKED WHAT WAS GOING ON.

Lk 15:27 HE SAID TO HIM, 'YOUR BROTHER HAS COME HOME, AND YOUR FATHER HAS KILLED THE FATTED CALF, BECAUSE HE HAS RECEIVED HIM BACK SAFE AND SOUND.'"

478   THE FATHER'S LOVE ALSO REACHES OUT TO THE SELF-RIGHTEOUS OLDER BROTHER *(Lk 15:28-30)*

Lk 15:28 "BUT HE WAS ANGRY, AND WOULD NOT GO IN. THEREFORE HIS FATHER CAME OUT, AND BEGGED HIM.

Lk 15:29 BUT HE ANSWERED HIS FATHER, 'YOU MUST KNOW, THESE MANY YEARS HOW I HAVE SERVED YOU, AND I NEVER DISOBEYED A COMMANDMENT OF YOURS, BUT YOU NEVER EVEN GAVE ME A GOAT, THAT I MIGHT CELEBRATE WITH MY FRIENDS.

Lk 15:30 BUT WHEN THIS, YOUR SON, CAME, WHO HAS SPLURGED YOUR LIFE SAVINGS ON PROSTITUTES, YOU KILL THE FATTED CALF FOR HIM.'"

479   A BOUNTIFUL GOD REPEATS HIS PROMISE AND GIVES A REASON TO CELEBRATE *(Lk 15:31-32)*

Lk 15:31 "HE SAID TO HIM, 'SON YOU ARE ALWAYS WITH ME, AND ALL THAT I HAVE IS YOURS.

> *Rom 8:7 (We are)...joint heirs with Christ...(everything that belongs to Jesus, belongs to us.)*

Lk 15:32 BUT IT WAS PROPER TO CELEBRATE AND BE GLAD, FOR THIS, YOUR BROTHER, WAS DEAD, AND IS ALIVE AGAIN. HE WAS LOST, AND NOW IS FOUND.'"

> *(If we only knew the divine potential that is in another person, we could not fall on our faces fast enough, to humble ourselves before him.)*

480   JESUS, THE "GOD OF OUR SALVATION," TELLS A PARABLE OF A SINNER ABOUT TO BE DISMISSED *(Lk 16:1-12)*

Lk 16:1 He also said to His disciples, "**THERE WAS A CERTAIN RICH MAN WHO HAD A MANAGER. AN ACCUSATION WAS MADE TO HIM THAT THIS MAN WAS WASTING THE RICH MAN'S POSSESSIONS.**

Lk 16:2   HE CALLED HIM, AND SAID TO HIM, 'WHAT IS THIS THAT I HEAR ABOUT YOU? GIVE AN ACCOUNTING OF YOUR MANAGEMENT, FOR YOU CAN NO LONGER BE MANAGER.'

Lk 16:3   THE MANAGER SAID WITHIN HIMSELF, 'WHAT WILL I DO, SEEING THAT MY LORD IS TAKING AWAY MY POSITION FROM ME? I DO NOT HAVE STRENGTH TO DIG. I AM ASHAMED TO BEG.' "

481   THE STEWARD BEGINS TO GIVE AWAY GOD'S WORLDLY POSSESSIONS (Lk 16:4-7)

Lk 16:4   "I KNOW WHAT I WILL DO, SO THAT WHEN I AM REMOVED FROM MANAGEMENT, THEY MAY RECEIVE ME INTO THEIR HOUSES.

Lk 16:5   CALLING EACH ONE OF HIS LORD'S DEBTORS TO HIM, HE SAID TO THE FIRST, 'HOW MUCH DO YOU OWE TO MY LORD?'

Lk 16:6   HE SAID, 'A HUNDRED GALLONS OF OIL.' HE SAID TO HIM, 'TAKE YOUR BILL, AND SIT DOWN QUICKLY AND WRITE FIFTY.'

Lk 16:7   THEN HE SAID TO ANOTHER, 'HOW MUCH DO YOU OWE?' HE SAID, 'A HUNDRED BUSHELS OF WHEAT.' HE SAID TO HIM, 'TAKE YOUR BILL, AND WRITE EIGHTY.' "

482   THE SHREWD MANAGER IS ADMIRED FOR HIS FORESIGHT IN PLANNING FOR HIS LATER LIFE (Lk 16:8,9)

Lk 16:8   "HIS LORD COMMENDED THE DISHONEST MANAGER BECAUSE HE HAD DONE WISELY. FOR THE CHILDREN OF THIS WORLD ARE, IN THEIR OWN GENERATION, WISER THAN THE CHILDREN OF THE LIGHT.

Lk 16:9   I TELL YOU, MAKE FOR YOURSELVES FRIENDS BY MEANS OF UNRIGHTEOUS MAMMON, SO THAT WHEN IT RUNS OUT, THEY MAY RECEIVE YOU INTO THE ETERNAL HOME."

483   LEARN TO SHARE THE MATERIAL GIFTS WHICH GOD HAS GIVEN YOU (Lk 16:10-12)

Lk 16:10 "HE WHO IS FAITHFUL IN VERY LITTLE IS FAITHFUL ALSO IN MUCH. HE WHO IS DISHONEST IN VERY LITTLE IS ALSO DISHONEST IN MUCH.

Lk 16:11 IF THEREFORE YOU HAVE NOT BEEN FAITHFUL IN THE UNRIGHTEOUS MAMMON, WHO WILL COMMIT TO YOUR TRUST THE TRUE RICHES?

Lk 16:12 IF YOU HAVE NOT BEEN FAITHFUL IN THAT WHICH IS ANOTHER'S (GOD'S), WHO WILL GIVE YOU THAT WHICH IS YOUR OWN?"

484   *YOU CANNOT ASPIRE TO BOTH THE KINGDOM OF GOD AND TO THE WORLD (Lk 16:13-15)*

Lk 16:13 "NO SERVANT CAN SERVE TWO MASTERS, FOR EITHER HE WILL HATE THE ONE, AND LOVE THE OTHER, OR ELSE HE WILL PREFER THE ONE, AND NEGLECT THE OTHER. YOU ARE NOT ABLE TO SERVE GOD AND MAMMON." *(money)*

Lk 16:14 The Pharisees, <u>who were lovers of money</u>, (the clue to interpreting the foregoing parable), also heard all these things, and they scoffed at Him.

Lk 16:15 He said to them, **"YOU ARE THOSE WHO JUSTIFY YOURSELVES IN THE SIGHT OF MEN, BUT GOD KNOWS YOUR HEARTS. FOR THAT WHICH IS EXALTED AMONG MEN IS AN ABOMINATION** *(awful)* **IN THE SIGHT OF GOD."**

485   *JESUS, THE "PATIENT TEACHER," TELLS ANOTHER PARABLE TO EXPLAIN THE DANGERS OF WEALTH (Lk 16:19-31)*

Lk 16:19 "NOW THERE WAS A CERTAIN RICH MAN, AND HE WAS CLOTHED IN PURPLE AND FINE LINEN, LIVING IN LUXURY EVERY DAY.

Lk 16:20 A CERTAIN BEGGAR, NAMED LAZARUS, WAS LAID AT HIS GATE, FULL OF SORES,

Lk 16:21 AND DESIRING TO BE FED WITH THE CRUMBS THAT FELL FROM THE RICH MAN'S TABLE. YES, EVEN THE DOGS CAME AND LICKED HIS SORES."

486   *THE LIFE OF THE RICH MAN AND THAT OF THE POOR MAN ARE CONTRASTED (Lk 16:22-24)*

Lk 16:22 "IT HAPPENED THAT THE BEGGAR DIED, AND THAT HE WAS CARRIED AWAY BY THE ANGELS TO ABRAHAM'S BOSOM. THE RICH MAN ALSO DIED, AND WAS BURIED.

Lk 16:23 AND IN HELL, HE LIFTED UP HIS EYES, BEING IN TORMENT, AND SAW ABRAHAM FAR OFF, AND LAZARUS AT HIS BOSOM.

Lk 16:24 HE CRIED AND SAID, 'FATHER ABRAHAM, HAVE MERCY ON ME, AND SEND LAZARUS, THAT HE MAY DIP THE TIP OF HIS FINGER IN WATER, AND COOL MY TONGUE! FOR I AM IN ANGUISH IN THESE FLAMES.' "

487   *A WIDE GULF SEPARATES THE SOULS IN HEAVEN FROM THOSE IN HELL (Lk 16:25,26)*

Lk 16:25 "BUT ABRAHAM SAID, 'SON, REMEMBER THAT YOU, IN YOUR LIFETIME, RECEIVED GOOD THINGS, AND LAZARUS, IN THE SAME WAY, BAD THINGS. BUT NOW HERE HE IS COMFORTED AND YOU ARE IN MISERY.

Lk 16:26 BESIDES ALL THIS, BETWEEN US AND YOU THERE IS A GREAT GULF, THAT THOSE WHO WANT TO PASS FROM HERE TO YOU ARE NOT ABLE, AND THAT NONE MAY CROSS OVER FROM THERE TO US.' "

488   *THE PEOPLE STILL LIVING SHOULD REPENT OF THEIR SINS AND PAY ATTENTION TO PAST SAINTS (Lk 16:27-29)*

Lk 16:27 "HE SAID, 'I ASK YOU THEREFORE, FATHER, THAT YOU WOULD SEND HIM TO MY FATHER'S HOUSE,

Lk 16:28 FOR I HAVE FIVE BROTHERS, THAT HE MAY TESTIFY TO THEM, SO THEY WILL NOT ALSO COME INTO THIS PLACE OF TORMENT.'

Lk 16:29 BUT ABRAHAM SAID TO HIM, 'THEY HAVE MOSES AND THE PROPHETS. LET THEM LISTEN TO THEM.' "

489   *JESUS, THE "COMING KING," TELLS US THAT THOSE WHO ARE PRE-OCCUPIED WILL EVEN IGNORE HIS OWN RESURRECTION (Lk 16:30,31)*

Lk 16:30 "HE SAID, 'NO, FATHER ABRAHAM, BUT IF ONE GOES TO THEM FROM THE DEAD, THEY WILL REPENT.'

Lk 16:31 HE SAID TO HIM, 'IF THEY DO NOT LISTEN TO MOSES AND THE PROPHETS, NEITHER WILL THEY BE PERSUADED IF ONE RISES FROM THE DEAD.' "

490   *ONE MUST REALIZE THE CONTINUAL GROWTH OF EVEN A NEW AND TINY FAITH (Lk 17:5,6)*

Lk 17:5   The apostles said to the Lord, "Increase our faith."

Lk 17:6 The Lord said, "IF YOU HAD FAITH LIKE A GRAIN OF MUSTARD SEED, YOU WOULD TELL THIS SYCAMORE TREE, 'BE UPROOTED, AND BE PLANTED IN THE SEA,' AND IT WOULD OBEY YOU."

491   DO NOT SEEK FAME WHILE THERE IS MUCH WORK TO DO (Lk 17:7-10)

Lk 17:7 "BUT WHO IS THERE AMONG YOU, HAVING A SERVANT PLOWING OR KEEPING SHEEP, THAT WILL SAY WHEN HE COMES IN FROM THE FIELD, 'COME IMMEDIATELY AND SIT DOWN AT THE TABLE.'

Lk 17:8 AND WILL NOT RATHER TELL HIM, 'PREPARE MY SUPPER, PUT ON YOUR APRON, AND SERVE ME, WHILE I EAT AND DRINK. AFTERWARD YOU SHALL EAT AND DRINK'

Lk 17:9 DOES HE THANK THAT SERVANT BECAUSE HE DID THE THINGS THAT WERE COMMANDED? I THINK NOT.

Lk 17:10 EVEN SO YOU ALSO, WHEN YOU HAVE DONE ALL THE THINGS THAT ARE EXPECTED OF YOU, SAY, 'WE ARE ONLY SERVANTS. WE HAVE MERELY DONE OUR DUTY.'"

492   JESUS WILL BRING GLORY TO GOD THROUGH THE DEATH OF HIS DEAR FRIEND LAZARUS (Jn 11:1-45)

Jn 11:1 Now a certain man was sick, Lazarus from Bethany, of the village of Mary and her sister, Martha.

Jn 11:2 It was that Mary who had anointed the Lord with ointment, and wiped His feet with her hair, whose brother, Lazarus, was sick.

Jn 11:3 The sisters therefore sent word to Him, saying, "Lord, behold, he for whom You have great affection is sick."

Jn 11:4 But when Jesus heard it, He said, "THIS SICKNESS IS NOT UNTO DEATH, BUT FOR THE GLORY OF GOD, THAT GOD'S SON MAY BE GLORIFIED BY IT."

493   HE DELAYS, THEN PROCEEDS TOWARD JERUSALEM THOUGH FOREWARNED OF DANGER (Jn 11:5-8)

Jn 11:5 Now Jesus loved Martha, and her sister, and Lazarus.

Jn 11:6 When therefore He heard that he was sick, He stayed two days in the place where He was.

Jn 11:7 Then after this He said to the disciples, **"LET US GO INTO JUDEA AGAIN."**

Jn 11:8 The disciples told Him, "Rabbi, the Jews were just trying to stone You, and are You going there again?"

494 *JESUS, THE "SUN OF RIGHTEOUSNESS," REVEALS THE BRILLIANCE OF HIS BEING (Jn 11:9-11)*

Jn 11:9 Jesus answered, **"ARE THERE NOT TWELVE HOURS OF DAYLIGHT?** *(50% of the earth's surface is in daylight at all times)* **IF A MAN WALKS IN THE DAYTIME, HE DOES NOT TRIP, BECAUSE HE CAN SEE THE "LIGHT OF THIS WORLD."**

> *Jn 8:12 ...I AM the "Light of the World"...*
>
> *Rev 22:16 ...I AM the "Bright and Morning Star"...*
>
> *Ps 84:11 For the Lord God is a "Sun and a Shield"...*

Jn 11:10 "BUT IF A MAN WALKS IN THE NIGHT, HE STUMBLES, BECAUSE THE LIGHT IS NOT IN HIM."

495 *JESUS CONSIDERS DEATH TO BE THE SAME AS SLEEP. (Jn 11:11-14)*

Jn 11:11 He said these things, and after that, He said to them, **"OUR FRIEND, LAZARUS, HAS FALLEN ASLEEP, BUT I AM GOING SO THAT I MAY AWAKE HIM OUT OF HIS SLEEP."**

Jn 11:12 The disciples therefore said, "Lord, if he has fallen asleep, he will recover."

Jn 11:13 Now Jesus had spoken of his death, but they thought that He spoke of being asleep.

Jn 11:14 So Jesus said to them plainly, **"LAZARUS IS DEAD."**

496 *NOT AFRAID THAT THE RABBIS MIGHT TRY TO KILL HIM, JESUS PROCEEDS ON HIS MISSION (Jn 11:15-17)*

Jn 11:15 "I AM GLAD FOR YOUR SAKES THAT I WAS NOT THERE, SO THAT YOU MAY BELIEVE. NEVERTHELESS, LET'S GO TO HIM."

Jn 11:16 Thomas therefore, who is called Didymus, said to his fellow disciples, "Let us go also, that we may die with Him."

Jn 11:17 So when Jesus came, He found that Lazarus had been in the tomb four days already.

497   HE APPROACHES THE BURIAL SITE TO FIND MANY IN MOURNING *(Jn 11: 17-22)*

Jn 11:18 Now Bethany was near Jerusalem, about two miles away.

Jn 11:19 Many of the Jews had joined the women around Martha and Mary, to console them concerning their brother.

Jn 11:20 Then when Martha heard that Jesus was coming, she went and met Him, but Mary stayed in the house.

Jn 11:21 Therefore Martha said to Jesus, "Lord, if You would have been here, my brother would not have died.

Jn 11:22 Even now I know that, whatever You ask of God, God will give You."

498   THE "IMMORTAL JESUS" DECLARES A VICTORY OVER DEATH *(Jn 11:23-26)*

Jn 11:23 Jesus said to her, **"YOUR BROTHER WILL RISE AGAIN."**

Jn 11:24 Martha said to Him, "I know that he will rise again in the resurrection at the last day." *(Dan 12:2)*

Jn 11:25 Jesus said to her, **"(BUT) I AM "THE RESURRECTION"... AND "THE LIFE!" HE WHO BELIEVES IN ME WILL LIVE** *(eternally)* **EVEN IF HE DIES** *(physically)*.

Jn 11:26 WHOEVER LIVES AND BELIEVES IN ME WILL NEVER DIE. *(will pass instantly from this life to the next life)* **DO YOU BELIEVE THIS?"**

499   *MARTHA MAKES A PROFESSION OF FAITH, MARY EXPRESSES HER DISAPPOINTMENT (Jn 11:27-32)*

Jn 11:27 She said to Him, "Yes, Lord. I have come to believe that You are the Christ, God's Son, who was to come into the world."

Jn 11:28 When she had said this she went away and called Mary, her sister secretly, saying, "The Teacher is here and is calling you."

Jn 11:29 When she heard this, she arose quickly, and went to Him.

Jn 11:30   Now Jesus had not yet come into the village, but was in the place where Martha met Him.

Jn 11:31   Then the Jews who were with Mary in the house and were consoling her, when they saw that she rose up quickly and went out, followed her, saying, "She is going to the tomb to weep there."

Jn 11:32   Therefore when Mary came to where Jesus was and saw Him, she fell down at His feet saying to Him, "Lord, if You would have been here, my brother would not have died."

500   THE LOVE OF JESUS FOR LAZARUS IS VERY OBVIOUS (Jn 11:33-36)

Jn 11:33   When Jesus saw her weeping, and the Jews weeping who came with her, He groaned in the spirit, and was troubled,

Jn 11:34   and said, **"WHERE HAVE YOU LAID HIM?"** They told Him, "Lord, come and see."

Jn 11:35   Jesus wept. *(shortest verse in the Bible)*

Jn 11:36   The Jews therefore said, "See how much affection He had for him!"

501   GOD'S MIRACLE WORKING POWER WILL BE SEEN (Jn 11:37-40)

Jn 11:37   Some of them said, "Could not this Man, who opened the eyes of him who was blind, have also kept this man from dying?"

Jn 11:38   Jesus therefore, again groaning in Himself, came to the tomb. Now it was a cave, and a stone lay against it.

Jn 11:39   Jesus said, **"TAKE AWAY THE STONE."** Martha, the sister of him who was dead, said to Him, "Lord, by this time there is a stench, for he has been dead four days."

Jn 11:40   Jesus said to her, **"DID I NOT TELL YOU THAT IF YOU BELIEVED, YOU WOULD SEE GOD'S GLORY?"**

502   JESUS, THE "FAITHFUL SON," HAS COMPLETE FAITH AND TRUST THAT THE FATHER'S GLORY WILL BE REVEALED THROUGH HIM (Jn 11:41,42)

Jn 11:41   So they took away the stone from the place where the dead man was lying. Jesus lifted up His eyes, and said, **"FATHER, I THANK YOU THAT YOU LISTEN TO ME.**

Jn 11:42   I KNOW THAT YOU ALWAYS LISTEN TO ME, BUT BECAUSE OF THE PEOPLE WHICH STAND AROUND I SAY THIS, THAT THEY MAY BELIEVE THAT

YOU SENT ME."

503   GOD, WHO CREATED LIFE, ALSO RESTORES LIFE, AND MANY FINALLY BELIEVE *(Jn 11:43-45)*

Jn 11:43 When He had said this, He cried with a loud voice, **"LAZARUS, COME FORTH."**

Jn 11:44 He who was dead came out, bound hand and foot with wrappings. His face was also wrapped around with a cloth. Jesus said to them, **"LOOSE HIM, AND LET HIM GO."**

Jn 11:45 Therefore many of the Jews, who came to Mary and saw what Jesus did, believed in Him.

> *(This is the third raising from the dead after the widow Nain's son, told to us briefly in Lk 7:11-17; then that of Jairus' daughter in a larger telling in Lk 8:41-56; and now the raising of Lazarus, taking up 45 verses in Jn 11. This is leading up to the resurrection of Jesus later, which will be given to us in far greater details.)*

504   THE PARANOID RELIGIOUS COUNCIL BECOMES CONCERNED AND ENVIOUS OVER THE REPUTATION OF JESUS, THE "SPOTLESS LAMB" *(Jn 11:46-48)*

Jn 11:46 But some of them went away to the Pharisees, and told them the things which Jesus had done.

Jn 11:47 The chief priests therefore and the Pharisees gathered a council and said, "What are we to do? For this Man does many miracles *(an event that creates faith)*.

Jn 11:48 If we leave Him alone like this, everyone will believe in Him, and the Romans will come and take away both our place *(position)* and our nation."

505   THE HOLY SPIRIT PROMPTS THE HIGH PRIEST TO SAY THAT IT IS BEST THAT JESUS SHOULD DIE TO SAVE ISRAEL *(Jn 11:49-52)*

Jn 11:49 But a certain one of them, Caiaphas, being high priest that year, said to them, "You know nothing at all,

Jn 11:50 nor do you consider that it is advantageous for us that one man should die for the people, and that the whole nation not perish."

Jn 11:51 Now he did not say this of himself, but being high priest that year, he prophesied that Jesus would die for the nation,

Jn 11:52 and not for the nation only, but that he might also gather together into one fold, all the children of God who are scattered.

506   *THEY CONSPIRE TO KILL JESUS, "THE HOLY GIVER," WHO NOW BECOMES A FUGITIVE (Jn 11:53,54)*

Jn 11:53 So from that day forward they took counsel that they might put Him to death.

Jn 11:54 Jesus therefore walked no more openly among the Jews, but departed from there into the country near the desert, to a city called Ephraim. He stayed there with His disciples.

507   *TEN LEPERS ARE CLEANSED OF THEIR SKIN DISEASE (Lk 17:11-19)*

Lk 17:11 It happened as He was on His way to Jerusalem, that He was passing along the border line between Samaria and Galilee.

Lk 17:12 As He entered into a certain village, ten men who were lepers met Him, who stood at a distance.

Lk 17:13 They lifted up their voices, saying, "Jesus, Master, have mercy on us!"

Lk 17:14 When He saw them, He said to them, **"GO AND SHOW YOURSELVES TO THE PRIESTS."** It happened that as they went, they were all healed.

508   *ONLY ONE RETURNS TO REVEAL HIS GRATITUDE (Lk 17:15-19)*

Lk 17:15 One of them, when he saw that he was made whole, turned back, glorifying God with a loud voice.

Lk 17:16 He fell on his face at Jesus' feet, giving Him thanks. And he was a Samaritan.

Lk 17:17 Jesus answered, **"WERE NOT TEN CLEANSED? BUT WHERE ARE THE OTHER NINE?**

Lk 17:18 WERE THERE NONE FOUND WHO RETURNED TO GIVE GLORY TO GOD, EXCEPT THIS STRANGER?"

Lk 17:19 Then He said to him, **"GET UP, AND GO YOUR WAY. YOUR FAITH HAS MADE YOU WHOLE."**

> *Ps 147:11 The Lord taketh pleasure in them that revere Him, in those that hope in His mercy.*

509 THE KINGDOM OF GOD BEGINS WITH AN INTERNAL AND SPIRITUAL CONDITION (Lk 17:20,21)

Lk 17:20 Being asked by the Pharisees when the Kingdom of God would come, He answered them, **"THE KINGDOM OF GOD DOES NOT COME BY VISUAL OBSERVATION.**

Lk 17:21 NEITHER WILL THEY SAY, 'LOOK HERE!' OR, 'LOOK THERE' FOR BEHOLD, THE KINGDOM OF GOD IS WITHIN YOU"

CHAPTER XV

FIRST PREDICTIONS OF THE END

510   HIS SECOND COMING WILL BE VERY EVIDENT AND SUDDEN (taken from Lk 17:22-25)

Lk 17:22   He said to the disciples, "THE DAYS WILL COME, WHEN YOU WILL DESIRE TO SEE ONE OF THE DAYS OF THE SON OF MAN, AND YOU WILL NOT SEE IT.

Lk 17:23   THEY WILL TELL YOU, 'LOOK, HERE!' OR 'LOOK, THERE!' DO NOT GO AFTER THEM, NOR FOLLOW THEM,

Lk 17:24   FOR AS LIGHTNING, WHICH FLASHES OUT OF ONE PART OF THE SKY SHINES TO THE OTHER PART OF THE SKY, SO ALSO WILL THE SON OF MAN COME IN HIS DAY.

Lk 17:25   BUT FIRST, HE MUST SUFFER MANY THINGS AND BE REJECTED BY THIS PRESENT GENERATION."

511   JESUS FORETELLS AN ABRUPT AND UNEXPECTED END FOR THOSE WHO BECOME TOO INVOLVED WITH AFFAIRS OF THIS WORLD (Lk 17:26-30)

Lk 17:26   "AS IT HAPPENED IN THE DAYS OF NOAH, EVEN SO WILL IT BE ALSO IN THE DAYS OF THE SON OF MAN.

Lk 17:27   THEY ATE, THEY DRANK, THEY MARRIED, THEY WERE GIVEN IN MARRIAGE, UNTIL THE DAY THAT NOAH ENTERED INTO THE ARK. THEN THE FLOOD CAME, AND DESTROYED THEM ALL.

Lk 17:28   IT WILL BE AS IT HAPPENED IN THE DAYS OF LOT. THEY ATE, THEY DRANK, THEY BOUGHT, THEY SOLD, THEY PLANTED, THEY BUILT.

Lk 17:29   BUT IN THE DAY THAT LOT WENT OUT FROM SODOM, IT RAINED FIRE AND SULFUR FROM THE SKY, AND DESTROYED THEM ALL.

Lk 17:30   IT WILL BE THE SAME WAY IN THE DAY THAT THE SON OF MAN RE-APPEARS."

Phil 2:12 ...work out your own salvation in fear and trembling.

512   JESUS, THE "ETERNAL LIFE," GIVES A WARNING ABOUT LOOKING BACK *(Lk 17:31-33)*

Lk 17:31 "IN THAT DAY, HE WHO WILL BE ON THE HOUSETOP, AND HIS GOODS IN THE HOUSE, LET HIM NOT GO DOWN TO TAKE THEM AWAY. LET HIM WHO IS IN THE FIELD LIKEWISE NOT TURN BACK.

Lk 17:32 REMEMBER LOT'S WIFE! *(Gen 19:26)*

Lk 17:33 WHOEVER SEEKS TO SAVE HIS LIFE SHALL LOSE IT, BUT WHOEVER LOSES HIS LIFE SHALL PRESERVE IT."

513   *THERE WILL COME A SIMULTANEOUS DAY AND NIGHT, WORLD-WIDE SEPARATION OF BELIEVERS FROM NON-BELIEVERS (Lk 17:34-37)*

Lk 17:34 "I TELL YOU, IN THAT NIGHT THERE WILL BE TWO PEOPLE IN ONE BED. THE ONE WILL BE TAKEN, AND THE OTHER WILL BE LEFT.

Lk 17:35 THERE WILL BE TWO GRINDING GRAIN TOGETHER. ONE WILL BE TAKEN, AND THE OTHER WILL BE LEFT.

Lk 17:36 TWO WILL BE IN THE FIELD, THE ONE TAKEN, AND THE OTHER LEFT."

Lk 17:37 They, answering, asked Him, "Where, Lord?" He said to them, **"WHERE THE BODY IS, THERE WILL THE VULTURES ALSO BE GATHERED TOGETHER."**

514   *JESUS, OUR "DEVOUT LORD," TELLS OF THE POWER OF PERSISTENT PRAYER (Lk 18:1-8)*

Lk 18:1   He also spoke a parable to them that they must always pray, and not give up,

Lk 18:2   saying, **"THERE WAS A JUDGE IN A CERTAIN CITY WHO DID NOT FEAR GOD, AND DID NOT RESPECT MAN.**

Lk 18:3   A WIDOW WAS IN THAT CITY, AND SHE OFTEN CAME TO HIM, SAYING, 'DEFEND ME FROM MY OPPONENT.'

Lk 18:4   HE WOULD NOT FOR A WHILE, BUT AFTERWARD HE SAID TO HIMSELF, 'THOUGH I NEITHER FEAR GOD, NOR RESPECT MAN,

Lk 18:5 YET BECAUSE THIS WIDOW BOTHERS ME, I WILL DEFEND HER, OR ELSE SHE WILL WEAR ME OUT BY HER CONTINUAL COMING.'"

515   GOD WILL ANSWER THOSE WHO CALL OUT TO HIM, BUT WILL PEOPLE CONTINUE IN THEIR FAITH UNTIL THE BITTER END? (Lk 18:6-8)

Lk 18:6 The Lord said, "LISTEN TO WHAT THAT UNRIGHTEOUS JUDGE SAYS.

Lk 18:7 WILL NOT GOD AVENGE HIS OWN CHOSEN ONES, WHO ARE CRYING OUT TO HIM DAY AND NIGHT, THOUGH HE IS PATIENT WITH THEM?

Lk 18:8 I TELL YOU THAT HE WILL AVENGE THEM QUICKLY. NEVERTHELESS, WHEN THE SON OF MAN COMES, WILL HE FIND FAITH ON EARTH?"

516   JESUS DRAWS ATTENTION TO THE PRAYER OF THE PROUD AND SELF-RIGHTEOUS PHARISEE IN MANY OF US (Lk 18:9-12)

Lk 18:9 He spoke also this parable to certain people who were convinced of their own righteousness, and who despised all others.

Lk 18:10 "TWO MEN WENT UP INTO THE TEMPLE TO PRAY, ONE WAS A PHARISEE, AND THE OTHER WAS A TAX COLLECTOR.

Lk 18:11 THE PHARISEE STOOD AND PRAYED TO HIMSELF LIKE THIS, 'GOD, I THANK YOU, THAT I AM NOT LIKE THE REST OF MEN, THIEVES, UNJUST, ADULTERERS, OR EVEN LIKE THIS TAX COLLECTOR.

Lk 18:12 I FAST TWICE A WEEK. I GIVE TITHES OF ALL THAT I GET.'"

517   JESUS, THE "FRIEND OF SINNERS," ADMIRES THE ATTITUDE OF THE HUMBLE REPENTENT (Lk 18:13,14)

Lk 18:13 "BUT THE TAX COLLECTOR, STANDING FAR AWAY, WOULD NOT EVEN LIFT UP HIS EYES TO HEAVEN, BUT BEAT HIS BREAST SAYING, 'GOD, BE MERCIFUL TO ME, A SINNER!'

Lk 18:14 I TELL YOU, THIS MAN WENT BACK TO HIS HOUSE APPROVED BY GOD RATHER THAN THE FORMER, FOR EVERYONE WHO EXALTS HIMSELF WILL BE HUMBLED, BUT HE WHO HUMBLES HIMSELF WILL BE EXALTED."

518   THE PHARISEES ASK THE "REVERENT LORD" TO INTERPRET THE LAW REGARDING DIVORCE (Mt 19:1-12; Mk 10:1-12)

Mk 10:1   He arose from there and came along the borders of Judea and beyond the Jordan...

Mt 19:2   Great multitudes followed Him, and He healed them there.

Mk 10:1   ...as He usually did, He was again teaching them.

Mt 19:3   The pharisees came to Him, testing Him, and saying, "Is it lawful for a man to divorce his wife for any reason?"

Mk 10:3   He answered, **"WHAT DID MOSES COMMAND YOU?"**

Mk 10:4   They said, "Moses allowed a certificate of divorce to be written, and to divorce her."

Mt 19:8   He said to them, **"MOSES, BECAUSE OF THE HARDNESS OF YOUR HEARTS, ALLOWED YOU TO DIVORCE YOUR WIVES, BUT FROM THE BEGINNING IT HAS NOT BEEN SO."**

519   NO ONE SHOULD ABOLISH THE BLESSINGS AND DISCIPLINE THAT MARRIAGE BRINGS (Mt 19:4-6; Mk 10:6-9)

Mt 19:4   He answered, **"HAVE YOU NOT READ THAT HE WHO MADE THEM FROM THE BEGINNING MADE THEM MALE AND FEMALE,**

Mt 19:5   **AND SAID, 'FOR THIS CAUSE A MAN SHALL LEAVE HIS FATHER AND MOTHER, AND SHALL JOIN TO HIS WIFE, AND THE TWO SHALL BECOME ONE FLESH?'** *(Gen 2:24)*

Mt 19:6   **SO THAT THEY ARE NO MORE TWO, BUT ONE FLESH. WHAT THEREFORE GOD HAS JOINED TOGETHER, DO NOT LET MAN TEAR APART."**

(Consider 1 Cor 7:1-16; Eph. 5:22-33 and 1 Pet. 3:1-7 for more on marriage)

520   THE WORLD IS FULL OF PEOPLE PROFESSING TO UPHOLD THE LAW (Mk 10:10; Lk 16:16,17)

Mk 10:10   In the house, His disciples asked Him again about the same matter.

Lk 16:16   **"THE LAW AND THE PROPHETS WERE UNTIL JOHN. FROM THAT TIME THE GOOD NEWS OF THE KINGDOM OF GOD IS PREACHED, AND EVERYONE IS FORCING HIS WAY INTO IT.**

Lk 16:17 BUT IT IS EASIER FOR HEAVEN AND EARTH TO PASS AWAY, THAN FOR EVEN ONE TINY DOT IN THE LAW TO BECOME VOID."

521   *ONE CANNOT BE TOO CAREFUL IN SELECTING A LIFETIME PARTNER (Mt 19:9; Mk 10:11,12; Lk 16:18)*

Mt 19:9 "I TELL YOU THAT WHOEVER DIVORCES HIS WIFE, EXCEPT FOR SEXUAL IMMORALITY, AND MARRIES ANOTHER, COMMITS ADULTERY. AND HE WHO MARRIES HER WHEN SHE IS DIVORCED COMMITS ADULTERY.

Mk 10:12 IF A WOMAN HERSELF DIVORCES HER HUSBAND, AND MARRIES ANOTHER, SHE COMMITS ADULTERY.

522   *IT IS BETTER FOR CERTAIN PEOPLE NOT TO MARRY (Mt 10:10-12)*

Mt 19:10 His disciples said to Him, "If this is the case of the man and his wife, it is not good to marry."

Mt 19:11 But He said to them, **"NOT ALL MEN CAN RECEIVE THIS SAYING, BUT THOSE TO WHOM IT IS GIVEN.**

Mt 19:12 FOR THERE ARE EUNUCHS WHO WERE BORN THAT WAY FROM THEIR MOTHER'S WOMB, AND THERE ARE EUNUCHS WHO WERE MADE IMPOTENT BY MEN. AND THERE ARE OTHERS WHO HAVE RENOUNCED MARRIAGE FOR THE SAKE OF THE KINGDOM OF HEAVEN. HE, WHO IS ABLE TO RECEIVE IT, LET HIM RECEIVE IT."

523   *SALVATION COMES BY CLINGING TO, TRUSTING IN, AND TOTALLY RELYING ON, OUR HEAVENLY FATHER, INSTINCTIVELY AS A CHILD (Mt 19:13-15; Mk 10:13-16; Lk 18:15-17)*

Lk 18:15 They were also bringing their babies to Him, that He might touch them. But when the disciples saw it, they rebuked them.

Mk 10:14 But when Jesus saw it, He was displeased, and said to them, **"ALLOW THE LITTLE CHILDREN TO COME TO ME! DO NOT FORBID THEM, FOR THE KINGDOM OF GOD BELONGS TO SUCH AS THESE.**

Mk 10:15 MOST CERTAINLY I TELL YOU, WHOEVER WILL NOT RECEIVE THE KINGDOM OF GOD LIKE A LITTLE CHILD, HE WILL IN NO WAY ENTER INTO IT."

Mk 10:16 He took them in His arms, and blessed them, laying His hands on them.

524   A RICH MAN ASKS JESUS, THE "LIVING GOD," HOW HE CAN BE SAVED (Mt 19:16-30; Mk 10:17-31; Lk 18:18-30)

Mt 19:16   Behold, one came to Him and said, "Good Teacher," what good thing shall I do, that I may gain eternal life?"

Mt 19:17   He said to him, "**WHY DO YOU CALL ME GOOD? NO ONE IS GOOD BUT ONE, THAT IS GOD. BUT IF YOU WANT TO ENTER INTO LIFE, KEEP THE COMMANDMENTS.**"

Mt 19:18   He said to Him, "Which ones?" Jesus said, "'**YOU SHALL NOT MURDER. YOU SHALL NOT COMMIT ADULTERY. YOU SHALL NOT STEAL. YOU SHALL NOT OFFER FALSE TESTIMONY.**

Mt 19:19   HONOR YOUR FATHER AND MOTHER. AND, YOU SHALL LOVE YOUR NEIGHBOR AS YOURSELF.'" *(Ex 20:13-16)*

525   THE MAN LEARNS THAT HE IS UNABLE TO FULFILL THE LAW AS HE PRO-FESSES (Mt 19:20-22; Mk 10:20-22; Lk 18:21-23)

Mt 19:20   The young man said to Him, "All these things I have observed from my youth. What do I still lack?"

Mk 10:21   Jesus looking at him kindly, said to him, "**ONE THING YOU LACK. GO, SELL WHATEVER YOU HAVE, AND GIVE TO THE POOR, AND YOU WILL HAVE TREASURE IN HEAVEN,' AND TAKING UP THE CROSS, COME, FOLLOW ME.**"

Mk 10:22   But his face fell at this saying and he went away sorrowful, for he was one who had great possessions.

(The wealthiest man in the world is the one who is the most easily contented.)

526   HAVING MUCH MONEY MAKES IT DIFFICULT TO ENTER INTO THE KINGDOM (Mt 19:23-26; Mk 10:23-37; Lk 18:24-27)

Mk 10:23   Jesus looked around, and said to His disciples, "**HOW DIFFICULT IT IS FOR THOSE WHO HAVE RICHES TO ENTER INTO THE KINGDOM OF GOD!**"

Mk 10:24   The disciples were amazed at His words. But Jesus repeated, "**CHILDREN, HOW HARD IT IS FOR THOSE WHO TRUST IN RICHES TO ENTER INTO THE KINGDOM OF GOD!**

Mk 10:25   IT IS EASIER FOR A CAMEL TO GO THROUGH A NEEDLE'S EYE THAN FOR A RICH MAN TO ENTER INTO THE KINGDOM OF GOD."

Prov 14:12 There is a way which seemeth right unto man, but the end thereof are the ways of death.

527   *BUT GOD'S GRACE GIVES US HOPE (Mt 19:25,26; Mk 10:26,27; Lk 18:26,27)*

Mk 10:26 They were surprised, saying to Him, "Then who can be saved?"

Mk 10:27 Jesus, looking at them, said, **"WITH MEN IT IS IMPOSSIBLE, BUT NOT WITH GOD, FOR ALL THINGS ARE POSSIBLE WITH GOD."**

528   *BLESSINGS ABOUND IN THIS LIFE AND AN EVEN GREATER FUTURE AWAITS US IN HEAVEN (Mt 19:27-30; Mk 10:28-31; Lk 18:28-30)*

Mt 19:27 Then Peter answered, "Look, we have left everything, and followed You. What then will we have?"

Mk 10:29 Jesus said, **"MOST CERTAINLY I TELL YOU, THERE IS NO ONE WHO HAS LEFT HOUSE, OR BROTHERS, OR SISTERS, OR FATHER, OR MOTHER, OR WIFE, OR CHILDREN, OR LAND, FOR MY SAKE, AND FOR THE GOSPEL,**

Mk 10:30 WHO WILL NOT RECEIVE ONE HUNDRED TIMES MORE NOW IN THIS LIFE; HOUSES, BROTHERS, SISTERS, MOTHERS, CHILDREN, AND LAND, WITH PERSECUTIONS, AND IN THE AGE TO COME ETERNAL LIFE."

Mt 19:28 Jesus said to them, **"I TELL YOU WHO HAVE FOLLOWED ME, THAT IN THE NEW CREATION WHEN THE SON OF MAN WILL SIT ON THE THRONE OF HIS GLORY, YOU ALSO WILL SIT ON TWELVE THRONES, JUDGING THE TWELVE TRIBES OF ISRAEL.**

Mk 10:31 BUT MANY WHO ARE FIRST *(privileged)* **WILL BE LAST, AND THE LAST** *(least favored will be)* **FIRST."**

529   *JESUS, OUR "DILIGENT GUIDE," RELATES THAT MANY WORKERS ARE CALLED TO SERVE IN THE WORK OF GOD (Mt 20:1-16)*

Mt 20:1 **"FOR THE KINGDOM OF HEAVEN IS LIKE A MAN WHO WAS THE MASTER OF A HOUSEHOLD, WHO WENT OUT EARLY IN THE MORNING TO HIRE LABORERS FOR HIS VINEYARD.**

Mt 20:2 **WHEN HE HAD AGREED WITH THE LABORERS FOR A DENARIUS A DAY, HE SENT THEM INTO HIS VINEYARD.**

Mt 20:3 HE WENT OUT ABOUT THE THIRD HOUR, AND SAW OTHERS STANDING IDLE IN THE MARKETPLACE.

Mt 20:4 TO THEM HE SAID, 'YOU ALSO GO INTO THE VINEYARD, AND WHATEVER IS RIGHT I WILL GIVE YOU.' SO THEY WENT THEIR WAY."

530   *MORE LABORERS ARE HIRED EVEN LATER (Mt 20:5-7)*

Mt 20:5 "AGAIN HE WENT OUT ABOUT THE SIXTH AND THE NINTH HOUR, AND DID LIKEWISE.

Mt 20:6 ABOUT THE ELEVENTH HOUR HE WENT OUT, AND FOUND OTHERS STANDING IDLE. HE SAID TO THEM, 'WHY DO YOU STAND HERE ALL DAY IDLE?'

Mt 20:7 THEY SAID TO HIM, 'BECAUSE NO ONE HAS HIRED US.' HE SAID TO THEM, 'YOU ALSO GO INTO THE VINEYARD, AND YOU WILL RECEIVE WHATEVER IS RIGHT.'"

531   *HEAVENLY REWARDS ARE THE SAME FOR A NEWCOMER AS FOR AN EARLY BELIEVER (Mt 20:8-12)*

Mt 20:8 "WHEN EVENING HAD COME, THE LORD OF THE VINEYARD SAID TO HIS MANAGER, 'CALL THE LABORERS AND PAY THEM THEIR WAGES, BEGINNING FROM THE LAST TO THE FIRST.'

Mt 20:9 WHEN THOSE WHO WERE HIRED AT ABOUT THE ELEVENTH HOUR CAME, THEY EACH RECEIVED A DENARIUS.

Mt 20:10 WHEN THE FIRST CAME, THEY SUPPOSED THAT THEY WOULD RECEIVE MORE, AND THEY LIKEWISE EACH RECEIVED A DENARIUS.

Mt 20:11 WHEN THEY RECEIVED IT, THEY MURMURED AGAINST THE MASTER OF THE HOUSEHOLD,

Mt 20:12 SAYING, 'THESE LAST HAVE SPENT ONE HOUR, AND YOU HAVE MADE THEM EQUAL TO US, WHO HAVE BORNE THE BURDEN OF THE DAY AND THE SCORCHING HEAT!'"

532   *GOD'S GREAT MERCY AND GENEROSITY BLESSES ALL ALIKE (Mt 20:13-16)*

Mt 20:13 "BUT HE ANSWERED ONE OF THEM, 'FRIEND, I AM DOING YOU NO WRONG. DID YOU NOT AGREE WITH ME FOR A DENARIUS?

Mt 20:14 TAKE THAT WHICH IS YOURS, AND GO YOUR WAY. IT IS MY DESIRE TO GIVE TO THIS LAST JUST AS MUCH AS TO YOU.

Mt 20:15 IS IT NOT LAWFUL FOR ME TO DO WHAT I WANT TO WITH WHAT I OWN? MUST YOU LOOK AT ME SCORNFULLY, BECAUSE I AM GENEROUS?

Mt 20:16 SO THE LAST WILL BE FIRST, AND THE FIRST LAST. FOR MANY ARE CALLED, BUT FEW ARE CHOSEN."

533   LARGE CROWDS GATHER IN JERUSALEM FOR THE YEAR'S MOST IMPORTANT CELEBRATION (Jn 11:55-57)

Jn 11:55   Now the Passover of the Jews was at hand. Many went up from the country to Jerusalem to purify themselves.

Jn 11:56   Then they sought Jesus and spoke one with another, as they stood in the temple, "What do you think, that He is not coming to the feast at all?"

Jn 11:57   Now the chief priests and the Pharisees had commanded that if anyone knew where He was, he should report it, that they might seize Him.

534   THE "PASSOVER LAMB" AGAIN SPEAKS ABOUT HIS DEATH AND LATER TRIUMPH OVER DEATH (Mt 20:17-19; Mk 10:32-34; Lk 18:31-34)

Mk 10:32 Many were on the way, going up to Jerusalem, and Jesus was going in front of them. They were amazed, and those who followed were afraid. He again took the twelve, and began to tell them the things that were going to happen to Him.

Mk 10:33 "BEHOLD, WE ARE GOING UP TO JERUSALEM. THE SON OF MAN WILL BE DELIVERED TO THE CHIEF PRIESTS AND THE SCRIBES. THEY WILL CONDEMN HIM TO DEATH, AND WILL DELIVER HIM TO THE PAGANS.

Mk 10:34 THEY WILL MOCK HIM, SPIT ON HIM, WHIP HIM, AND KILL HIM. AND (*not after* three days, but) **ON** THE THIRD DAY HE WILL RISE AGAIN.

Lk 18:31 ...ALL THE THINGS THAT ARE WRITTEN THROUGH THE PROPHETS CONCERNING THE SON OF MAN WILL BE ACCOMPLISHED."

Lk 18:34 They understood none of these things. This saying was hidden from them, and they did not comprehend the things that were said.

535   THE MOTHER OF JAMES AND JOHN HAS A SELFISH AMBITION FOR HER TWO SONS (Mt 20:20-22; Mk 10:35-40)

Mt 20:20 Then the mother of the sons of Zebedee came to Him with her sons, kneeling and asking a certain favor of Him.

Mt 20:21 He said to her, **"WHAT DO YOU WANT?"** She said to Him, "Command that these, my two sons, may sit one on Your right hand, and one on Your left hand, in Your Kingdom."

Mt 20:22 But Jesus answered, **"YOU DO NOT KNOW WHAT YOU ARE ASKING. ARE THEY ABLE TO DRINK THE CUP** *(of suffering)* **THAT I AM ABOUT TO DRINK, AND BE BAPTIZED WITH THE BAPTISM THAT I AM TO BE BAPTIZED WITH?"**

536   THE CHOSEN HAVE THEIR SPECIAL PLACE IN HEAVEN SELECTED BEFORE THEY WERE BORN (Mt 20:23,24; Mk 10:39-41)

Mk 10:39 They said to Him, "We are able." Jesus said to them, **"YOU SHALL INDEED DRINK THE CUP THAT I DRINK, AND YOU SHALL BE BAPTIZED WITH THE BAPTISM THAT I AM BAPTIZED WITH,**

Mk 10:40 BUT TO SIT AT MY RIGHT HAND AND AT MY LEFT HAND IS NOT MINE TO GIVE, BUT FOR WHOM IT HAS BEEN PREPARED."

Mk 10:41 When the ten heard it, they began to be resentful towards James and John.

537   DISCIPLES ARE CALLED NOT TO RULE, BUT TO DEDICATE THEIR LIVES FOR OTHERS (Mt 20:25-28; Mk 10:42-45)

Mk 10:42 Jesus summoned them, and said to them, **"YOU KNOW THAT THEY WHO ARE RECOGNIZED AS RULERS OVER THE NATIONS LORD IT OVER THEM, AND MEN DO EXERCISE AUTHORITY OVER THEM.**

Mt 20:26 BUT IT SHALL NOT BE SO AMONG YOU, FOR WHOEVER DESIRES TO BECOME GREAT AMONG YOU, SHALL BE YOUR SERVANT.

Mk 10:44 WHOEVER OF YOU WANTS TO BECOME FIRST AMONG YOU, SHALL BE BONDSERVANT OF ALL.

Mk 10:45 FOR THE SON OF MAN CAME NOT TO BE SERVED, BUT TO SERVE, AND TO GIVE HIS LIFE A RANSOM FOR MANY."

538   A PERSISTENT BLIND BEGGAR RECOGNIZES JESUS, THE "SERVANT KING," AND PLEADS FOR MERCY (Mt 20:29-34; Mk 10:46-52; Lk 18:35-43)

Mk 10:46   He went out from Jericho, with His disciples and a great many people. The son of Timaeus, Bartimaeus, a blind beggar, was sitting by the road.

Lk 18:36   Hearing many people going by, he asked what this meant.

Lk 18:37   They told him that Jesus of Nazareth was passing by.

Lk 18:38   He cried out, "Jesus, You "Son of David," have mercy on me!"

Lk 18:39   Those who led the way rebuked him, that he should be quiet, but he cried out all the more, "You son of David, have mercy on me!"

> *Acts 2:21 It will be, that whoever will call on the name of the Lord will be saved.*

539   HEALING IS OBTAINED THROUGH ONE'S EAGERNESS TO BELIEVE IN JESUS (Mt 20:32-34; Mk 10:49-52; Lk 18:40-43)

Mk 10:49   Jesus stopped, and said, **"CALL HIM."** They called the blind man, saying to him, "Cheer up! Get up. He is calling you!"

Mk 10:50   He, casting away his cloak, sprang up, and came to Jesus.

Mk 10:51   Jesus asked him, **"WHAT DO YOU WANT ME TO DO FOR YOU?"** The blind man said to Him, "Lord, that I may see again."

Lk 18:42   Jesus said to him, **"RECEIVE YOUR SIGHT. YOUR FAITH HAS HEALED YOU."** *(God is not moved by our need. He is moved by our faith in Him.)*

Lk 18:43   Immediately he received his sight, and followed Him, glorifying God. All the people, when they saw it, praised God. *(It is helpful to acknowledge the Lord publicly.)*

> *Ps 147:11 The Lord taketh pleasure in them that fear Him, in those that hope in His mercy.*

540   A RICH MAN BECOMES CURIOUS AND DETERMINED TO SEE JESUS, THE "LOVER OF SINNERS" (Lk 19:1-10)

Lk 19:2   There was a man named Zacchaeus. He was a chief tax collector, and he was rich.

Lk 19:3   He was trying to see who Jesus was and could not because of the crowd, because he was short.

Lk 19:4 He ran on ahead, and climbed up into a sycamore tree to see Him, for Jesus was to pass that way.

541   *JESUS INVITES HIMSELF TO BE THE GUEST OF ZACCHAEUS WHOM PEOPLE DESPISE (Lk 19:5-7)*

Lk 19:5 When Jesus came to the place, He looked up and saw him, and said to him, **"ZACCHAEUS, HURRY AND COME DOWN, FOR TODAY I MUST STAY AT YOUR HOUSE."**

Lk 19:6 He hurried, came down, and received Him joyfully.

Lk 19:7 When they saw it, they all murmured, saying, "He has gone in to lodge with a man who is a sinner."

542   *TRUE REPENTANCE RESULTS IN A JOYFUL LIBERATION (Lk 19:8-10)*

Lk 19:8 Zacchaeus said to the Lord, "Behold, Lord, half of my goods I give to the poor. And if I have taken anything from anyone, I will restore him four times as much."

Lk 19:9 Jesus said to him, **"TODAY, SALVATION HAS COME TO THIS HOUSE, BECAUSE HE ALSO IS A SON OF ABRAHAM.**

Lk 19:10 FOR THE SON OF MAN CAME TO SEEK AND TO SAVE THAT WHICH WAS LOST."

543   *EXPECTING THAT JESUS WOULD BE MADE "MESSIANIC KING," HE TELLS A PARABLE INDICATING THE KINGDOM COULD BE DELAYED (Lk 19:11-28)*

Lk 19:11 As they heard these things, He went on and told a parable, because He was near Jerusalem, and they supposed that the Kingdom of God would happen immediately.

Lk 19:12 He said therefore, **"A CERTAIN NOBLEMAN WENT INTO A FAR COUNTRY TO RECEIVE FOR HIMSELF A KINGDOM, AND TO RETURN."**

544   *JESUS EXPECTS ALL CHRISTIANS TO BE MINISTERING (Lk 19:13,14)*

Lk 19:13 "HE CALLED TEN SERVANTS OF HIS, AND GAVE EACH OF THEM A MINA COIN AND TOLD THEM, 'CONDUCT BUSINESS UNTIL I COME.'

Lk 19:14 BUT HIS CITIZENS HATED HIM, AND SENT AN ENVOY AFTER HIM,

SAYING, 'WE DO NOT WANT THIS MAN TO REIGN OVER US.' "

545   *HE RETURNS AS "EXALTED MONARCH" TO REWARD THOSE WHO WERE PRODUCTIVE (Lk 19:15-19)*

Lk 19:15 "IT HAPPENED WHEN HE HAD COME BACK AGAIN, HAVING RECEIVED THE KINGDOM, THAT HE COMMANDED THESE SERVANTS TO WHOM HE HAD GIVEN THE MONEY TO BE CALLED TO HIM, THAT HE MIGHT KNOW WHAT THEY HAD GAINED BY CONDUCTING BUSINESS.

Lk 19:16 THE FIRST CAME BEFORE HIM, SAYING, 'LORD, YOUR MINA HAS MADE TEN MORE MINAS.'

Lk 19:17 HE SAID TO HIM, 'WELL DONE, YOU GOOD SERVANT! BECAUSE YOU WERE FOUND FAITHFUL WITH VERY LITTLE, YOU SHALL HAVE AUTHORITY OVER TEN CITIES.'

Lk 19:18 THE SECOND CAME, SAYING, 'YOUR MINA, LORD, HAS MADE FIVE MINAS.'

Lk 19:19 SO HE SAID TO HIM, 'AND YOU ARE TO BE OVER FIVE CITIES.' "

546   *BUT AN IDLE SERVANT IS SCOLDED FOR NOT GETTING MORE INVOLVED (Lk 19:20-23)*

Lk 19:20 "ANOTHER CAME SAYING, 'LORD, BEHOLD, YOUR MINA WHICH I KEPT LAID AWAY IN A CLOTH,

Lk 19:21 FOR I FEARED YOU, BECAUSE YOU ARE A HARD MAN. YOU TAKE UP THAT WHICH YOU DID NOT LAY DOWN, AND REAP THAT WHICH YOU DID NOT SOW.'

Lk 19:22 HE SAID TO HIM, 'OUT OF YOUR OWN MOUTH WILL I JUDGE YOU, YOU WICKED SERVANT! YOU KNEW THAT I AM AN EXACTING MAN, TAKING UP THAT WHICH I DID NOT LAY DOWN, AND REAPING THAT WHICH I DID NOT SOW.

Lk 19:23 THEN WHY DID YOU NOT DEPOSIT MY MONEY IN THE BANK, AND AT MY COMING, I MIGHT HAVE EARNED INTEREST ON IT?' "

547 THOSE WHO DO NOT SERVE THE "LIGHT FROM HEAVEN" WILL BE PUNISHED FOR THEIR LAZINESS (Lk 19:24-28)

Lk 19:24 "HE SAID TO THOSE WHO STOOD BY, 'TAKE THE MINA AWAY FROM HIM, AND GIVE IT TO HIM WHO HAS THE TEN MINAS.'

Lk 19:25 THEY SAID TO HIM, 'LORD, HE HAS TEN MINAS!'

Lk 19:26 'FOR I TELL YOU THAT TO EVERYONE WHO HAS, WILL MORE BE GIVEN. BUT FROM HIM WHO DOES NOT HAVE MUCH, EVEN THAT WHICH HE HAS WILL BE TAKEN AWAY FROM HIM.

Lk 19:27 BUT BRING THOSE ENEMIES OF MINE WHO DID NOT WANT ME TO REIGN OVER THEM HERE, AND KILL THEM BEFORE ME.' "

Lk 19:28 Having said these things, He went on ahead, going up to Jerusalem.

CHAPTER XVI

HIS ROYAL ENTRY INTO JERUSALEM

548 *THE "INDESCRIBABLE LORD" GIVES INSTRUCTIONS IN PREPARATION FOR HIS ENTRANCE INTO THE CAPITAL CITY (taken from Mt 21:1-6; Mk 11:1-7; Lk 19:29-35)*

Mt 21:1 When they drew near to Jerusalem and came to Bethphage, near the Mount of Olives, then Jesus sent two disciples,

Lk 19:30 "GO YOUR WAY INTO THE VILLAGE AHEAD OF YOU, AS YOU ENTER, YOU WILL FIND A DONKEY'S COLT TIED WHEREON NO MAN EVER YET SAT. UNTIE IT AND BRING IT.

Mt 21:3 IF ANYONE SAYS ANYTHING TO YOU. YOU SHALL SAY, 'THE LORD NEEDS IT,' AND IMMEDIATELY HE WILL LET YOU HAVE IT."

549 *THE TWO DISCIPLES BRING THE COLT FOR JESUS TO RIDE ON (Mt 21:6,7; Mk 11:4-6; Lk 19:32-35)*

Lk 19:32 Those who were sent went away, found things just as He had told them.

Lk 19:33 As they were untying the colt, its owners said to them, "Why are you untying my colt?"

Lk 19:34 They said, "The Lord needs it."

Mk 11:6 ...and he let them go.

Lk 19:35 They brought it to Jesus. They threw their cloaks on the colt, and helped Jesus get on.

550 *UNLIKE THE VICTORIOUS ROMAN CONQUERORS POMPOUSLY PARADING BACK INTO ROME, JESUS, THE "HUMBLE LEADER," MAKES A MODEST ENTRY INTO JERUSALEM (Mt 21:4,5; Jn 12:14-16)*

Mt 21:4 All this was done, that it might be fulfilled which was spoken through the prophet, saying,

Mt 21:5   "Tell the daughter of Zion, behold, your King comes to you, humble, and riding on a donkey, on a colt, the foal of a donkey." (Zec 9:9)

Jn 12:16   His disciples did not understand these things at first, but when Jesus was glorified, then they remembered that this had been written about Him, and that they had done these things for Him.

551   MANY WHO HEARD OF THE RAISING OF LAZARUS WANT TO SEE JESUS, THE "RIVER OF LIFE" *(Mt 21:8-11; Mk 11:9-11; Lk 19:36-40; Jn 12:17,18)*

Jn 12:17   Many therefore who were with Him when He called Lazarus out of the tomb and raised him from the dead were testifying about it.

Jn 12:18   For this cause also the people went and met Him, because they heard that He had done this wonder.

Lk 19:37   As He was now getting near, at the descent from the Mount Olives, a great many of His disciples began to rejoice and praise God with a loud voice for all the mighty works which they had seen.

552   THE PEOPLE BEGIN TO HONOR THE "MEEK AND MILD LEADER" AS SENT FROM GOD *(Mt 21:8; Mk 11:8,9; Lk 19:36; Jn 12:13)*

Mt 21:8   A very large crowd spread their clothes on the road. Others cut branches from the palm trees, and spread them on the road.

Jn 12:13   Some took those branches of the palm trees and went out to meet Him, and cried out, "Hosanna! Blessed is He who comes in the name of the Lord, the "King of Israel!" "

Mk 11:9   Those who went in front of Him, and those who followed, cried out, "Hosanna!"

553   THEY ARE UNABLE TO CONTAIN THEMSELVES AS THEY HAIL JESUS AS THEIR KING *(Mt 21:9; Mk 11:10; Lk 19:38)*

Lk 19:38   "Blessed is the King who comes in the name of the Lord! Peace in heaven, and glory in the highest!"

Mk 11:10   "Blessed is the kingdom of our father David. Hosanna in the highest!"

Mt 21:9   ...they kept shouting, "Hosanna to the son of David!" *(Ps 118:26)*

554   HE ENTERS THE CITY WHICH IS OVERJOYED TO RECEIVE HIM (Mt 21:10,11; Jn 12:19)

Mt 21:10   When He had come into Jerusalem, all the city was stirred up, saying, "Who is this?"

Mt 21:11   The people said, "This is the Prophet, Jesus, from Nazareth of Galilee."

Jn 12:19   The Pharisees therefore said among themselves, "See how the whole world is following Him."

555   AS THEIR EXALTING CANNOT BE AVOIDED, JESUS REACHES THE TEMPLE AND OBSERVES WHAT IS GOING ON (Mk 11:11; Lk 19:39,40)

Lk 19:39   Some of the Pharisees from the multitude said to Jesus, "Teacher, rebuke Your disciples!"

Lk 19:40   He answered them, **"I TELL YOU THAT IF THESE WERE SILENT, THE STONES WOULD CRY OUT."**

Mk 11:11   Jesus entered into the temple in Jerusalem. When He had looked around at everything, it being now evening, He went out to Bethany with the twelve.

556   JESUS CURSES A FRUITLESS FIG TREE (Mt 21:18,19; Mk 11:12-14)

Mk 11:12   The next day, when they had come out from Bethany, He was hungry.

Mk 11:13   Seeing a fig tree afar off having leaves He came to see if perhaps He might find fruit on it. When He came to it, He found nothing but leaves, for it was not the season for figs. *(leaves are words; fruits are deeds)*

Mt 21:19   He said to it, **"LET THERE BE NO FRUIT FROM YOU FOREVER!"**

Mk 11:14   Jesus told it, **"MAY NO ONE EVER EAT FRUIT FROM YOU AGAIN!"** and His disciples heard it. *(Israel is often referred to as the fig tree.)*

557   JESUS, THE "MORNING STAR," SHEDS TEARS OVER JERUSALEM (Lk 19:41-44)

Lk 19:41   When He drew near, He saw the city and wept over it,

Lk 19:42   saying, **"IF YOU, EVEN YOU, HAD KNOWN TODAY THE THINGS WHICH COULD BRING YOU PEACE! BUT NOW, THEY ARE HIDDEN FROM YOUR EYES.**

Lk 19:43   FOR THE DAYS WILL COME ON YOU, WHEN YOUR ENEMIES WILL THROW

UP A BARRICADE AGAINST YOU, SURROUND YOU, HEM YOU IN ON EVERY SIDE,

Lk 19:44 AND WILL DASH YOU AND YOUR CHILDREN WITHIN YOU TO THE GROUND. THEY WILL NOT LEAVE IN YOU ONE STONE ON ANOTHER. ALL BECAUSE YOU DID NOT KNOW THE TIME OF MY VISITATION." *(Also see #435)*

558   AN OTHERWISE GENTLE AND LOVING JESUS ANGRILY DRIVES OUT THE PROFITEERS FROM THE TEMPLE A SECOND TIME *(Mt 21:12,13; Mk 11:15-17; Lk 19:45,46)*

Mk 11:15 They came again to Jerusalem, and Jesus entered into the temple and began to drive out those who sold and those who bought in the temple. He overthrew the tables of the money changers, and the seats of those who sold doves.

Mk 11:16 He would not allow anyone to carry even a container through the temple yard.

Mk 11:17 He taught, saying to them, **"IS IT NOT WRITTEN, 'MY HOUSE WILL BE CALLED A HOUSE OF PRAYER FOR ALL NATIONS?' BUT YOU HAVE MADE IT A DEN OF ROBBERS!"** *(Jer 7:11)*

(No one should passively ignore abuses against God, or his fellow man.)

559   OVER THE STUBBORN UNBELIEF OF THE RULERS, THE "LORD OF ALL" HEALS AND TEACHES THOSE HUNGRY FOR HIS MESSAGE *(Mt 21:14; Mk 11:18; Lk 19:47,48)*

Mt 21:14 The blind and the lame came to Him in the temple, and He healed them.

Lk 19:47 He was teaching daily in the temple, but the chief priests and the scribes and the leading men among the people sought to destroy Him.

Lk 19:48 They could not find how they might do it, for all the people hung on to every word that He said.

Mk 11:18 …For they feared Him, because all the people were impressed at His teaching.

560   THE PLAIN AND SIMPLE PRAISE OF CHILDREN IS PLEASING TO GOD *(Mt 21:15-17; Mk 11:19)*

Mt 21:15 But when the chief priests and the scribes saw the wonderful things that He did, and the children cheering in the temple and saying, "Hosanna to the "Son of David," they became bitter,

Mt 21:16 and said to Him, "Do You hear what these are saying?" Jesus said to them, **"YES. DID YOU EVER READ, 'OUT OF THE MOUTH OF BABES AND NURSING BABIES YOU**

HAVE PERFECTED PRAISE?'" *(Ps 8:2)*

Mk 11:19 When evening came, He went out of the city.

561   THE DISCIPLES FIND THE UNFRUITFUL FIG TREE COMPLETELY DRIED UP, TO LEARN MORE ABOUT THEIR "CAPABLE LEADER" (Mt 21:20-22; Mk 11:20,21)

Mk 11:20 As they passed by in the morning, they saw the fig tree withered away from the roots.

Mk 11:21 Peter, remembering, said to Him, "Rabbi, look! The fig tree which You cursed has dried up."

Mt 21:20 When the disciples saw it, they marveled, saying, "How did the fig tree wither away so quickly?"

562   ALLOW GOD'S INFINITE ABILITIES TO FLOW THROUGH YOU BY DEVELOPING YOUR FAITH (Mt 21:21; Mk 11:22,23)

Mk 11:22 Jesus answered them, **"HAVE FAITH IN GOD!**

Mt 21:21 MOST CERTAINLY I TELL YOU, IF YOU HAVE FAITH, YOU WILL NOT ONLY DO WHAT WAS DONE TO THIS FIG TREE, BUT EVEN IF YOU TOLD THIS MOUNTAIN, 'BE TAKEN UP AND CAST YOURSELF INTO THE SEA,'

Mk 11:23 AND DO NOT DOUBT IN YOUR HEART, BUT BELIEVE THAT WHAT YOU SAY IS HAPPENING, IT SHALL GIVEN TO YOU."

563   JESUS, THE "SOURCE OF WISDOM," GIVES A FORMULA FOR CHANGING OBSTACLES INTO STEPPING STONES (Mt 21:22; Mk 11:24-26)

Mk 11:24 "THEREFORE I TELL YOU, ALL THINGS WHATEVER YOU PRAY AND ASK FOR, BELIEVE THAT YOU HAVE RECEIVED THEM, AND YOU SHALL HAVE THEM.

Mk 11:25 WHENEVER YOU STAND TO PRAY, FORGIVE, IF YOU HAVE ANYTHING AGAINST ANYONE, SO THAT YOUR FATHER WHO IS IN HEAVEN, MAY ALSO FORGIVE YOU YOUR TRANSGRESSIONS.

Mk 11:26 BUT IF YOU DO NOT FORGIVE, NEITHER WILL YOUR FATHER IN HEAVEN FORGIVE YOU YOUR TRANSGRESSIONS."

564 *THE AUTHORITY OF JESUS IS AGAIN CHALLENGED BY THE COUNCIL OF RELIGIOUS LEADERS (Mt 21:23-27; Mk 11:27-33; Lk 20:1-8)*

Lk 20:1 It happened on one of those days, as He was teaching the people in the temple and preaching the Good News, that the priests and scribes came to Him with the elders.

Lk 20:2 They asked Him, "Tell us, by what authority do you do these things? Or who is giving You this right?"

Mk 11:29 Jesus said to them, **"I WILL ASK YOU ONE QUESTION. ANSWER ME, AND I WILL TELL YOU BY WHAT AUTHORITY I DO THESE THINGS.**

Mk 11:30 THE BAPTISM OF JOHN, WAS IT FROM HEAVEN, OR FROM MEN? ANSWER ME."

565 *THEY ARE UNABLE TO ANSWER THE QUESTION ABOUT THE ORIGIN OF THE "FOUNTAIN OF HOLINESS" (Mt 21:25-27; Mk 11:31-33; Lk 20:5-8)*

Lk 20:5 They reasoned among themselves, saying, "If we say, 'From heaven,' He will say, 'Why did you not believe Him?'

Lk 20:6 But if we say, 'From men,' all the people will stone us, for they are persuaded that John was a prophet."

Lk 20:7 They answered that they did not know where it was from.

Lk 20:8 Jesus said to them, **"NEITHER WILL I TELL YOU BY WHAT AUTHORITY I DO THESE THINGS."**

566 *JESUS OFFERS THREE PARABLES ON UNFRUITFULNESS, BEGINNING WITH TWO DISRESPECTFUL SONS (Mt 21:28-32)*

Mt 21:28 "BUT WHAT DO YOU THINK? A MAN HAD TWO SONS, AND HE CAME TO THE FIRST, AND SAID, 'SON, GO WORK TODAY IN MY VINEYARD.'

Mt 21:29 HE ANSWERED, 'I WILL NOT,' BUT AFTERWARD HE CHANGED HIS MIND, AND WENT.

Mt 21:30 HE CAME TO THE SECOND, AND SAID THE SAME THING. HE ANSWERED, 'I WILL GO, SIR,' BUT HE DID NOT GO."

567   HE CONTRASTS THE POOR PRACTICES OF THE RELIGIOUS LEADERS WITH TRUE REPENTANCE (Mt 21:31,32)

Mt 21:31 "WHICH OF THE TWO DID THE WILL OF HIS FATHER?" They said to Him, "The first." Jesus said to them, **"MOST CERTAINLY I TELL YOU, THAT THE TAX COLLECTORS AND THE PROSTITUTES ARE ENTERING INTO THE KINGDOM OF GOD BEFORE YOU.**

Mt 21:32 FOR JOHN CAME TO YOU IN THE WAY OF RIGHTEOUSNESS, AND YOU DID NOT BELIEVE HIM, BUT THE TAX COLLECTORS AND THE PROSTITUTES BELIEVED HIM. WHEN YOU SAW IT, YOU DID NOT EVEN REPENT AFTERWARD, THAT YOU MIGHT BELIEVE HIM."

568   A PICTURE STORY SYMBOLIZING THEIR REJECTION OF THE "SOVEREIGN LORD" IS TOLD (Mt 21:33-46; Mk 12:1-12; Lk 20:9-19)

Mt 21:33 "HEAR ANOTHER PARABLE. THERE WAS A MAN WHO WAS A MASTER OF A HOUSEHOLD, WHO PLANTED A VINEYARD, PUT A HEDGE ABOUT IT, DUG A WINEPRESS IN IT, BUILT A TOWER, LEASED IT OUT TO FARMERS, AND WENT INTO ANOTHER COUNTRY.

Mt 21:34 WHEN THE HARVEST SEASON DREW NEAR, HE SENT HIS SERVANTS TO THE FARMERS, TO RECEIVE HIS SHARE.

Mt 21:35 THE FARMERS TOOK HIS SERVANTS, BEAT ONE, KILLED ANOTHER, AND STONED ANOTHER.

Mt 21:36 AGAIN, HE SENT OTHER SERVANTS MORE THAN THE FIRST, AND THEY TREATED THEM THE SAME WAY."

569   EVEN THE AUTHORITY OF THE VERY SON OF GOD IS DENIED IN THEIR ATTEMPT TO MAINTAIN THEIR OWN KINGDOM (Mt 21:37-39; Mk 12:6-8; Lk 20:15-17)

Mt 21:37 "BUT AFTERWARD HE SENT THEM HIS OWN SON *(Jesus)* **SAYING, 'SURELY THEY WILL RESPECT MY SON.'**

Mt 21:38 BUT THE FARMERS, WHEN THEY SAW THE SON, SAID AMONG THEMSELVES, 'THIS IS THE HEIR. COME, LET'S KILL HIM, AND SEIZE HIS INHERITANCE.'

Mt 21:39 SO THEY TOOK HIM, AND THREW HIM OUT OF THE VINEYARD, AND KILLED HIM."

570 THEIR RENUNCIATION BRINGS ABOUT THE OWNER'S ANGER AND OPENS AN INVITATION TO OTHER PEOPLE (Mt 21:40-46; Mk 12:9-12; Lk 20:13-19)

Mt 21:40 "WHEN THEREFORE THE LORD OF THE VINEYARD COMES, WHAT WILL HE DO TO THOSE FARMERS?"

Mt 21:41 They told Him, "He will mercilessly destroy those wicked men, and will lease out the vineyard to other farmers, who will give him the rent money in its season."

Mt 21:42 Jesus said to them, **"DID YOU EVER READ IN THE SCRIPTURES, THE STONE WHICH THE BUILDERS REJECTED, THE SAME WAS MADE THE CHIEF CORNER STONE. THIS IS FROM THE LORD. IT IS MARVELOUS IN OUR EYES?"**

571 THOSE WHO TURN AWAY FROM JESUS AND ALL HE STANDS FOR WILL LOSE THEIR STATUS (Mt 21:43-46; Mk 12:14; Lk 20:18,19)

Lk 20:18 "EVERYONE WHO FALLS ON THAT STONE WILL BE BROKEN TO PIECES, AND IT WILL CRUSH WHOMEVER IT FALLS ON TO DUST.

Mt 21:43 THEREFORE I TELL YOU, THE KINGDOM OF GOD WILL BE TAKEN AWAY FROM YOU, AND WILL BE GIVEN TO A NATION BRINGING FORTH ITS FRUIT."

Lk 20:19 The chief priests and the scribes sought to lay hands on Him that very hour, for they knew He had spoken this parable against them.

Mt 21:46 Though they sought to seize Him, they feared the multitudes, because the crowd considered Him to be a prophet.

572 GOD EXTENDS AN OPEN INVITATION TO THE WEDDING FEAST OF HIS OWN DEAR SON (Mt 22:1-14; Lk 14:15-24)

Mt 22:1 Jesus answered and spoke again in a parable to them, saying,

Mt 22:2 "THE KINGDOM OF HEAVEN IS LIKE A CERTAIN KING, WHO PREPARED A MARRIAGE FEAST FOR HIS SON,

Mt 22:3 AND SENT OUT HIS SERVANTS TO CALL THOSE WHO WERE INVITED TO THE MARRIAGE FEAST. BUT THEY WOULD NOT COME."

573   THE LORD PERSISTS IN HIS INVITATION WHICH IS NOT ACCEPTED BY THOSE WHO ARE PRIVILEGED AND TOO BUSY TO ATTEND (Mt 22:4,5; Lk 14:18-20)

Mt 22:4   "AGAIN HE SENT OUT OTHER SERVANTS, SAYING, 'TELL THOSE WHO ARE INVITED, "BEHOLD, I HAVE PREPARED MY DINNER. MY CATTLE AND MY FATLINGS ARE KILLED, AND ALL THINGS ARE READY. COME TO THE MARRIAGE FEAST!'

Lk 14:18   THEY ALL BEGAN TO MAKE EXCUSES. "THE FIRST SAID TO HIM, 'I HAVE BOUGHT A FIELD, AND I MUST GO AND SEE IT. PLEASE HAVE ME EXCUSED.'

Lk 14:19   ANOTHER SAID, 'I HAVE BOUGHT FIVE YOKE OF OXEN, AND I MUST GO TRY THEM OUT. PLEASE HAVE ME EXCUSED.' "

Lk 14:20   "ANOTHER SAID, 'I HAVE MARRIED A WIFE, AND THEREFORE I CANNOT COME.' "

574   GOD DESTROYS THOSE WHO IGNORE HIS OFFER AND WHO ABUSE HIS MESSENGERS (Mt 22:6,7; Lk 14:20)

Mt 22:6   "AND THEY GRABBED HIS SERVANTS, AND TREATED THEM SHAMEFULLY, AND KILLED THEM.

Mt 22:7   WHEN THE KING HEARD ABOUT THAT, HE WAS ANGRY, AND SENT HIS ARMIES, DESTROYED THOSE MURDERERS, AND BURNED THEIR CITY."
(as happened in 70 A.D.)

575   THE REFUSAL BY HIS OWN PEOPLE CAUSES THE KING TO EXTEND A UNIVERSAL APPEAL TO ALL (Mt 22:8,9; Lk 14:21)

Mt 22:8   "THEN HE SAID TO HIS SERVANTS, 'THE WEDDING IS READY, BUT THOSE WHO WERE INVITED WERE NOT WORTHY.

Mt 22:9   GO THEREFORE TO THE HIGHWAYS, AND AS MANY AS YOU MAY FIND, INVITE TO THE MARRIAGE FEAST.

Lk 14:21 GO OUT QUICKLY INTO THE STREETS AND LANES OF THE CITY, AND BRING IN THE POOR, THE CRIPPLED, THE BLIND, AND LAME.' "

576   EVEN THE MOST UNLIKELY SHALL RECEIVE THEIR BLESSINGS WHILE THOSE PREVIOUSLY INVITED WILL BE LEFT OUT (Mt 22:10; Lk 14:22-24)

Lk 14:22 "THE SERVANT SAID, 'LORD, IT IS DONE AS YOU COMMANDED, AND THERE IS STILL ROOM.'

Lk 14:23 THE LORD SAID TO THE SERVANT, 'GO OUT INTO THE HIGHWAYS AND HEDGES, AND <u>COMPEL</u> THEM TO COME IN, THAT MY HOUSE MAY BE FILLED.

Lk 14:24 FOR I TELL YOU THAT NONE OF THOSE MEN WHO WERE INVITED WILL TASTE OF MY SUPPER.'"

577   A SEVERE PENALTY IS GIVEN THOSE WHO THROUGH THEIR OWN NEGLECT DO NOT COME SPIRITUALLY PREPARED (Mt 22:11-14)

Mt 22:11 "BUT WHEN THE KING CAME IN TO SEE THE GUESTS, HE SAW THERE A MAN WHO DID NOT HAVE ON PROPER WEDDING CLOTHING,

Mt 22:12 AND HE SAID TO HIM, 'FRIEND, HOW DID YOU COME IN HERE NOT WEARING WEDDING CLOTHING?' HE WAS SPEECHLESS.

Mt 22:13 THEN THE KING SAID TO THE SERVANTS, 'BIND HIM HAND AND FOOT, TAKE HIM AWAY, AND THROW HIM INTO OUTER DARKNESS, THERE IS WHERE THE WEEPING AND GRINDING OF TEETH WILL BE.'

Mt 22:14 FOR MANY ARE CALLED, BUT FEW ARE CHOSEN."

578   VARIOUS OFFICIALS THEN COME TO THE "TREASURE OF TRUTH" WITH CLEVER QUESTIONS HOPING TO HAVE HIM SLIP UP (Mt 22:15-22; Mk 12:13-17; Lk 20:20-26)

Mk 12:13 They sent some of the Pharisees and of the Herodians to Him...

Lk 20:20 They watched Him, and sent out spies, who pretended to be righteous, that they might trap Him in something He said, so as to deliver Him up to the power and authority of the governor.

Mk 12:14 When they had come, they asked Him, "Teacher, we know that You are honest, and do not fear anyone, and You are not partial to anyone, but truly teach the way of God. Is it lawful to pay taxes to Caesar, or not?"

579   JESUS TELLS US TO OBEY MAN-MADE AS WELL AS GOD'S LAW (Mt 22:18-22; Mk 12:15-17; Lk 20:23-26)

Mk 12:15 "Shall we give, or shall we not give?" But He, knowing their hypocrisy, said to them, **"WHY DO YOU TEST ME? BRING ME A DENARIUS, THAT I MAY SEE IT."**

Mk 12:16 They brought it. He said to them, **"WHOSE IS THIS IMAGE AND INSCRIPTION?"** They said to Him, "Caesar's."

Mk 12:17 Jesus answered them, **"RENDER TO CAESAR THE THINGS THAT ARE CAESAR'S, AND TO GOD THE THINGS THAT ARE GOD'S."**

Lk 20:26 They were not able to trap Him in His words before the people. They marveled at His answer, and became silent.

580   THE PRACTICAL SADDUCEES ASK ABOUT MARRIAGE IN A LIFE AFTER DEATH IN WHICH THEY DO NOT BELIEVE (Mt 22:23-33; Mk 12:18-23; Lk 20:27-40)

Mt 22:23 On that day the Sadducees, those who say that there is no resurrection, came to Him. They asked Him,

Mt 22:24 saying, "Teacher, Moses said, 'If a man dies, having no children, his brother shall marry his wife, and raise up children for his brother.' *(Deut 25:5)*

Mt 22:25 Now there were seven brothers. The first married and died, and having no children left his wife to his brother.

Mt 22:26 In the same way, the second also, and the third, to the seventh.

Mt 22:27 After them all, the woman died.

Mt 22:28 In the resurrection, therefore, whose wife will she be of the seven? For they all had married her."

581   JESUS SHOWS UP THEIR LACK OF KNOWLEDGE ABOUT HEAVEN WHICH HAS NO PHYSICAL NECESSITIES (Mt 22:29,30; Mk 12:24,25; Lk 20:34-36)

Mk 12:24 Jesus answered them, **"IS IT BECAUSE YOU ARE MISTAKEN AND DO NOT KNOW THE SCRIPTURES, NOR THE POWER OF GOD?"**

Lk 20:34 Jesus said to them, **"THE CHILDREN OF THIS AGE MARRY, AND ARE GIVEN IN MARRIAGE.**

Lk 20:35 BUT THOSE WHO ARE CONSIDERED WORTHY TO ATTAIN TO THAT WORLD AND THE RESURRECTION FROM THE DEAD, NEITHER MARRY, NOR ARE GIVEN IN MARRIAGE.

Lk 20:36 FOR THEY CANNOT DIE ANY MORE, FOR THEY ARE LIKE THE ANGELS, AND ARE CHILDREN OF GOD, BEING CHILDREN OF NEW LIFE."

582   HE PINPOINTS WHERE THE INSPIRED WORD OF GOD SAYS THAT THOSE WHO ARE DECEASED ARE STILL LIVING (Mt 22:31,32; Mk 12:26,27; Lk 20:37,38)

Mt 22:31 "BUT CONCERNING THE RESURRECTION OF THE DEAD...

Mk 12:26 ...HAVE YOU NOT READ IN THE BOOK OF MOSES, ABOUT THE BUSH, WHEN GOD SPOKE TO HIM, SAYING, 'I AM THE GOD OF ABRAHAM, THE GOD OF ISAAC, AND THE GOD OF JACOB?' *(Ex 3:6)*

Lk 20:38 NOW, HE IS NOT THE GOD OF THE DEAD, BUT OF THE LIVING, FOR ALL ARE ALIVE TO HIM.

Mk 12:27 ...YOU ARE THEREFORE BADLY MISTAKEN."

583   JESUS, "OUR CONFIDENCE," SUCCEEDS IN SILENCING THE SADDUCEES (Mt 22:33,34; Lk 20:39,40)

Mt 22:33   When the multitudes heard it, they were moved by His teaching.

Lk 20:39   Some of the scribes answered, "Teacher, You speak well."

Mt 22:34   But the Pharisees, when they heard that He had silenced the Sadducees, gathered themselves together.

584   A TEACHER OF THE LAW MAKES ONE LAST ATTEMPT BY ASKING ABOUT THE MOST IMPORTANT COMMANDMENT (Mt 22:35-40; Mk 12:28-30)

Mt 22:35   One of them, a lawyer, asked Him a question, testing Him.

Mt 22:36   "Teacher, which is the greatest commandment in the law?"

585   NO COMMANDMENT EXCEEDS THAT OF LOVING GOD *(Mt 22:37,38; Mk 12:29,30; Lk 10:27,28)*

Mk 12:29 Jesus answered, **"THE GREATEST IS THIS, 'HEAR, O ISRAEL, THE LORD OUR GOD, <u>THE LORD IS ONE</u>,'** *(said by devout Jews daily, and repeated by Jesus, "Shma Israel, Adonai Elohenu, Adonai Echad.")*

Mk 12:30 YOU SHALL LOVE THE LORD YOUR GOD WITH ALL YOUR HEART, AND WITH ALL YOUR SOUL, AND WITH ALL YOUR MIND, AND WITH ALL YOUR STRENGTH.' *(Deut 6:5)*

Mt 22:38 THIS IS THE FIRST AND GREAT COMMANDMENT."

586   AND THE LOVE OF GOD IS COMPARABLE TO THE LOVE OF NEIGHBOR *(Mt 22:39,40; Mk 12:31)*

Mt 22:39 "THE SECOND IS LIKE UNTO IT, 'YOU SHALL LOVE YOUR NEIGHBOR AS YOURSELF.' *(Lev 19:18)*

Mt 22:40 THE WHOLE LAW AND THE PROPHETS DEPEND ON THESE TWO COMMANDMENTS.

Mk 12:31 THERE IS NO OTHER COMMANDMENT GREATER THAN THESE."

587   A SCRIBE'S UNDERSTANDING OF GOD'S COMMANDMENTS BRINGS HIM CLOSE TO THE KINGDOM OF HEAVEN *(Mk 12:32-24)*

Mk 12:32 The scribe said to Him, "Truly, teacher, You have said well that God is One, and there is none other but He,

Mk 12:33 and to love Him with all our heart, and with all our understanding, with all our soul, and with all our strength. And to love our neighbor as ourself. These are more important than all burnt offerings and sacrifices."

Mk 12:34 When Jesus saw that he answered wisely, He said to him, **"YOU ARE NOT FAR FROM THE KINGDOM OF GOD."**

588   JESUS, THE "BLESSED LORD," THEN ASKS A QUESTION ABOUT DAVID'S SON AND ABOUT DAVID'S LORD *(Mt 22:41-46; Mk 12:35-37; Lk 20:41-44)*

Mt 22:41 Now while the Pharisees were gathered together, Jesus asked them a question,

Mt 22:42 saying, **"WHAT DO YOU THINK OF THE CHRIST? WHOSE SON IS HE?"** They said to Him, "Of David."

Mt 22:43 He said to them, **"HOW THEN DOES DAVID, IN THE SPIRIT, CALL HIM LORD?"**

589　　*THE "ELOQUENT TEACHER" SILENCES THOSE WHO SOUGHT TO HARASS HIM (Mt 22:44-46; Mk 12:36,37; Lk 20:42-44)*

Lk 20:42 **"DAVID HIMSELF SAYS IN THE BOOK OF PSALMS, 'THE LORD SAID TO MY LORD, SIT AT MY RIGHT HAND,** *(Ps 110:1)*

Lk 20:43 **UNTIL I MAKE YOUR ENEMIES A FOOTSTOOL FOR YOUR FEET.'**

Mt 22:45 **IF THEN DAVID CALLS HIM LORD, HOW IS HE HIS SON?"**

Mt 22:46 No one was able to answer Him a word, neither did any man dare ask Him any more questions from that day forth.

590　　*JESUS ENDORSES THEIR INTERPRETATIONS OF HOLY SCRIPTURE, BUT CRITICIZES THEIR BEHAVIOR AND BAD EXAMPLE (Mt 23:1-12; Lk 20:45-47)*

Mt 23:1 Then Jesus spoke to the multitudes and to His disciples,

Mt 23:2 saying, **"THE SCRIBES AND THE PHARISEES SIT ON MOSES' SEAT.**

Mt 23:3 **ALL THINGS, THEREFORE, WHATEVER THEY TELL YOU TO OBSERVE, OBSERVE AND DO. BUT DO NOT DO THEIR WORKS, FOR THEY SAY, AND DO NOT DO."**

591　　*THEY ABUSE OTHERS AND MAKE RELIGION A BURDEN WHILE EXEMPTING THEMSELVES (Mt 23:4; Mk 12:40; Lk 20:47)*

Mk 12:40 **"THESE ARE THOSE WHO DEVOUR WIDOWS' HOUSES, AND FOR A PRETENSE MAKE LONG PRAYERS. THESE WILL RECEIVE THE GREATER CONDEMNATION.**

Mt 23:4 **FOR THEY BIND HEAVY BURDENS THAT ARE GRIEVOUS TO BE CARRIED, AND LAY THEM ON MEN'S SHOULDERS. BUT THEY THEMSELVES WILL NOT LIFT A FINGER TO HELP THEM."**

592   THEY ARE ALSO GUILTY OF PRETENTIOUS SHOWMANSHIP IN THEIR SELF-EXALTED VANITY (Mt 23:5-7; Mk 12:38,39; Lk 20:46)

Mt 23:5   "ALL THEIR WORKS THEY DO TO BE SEEN BY MEN. THEY MAKE BROAD THEIR PHYLACTERIES *(a collection of scriptures which they carry),* **ENLARGE THE FRINGES OF THEIR GARMENTS,**

Mt 23:6   AND LOVE THE PLACE OF HONOR AT FEASTS, THE BEST SEATS IN THE SYNAGOGUES,

Mt 23:7   THE SALUTATIONS IN THE MARKETPLACES, AND TO BE CALLED 'RABBI, RABBI' BY MEN."

> *Mic 6:8 ...what doth the Lord require of thee, but to do justly, to love mercy, and to walk humbly with thy God?*

593   THE "HOLY WORD OF GOD" CAUTIONS EVERYONE TO BE HUMBLE BY NOT ACCEPTING CERTAIN TITLES RESERVED FOR THE HOLY TRINITY (Mt 23:8-12)

Mt 23:9   "CALL NO MAN ON EARTH YOUR FATHER, FOR ONE IS YOUR FATHER, HE WHO IS IN HEAVEN. *(Jehovah Abba)*

Mt 23:10 NEITHER BE CALLED MASTERS, FOR ONE IS YOUR MASTER, THE CHRIST. *(Yeshua Ha Meshiach)*

Mt 23:8   DO NOT YOU BE CALLED 'RABBI,' FOR ONE IS YOUR TEACHER *(the Holy Spirit—Ruach Ha Kodesh)* **AND ALL OF YOU ARE BROTHERS."**

> *(As told to me when I was much younger; "If you have even a single thought about God, you are already on the road to becoming a theologian.")*

594   HUMILITY, AND SUBMISSION TO OTHERS, ARE THE CHIEF ATTRIBUTES OF THOSE WHO CHOOSE TO SERVE JESUS (Mt 23:11,12)

Mt 23:11   "BUT HE WHO IS GREATEST AMONG YOU MUST BE YOUR SERVANT.

Mt 23:12 WHOEVER EXALTS HIMSELF WILL BE HUMBLED, AND WHOEVER HUMBLES HIMSELF WILL BE EXALTED."

595   JESUS COMPARES THE GIFTS OF THOSE WHO GIVE FROM THEIR SURPLUS TO ONE WHO GIVES OUT OF HER OWN NEEDS (Mk 12:41-44; Lk 21:1-4)

Mk 12:41 Jesus sat down opposite the treasury, and saw how the multitude cast money into the collection box. Many who were rich cast in much.

Mk 12:42 A poor widow came, and she cast in two small brass coins, which equal a penny.

Mk 12:43 He called His disciples to Himself, and said to them, **"MOST CERTAINLY I TELL YOU, THIS POOR WIDOW GAVE MORE THAN ALL THOSE WHO ARE GIVING INTO THE TREASURY.**

Lk 21:4   FOR ALL THESE PUT IN GIFTS FOR GOD FROM THEIR ABUNDANCE, BUT SHE, OUT OF HER POVERTY, PUT IN ALL THAT SHE HAD TO LIVE ON."

Acts 20:35 ...It is more blessed to give than to receive.

CHAPTER XVII

THE OLIVET DISCOURSE

This "End-of-Time" chapter is often referred to as the "Olivet Discourse." It is a discourse because it begins with a give-and-take discussion between Jesus and His disciples. It is called the Olivet Discourse because it takes place on the Mount of Olives.

This portion is part of an earlier project in which some attempt was made on my part to further amplify the words of Jesus, by inserting numerous explanatory remarks (in parentheses). Also included are more cross-references than usual from other parts of the Bible, to elaborate and endorse each paragraph, or main point being made.

As you will see, this is an advanced teaching intended for mature Christians, which may explain why Jesus gave it to us so late in His gospel drama. This is offered in the original King James Version (KJV), before we started using the World English Bible (WEB) which you have been reading.

Jesus speaks in this chapter of the coming last seven years of man's existence on earth such as we know it. This is a most difficult time of suffering known as the "Tribulation" period. In the last couple centuries there has developed a new theory that the Christian will be "raptured" into glory before that terrible time comes upon us. Those who share this opinion are referred to as "pre-trib believers." There are others who believe in the post-tribulation "catching away" of the saints—that the believers will actually go through those troublesome days, to be raptured only at the end. These call themselves "post-tribbers."

Both groups believe that a rapture will take place, but disagree on its timing. I have precious dear friends in opposing camps who are insistent about their separate view points. But whether it is "pre," or "post," this chapter is dedicated to searching out what Jesus has to say on this topic. And He does address the subject of "the timing" of the rapture in this section.

As you will learn, Jesus seems to lean towards a post-tribulation rapture in this Olivet Discourse. So many people have heard only the pre-trib rapture position all their lives that it may be difficult to recognize any other opinion. So…may I request that as you read this portion, that you "assume" and "presume" a post-tribulation point of view for now, and go along with the Lord's very words. In the end you will be free to form your own opinion.

Years ago I was writing a book about the End-of-Times, and the timing of the rapture, which is now being condensed for you here, in this chapter XVII.

596   JESUS WITHDRAWS FROM THE LAVISH TEMPLE REBUILT BY HEROD TO PACIFY THE JEWS *(taken from Mt 24:1; Mk 13:1; Lk 21:5)*

Mt 24:1 And Jesus went out, and departed from the temple. His disciples came to Him to show Him the buildings of the temple.

Mk13:1   …one of His disciples saith unto Him, see what manner of stones and what buildings are here!

Lk 21:5 And as some spake of the temple, how it was adorned with goodly *(colorful)* stones and gifts…

> *1 Ki 8:27…behold, the heaven and heaven of heavens cannot contain Thee, how much less this house that I have builded.*

597   JESUS, THE "GREATEST PROPHET," MAKES A STARTLING PREDICTION ABOUT THEIR TEMPLE'S ABSOLUTE DESTRUCTION *(Mt 24:2; Mk 13:2; Lk 21:6)*

Mk 13:2   And Jesus answering said unto him, **"SEEST THOU THESE GREAT BUILDINGS?**…

Mt 24:2   …**VERILY I SAY UNTO YOU…** *(I tell you solemnly)*

Lk 21:6   **AS FOR THESE THINGS WHICH YE BEHOLD, THE DAYS WILL COME, IN WHICH THERE SHALL NOT BE LEFT ONE STONE UPON ANOTHER, THAT SHALL NOT BE** *(separated and)* **THROWN DOWN."** *(as happened 40 years later)*

> *1 Cor 3:16 Know ye not that ye are the temple of God, and that the Spirit of God dwelleth in you?*

598   HIS EARLIEST AND MOST EXPERIENCED DISCIPLES ARE PROMPTED TO ASK A MULTIPLE PART QUESTION ABOUT THE NEAR AND DISTANT FUTURE *(Mt 24:3; Mk 13:3,4; Lk 21:7)*

Mk 13:3   And later as He sat upon the Mount of Olives, over against *(across from)* the temple, Peter and James, John and Andrew, asked Him privately…

Lk 21:7   saying, "Master…

Mk 13:4   tell us, (1) when shall these things be?

Lk 21:7   and (2) what sign will there be when these things come to pass?

Mt 24:3   …and (3) what shall be the sign *(indication)* of Thy coming? *(return to earth)* and (4) of the end of the world?"

> Jer 33:3 Call unto me, and I will answer thee, and show thee great and mighty things, which thou knowest not.
>
> Dan 2:28 But there is a God in heaven who revealeth secrets, and maketh known... what shall be in the latter days...

599   JESUS STARTS BY CAUTIONING THEM ABOUT MANY SELF-PROCLAIMED SAVIORS AS THE FIRST SIGN (Mt 24:5; Mk 13:5,6; Lk 21:8)

Mk 13:5   And Jesus answering them began to say, "**TAKE HEED** *(be cautious)* **LEST ANY MAN DECEIVE YOU.**

Mt 24:5   **FOR MANY** *(misleading impersonators)* **SHALL COME IN MY NAME, SAYING 'I AM CHRIST'** *(the Messiah)* **AND SHALL DECEIVE** *(fool)* **MANY.**

Lk 21:8   **...AND 'THE TIME** *(the end of the world)* **DRAWETH NEAR.' GO YE NOT THEREFORE AFTER** *(do not follow)* **THEM."**

> *1 Jn 2:18 Little children, it is the last time, and as ye have heard that Anti-Christ shall come, even now are there many anti-christs, whereby we know that it is the last days.*
>
> *2 Jn 1:7 For many deceivers are entered into the world, who confess not that Jesus Christ is come in the flesh. This is a deceiver and an anti-christ.*

600   BELIEVERS ARE NOT TO FEAR WARS AND REBELLIONS, WHICH ARE MERELY EARLY INDICATIONS OF THE END (Mt 24:6; Mk 13:7; Lk 21:9)

Mk 13:7   "**AND WHEN YE SHALL HEAR OF WARS, AND RUMORS OF WARS...**

Lk 21:9   **...AND COMMOTIONS,** *(civil disturbances)* **BE NOT TERRIFIED** *(scared)* **FOR THESE THINGS** *(conflicts)* **MUST FIRST COME TO PASS...**

Mt 24:6   **...BUT THE END IS NOT YET."** *(not immediate)*

> *2 Tim 3:1 Know this also, that in the last days perilous (dangerous) times shall come.*

601   BUT MAJOR WARS, ACCOMPANIED BY EARTH-SHAKING DISASTERS WHICH ARE NOT MAN-MADE, WILL BE OUR ACTUAL CLUES AS TO THE VERY BEGINNING OF THE END (Mt 24:7,8; Mk 13:8; Lk 21:10,11)

Lk 21:10   Then said He unto them, "**NATION SHALL RISE AGAINST** *(attack)* **NATION, AND KINGDOM AGAINST KINGDOM,**

Lk 21:11 AND GREAT *(violent)* EARTHQUAKES SHALL BE IN DIVERS *(various)* PLACES, AND FAMINES *(mass starvation)* PESTILENCES *(deadly epidemics)*, AND FEARFUL SIGHTS AND GREAT SIGNS *(cosmic phenomena)* SHALL THERE BE FROM HEAVEN.

> *Joel 2:30 And I will show wonders in the heavens and in the earth, blood, and fire, and pillars of smoke.*

> *Pr 3:24-26 When thou liest down, thou shalt not be afraid; yea, thou shalt lie down, and thy sleep shall be sweet...Be not afraid of sudden fear, neither of the desolation of the wicked, when it cometh...For the Lord shall be thy confidence, and shall keep thy foot from being taken.*

Mt 24:8 ALL THESE *(this combination)* ARE *(just)* THE BEGINNING OF SORROWS." *(the beginning of the Tribulation)*

> *Dan 11:32 ...but the people who do know their God shall be strong, and do exploits.*

> *Ps 91:3,5,7,10,11 Surely he shall deliver thee from the snare of the fowler and from the noisesome pestilence...Thou shalt not be afraid of the terror by night, nor of the arrow that flieth by day...A thousand shall fall at thy side, and ten thousand at thy right hand, but it shall not come nigh thee...There shall no evil befall thee, neither shall any plague come nigh thy dwelling place...For He shall give His angels charge over thee...*

602 *JESUS ALERTS HIS FAITHFUL FOLLOWERS TO EXPECT RELIGIOUS AND SECULAR TRIALS AND MISTREATMENT (Mk 13:9; Lk 21:12)*

Mk 13:9 "BUT TAKE HEED *(be advised)* TO YOURSLEVES, FOR...

Lk 21:12 ...BEFORE ALL THESE, THEY SHALL LAY HANDS ON *(arrest)* YOU, AND PERSECUTE *(oppress)* YOU, DELIVERING *(dragging)* YOU UP TO THE SYNAGOGUES AND INTO PRISONS...

Mk 13:9 ...THEY SHALL DELIVER YOU UP TO THE COUNCILS *(civil courts)* AND IN THE SYNAGOGUES *(houses of worship)* YE SHALL BE BEATEN..."

> *Jn 16:2 They shall put you out of the synagogues, yea, the time cometh, that whosoever killeth you will think that he doeth God service.*

> *Rev 2:10 Fear none of those things which thou shalt suffer: behold, the devil shall cast some of you into prison, that ye may be tried; and ye shall have tribulation ten days. Be thou faithful unto death, and I will give thee a crown of life.*

> *2 Tim 3:12 Yea, and all that will live godly in Christ Jesus shall suffer persecution.*

603 BELIEVERS WILL BE GIVEN AN OPPORTUNITY TO DECLARE WHERE THEY STAND REGARDING THEIR "LORD AND SAVIOR" (Mk 13:9,10; Lk 21:13)

Mk 13:9 "...AND YE SHALL BE BROUGHT BEFORE RULERS AND KINGS *(highest authorities)* **FOR MY SAKE...** *(on my account)*

Lk 21:13 AND IT SHALL TURN TO YOU *(your opportunity)* **FOR A TESTIMONY** *(to bear witness)*

Mk 13:9 ...AGAINST THEM. *(against their lifestyle)*

Rev 12:11 And they overcame him (Satan) by the blood of the lamb (Jesus), and by the word of their testimony, and they loved not their lives unto the death.

Ezek 33:9 Nevertheless, if thou warn the wicked of his way to turn from it, if he does not turn from his ways, he shall die in his iniquity, but thou hast delivered thy soul.

Mk 13:10 AND THE GOSPEL *(Good News)* **MUST FIRST BE PUBLISHED** *(preached)* **AMONG ALL NATIONS."** *(throughout the world)*

Jn 9:4 "I must work the works of Him that sent me, while it is day, the night cometh, when no man can work.

604 CHRISTIANS ARE TO MAINTAIN THEIR COMPOSURE BY TRUSTING AND RELYING ON THE HOLY SPIRIT TO GUIDE THEM, TO CONVINCE AND TO CONVICT OTHERS (Mk 13:11; Lk 21:14,15)

Mk 13:11 "BUT WHEN THEY SHALL LEAD YOU, AND DELIVER YOU UP *(to trial)* **TAKE NO THOUGHT** *(do not worry)* **BEFOREHAND WHAT YE SHALL SPEAK, NEITHER DO YE PREMEDITATE.** *(practice)* **BUT WHATSOEVER SHALL BE GIVEN** *(occur to)* **YOU IN THAT HOUR, THAT SPEAK YE.** *(simply say)* **FOR IT IS NOT YE THAT SPEAK, BUT THE HOLY GHOST.** *(speaking through you)*

Lk 21:14 SETTLE IT THEREFORE IN YOUR HEARTS NOT TO MEDITATE *(rehearse)* **BEFORE WHAT YE SHALL ANSWER...** *(in your defense)*

Lk 21:15 FOR I WILL GIVE YOU A MOUTH *(an eloquence)* **AND** *(divine)* **WISDOM WHICH ALL YOUR ADVERSARIES** *(opponents)* **SHALL NOT BE ABLE TO GAINSAY** *(contradict)* **NOR RESIST."**

Jer 1:17,19 Thou therefore gird up thy loins, and arise, and speak unto them all that I command thee. Be not dismayed at their faces, lest I confound thee before them...And they shall fight against thee, but they shall not prevail against thee, for I am with thee, saith the Lord, to deliver thee.

(Elaborating remarks in parentheses, such as in this chapter, along with cross-references (X-refs) can be added by just about anyone, to amplify the entire Gospels.)

605   UNLIKE INTERNATIONAL CONFLICTS AND CIVIL WARS, THE FINAL STRUGGLE BECOMES MUCH MORE <u>INDIVIDUAL AND PERSONAL</u> *(Mt 24:9; Mk 13:12; Lk 21:16)*

Mk 13:12 "NOW *(even)* **THE BROTHER SHALL BETRAY** *(turn in)* **THE BROTHER TO DEATH, AND THE FATHER THE** *(his own)* **SON, AND CHILDREN SHALL RISE UP AGAINST** *(defy)* **THEIR PARENTS, AND SHALL CAUSE THEM TO BE PUT TO DEATH.** *(not the Muslim Jihadist, but closer to home than that)*

Lk 21:16 AND YE SHALL BE BETRAYED *(sold out)* **BOTH BY PARENTS, AND BRETHREN, AND KINSFOLKS, AND FRIENDS…** *(All of this over where each person stands, for, or against Christ.)*

> *Mt 10:34, 36 Think not that I am come to send peace on earth, I came not to send peace, but a sword…And a man's foes shall be they of his own household.*
>
> *Lk 12:52 For, from henceforth there shall be five in one house divided, three against two, and two against three.*
>
> *Rev 12:13,17 And when the dragon saw that he was cast unto the earth, he persecuted the woman which brought forth the "Man Child"…he went to make war with the remnant of her seed, which keep the commandments of God, and have the testimony of Jesus Christ. (obviously referring to Christians)*
>
> *1 Th 3:4 For verily, when we were with you, we told you before that we should suffer tribulation…*
>
> *Jn 16:12 I have yet many things to say unto you, but ye cannot bear them now.*

Mt 24:9   THEN SHALL THEY DELIVER YOU UP *(throughout this discourse Jesus stresses the word <u>you</u> which must be referring to us, and not to late converts)* **TO BE AFFLICTED.** *(abused)*

> *2 Cor 4:8,9 We are troubled on every side, yet not distressed; we are perplexed, but not in despair…persecuted, but not forsaken, cast down but not destroyed.*
>
> *Ps 34:19 Many are the afflictions of the righteous, but the Lord will deliver you out of them all.*
>
> *Dan 7:21,22 I beheld, and the same horn made war with the saints, and prevailed against them; until the Ancient of Days came, and judgment was given to the saints*

of the most High; and the time came that the saints possessed the kingdom.

Jn 16:33 ...in the world ye shall have tribulation, but be of good cheer, I have overcome the world.

Lk 21:16 ...AND SOME OF YOU (*told even to His foremost disciples*) **SHALL THEY CAUSE TO BE PUT TO DEATH."**

Ps 116:15 Precious in the sight of the Lord is the death of His saints.

Rev 14:15 ...Thrust in thy sickle, and reap: for the time is come for thee to reap; for the harvest of the earth is ripe.

Rev 14:13 ...Blessed are the dead which die in the Lord from henceforth; Yea saith the Spirit, that they may rest from their labors; and their works do follow them.

Mt 10:28 And fear not them which kill the body, but are not able to kill the soul, but rather fear Him which is able to destroy both soul and body in hell.

Rev 20:4 ...and I saw the souls of them that were beheaded for the witness of Jesus, and for the word of God, and which had not worshipped the beast (the Anti-Christ), neither his image, neither had received his mark upon their foreheads, or in their hands...

(According to this belated Rev 20:4, Christians must still be in the Tribulation because the beast and his mark do not come along, except in the Tribulation!)

(And furthermore, very late in Revelation, we find that the very next verse, Rev 20:5, goes on to say "...This is the first resurrection." If we are to believe our Bibles, and this is indeed the first resurrection, then there could not have been an earlier one, at the beginning of the Tribulation!)

Rev 7:14 ...These are they which came out of great Tribulation, and have washed their robes, and made them white in the blood of the Lamb.

606   *MANY DECEIVERS WILL ATTEMPT TO MISLEAD THE FLOCK, WHICH BRINGS ABOUT A MORE RAPID SEPARATION OF THE GOOD FROM THE EVIL ONES (Mt 24:10-12)*

Mt 24:10 "AND THEN SHALL MANY BE OFFENDED (*reject Christ*) **AND SHALL BETRAY ONE ANOTHER, AND SHALL HATE ONE ANOTHER.**

2 Tim 3:2,3,4 For men shall be lovers of their own selves; covetous, boasters, proud, blasphemers, disobedient to parents, unthankful, unholy...without natural affection, trucebreakers, false accusers, without self-control, fierce, despisers of those that are good…traitors, headstrong, conceited, lovers of pleasure rather than lovers of God.

Mt 24:11 AND <u>MANY</u> FALSE PROPHETS SHALL RISE AND SHALL DECEIVE <u>MANY</u>. *(into heresy and defections)*

Isa 30:10 …speak unto us smooth things…

Lk 6:44 For every tree is known by its fruit…

2 Tim 3:13 But evil men shall wax worse and worse deceiving and being deceived.

Eph 5:6 Let no man deceive you with vain words…

Eph 4:14 That we henceforth be no more children, tossed to and fro, and carried about with every wind of doctrine, by the sleight of men, and cunning craftiness, whereby they lie in wait, to deceive.

Mt 24:12 AND BECAUSE INIQUITY *(evil)* **SHALL ABOUND** *(increase)* **THE LOVE OF MANY SHALL WAX** *(grow)* **COLD."** *(We should not be surprised if society becomes much worse leading up to these End-Times conditions)*

Joel 3:14 Multitudes, multitudes in the valley of decision. The day of the Lord is near, in the valley of decision.

2 Pet 3:4 (People who had believed in the pre-tribulation rapture still say)…Where is the promise of His coming? For since the fathers fell asleep, all things continue as they were from the beginning of the creation.

Rev 22:11 He that is unjust, let him be unjust still.. he that is holy let him be holy still.

Dan 12:10 Many shall be purified and made white, and tried; but the wicked shall do wickedly. None of the wicked shall understand; but the wise shall understand.

Ps 37:1 Fret not thyself because of evil-doers, neither be thou envious against the workers of iniquity.

Dan 12:4 …many shall run to and fro (have busy lives), and knowledge shall be increased (substantially).

607   IN SPITE OF BITTER HATRED, HIS FOLLOWERS MUST REMAIN STEADFAST TO THE VERY END *(Mt 24:13; Mk 13:13; Lk 21:17-19)*

Lk 21:17 "<u>AND YE</u> *(My beloved)* **SHALL BE HATED OF** *(by)* **ALL MEN FOR MY NAME'S SAKE.** *(because you are Christians)*

Jn 15:20 Remember the word that I said unto you, the servant is not greater than his Lord. If they have persecuted Me, they will also persecute you...

Ac 14:22 Confirming the souls of the disciples and exhorting them to continue in the faith, and that we must through much tribulation enter into the kingdom of God.

(If you are still "presuming" a Post-Tribulation rapture along with us, you can see in this chronological order how Jesus elaborates on some of the difficulties we will experience—and so far He has not mentioned anything about a pre-tribulation rapture.)

Mt 24:13 BUT HE THAT SHALL ENDURE *(keeps loving)* **UNTIL THE END, THE SAME SHALL BE SAVED.** *(unto eternal life)*

Gal 6:9 And let us not be weary in well doing, for in due season we shall reap, if we faint not.

Rom 8:18 For I reckon that the sufferings of this present time are not worthy to be compared with the glory which shall be revealed in us.

2 Tim 2:3 Thou therefore endure hardness, as a good soldier of Jesus Christ.

Rev 3:11 Behold, I come quickly, hold that fast which thou hast, that no man take thy crown.

Lk 21:18 BUT THERE SHALL NOT A HAIR OF YOUR HEAD PERISH. *(be lost)*

Lk 21:19 IN YOUR PATIENCE *(perseverance)* **POSSESS YE** *(gain)* **YOUR SOULS."**

Amos 4:12 ...prepare to meet thy God...

1 Cor 2:9 But as it is written, eye hath not seen, nor ear heard, neither have entered into the heart of man, the things which God hath prepared for them that love Him. (Who is Jesus telling this hard message to, if everyone was raptured earlier? He is not talking to the Pharisees, or to Jews, nor to new believers but to His earliest and most mature followers, namely Peter, James, John, and Andrew as revealed in Mk 13:3 above in Caption #598)

608	*JESUS SAYS THAT HIS HOLY AMBASSADORS ARE TO SPREAD THE GOSPEL FOR ALL TO CHOOSE, <u>BEFORE THE END CAN COME</u> (Mt 24:14)*

Mt 24:14 "AND THIS GOSPEL OF THE KINGDOM SHALL BE PREACHED *(be made known)* **IN ALL THE WORLD FOR A WITNESS** *(of Jesus)* **UNTO ALL NATIONS. AND** *(<u>only</u>)* **THEN SHALL THE END** *(of the world)* **COME."**

(And you have a mandate to preach the Gospel without compromise.)

Pr 28:1 The wicked flee when no man pursueth, but the righteous are bold as a lion.
Jer 8:20 The harvest is past, the summer is ended, and we are not saved.

Lk 14:23 …Go out into the highways and hedges and compel them to come in…

Mt 10:23 When they persecute you in one city, flee to another…(but keep on witnessing)

609 AS THE MIDDLE OF THE TRIBULATION IS REACHED, THE PENDING DESTRUCTION OF JERUSALEM, AND THE ANTI-CHRIST BEING REVEALED, ARE CLEAR INDICATIONS THAT THOSE SENSITIVE TO HIS SPIRIT ARE TO ESCAPE TO, AND TAKE REFUGE IN, THE HIGH COUNTRY (Mt 24:15,16; Mk 13:14; Lk 21:20,21)

Lk 21:20 "AND WHEN YE SHALL SEE JERUSALEM COMPASSED WITH (surrounded by) **ARMIES, THEN KNOW THE DESOLATION** (its utter destruction) **THEREOF IS NIGH.** (about to happen)

Rev 11:2 …And the Holy City shall they tread under foot forty and two months.

Zec 12:3 And in that day will I make Jerusalem a burdensome stone for all people. All that burden themselves with it shall be cut in pieces, though all the people of the earth be gathered together against it.

(Ever since Salem was first mentioned in Gen 14:18, under king Melchizedek, Jerusalem has suffered 37 major wars. It has changed hands 85 times. It has been totally destroyed right to the ground 18 times. Jerusalem is the focal point between Europe, Africa and Asia. No city on earth has been fought over more than Jerusalem. It is well known in history, it will be significant in the future.)

Ezek 5:5 …This is Jerusalem: I have set it in the midst of the nations…

Mk 13:14 BUT WHEN YE SHALL SEE THE "ABOMINATION OF DESOLATION" (detestable sacrilege) **SPOKEN OF** (described) **BY DANIEL THE PROPHET** (in Dan 9:27 & 11:31), **STANDING WHERE IT OUGHT NOT…** (where it does not belong)

Dan 12:11 And from the time (most likely beginning in #602) that the daily sacrifice (communion service which is a re-enactment of the sacrifice of Jesus on Calvary) shall be taken away (as celebrated several thousand times daily world-wide in Orthodox, Catholic, Coptic, and a few other denominations) and the abomination that maketh desolate is set up, there shall be 1,290 days.

1 Th 5:3 For when they shall say, Peace and safety; then sudden destruction cometh upon them, as travail upon a woman with child; and they shall not escape.

2 Th 2:2,3 That ye be not soon shaken in mind, or be troubled, neither by spirit, nor by *word, nor by letter as from us, that <u>the day of Christ</u> (and the rapture) is at hand…Let no man deceive you by any means, for <u>that day shall not come</u>, except there come 1) a falling away of some Christians first, and 2) <u>that man of sin (the Antichrist) be revealed</u>, the son of perdition.*

Mt 24:15 …IN THE HOLY PLACE. WHOSO READETH, LET HIM *(try to)* UNDERSTAND. *(take special notice)*

Dan 9:27 And he (the Anti-christ) shall confirm the covenant with many for one week (figuratively seven days representing seven years), and in the midst of the week he shall cause the sacrifice and the oblation (holy communion offering?) to cease…

Rev 13:5 And there was given unto him a mouth speaking great things and blasphemies; and power was given unto him to continue forty and two months.

Rev 14:9,10 And the third angel followed them, saying with a loud voice, If any man worship the beast and his image, and receive his mark in his forehead, or in his hand…The same shall drink of the wine of the wrath of God…"

(The "Anti-Christ" will be Satan incarnated. More about him is found in Dan 7:21,25; 8:11, 23-25; 9:26,27; 11:3, 21-45; 2 Thes 2:3-10; all of Rev 13; & 19:19,20; 20:10.)

Mt 24:16 THEN, LET THEM WHICH BE IN JUDEA FLEE INTO *(take refuge in)* THE MOUNTAINS." *(not raptured into the sky)*

Zech 14:5 And ye shall flee to (find sanctuary in) the valley of the mountains…and all the saints with thee.

*Rev 3:10 Because thou has kept the word of My patience, I also will keep thee from the hour of temptation, which shall come upon all the world, to try them that dwell upon the earth. (This Rev 3:10 verse belongs here, in the middle of the Tribulation, and not at the beginning of the Tribulation.)

Rev 18:4 And I heard another voice from heaven, saying, Come out of her My people, that ye be not partakers of her sins, and that ye receive not of her plagues.

(The flood did not come until after Noah and his family got into the ark. Fire and brimstone did not fall on Sodom and Gomorrah until Lot and his family were safely out. And God will lead His faithful into the mountains before His anger is poured out on godless heathen.)

Ps 23:4 Yea though I walk through the valley of shadow of death, I will fear no evil for Thou art with me; Thy rod and Thy staff they comfort me.

Pr 22:3 A prudent man foreseeth the evil and hideth himself…

610 JESUS, THE "OWNER OF ALL THINGS," URGES US TO QUICKLY ABANDON EVERYTHING TO AVOID GOD'S COMING EXTREME WRATH UPON THE WICKED (Mt 24:17,18; Mk 13:15,16; Lk 21:21,22)

Mk 13:15 "AND LET HIM THAT IS ON THE HOUSETOP NOT GO DOWN (waste time going) **INTO THE HOUSE, NEITHER ENTER THEREIN, TO TAKE** (collect) **ANYTHING OUT OF HIS HOUSE.**

Mt 24:18 NEITHER LET HIM WHICH IS IN THE FIELD RETURN BACK TO TAKE (bring even) **HIS CLOTHES.**

> *Gen 19:26 But his wife looked back from behind him, and she became a pillar of salt.*

Lk 21:21 ...AND LET THEM WHICH ARE IN THE MIDST OF IT (the city) **DEPART OUT. AND LET NOT THEM THAT ARE IN THE COUNTRIES ENTER THEREINTO.**

> *Rev 12:14 And to the woman were given two wings of a great eagle, that she might fly into the wilderness, into her place, where she is nourished for a time, and times, and half a time (3.5 years), from the face of the serpent.*

> *(If God protected the Hebrew nation and fed them manna for forty years in the Sinai desert, He can certainly take care of us and feed us in the mountain areas, during the latter three and a half years of the Tribulation.)*

> *Rev 8:1 And when he had opened the seventh seal, there was silence in heaven about the space of half an hour.*

Lk 21:22 FOR THESE BE THE DAYS OF (God's) **VENGEANCE** (severe punishment) **THAT ALL THINGS WHICH ARE WRITTEN** (which were prophesied) **MAY BE FULFILLED."** (on unrepentant sinners)

> *Zep 2:3 Seek ye the Lord, all ye meek of the earth…it may be ye shall be hid (this means hidden, not raptured up) in the day of the Lord's anger.*

> *Mic 5:15 And I will execute vengeance in anger and fury upon the heathen, such as they have not heard.*

> *Col 3:6 For which things' sake the wrath of God cometh on the children of disobedience*

611 THOSE WHO DECLINE GOD'S MERCY AND GRACE ARE 'LEFT BEHIND' TO SUFFER IMMENSE PERSONAL SUFFERING AND ANGUISH (Mt 24:19; Mk 13:17; Lk 21:23,24)

Lk 21:23 "BUT WOE UNTO THEM THAT ARE WITH CHILD AND TO THEM THAT

GIVE SUCK *(nursing)* **IN THOSE DAYS! FOR THERE SHALL BE GREAT DISTRESS** *(incredible problems)* **IN THE LAND, AND WRATH** *(God's extreme anger)* **UPON THIS PEOPLE.**

> *Isa 65:2,3 I have spread out my hands all the day unto a rebellious people, which walketh in a way that was not good, after their own thoughts…a people that provoketh me to anger continually to My face…*

> *Jer 30:7 …it is even a time of Jacob's trouble; but he shall be saved out of it.*

> *Dan 12:1 …and there shall be a time of trouble, such as never was since there was a nation even to that same time; and at that time thy people shall be delivered, every one that shall be found written in the book.*

Lk 21:24 AND THEY SHALL FALL *(be slain)* **BY THE EDGE OF THE SWORD, AND SHALL BE LED AWAY CAPTIVE INTO ALL NATIONS, AND JERUSALEM SHALL BE TRODDEN DOWN OF** *(trampled under by)* **THE GENTILES** *(non-believers)* **UNTIL THE TIMES OF THE GENTILES BE FULFILLED."** *(be over)*

> *Lk 19:44 …because thou knewest not the time of My visitation.*

> *Jer 19:15 Thus saith the Lord of hosts, the God of Israel; Behold, I will bring upon this city and upon all her towns all the evil that I have pronounced against it, because they have hardened their necks, that they might not hear My words.*

612   JESUS TELLS US TO PRAY SPECIFICALLY FOR OUR TIMELY EVACUATION AND SAFETY, AS GOD'S TERRIBLE FURY ON THE UNHOLY WILL INCREASE (Mt 24:20-22; Mk 13:18-20)

Mt 24:20 "BUT PRAY YE *(beforehand)* **THAT YOUR FLIGHT** *(to the mountains)* **BE NOT IN THE WINTER, NEITHER ON THE SABBATH DAY.**

> **1 Th 5:9 For God hath not appointed us to wrath…(This verse also properly belongs where it is placed here in the middle of the tribulation, when we are to flee to the mountains and not before the Tribulation begins.)*

> *Lk 21:36 Watch ye therefore, and pray always, that ye may be accounted <u>worthy to escape</u> (not raptured up from) all these things that shall come to pass…*

> *Jn 17:15 I pray not that you would take them from the world, but that you would keep them from the evil one.*

> *Rev 15:2 And I saw…them that had gotten <u>the victory over the beast</u> (the Anti-christ), and over his image, and over his mark, and over the number of his name…*

Ps 34:7,8 The angel of the Lord encampeth round about them that fear Him and delivereth them...O taste and see that the Lord is good, blessed is the man that trusteth in Him.

Mt 24:21 FOR THEN SHALL BE <u>GREAT TRIBULATION</u> *(great suffering)* **SUCH AS WAS NOT SINCE THE BEGINNING OF THE WORLD...**

Mk 13:19 ...WHICH GOD CREATED UNTO THIS TIME, NEITHER SHALL BE.

(With the believers safe and protected in the mountains, the dreadful punishments of God upon the ungodly are described in the <u>harsh and brutal "seals"</u> which intensify beginning with Rev 6:1, and in the <u>shocking and awful "trumpets"</u> beginning with Rev 8:6, and in the <u>fierce and horrifying "vials or bowls"</u> beginning with Rev 16:1.)

Rev 16:1,6 And I heard a great voice out of the temple saying to the seven angels, Go your ways, and pour out the vials of the wrath of God upon the earth...For they have shed the blood of saints and prophets, and thou hast given them blood to drink; for they are worthy.

Rev 9:5,6 And to them (the locusts) it was given that they should not kill them (the wrongdoers), but that they should be tormented five months, and their torment was the torment of the scorpion, which striketh a man...And in those days shall men seek death, and shall not find it, and shall desire to die, and death shall flee from them.

Rev 8:13 And I beheld, and heard an angel flying through the midst of heaven, saying with a loud voice, "Woe, woe, woe, to the inhabitors of the earth..."

Rev 16:9,10 And men were scorched with great heat, and blasphemed the name of God, which hath power over these plagues, and they repented not to give Him glory...and they gnawed their tongues for pain.

Mk 13:20 AND EXCEPT THAT THE LORD HAD SHORTENED *(reduced)* **THOSE DAYS, NO FLESH** *(no human beings)* **SHOULD BE SAVED** *(survive)* **BUT FOR THE ELECT'S SAKE, WHOM HE HATH CHOSEN, HE HATH SHORTENED THE DAYS."**

Ps 145:20 The Lord preserveth all them that love Him: but all the wicked will He destroy.

Isa 26:3 Thou wilt keep him in perfect peace, whose mind is stayed on Thee, because he trusteth in Thee.

Lk 18:8 ...when the Son of Man cometh, shall He find faith on the earth? (This would be impossible if we were already raptured.)

613 *AVOID ANYONE ATTEMPTING TO DIRECT GOD'S CHILDREN TO COUNTERFEIT MESSIAHS AND IMPRESSIVE MAGICIANS (Mt 24:23,24; Mk 13:21,22)*

Mk 13:21 "AND THEN IF ANY MAN SHALL SAY TO YOU, 'LOOK, HERE IS CHRIST' *(the Messiah)* **OR, 'LOOK, HE IS THERE,' BELIEVE HIM NOT.**

Mt 24:24 FOR THERE SHALL ARISE *(emerge)* **FALSE CHRISTS** *(imitators)* **AND FALSE** *(lying)* **PROPHETS, AND SHALL SHOW** *(perform)* **GREAT SIGNS AND WONDERS** *(colossal tricks)* **INSOMUCH THAT IF IT WERE POSSIBLE, THEY SHALL DECEIVE...** *(lead astray)* (Deut 13:1)

Mk 13:22 ...SEDUCE *(persuade)* **EVEN <u>THE ELECT</u>..."** *(His most devoted)*

> *(It is unfair for some pre-trib preachers to keep using the Jewish nation as the fall guys, only to exempt themselves in an early rapture, away from the difficulties to come. According to Lk 18:7, Col 3:12 and Titus 1:1, the elect are the followers of Jesus, not the Hebrew nation.)*

> *2 Tim 3:13 But evil men and seducers shall wax worse, deceiving, and being deceived.*

> *Mt 3:7 ...you brood of vipers, who warned you of the wrath to come?*

614 *IGNORE RUMORS ABOUT THE LORD HAVING ALREADY RETURNED, BECAUSE HIS SECOND COMING WILL BE QUICK AND OBVIOUS FOR THE ENTIRE WORLD TO SEE SIMULTANEOUSLY (Mt 24:25-27; Mk 13:23)*

Mt 24:26 "WHEREFORE IF THEY SHALL SAY UNTO YOU, 'BEHOLD, HE *(the Lord having returned)* **IS IN THE DESERT' GO NOT FORTH, 'BEHOLD HE IS IN THE SECRET CHAMBERS,'** *(their special group)* **BELIEVE IT NOT.**

Mt 24:27 FOR AS THE LIGHTNING COMETH OUT OF THE EAST AND SHINETH *(flashes)* **EVEN UNTO THE WEST, SO** *(suddenly and most visibly)* **SHALL ALSO THE COMING OF THE SON OF MAN BE.** *(for all to witness)*

> *Rev 3:3 ...I will come on thee as a thief, and thou shalt not know what hour I will come upon thee.*

> *(According to Mt 24:36 no one knows the day nor the hour. However, Mt 24:32,33 tells us that we will know the approximate season.)*

Mk 13:23 BUT TAKE YE HEED. *(be on guard)* **BEHOLD** *(take notice)* **I HAVE FORETOLD YOU ALL THINGS."** *(in advance)*

> *Rev 1:19 Write the things which thou has seen, and the things which are, and the things which shall be hereafter.*

1 Pet 4:7 But the end of all things is at hand; be ye therefore sober and <u>watch unto prayer</u>.

Rev 22:10 "Do not seal up the words of the prophecy of this book, for the time is at hand."

(There is only one way to prepare for the Last Days, and that is to learn to rely on God to guide us, to provide for us and to protect us, through thick and thin.)

1 Th 5:11 Wherefore comfort yourselves together, and edify one another, even as also ye do.

615   MANY BECOME TROUBLED AND TERRIFIED AS GOD USES HIS CREATION TO BRING HIS JUDGMENT UPON A SINFUL WORLD (Mt 24:28; Lk 21:25,26)

Lk 21:25 "AND THERE SHALL BE *(unusual)* **SIGNS IN THE SUN AND IN THE MOON, AND IN THE STARS. AND UPON THE EARTH DISTRESS OF** *(misery and despair upon all)* **NATIONS, WITH PERPLEXITY** *(mass confusion)* **THE SEA AND THE WAVES ROARING.** *(Isa 13:10)*

Lk 21:26 MEN'S HEARTS FAILING THEM FOR FEAR, AND FOR LOOKING AFTER *(fearfully anticipating)* **THOSE THINGS WHICH ARE COMING** *(next)* **ON THE EARTH...**

Rev 6:15-17 ...men hid themselves in the dens and in the rocks of the mountains; and said to the mountains and rocks, "Fall on us, and hide us from the face of Him that sitteth on the throne, and from the wrath of the Lamb(Jesus)...for the great day of His wrath is come; and who shall be able to stand?"

Rev 18:17 For in one hour such great riches will come to nothing...(The Bible tells us in Rev 6:8 that one fourth "of mankind" is killed, leaving 75%. Later, in Rev 9:15 and 18 another one third "of men" are slain.

Isa 4:1 And in that day seven women shall take hold of one man, saying, We will eat our own bread, and wear our own apparel; only let us be called by thy name, to take away our reproach.

Mt 24:28 FOR WHEREVER THE CARCASS *(dead body)* **IS, THERE WILL THE EAGLES** *(some translations say vultures and some buzzards)* **BE GATHERED TOGETHER."** *(to scavenge the goods of the deceased?)*

Zep 1:13 Therefore their goods shall become booty, and their houses a desolation...

Lk 12:15 "Beware! Keep yourselves from covetousness, for a man's life does not consist of the abundance of the things which he possesses."

616 *SOON AFTER THAT TIME OF UNBEARABLE DIFFICULTY THE WORLD IS THROWN INTO DARKNESS, THEN ALL MANKIND IS GIVEN TO SEE THE SYMBOL OF OUR LONG AWAITED "BLESSED HOPE" (Mt 24:29,30; Mk 13:24,25; Lk 21:26)*

Mt 24:29 "IMMEDIATELY AFTER THE TRIBULATION *(that time of trouble)* **OF THOSE DAYS** *(no rapture yet)* **SHALL THE SUN BE DARKENED AND THE MOON SHALL NOT GIVE HER LIGHT…**

Mk 13:25 AND THE STARS OF HEAVEN SHALL FALL *(be driven from their courses)* **AND THE POWERS THAT ARE IN HEAVEN SHALL BE SHAKEN.** *(disrupted)*

> *Acts 2:19,20 And I will shew wonders in heaven above, and signs in the earth beneath, blood, and fire, and vapor of smoke…The sun shall be turned into darkness, and the moon into blood, <u>before</u> that great and notable day of the Lord come.*

Mt 24:30 AND THEN SHALL APPEAR THE SIGN *(the cross?)* **OF THE SON OF MAN IN HEAVEN** *(through all that darkness)* **AND THEN SHALL ALL THE TRIBES** *(even the smallest groups)* **OF THE EARTH MOURN…"** *(the wicked in regret, and those saved for all the additional good they could have done)*

> *Rev 1:7 Behold, He cometh with clouds, and every eye shall see Him, and they also which pierced Him, and all kindreds of the earth shall wail because of Him…*

> *Heb 9:28 So Christ was once offered to bear the sins of many, and unto them that look for Him shall He appear the second time…(not a second and third time)*

> *Rev 22:12 And, behold, I come quickly (suddenly, not necessarily soon); and My reward is with Me, to give every man according to his work…*

617 *AS THE PERSECUTION APPROACHES SO DOES OUR ETERNAL GLORIFICATION DRAW NEAR (Mt 24:33; Lk 21:28)*

Lk 21:28 "AND WHEN THESE THINGS BEGIN TO COME TO PASS, THEN LOOK UP, AND LIFT UP YOUR HEADS, FOR YOUR REDEMPTION DRAWETH NIGH.

> **Jn 14:3 And if I go and prepare a place for you, I will come again, and receive you unto Myself, that where I am, there ye may be also.*

> *Rev 10:1,3,6 And I saw another mighty angel come down from heaven…and cried with a loud voice…that there should be time no longer…*

> *2 Thes 2:8 And then shall that wicked be revealed, whom the Lord shall consume with the Spirit of His mouth, and shall destroy with the brightness of His coming.*

Mt 24:33 SO LIKEWISE YE, WHEN YE SHALL SEE ALL THESE THINGS, KNOW THAT IT IS NEAR, EVEN AT THE DOORS."

Rev 14:7 ...Fear God, and give glory to Him, for the hour of His judgment is come.

Rev 20:10,12,15 And the devil that deceived them was cast into the lake of fire and brimstone, where the beast and the false prophet are (a trilogy of evil), and shall be tormented day and night forever and ever...and the dead were judged out of those things which were written in the books, according to their works...And whosoever was not found in the book of life was cast into the lake of fire.

Rev 21:8 But the fearful, and unbelieving, and abominable, and murderers, and whoremongers, and sorcerers, and idolaters, and all liars, shall have their part in the lake which burneth with fire and brimstone; which is the second death.

(The Anti-Christ, who most likely appears on the scene with the first persecution of the Christians in #602, is unmistakenly revealed in the middle of the Tribulation when he proclaims himself as God in the temple in #609b, then is finally consumed with the brightness of the Lord's coming in #618.)

618   THE INNOCENT "BETHELEM BABE" RETURNS IN AWESOME SPLENDOR AS THE "KING OF GLORY," WHICH IS QUICKLY FOLLOWED BY THE RAPTURE OF THE SAINTS (Mt 24:30,31; Mk 13:26,27; Lk 21:27)

Mt 24:30 "...AND THEY SHALL SEE THE SON OF MAN COMING IN THE CLOUDS OF HEAVEN—WITH (overwhelming) **POWER AND GREAT** (immense) **GLORY.**

Rev 19:11,13,14,16 And I saw heaven opened, and behold a white horse; and He that sat upon him was called "Faithful and True"...And He was clothed with a vesture dipped in blood; and His name is called the "Word of God"...and the armies which were in heaven (the saints of history?) followed Him upon white horses, clothed in fine linen, white and clean...And He hath on His vesture and on His thigh a name written, "KING OF KINGS" and "LORD OF LORDS."

1 Th 3:13 ...at the coming of our Lord Jesus Christ with all His saints.

Rev 22:13 I AM the "Alpha and Omega," the "Beginning and the End," the "First and the Last."

Mt 24:31 AND HE SHALL SEND HIS ANGELS WITH A GREAT SOUND (blast) **OF A TRUMPET. AND THEY SHALL** (finally) **GATHER** (rapture) **HIS ELECT FROM THE FOUR WINDS...** (North, South, East, West)

*1 Th 4:16,17 For the Lord Himself shall descend from heaven with a shout, with the

voice of the archangel, and <u>with the trump of God</u> (referred to in this previous verse Mt 24:31), and the dead in Christ shall rise first…then we which are alive and remain shall be "caught up" together with them in the clouds (this is known as the catching away) to meet the Lord in the air, and so shall we ever be with the Lord.

*1 *Cor 15:51,52 Behold, I show you a mystery, We shall not all sleep, but we shall all be changed…in a moment, in the twinkling of an eye, <u>at the last trump</u> (if the Bible says that this rapture comes at the last trumpet, then this must be after the seven trumpets beginning in Rev 8:6, towards the end of the Tribulation) for the trumpet shall sound, and the dead shall be raised incorruptible, and we shall be changed.*

(The five Bible references referred to in this chapter, marked with an * asterisk are the most often quoted passages by those who believe in a pre-tribulation rapture, in an attempt to prove their point. Yet not a single one of them specifically says that such a rapture occurs <u>before</u> the Tribulation. With all due respect, these Biblical cross-references belong where they are placed in this sequence—and not as hoped for at the very beginning of the Tribulation.)

(In this entire Olivet Discourse Jesus does not make any reference to an early rapture. But He does refer to His one and only return at the very End-of-Time in Mt 24:30, with the rapture of the saints taking place simultaneously, in the very next verse in Mt 24:31 above.)

* (Another Bible verse offered by pre-tribulation believers is Rev 4:1, which deserves its own asterisk. However, You will find that Revelation 4:1 is not an indication of <u>our</u> pre-tribulation rapture, as some televangelists keep broadcasting, but only of John's "temporary rapture," so that the Lord could tell him what is coming on the earth. This is told to us specifically as follows, "Come up hither, and I will show thee (John) things which must be hereafter."

(Besides, his visit to heaven was in the spirit and not in the body, as told to us very clearly in verse 2, "And immediately I was in the Spirit…" You may look at these verses as long as you wish. But in no way will you find that these even remotely suggest that they have any reference to our own early rapture—as pre-trib believers too often insist.)

(I must have read these chief references of theirs over 100 times in my 33 years in Biblical research, and must say that I have not yet been able to find any proof of a pre-trib rapture in any of these, on which to base such a very important verdict. And I, here and now, challenge the reader to attempt to find, <u>and underline</u>, any wording in these references <u>which specifically</u> says, that the rapture happens <u>before</u> the Tribulation.)

(You will find no such reference. In Biblical interpretation we must separate actual fact, from wishful personal opinion—especially if such speculation contradicts what Jesus has told us in his many Gospel messages.)

Mk 13:27 *(and the angels shall gather His saints, as given to us in the preceeding Mt 24:31)…*

FROM THE UTTERMOST PART *(most remote regions)* **OF THE EARTH,** *(and He shall send them)* **TO THE UTTERMOST PART** *(further reaches)* **OF HEAVEN."**

Mt 13:43 Then shall the righteous shine forth <u>as the sun</u> in the kingdom of their Father. Who hath ears to hear, let him hear.

Dan 12:3 And they that be wise shall shine as the brightness of the firmament, and they that turn many to righteousness <u>as the stars</u> for ever and ever.

Jas 1:17 Every good gift and every perfect gift is from above, and cometh down from <u>the Father of Lights</u>...And God is also referred to as the "<u>Ancient of Days</u>," which can be found in Dan 7:9,13 and 22.

Isa 48:13 ...My right hand has spread the heavens...

Ps 19:1 The heavens declare the glory of God, and the firmament sheweth His handywork.

(Those who believe in the pre-tribulation rapture are inclined to say that the persecution during the Tribulation is against the Jews, and not against the Christians. To that I repeat, Jesus was not talking to the Jews, but was looking right at Peter, Andrew, James and John (His very earliest Christians) when He said, "...before all these, they shall lay their hands on <u>you</u>, and persecute <u>you</u>, delivering <u>you</u> up..." Lk 21:12 "And <u>you</u> shall be betrayed by parents, and brethren, and kinsfolk, and friends..." Lk 21:16 "And <u>you</u> shall be hated of all men for My name's sake." Lk 21:17 "But pray that <u>your</u> flight be not in the winter, neither on the Sabbath day." Mt 24:20)

(The assumption that the persecution in the Tribulation is of the Jews, and not of the Christians, is totally contrary to what Jesus took time to reveal to us. Using the Jews as a scapegoat is just a cheap cop-out, not at all based on Sacred Scripture.)

THE POST-TRIBULATION RAPTURE CLARIFIED

We hear constantly in pre-trib circles that the Christian is not on earth between Revelation 4 and Revelation 18. The following is being submitted, which according to your Bible, will disprove that way of thinking. These put the Christians directly in the Tribulation; Rev 6:9-11; 7:3,13,14; 9:4; 12:6,11,13,14,17; 13:7; 14:12,13; 15:2; 17:5,6; 18:4, 24 and in 20:4.

Christians in the Tribulation is also made very obvious as early as Deut 4:30,31 and continuing in Ps 91:7-9; Dan 7:21,22,25; 8:23,24; 11:32,33; 12:10,12; Lk 21:36; Jn 16:33; Acts 14:22; Rom 8:36; 1 Th 3:3,4 and in 2 Tim 3:12.

The idea that mature Christians are already in heaven while new Christians are still on earth being perfected is not at all scriptural. The seasoned believer will be particulatly needed in the End-of-Times to spread God's messages, to win the many which are lost, and to teach and disciple those latecomers. Writing about the Last Days, Daniel says that in spite of the persecution, "And they that understand shall instruct many..." Daniel 11:33. So, where will the advanced Christian be? He will be badly needed right here, instructing those newcomers.

It was not intended to leave out the "Millennium" or thousand year reign on the earth. It is just that Jesus did not mention it in the Olivet Discourse. However, there is reason to believe that a millennium will take place. It will begin with the dead, then the living, rising to meet Him "in the air." Jesus does not come just to turn back away. This is when He continues to earth as promised "...at the coming of our Lord Jesus Christ <u>with all His saints</u>." (1 Thes 3:13) We will then reign with Him for that thousand years—after the earth has been purged of all its evil, sinful, abominable, perverse, depraved, degenerate, vile, immoral, devilish, self-indulgent, unspeakable, nefarious ways.

Many theologians have expressed their belief in the "post-tribulation" rapture. Among some notables are John Huss, John Calvin, John Knox, Martin Luther, William Tyndale, John Wesley, John Bunyan, Isaac Newton, William Booth, Charles W. Spurgeon, Matthew Henry, Alexander Cruden, Jonathan Edwards, C. S. Lovett, Charles Finney, Charles R. Erdman, William Hendriksen, Robert H. Gundry, Henry T. Hudson, Dale Moody, Robert F. Youngblood and A.W. Pink, to name a few. Aside from these, a great many who once believed in pre-trib now believe in the post-tribulation rapture.

You will find that the pre-trib opinion is primarily an American notion which is not shared much by knowledgeable Christians in other countries, nor in prior centuries. It is time to ponder the Word of God more intently, to discover what it has truly been telling us right along.

Most importantly, we have to believe what Jesus emphasized throughout the Olivet Discourse, expecially in captions #602 to #612. This you can also read very clearly in your own Bible in Mt 24:9-27; Mk 13:9-23 and in Lk 21:12-24. And do take time to read evidence of our being here throughout the Tribulation, in the many verses listed for you in the first two paragraphs above.

ADDENDUM

So, there you have it, the unfolding of the End-of-Times in Jesus' own words. You may have noticed in this discourse that the first half of the Tribulation (believed by many to be 3.5 years) is a persecution of the Christians (given to us in Mt 24:9-13; Mk 13:9-13 and Lk 21:12-19 in paragraphs #602 to #607). But the second half becomes God's terrible anger on the evildoers.

The first half is known as the "Tribulation." But Jesus refers to the severe second half of #610 to #612, as the "Great Tribulation," which is emphasized in Mt 24:21 in #612, against the wicked.

Also notice that John, who was present at the Olivet Discourse (Mk 13:3 in #598), does not tell us anything about End-Time events in his gospel. This could be because by the time he wrote his gospel in 90 to 95 A.D., he may have read that the other gospel writers had already covered the subject in their writings. However, John more than makes up for it when he later gives us the entire "Book of the Revelation (always singular) of Jesus Christ," which deals with the End-of-Times, for the most part, with many of its key verses already quoted for you in this last chapter.

Prophecy is history written in advance. Since so many prophecies in the Old Testament have come true in the life of Jesus, there is every reason to believe that the prophecies that He gave us concerning the End-of-Times which you have just read, will also happen.

We apologize for the foregoing dreadful and gloomy End-of-Time conditions described in this section. But this is in the middle of Jesus' own biography. And it must be His will that we include it all. We have sought to quote His very words—just as you will find it in your own Bible. This is also in the exact order that Jesus gave to us.

And what should be our response to the severity of the Last Days. Exactly what we are told in Rev 22:20 "...Amen. Even so, come, Lord Jesus!"

If you have found that this End-of-Time has been too lengthy and laborious to wade through, you may want to skip this chapter if desired, in your future reading(s) of this book.

Now you have it. The digest of a book, within a book. Forgive me, but I have long felt a need to correct the erroneous presupposition of a pre-trib escape, which is contrary to what the Lord Jesus has clearly revealed to us about End-Time persecution.

I really do see the Lord emphasizing the post-tribulation position in this Olivet Discourse, Chapter XVII. It is most likely that someone else will see the pre-tribulation rapture through it all. To that I say that reasonable men can collide and still walk away friends. Especially since they are both Christian brothers and committed to the Lord, and to the building of His kingdom.

A BRIEF END-TIMES SUMMARY

A quick blueprint of the major events in the Tribulation—and the Timing of the Rapture

A. **Pre-Tribulation Happenings:**
   1. Many anti-christs showing up. Found in Mt 24:5 in #599
   2. Wars and rumors of wars. Mk 13:7 in #600
   3. Revolutions and civil disturbances. Lk 21:9 in #600
B. **Indications that the Tribulation has Begun:**
   1. The combination of wars, earthquakes, famines, pestilences, fearful sights and great signs from heaven , all occurring simultaneously. Lk 21:10, 11 in #601
   2. All these will signal the beginning of the Tribulation. Mt 24:7,8 I #601
C. **Christians are Persecuted in the First Half of the Tribulation:**
   1. Shall be arrested, put into prison, and shall be beaten. Mk 13:9; Lk 21:12 in #602
   2. This will present an opportunity to witness to your persecutors. Lk 2:13-15 in #603
   3. Betrayed by relatives and friends. Mk 13:12; Lk 21:16 in #605a,b
   4. Some of you shall they cause to be put to death. Lk 21:16 in #605c
   5. Defections as the love of many grows cold. Mt 24:10-12 #606
   6. Believers will be hated by many. Lk 21:17 in #607
   7. But world-wide evangelism must take place before the very end. Mt 24:14 in #608
D. **Obvious Events Signal the Middle of the Tribulation Period:**
   1. When you see Jerusalem surrounded by armies. Lk 21:20 in #609a
   2. When the Anti-Christ desecrates the Holy Place. Mt 24:15 in #609b
   3. Then flee to safety, to the mountains. Mt 24:16 in #609c; and Mt 24:20 in #612a
E. **God's Severe Wrath is then Poured out on the Wicked in the Second Half:**
   1. For these are the days of vengeance, to fulfill prophecy. Lk 21:22 in #610b
   2. There is great anguish and misery in the land. Lk 21:23 in #611a
   3. Jerusalem is trodden down by the infidels. Lk 21:24 in #611b
   4. The painful Tribulation intensifies into the "Great Tribulation" resulting in immense suffering for the wicked heathen. Mt 24:21 in #612
F. **Tell-Tale Signs That The End is Nearing:**
   1. Many false christs and prophets attempt to deceive believers. Mt 24:24 in #613
   2. Signs in the sun and moon, distress and perplexity of nations, the sea and waves roaring. Lk 21:25,26 in #615a
   3. Survivors plunder the goods of those who are deceased. Mt 24:28 in #615b
   4. The sun is darkened and the moon will not give its light. Mt 24:29 in #616a
   5. The powers that are in heaven will be shaken. Mk 13:25 in #616a
   6. And then shall appear the sign of the Son of Man. Mt 24:30 in #616a
   7. Everyone on earth mourns. Mt 24:30b in #616b
G. **The King of Kings Finally Returns to 'Catch Away' His Precious Saints:**
   1. Jesus returns with power and great glory. Mt 24:30 in #618a
   2. Which is when the rapture occurs. Mt 24:31 after verse 30 in #618b
   3. He gathers His saints from the uttermost parts of the earth. Mk 13:27a in #618c
   4. and sends them to the uttermost parts of heaven. (Into a new galactic expansion?) See Mk 13:27b in caption #618c.

CHAPTER XVIII

CONTINUING CAUTIONARY ADVICE

Now back to our World English Bible (W.E.B.) which is a more modern translation

619 JESUS USES THE ANALOGY OF ISRAEL BECOMING A NATION AGAIN TO INDICATE THE NEARNESS OF THE END (taken from Mt 24:32,33; Mk 13:28,29; Lk 21:29-31)

Lk 21:29 He told them a parable. **"SEE THE FIG TREE, AND ALL THE TREES.** *(And all the other ethnic groups gaining their independence. Since World War II more than 80 former colonies have gained their independence.)*

Lk 21:30 WHEN THEY ARE BUDDING, YOU SEE IT AND KNOW BY YOUR OWN SELVES THAT THE SUMMER IS ALMOST NEAR.

Mk 13:29 EVEN SO YOU ALSO, WHEN YOU SEE THESE THINGS COMING TO PASS, KNOW THAT IT *(the End-of-Time)* **IS NEAR, EVEN AT THE DOOR."**

620 EACH GENERATION WILL HAVE ITS TRIBULATION AS THE LORD'S TEACHINGS ARE FOREVER (Mt 24:34,35; Mk 13:30,31; Lk 21:32,33)

Mt 24:34 "MOST CERTAINLY I TELL YOU, THIS GENERATION WILL NOT PASS AWAY, UNTIL ALL THESE THINGS ARE ACCOMPLISHED. *(Told to people then hearing this message, and to those now reading it.)*

Mt 24:35 HEAVEN AND EARTH WILL PASS AWAY, BUT MY WORDS WILL NOT PASS AWAY."

621 BE READY, BOTH PHYSICALLY AND SPIRITUALLY, PRAYING AND SERVING ALWAYS (Lk 21:34-36)

Lk 21:34 "SO BE CAREFUL, OR YOUR HEARTS WILL BE LOADED DOWN WITH FROLICKING, DRUNKENNESS, AND CARES OF THIS LIFE AND THAT DAY WILL COME ON YOU SUDDENLY.

Lk 21:35 FOR IT WILL COME LIKE A TRAP, ON ALL THOSE WHO DWELL ON THE

FACE OF THE EARTH.

Lk 21:36 THEREFORE BE WATCHFUL ALL THE TIME, PRAYING THAT YOU MAY BE ACCOUNTED WORTHY TO ESCAPE ALL THESE THINGS THAT WILL HAPPEN, AND TO STAND BEFORE THE SON OF MAN."

622   MANY WILL REMAIN PREOCCUPIED WITH DAILY CARES OF THIS LIFE UNTIL DISASTER IS UPON THEM (Mt 24:36-39; Mk 13:32,33)

Mt 24:36 "BUT NO ONE KNOWS OF THAT DAY AND HOUR, NOT EVEN THE ANGELS OF HEAVEN, BUT MY FATHER ONLY.

Mt 24:37 AS THE DAYS OF NOAH WERE, SO WILL BE THE COMING OF THE SON OF MAN.

Mt 24:38 FOR AS IN THOSE DAYS WHICH WERE BEFORE THE FLOOD THEY WERE EATING AND DRINKING, MARRYING AND GIVING IN MARRIAGE, UNTIL THE DAY THAT NOAH ENTERED INTO THE ARK. *(Gen 7:7)*

Mt 24:39 AND THEY DID NOT KNOW UNTIL THE FLOOD CAME AND SWEPT THEM ALL AWAY. SO WILL BE THE COMING OF THE SON OF MAN.

Mk 13:33 WATCH, KEEP ALERT, AND PRAY, FOR YOU DO NOT KNOW WHEN THAT TIME IS."

623   JESUS, THE "NARROW DOOR," APPEALS TO US TO LIVE EACH MOMENT AS IF IT WERE OUR LAST (Mt 24:42-44; Mk 13:34-37; Lk 12:39,40)

Mt 24:42 "WATCH THEREFORE, FOR YOU DO NOT KNOW IN WHAT HOUR YOUR LORD COMES.

Mt 24:43 BUT KNOW THIS, THAT IF THE MASTER OF THE HOUSE HAD KNOWN IN WHAT WATCH OF THE NIGHT THE THIEF WAS COMING, HE WOULD HAVE STAYED UP, AND WOULD NOT HAVE ALLOWED HIS HOUSE TO BE BROKEN INTO.

Mt 24:44 THEREFORE ALSO <u>BE READY</u>, FOR AT AN HOUR THAT YOU DO NOT EXPECT, THE SON OF MAN WILL COME."

624   BE READY ALWAYS, AND EVER SERVING, FOR THE LORD MUST NOT FIND YOU IN SLUMBER (Mk 13:34-37; Lk 12:39,40)

Mk 13:34 "IT IS LIKE A MAN TRAVELING TO ANOTHER COUNTRY HAVING LEFT

HIS HOUSE, AND GIVEN AUTHORITY TO HIS SERVANTS, AND TO EACH ONE HIS WORK. AND ALSO COMMANDED THE DOORKEEPER TO KEEP WATCH.

Mk 13:35 WATCH THEREFORE, FOR YOU DO NOT KNOW WHEN THE LORD OF THE HOUSE IS COMING, WHETHER DURING THE EVENING, OR AT MIDNIGHT, OR WHEN THE ROOSTER CROWS, OR IN THE MORNING,

Mk 13:36 LEST COMING SUDDENLY HE MIGHT FIND YOU SLEEPING.

Mk 13:37 WHAT I TELL YOU, I SAY TO ALL, WATCH."

625   *THOSE RADIATING HIS LOVE AND WHO LOOK EAGERLY FOR HIS RETURN RECEIVE A GRATIFYING REWARD (Lk 12:35-38)*

Lk 12:35 "YOU MUST BE DRESSED AND YOUR LAMPS BURNING.

Lk 12:36 BE LIKE MEN WATCHING FOR THEIR LORD, WHEN HE RETURNS FROM THE MARRIAGE FEAST, THAT WHEN HE COMES AND KNOCKS, THEY MAY IMMEDIATELY OPEN TO HIM.

Lk 12:37 BLESSED ARE THOSE SERVANTS WHOM THE LORD WILL FIND WATCHING WHEN HE COMES. MOST CERTAINLY I TELL YOU, THAT HE WILL TIE AN APRON AROUND HIMSELF, AND MAKE THEM SIT DOWN, AND WILL WAIT UPON THEM AND SERVE THEM.

Lk 12:38 THEY WILL BE BLESSED IF HE RETURNS IN THE SECOND OR THIRD WATCH, AND FINDS THEM WATCHING."

626   *THE GOOD AND FAITHFUL SERVANTS ARE THOSE WHO ACTUALLY TEACH OTHERS DURING THE MASTER'S ABSENCE (Mt 24:45-51; Lk 12:41-46)*

Lk 12:41 Peter said to Him, "Lord, are You telling this parable to us, or to everybody?"

Mt 24:45 "WHO THEN IS THE FAITHFUL AND WISE SERVANT WHOM HIS LORD HAS SET OVER HIS HOUSEHOLD, TO GIVE THEM THEIR FOOD AT THE PROPER TIME?

Mt 24:46 BLESSED IS THAT SERVANT WHOM HIS LORD FINDS DOING SO WHEN HE COMES.

Mt 24:47 MOST CERTAINLY I TELL YOU THAT HE WILL MAKE HIM RULER OVER ALL HIS PROPERTY."

627   BUT THE LAZY AND NEGLECTFUL WHO ABUSE THEIR STEWARDSHIP RECEIVE A GRIEVOUS PUNISHMENT (Mt 24:50,51; Lk 12:45,46)

Lk 12:45 "BUT IF THAT SERVANT SAYS IN HIS HEART, 'MY LORD DELAYS HIS COMING,' AND BEGINS TO BEAT THE MENSERVANTS AND THE MAIDSERVANTS, AND TO EAT AND DRINK, AND TO BE DRUNKEN,

Mt 24:50 THE LORD OF THAT SERVANT WILL COME IN A DAY WHEN HE DOES NOT EXPECT IT, AND IN AN HOUR WHEN HE DOES NOT KNOW IT,

Mt 24:51 AND WILL CUT HIM IN PIECES, AND GIVE HIM HIS PORTION WITH THE HYPOCRITES. THERE IS WHERE THE WEEPING AND GRINDING OF TEETH WILL BE."

628   ETERNAL PENALTIES AND ETERNAL REWARDS ARE COMMENSURATE WITH EACH PERSON'S UNDERSTANDING AND APPLICATION (Lk 12:47,48)

Lk 12:47 "THAT SERVANT WHO KNEW HIS LORD'S WILL, AND DID NOT PREPARE NOR DO WHAT HE WANTED, WILL BE BEATEN WITH MANY STRIPES,

Lk 12:48 BUT HE WHO DID NOT KNOW, AND DID THINGS WORTHY OF STRIPES, WILL BE BEATEN WITH FEW STRIPES. TO WHOMEVER MUCH IS GIVEN, OF HIM MUCH WILL BE REQUIRED. AND TO WHOM MUCH WAS ENTRUSTED, OF HIM MORE WILL BE EXPECTED."

629   JESUS, THE "MAN OF SORROWS," DREADS THE INTENSE SUFFERING WHICH HE IS ABOUT TO BEAR (Lk 12:49-53)

Lk 12:49 "I CAME TO SET THE WORLD ON FIRE. AND I WISH IT WAS ALREADY STARTED.

Lk 12:50 BUT I HAVE A BAPTISM TO BE RECEIVED, AND HOW DISTRESSED I AM UNTIL IT IS OVER!

Lk 12:51 DO YOU THINK THAT I HAVE COME TO BRING PEACE IN THE EARTH? I TELL YOU, NO, BUT RATHER DIVISION.

Lk 12:52 FOR FROM NOW ON, THERE WILL BE FIVE IN ONE HOUSE DIVIDED, THREE AGAINST TWO, AND TWO AGAINST THREE.

Lk 12:53 THEY WILL BE DIVIDED, FATHER AGAINST SON, AND SON AGAINST FATHER, MOTHER AGAINST DAUGHTER, AND DAUGHTER AGAINST HER MOTHER, MOTHER-IN-LAW AGAINST HER DAUGHTER-IN-LAW, AND

DAUGHTER-IN-LAW AGAINST HER MOTHER-IN-LAW."

630 *TAKE TIME NOW TO SETTLE WITH ANYONE WHO HAS ANYTHING AGAINST YOU, BEFORE THE LAST JUDGMENT (Lk 12:57-59)*

Lk 12:57 "WHY DO YOU NOT JUDGE FOR YOURSELVES WHAT IS THE RIGHT THING TO DO?

Lk 12:58 FOR WHEN YOU ARE GOING WITH YOUR ADVERSARY BEFORE THE JUDGE, TRY DILIGENTLY ON THE WAY TO SETTLE WITH HIM, LEST PERHAPS HE DRAG YOU BEFORE THE JUDGE. AND THE JUDGE DELIVER YOU TO THE OFFICER, AND THE OFFICER THROW YOU INTO PRISON.

Lk 12:59 I TELL YOU, YOU WILL BY NO MEANS GET OUT OF THERE UNTIL YOU HAVE PAID THE VERY LAST PENNY."

631 *IN THE STORY OF THE TEN FIANCEES, JESUS, THE "BRIDEGROOM," ILLUSTRATES THE DIFFERENT BEHAVIORS OF THOSE WAITING FOR HIS RETURN (Mt 25:1-13)*

Mt 25:1 "THEN THE KINGDOM OF HEAVEN WILL BE LIKE TEN VIRGINS, WHO TOOK THEIR LAMPS, AND WENT OUT TO MEET THE BRIDEGROOM.

Mt 25:2 FIVE OF THEM WERE FOOLISH *(comfortable, careless, complacent church goers)*, AND FIVE WERE WISE *(caring, compassionate, committed christians)*.

Mt 25:3 THOSE WHO WERE FOOLISH, WHEN THEY TOOK THEIR LAMPS, TOOK NO OIL WITH THEM,

Mt 25:4 BUT THE WISE TOOK OIL *(could mean the Holy Spirit with His transforming powers)* IN THEIR VESSELS WITH THEIR LAMPS."

632 *THE EXPECTATION THAT JESUS IS ABOUT TO RETURN WILL CAUSE ALL CHRISTIANS TO QUICKLY ATTEMPT TO SHARE HIS LOVE WITH OTHERS (Mt 25:5-7)*

Mt 25:5 "NOW WHILE THE BRIDEGROOM WAS DELAYED, THEY ALL SLUMBERED AND SLEPT.

Mt 25:6 BUT AT MIDNIGHT THERE WAS A CRY, 'BEHOLD! THE BRIDEGROOM IS COMING! COME OUT TO MEET HIM!'

Mt 25:7 THEN ALL THOSE VIRGINS AROSE, AND TRIMMED THEIR LAMPS."

633 SINCE PREPAREDNESS IS NOT TRANSFERRABLE, THE FOOLISH ONES SCRAMBLE LATE TO CATCH UP SPIRITUALLY (Mt 25:8-10).

Mt 25:8 "THE FOOLISH SAID TO THE WISE, 'GIVE US SOME OF YOUR OIL, FOR OUR LAMPS ARE GOING OUT.'

Mt 25:9 BUT THE WISE ANSWERED, SAYING, 'NO, THERE IS NOT ENOUGH FOR US AND YOU. *(one person's faith cannot save another)* **YOU GO RATHER TO THOSE WHO SELL, AND BUY FOR YOURSELVES.'**

Mt 25:10 WHILE THEY WENT AWAY TO BUY, THE BRIDEGROOM CAME, AND THOSE WHO WERE READY WENT IN WITH HIM TO THE MARRIAGE FEAST, AND THE DOOR WAS SHUT."

Rev 19:7 Let us be glad and rejoice, and give honor to Him, for the marriage of the Lamb is come, and His wife hath made herself ready.

634 THOSE WHO WAITED TILL THE LAST HOUR TO GET THEIR LIFE IN ORDER COULD SUFFER ETERNAL DAMNATION (Mt 25:11-13)

Mt 25:11 "AFTERWARD THE OTHER VIRGINS ALSO CAME, SAYING, 'LORD, LORD, OPEN TO US.'

Mt 25:12 BUT HE ANSWERED, 'MOST CERTAINLY I TELL YOU, I DO NOT KNOW YOU.'

Mt 25:13 WATCH THEREFORE, FOR YOU DO NOT KNOW THE DAY NOR THE HOUR IN WHICH THE SON OF MAN IS COMING."

1 Pet 4:18 And if the righteous scarcely be saved, what shall happen to the ungodly and the sinner?

635 GOD GIVES SPIRITUAL GIFTS ACCORDING TO OUR DIFFERENT ABILITIES (Mt 25:14,15)

Mt 25:14 "FOR IT IS LIKE A MAN GOING INTO ANOTHER COUNTRY, WHO CALLED HIS OWN SERVANTS, AND ENTRUSTED HIS GOODS TO THEM.

Mt 25:15 TO ONE HE GAVE FIVE TALENTS, TO ANOTHER TWO, TO ANOTHER ONE, TO EACH ACCORDING TO HIS OWN ABILITY. THEN HE WENT ON HIS JOURNEY."

636   *TWO CHRISTIANS ARE IN DUTIFUL SERVICE WHILE ANOTHER IS NOT (Mt 25:16-18)*

Mt 25:16 "IMMEDIATELY HE WHO RECEIVED THE FIVE TALENTS WENT AND TRADED WITH THEM, AND EARNED ANOTHER FIVE TALENTS.

> *Pr. 11:30 He that winneth souls is wise.*

Mt 25:17 IN THE SAME WAY, HE ALSO WHO GOT THE TWO GAINED ANOTHER TWO.

> *1 Thes 2:20 For you (a convert) are our glory and joy.*

Mt 25:18 BUT HE WHO RECEIVED ONLY ONE, WENT AWAY AND DUG IN THE EARTH, AND HID HIS LORD'S MONEY."

> *(If eternity is so very great and everlasting for you, then it could be equally so for many others whom you can save from the jaws of hell.)*

637   *THE LORD RETURNS TO MIGHTILY REWARD THE SERVANT WHO HAD WON OVER FIVE OTHER SOULS (Mt 25:19-21)*

Mt 25:19 "NOW AFTER A LONG TIME THE LORD OF THOSE SERVANTS CAME, AND RECONCILED ACCOUNTS WITH THEM.

Mt 25:20 HE WHO RECEIVED THE FIVE TALENTS CAME AND BROUGHT ANOTHER FIVE TALENTS, SAYING, 'LORD, YOU DELIVERED TO ME FIVE TALENTS. LOOK, I HAVE GAINED ANOTHER FIVE TALENTS BESIDES THEM.'

Mt 25:21 HIS LORD SAID TO HIM, 'WELL DONE, GOOD AND FAITHFUL SERVANT. YOU HAVE BEEN FAITHFUL OVER A FEW THINGS, I WILL SET YOU OVER MANY THINGS. ENTER INTO THE JOY OF YOUR LORD.' "

> *(As a grandma once said, "You will enter heaven leaning on the arms of those you have brought with you.)*

638   *JESUS, OUR "ETERNAL REWARD," COMMENDS EVEN THE SERVANT WHO HAS LIMITATIONS (Mt 25:22-23)*

Mt 25:22 "HE ALSO WHO GOT THE TWO TALENTS CAME AND SAID, 'LORD, YOU DELIVERED TO ME TWO TALENTS. BEHOLD, I HAVE GAINED ANOTHER TWO TALENTS BESIDES THEM.'

Mt 25:23 HIS LORD SAID TO HIM, 'WELL DONE, GOOD AND FAITHFUL SERVANT. YOU HAVE BEEN FAITHFUL OVER A FEW THINGS, I WILL SET YOU OVER MANY THINGS. ENTER INTO THE JOY OF YOUR LORD.' "

(God will ask you, "Who did you bring with you, into My kingdom?")

639   *BUT HE CONDEMNS THE ONE WHO KEPT HIS FAITH TO HIMSELF (Mt 25:24-26)*

Mt 25:24 "HE ALSO WHO HAD RECEIVED THE ONE TALENT CAME AND SAID, 'LORD, I KNEW YOU THAT YOU ARE A HARD MAN, REAPING WHERE YOU DID NOT SOW, AND GATHERING WHERE YOU DID NOT SCATTER.

Mt 25:25 I WAS AFRAID, AND WENT AWAY AND HID YOUR TALENT IN THE EARTH. HERE, YOU HAVE WHAT IS YOURS.'

(The Lord could be asking you, "Do you not care that he should pass you by?")

Mt 25:26 "BUT HIS LORD ANSWERED HIM, 'YOU WICKED AND LAZY SERVANT. YOU KNEW THAT I REAP WHERE I DID NOT SOW, AND GATHER WHERE I DID NOT SCATTER."

(Avoid the cardinal sins of sloth, pride, envy, anger, gluttony, greed, and lust.)

640   *EVEN WORKING WITH OTHER MINISTRIES COULD HAVE BROUGHT IN SOME BENEFITS (Mt 25:27,28)*

Mt 25:27 "YOU OUGHT THEREFORE TO HAVE DEPOSITED MY MONEY WITH THE BANKERS, AND AT MY COMING I SHOULD HAVE RECEIVED BACK MY OWN WITH INTEREST.

Mt 25:28 TAKE AWAY THEREFORE THE TALENT FROM HIM, AND GIVE IT TO HIM WHO HAS THE TEN TALENTS."

(Jesus keeps telling us that there is an urgency to evangelize others. Yet, some 92% of Christians have never made any attempt at leading another person to the Lord.)

641   *THE UNPROFITABLE ONE IS CAST FROM THE "GLORIOUS LIGHT," AND BECOMES EXTREMELY REMORSEFUL (Mt 25:29,30)*

Mt 25:29 "FOR TO EVERYONE WHO HAS WILL BE GIVEN, AND HE WILL HAVE AN ABUNDANCE. BUT FROM HIM WHO DOES NOT HAVE MUCH, EVEN THAT WHICH HE HAS WILL BE TAKEN AWAY.

Mt 25:30 AND THROW OUT THIS UNPROFITABLE SERVANT INTO OUTER DARKNESS, WHERE THERE WILL BE WEEPING AND GNASHING OF TEETH."

(Never hesitate to love someone and talk to him or her about the Lord. If you know only 10% what there is to know about Christianity, you could know 100% more than the person you are talking to.)

642   *JESUS GIVES US A PREVIEW OF THE LAST JUDGMENT IN THE SEPARATION OF HIS SERVANTS FROM THE SELFISH (Mt 25:31-46)*

Mt 25:31 "BUT WHEN THE SON OF MAN COMES IN HIS GLORY, AND ALL THE HOLY ANGELS WITH HIM, THEN HE WILL SIT ON HIS THRONE OF GLORY.

Mt 25:32 BEFORE HIM ALL THE NATIONS WILL BE GATHERED. AND HE WILL SEPARATE THEM ONE FROM ANOTHER, AS A SHEPHERD SEPARATES THE SHEEP FROM THE GOATS.

Mt 25:33 HE WILL SET THE SHEEP ON HIS RIGHT HAND, BUT THE GOATS ON THE LEFT."

643   *THE OBEDIENT WHO WERE CHARITABLE TO OTHERS RECEIVE THEIR INHERITANCE AS MODEL CHILDREN OF A BENEVOLENT FATHER (Mt 25:34-36)*

Mt 25:34 "THEN THE KING WILL TELL THOSE ON HIS RIGHT HAND, 'COME, BLESSED OF MY FATHER. INHERIT THE KINGDOM PREPARED FOR YOU FROM THE BEGINNING OF THE WORLD.

Mt 25:35 FOR I WAS HUNGRY, AND YOU GAVE ME FOOD TO EAT. I WAS THIRSTY, AND YOU GAVE ME DRINK. I WAS A STRANGER, AND YOU TOOK ME IN.

Mt 25:36 I WAS NAKED, AND YOU CLOTHED ME. I WAS SICK, AND YOU VISITED ME. I WAS IN PRISON, AND YOU CAME TO ME.'"

(Jesus could be telling us where to reach those most likely to respond to His call.)

644   *THOSE WHO SHARE GOD'S MANY BLESSINGS BECOME PLEASANTLY SURPRISED THAT THEY HAVE KNOWN THEIR SAVIOR (Mt 25:37-40)*

Mt 25:37 "THEN THE RIGHTEOUS WILL ANSWER HIM, SAYING, 'LORD, WHEN DID WE SEE YOU HUNGRY, AND FEED YOU, OR THIRSTY, AND GIVE YOU A DRINK?

Mt 25:38 WHEN DID WE SEE YOU AS A STRANGER, AND TAKE YOU IN, OR NAKED AND CLOTHE YOU?

Mt 25:39 WHEN DID WE SEE YOU SICK, OR IN PRISON, AND COME TO YOU?'

Mt 25:40 THE KING WILL ANSWER THEM, 'MOST CERTAINLY I TELL YOU, INASMUCH AS YOU DID IT TO ONE OF THE LEAST OF THESE MY BROTHERS, YOU DID IT TO ME.'"

> *Jms 1:27 Pure religion and undefiled before our God and Father is this; to visit the orphans and widows in their affliction, and to keep oneself unspotted from the world.*

645   AN ANGRY GOD REMEMBERS THE NEGLIGENCE OF LUKEWARM CHRISTIANS AND OF THOSE LOOKING AFTER THEIR OWN WELL-BEING (Mt 25:41-43)

Mt 25:41 "THEN HE WILL SAY TO THOSE ON THE LEFT SIDE, 'DEPART FROM ME, YOU CURSED, INTO THE ETERNAL FIRE WHICH IS PREPARED FOR THE DEVIL AND HIS ANGELS,

Mt 25:42 FOR I WAS HUNGRY AND YOU DID NOT GIVE ME FOOD TO EAT, I WAS THIRSTY, AND YOU GAVE ME NO DRINK,

> *Rev 3:16 Because you are lukewarm, and neither hot nor cold, I will vomit you out of My mouth.*

Mt 25:43 I WAS A STRANGER, AND YOU DID NOT TAKE ME IN, NAKED, AND YOU DID NOT CLOTHE ME, SICK, AND IN PRISON, AND YOU DID NOT VISIT ME."

> *Jms 2:20 But do you want to know vain man, that faith without works is dead?*

646   JESUS, AS THE "EVER LOVING GOD," REPEATS THE FATHER'S BASIC MESSAGE FOR ALL TO CLEARLY UNDERSTAND (Mt 25:44-46)

Mt 25:44 "THEN THEY WILL ALSO ANSWER SAYING, 'LORD, WHEN DID WE SEE YOU HUNGRY, OR THIRSTY, OR A STRANGER, OR NAKED, OR SICK, OR IN PRISON, AND DID NOT HELP YOU?'

Mt 25:45 THEN HE WILL ANSWER THEM, SAYING, 'MOST CERTAINLY I TELL YOU, INASMUCH AS YOU DID NOT DO IT TO ONE OF THE LEAST OF THESE, YOU DID NOT DO IT TO ME.'

Mt 25:46 THESE WILL GO AWAY INTO <u>ETERNAL PUNISHMENT</u>, BUT THE RIGHTEOUS INTO <u>ETERNAL LIFE</u>." *(Dan 12:2)*

1 Pet 4:17 For the time has come for judgment to begin with the household of God. And if it begins with us, what will be the end for those who do not obey the gospel of God?

647 *AS THE THREE MAGI FROM THE EAST CAME TO SEE JESUS AT HIS BIRTH, THE GREEKS FROM THE WEST COME TO SEE HIM TO HIS GRAVE (Jn 12:20-50)*

Jn 12:20 Now there were certain Greeks among those that went up to worship at the feast.

Jn 12:21 Therefore these came to Philip, who was from Bethsaida of Galilee, and asked him, saying, "Sir, we want to see Jesus."

Jn 12:22 Philip came and told Andrew, and in turn, Andrew came with Philip, and they told Jesus.

648 *JESUS SHARES WITH US THE PRIMARY GOSPEL MESSAGE—THE GREAT MYSTERY OF LIVING A LIFE OF SELF-DENIAL—TO BENEFIT ANOTHER (Jn 12:23-26)*

Jn 12:23 Jesus answered them, **"THE TIME HAS COME FOR THE SON OF MAN TO BE GLORIFIED.**

Jn 12:24 MOST CERTAINLY I TELL YOU, UNLESS A GRAIN OF WHEAT FALLS INTO THE EARTH AND DIES, IT REMAINS BUT A SINGLE GRAIN. BUT IF IT DIES, IT BEARS MUCH FRUIT!

Jn 12:25 HE WHO LOVES HIS LIFE WILL LOSE IT. HE WHO HATES HIS LIFE IN THIS WORLD WILL KEEP IT TO ETERNAL LIFE.

Jn 12:26 IF ANYONE SERVES ME, LET HIM FOLLOW ME. WHERE I AM, THERE WILL MY SERVANT ALSO BE. IF ANYONE SERVES ME, THE FATHER WILL HONOR HIM."

> *(The Ten Commandments which are listed from Exodus 20:3 and from Deut 5:7 tell us of some things not to do, such as "Thou shalt have no other gods before me. Thou shalt not kill. Thou shalt not steal. Thou shalt not…Thou shalt not…Thou shalt not…etc. But Jesus gives us a hundred positive things to do; such as, to love, to pray, to give, to forgive, to fast, to be humble, to worship, to sacrifice, to witness, to teach, to serve, etc. etc.)*

649 *GOD THE FATHER, AFFIRMS THAT HIS "MODEL SON" WILL BE SANCTIFIED (Jn 12:27-29)*

Jn 12:27 "NOW MY SOUL IS TROUBLED. WHAT SHALL I SAY? 'FATHER, SAVE ME FROM THIS HOUR?' BUT IT IS FOR THIS CAUSE THAT I CAME!

Jn 12:28 FATHER, GLORIFY YOUR NAME!" Then there came a voice out of heaven, saying, *"I HAVE BOTH GLORIFIED IT, AND WILL GLORIFY IT AGAIN."*

Jn 12:29 The people therefore, who stood by and heard it, said that it had thundered. Others said, "An angel has spoken to Him."

650   *THE GREAT LOVE OF JESUS THROUGH HIS CRUCIFIXION WILL OVERCOME SATAN'S WORKS AND INFLUENCE ON EARTH (Jn 12:30-33)*

Jn 12:30 Jesus answered, **"THIS VOICE DID NOT COME FOR MY SAKE, BUT FOR YOUR SAKES.**

Jn 12:31 NOW IS THE JUDGMENT OF THIS WORLD. NOW THE PRINCE OF THIS WORLD *(Satan)* **WILL BE CAST OUT.**

Jn 12:32 AND I, WHEN I AM LIFTED UP FROM THE EARTH, WILL DRAW ALL PEOPLE TO MYSELF."

Jn 12:33 He said this, signifying by what kind of death He should die.

651   *JESUS, THE "BRIGHT AND MORNING STAR," TELLS US TO WALK IN THE LIGHT SO THAT WE WILL BECOME LIKE HIM (Jn 12:34-36)*

Jn 12:34 The people answered Him, "We have heard out of the law that the Christ remains forever. How do You say, 'The Son of Man must be lifted up?' Who is this Son of Man?"

Jn 12:35 Jesus therefore said to them, **"YET A LITTLE WHILE THE LIGHT IS WITH YOU. WALK WHILE YOU HAVE THE LIGHT, THAT DARKNESS DOES NOT OVERTAKE YOU. HE WHO WALKS IN THE DARKNESS DOES NOT KNOW WHERE HE IS GOING.**

Jn 12:36 WHILE YOU HAVE THE LIGHT, BELIEVE IN THE LIGHT, THAT YOU MAY BECOME CHILDREN OF THE LIGHT." Jesus said these things, and He departed and hid Himself from them.

> *1 Thes 5:5 Ye are all the children of light, and the children of the day; we are not of the night, nor of darkness.*

652   *THE PROPHECY FROM ISAIAH OF OLD IS RECALLED (Jn 12:37-43)*

Jn 12:37 But though He had done so many signs before them, yet they did not believe in Him,

Jn 12:38 that the word of Isaiah the prophet might be fulfilled, which he spoke, "Lord, who has believed our report? To whom has the "Arm of the Lord" been revealed?" *(Isa 53:1)*

653   THOSE REFUSING TO REFORM THEIR LIVES STAY IN SPIRITUAL DARKNESS AND ARE UNABLE TO UNDERSTAND HOLY SCRIPTURE (Jn 12:39-41)

Jn 12:39 For this cause they could not believe, for Isaiah also said,

Jn 12:40 "He has blinded their eyes and He hardened their heart, lest they should see with their eyes, and perceive with their heart, and would turn back to me, and I would heal them."

Jn 12:41 Isaiah said these things when he foresaw His glory, and spoke of Him. *(Isa 6:10)*

654   MANY PEOPLE OF STATUS BELIEVE IN JESUS, BUT ARE AFRAID TO ADMIT IT OPENLY, PREFERRING POPULAR ACCEPTANCE (Jn 12:42,43)

Jn 12:42 Nevertheless even of the rulers many believed in Him, but because of the Pharisees they did not confess it, so that they would not be put out of the synagogue,

Jn 12:43 for they loved men's praises more than God's praise.

> *Rom 2:28,29 For he is not a Jew, which is one outwardly; neither is that circumcision, which is outward in the flesh...But he is a Jew, which is one inwardly, and circumcision is that of the heart; in the spirit, and not in the letter, whose praise is not of men, but of God.*

655   IN HIS LAST PUBLIC APPEAL, JESUS SHOUTS OUT HIS IDENTITY AND PURPOSE FOR ALL TO CLEARLY UNDERSTAND (Jn 12:44-47)

Jn 12:44 Jesus cried out and said, **"WHOEVER BELIEVES IN ME, BELIEVES NOT ONLY IN ME, BUT IN HIM WHO SENT ME.**

Jn 12:45 HE WHO SEES ME, ALSO SEES HIM WHO SENT ME.

Jn 12:46 I HAVE COME AS A LIGHT INTO THE WORLD, THAT WHOEVER BELIEVES IN ME MAY NOT REMAIN IN DARKNESS.

Jn 12:47 IF ANYONE LISTENS TO MY SAYINGS, AND DOES NOT BELIEVE, I DO NOT JUDGE HIM. FOR I CAME NOT TO JUDGE THE WORLD, BUT TO SAVE THE WORLD!"

> *(Jesus came not as a God of judgment and punishment, but as a God of love, of joy, of peace, and of mercy, which He is anxious to lavish upon us.)*

656   JESUS, THE "SPIRITUAL LIGHT," SPEAKS THE RIGHT MESSAGES AS GIVEN TO HIM BY HIS HEAVENLY FATHER (Jn 12:48-50)

Jn 12:48 "HE WHO REJECTS ME, AND DOES NOT RECEIVE MY SAYINGS, HAS ONE WHO JUDGES HIM. THE WORDS THAT I SPOKE, THE SAME WILL JUDGE HIM IN THE LAST DAY.

Jn 12:49 FOR I SPOKE NOT FROM MYSELF, BUT THE FATHER WHO SENT ME. HE GAVE ME INSTRUCTIONS, WHAT I SHOULD SAY, AND HOW I SHOULD SAY IT.

Jn 12:50 I KNOW THAT HIS COMMANDMENT MEANS ETERNAL LIFE. THE THINGS THEREFORE WHICH I SPEAK, ARE JUST AS THE FATHER TOLD ME. AND THAT I SPEAK."

657   JESUS WILL NOT BE QUICKLY EXECUTED BUT WILL BECOME A "LIVING SACRIFICE" ON A CROSS (Mt 26:1,2)

Mt 26:1 It happened, when Jesus had finished all these words, that He said to His disciples,

Mt 26:2 "YOU KNOW THAT AFTER TWO DAYS THE PASSOVER IS COMING, AND THE SON OF MAN WILL BE DELIVERED UP TO BE CRUCIFIED."

658   LUKE SUMMARIZES JESUS' LAST WEEK IN JERUSALEM (Lk 21:37,38)

Lk 21:37 Every day Jesus was teaching in the temple, and every night He would go out and spend the night on the mount that is called Olivet.

Lk 21:38 All the people came early in the morning to Him in the temple, in order to hear Him.

659   FEAR OF THE PEOPLE CAUSES THE RELIGIOUS LEADERS TO DELAY THEIR ATTEMPT TO KILL THE "SEEKER OF THE LOST" (Mt 26:3-5; Mk 14:1,2; Lk 22:1,2)

Mk 14:1 It was now two days before the feast of the Passover and the unleavened bread, and the chief priests and the scribes sought how they might seize Him.

Mt 26:3 Then the chief priests, the scribes, and the elders of the people were gathered in the court of the high priest, who was called Caiaphas.

Mt 26:4 They took counsel together how they might take Jesus by deceit, and kill Him.

Mt 26:5 But they said, "Not during the Passover, lest a riot occur among the people."

660   *JESUS IS HONORED AT A SPECIAL MEAL, WITH A FRAGRANT GIFT (Mt 26:6-13; Mk 14:3-9; Jn 12:1-8)*

Jn 12:1   Jesus came to Bethany where Lazarus was, who had been dead, whom He raised from the dead.

Jn 12:2   So they made Him a supper there. Martha served, but Lazarus was one of those who sat at the table with Him.

Jn 12:3   Mary therefore took a pound of ointment of pure nard, very precious, and anointed the feet of Jesus, then wiped His feet with her hair. The house was filled with the fragrance of the ointment.

661   *OBJECTIONS ARE VOICED OVER THE EXTRAVAGANCE OF A YEAR'S WAGES BEING WASTED ON "HOLY ROYALTY" (Mt 26:8-10; Mk 14:4-6; Jn 12:4-6)*

Mk 14:4   But there were some who were indignant among themselves, saying, "Why has this ointment been wasted?

Jn 12:4   Then Judas Iscariot, Simon's son, one of His disciples, who would betray Him, said,

Jn 12:5   "Why was this ointment not sold for three hundred denarius, and given to the poor?"

Jn 12:6   Now he said this, not because he cared for the poor, but because he was a thief. Having the money box, used to steal what was put into it.

662   *IN DEFENDING MARY'S UNSELFISH DEED, JESUS DRAWS ATTENTION TO HER LOVING GESTURE (Mt 26:11-13; Mk 14:6-9; Jn 12:7,8)*

Mk 14:6   But Jesus said, "LEAVE HER ALONE. WHY DO YOU TROUBLE HER? SHE HAS DONE A GOOD DEED FOR ME.

Mk 14:7   FOR YOU ALWAYS HAVE THE POOR WITH YOU, AND WHENEVER YOU WANT TO, YOU CAN DO THEM GOOD. BUT YOU WILL NOT ALWAYS HAVE ME. *(Deut 15:11)*

Mk 14:8   SHE HAS DONE WHAT SHE COULD. SHE HAS ANOINTED MY BODY BEFOREHAND FOR MY BURIAL.

Mk 14:9   MOST CERTAINLY I TELL YOU, WHEREVER THIS GOSPEL WILL BE PREACHED THROUGHOUT THE WHOLE WORLD, THAT WHICH THIS WOMAN HAS DONE WILL BE SPOKEN OF, AS A MEMORIAL TO HER."

663   *SENSING THE THREAT TO THEIR PRESTIGE, THE ELDERS PLOT TO KILL LAZARUS AS WELL (Jn 12:9-11)*

Jn 12:9 A large crowd therefore of the Jews learned that He was there, and they came, not for Jesus' sake only, but that they might see Lazarus also, whom Jesus had raised from the dead.

Jn 12:10 But the chief priests conspired to put Lazarus to death also,

Jn 12:11 because on account of him many of the Jews were turning away and believing in Jesus.

664   *JUDAS DECIDES TO BETRAY RATHER THAN SERVE THE LORD, AND THUS SELLS HIS ETERNAL SOUL (Mt 26:14-16; Mk 14:10,11; Lk 22:3-6)*

Lk 22:3 Satan entered into Judas, who was surnamed Iscariot, who was numbered with the twelve.

Lk 22:4 He went his way, and talked with the chief priests and captains about how he might deliver Him to them.

Lk 22:5 They were glad, and agreed to give him money.

Mt 26:15 He said, "What are you willing to give me that I should deliver Him to you?" They counted out for him thirty pieces of silver.

Lk 22:6 He consented, and sought an opportunity to deliver Him to them, away from the multitude.

> *Mk 8:36 For what shall it profit a man, if he shall gain the whole world, and lose his own soul.*

CHAPTER XIX

THE LAST SUPPER

665   JESUS SENDS TWO DISCIPLES INTO THE CITY TO ARRANGE FOR THEIR MEMORIAL MEAL (taken from Mt 26:17-19; Mk 14:12-16; Lk 22:7-14)

Lk 22:7   The day of unleavened bread came, on which the Passover must be sacrificed.

Lk 22:8   He sent Peter and John, saying, **"GO AND PREPARE THE PASSOVER FOR US, THAT WE MAY EAT."**

Lk 22:9   They said to Him, "Where do You want us to prepare it?"

666   THE DISCIPLES FOLLOW THE LORD'S INSTRUCTIONS AND GET THINGS READY FOR THE IMPORTANT CELEBRATION (Mt 26:18,19; Mk 14:14-16; Lk 22:10-13)

Lk 22:10 He said to them, **"WHEN YOU HAVE ENTERED INTO THE CITY, A MAN CARRYING A PITCHER OF WATER WILL MEET YOU. FOLLOW HIM INTO THE HOUSE WHICH HE ENTERS.**

Lk 22:11 TELL THE MASTER OF THE HOUSE, 'THE TEACHER SAYS TO YOU, WHERE IS THE GUEST ROOM, WHERE I MAY EAT THE PASSOVER WITH MY DISCIPLES?'

Mk 14:15 HE WILL HIMSELF SHOW YOU A LARGE UPPER ROOM FURNISHED AND READY. PREPARE EVERYTHING FOR US THERE."

Mk 14:16 His disciples went out, and came into the city, and found things as He had said to them, and they prepared the Passover.

667   JESUS, OUR "SWEET LORD," HAS INFINITE LOVE FOR HIS DISCIPLES (Mt 26:20; Mk 14:17; Lk 22:14; Jn 13:1,2)

Jn 13:1   Before the feast of the Passover, Jesus, knowing that His time had come when He would depart from this world to the Father, having loved His own who were in the world, He would love them to the end. *(to the utmost)*

Mt 26:20   Now when evening had come, He was reclining at the table with the twelve disciples,

Jn 13:2   …the devil having already put into the heart of Judas Iscariot, Simon's son, to betray Jesus.

668   *THE ONE WHOSE SANDALS WE ARE NOT FIT TO CARRY, NOW STOOPS TO WASH THE FEET OF THE DISCIPLES (Jn 13:3-12)*

Jn 13:3   Jesus, knowing that the Father had given all things into His hands, and that He came forth from God, and was going to God,

Jn 13:4   arose from supper, and laid aside His outer garments. He took a towel, and wrapped it around His waist.

Jn 13:5   Then He poured water into a basin, and began to wash the disciples' feet, and to wipe them with the towel that was wrapped around Him.

669   *ANY AND ALL LEADERS OF HIS FLOCKS MUST COME UNDER AUTHORITY (Jn 13:6-8)*

Jn 13:6   Then He came to Simon Peter. He said to Him, "Lord, do You wash my feet?"

Jn 13:7   Jesus answered him, **"YOU DO NOT KNOW WHAT I AM DOING NOW, BUT YOU WILL UNDERSTAND LATER."**

Jn 13:8   Peter said to Him, "You will never wash my feet!" Jesus answered him, **"IF I DO NOT WASH YOU, YOU WILL HAVE NO PART WITH ME."**

670   *PETER CONTINUES TO PROTEST, NOT RECOGNIZING THE NEED TO REPENT ON A DAILY BASIS (Jn 13:9-12)*

Jn 13:9   Simon Peter said to Him, "Lord, not my feet only, but also my hands and my head!"

Jn 13:10   Jesus said to him, **"SOMEONE WHO HAS BATHED IS COMPLETELY CLEAN, BUT ONLY NEEDS TO HAVE HIS FEET WASHED. YOU ARE CLEAN, BUT NOT ALL OF YOU."**

Jn 13:11   For He knew him who would betray Him, therefore He said, **"YOU ARE NOT ALL CLEAN."**

Jn 13:12   So when He had washed the feet of all twelve, He put His outer garment back on, and sat down again and said to them, **"DO YOU KNOW WHAT I HAVE DONE TO YOU?"**

671   EVERY DISCIPLE SHOULD HUMBLE HIMSELF BEFORE OTHERS BY DEMONSTRATING SIMILAR ACTS OF SERVICE (Jn 13:13-15)

Jn 13:13 "YOU CALL ME, 'TEACHER' AND 'LORD.' YOU SAY SO CORRECTLY, FOR SO I AM.

Jn 13:14 IF I THEN, YOUR LORD AND TEACHER, HAVE WASHED YOUR FEET, YOU ALSO OUGHT TO WASH ONE ANOTHER'S FEET.

Jn 13:15 FOR I HAVE GIVEN YOU AN EXAMPLE, THAT YOU ALSO SHOULD DO AS I HAVE DONE TO YOU."

672   SACRIFICIAL LOVE IS A NECESSARY CHARACTERISTIC FOR ALL TRUE FOLLOWERS OF JESUS (Jn 13:16,17)

Jn 13:16 "MOST CERTAINLY I TELL YOU, A SERVANT IS NOT GREATER THAN HIS LORD, NEITHER ONE WHO IS SENT GREATER THAN HE WHO SENT HIM.

Jn 13:17 IF YOU KNOW THESE THINGS, BLESSED ARE YOU IF YOU DO THEM."

673   THE BETRAYAL OF JESUS, THE "ETERNAL ONE," IS ANOTHER FULFILLMENT OF PROPHECY (Jn 13:18-21)

Jn 13:18 "I DO NOT SPEAK CONCERNING ALL OF YOU. I KNOW WHOM I HAVE CHOSEN. BUT THAT THE SCRIPTURE MAY BE FULFILLED WHICH SAYS, 'HE WHO EATS BREAD WITH ME HAS LIFTED UP HIS HEEL AGAINST ME.'

Jn 13:19 I TELL YOU THIS NOW BEFORE IT HAPPENS, SO THAT WHEN IT HAPPENS, YOU MAY BELIEVE THAT I AM HE.

Jn 13:20 MOST CERTAINLY I TELL YOU, HE WHO RECEIVES WHOMEVER I SEND, RECEIVES ME. AND HE WHO RECEIVES ME, RECEIVES HIM WHO SENT ME."

674   THEY BEGIN THEIR LAST SUPPER, WHICH IS ALSO KNOWN AS THE LORD'S SUPPER (Mt 26:20-35; Mk 14:18-26; Lk 22:14-23; Jn 13:21-35)

Lk 22:14 When the hour had come…

Lk 22:15 He said to them, "I HAVE EARNESTLY DESIRED TO EAT THIS PASSOVER WITH YOU BEFORE I SUFFER,

Lk 22:16 FOR I TELL YOU, I WILL NO LONGER BY ANY MEANS EAT OF IT UNTIL

THE PASSOVER IS FULFILLED, IN THE KINGDOM OF GOD."

675   JESUS ANNOUNCES THERE IS AN ENEMY IN THEIR PRESENCE (Mt 26:21-25; Mk 14:18-21; Lk 22:21-23; Jn 13:21-30)

Lk 22:21 "BUT BEHOLD, THE HAND OF HIM WHO BETRAYS ME IS WITH ME AT THIS TABLE.

Lk 22:22 THE SON OF MAN WILL GO, AS IT HAS BEEN PROPHESIED, BUT WOE TO THAT MAN THROUGH WHOM HE IS BETRAYED!"

Jn 13:21 When Jesus had said this, He was troubled in spirit, and testified, **"MOST CERTAINLY I TELL YOU THAT ONE OF YOU WILL BETRAY ME."** *(Ps 41:9)*

Lk 22:23 They began to question among themselves, which one of them would do such a thing.

Mt 26:22 They were exceedingly sorrowful, and each began to ask Him, "It is not me, is it, Lord?"

676   THE "RIGHTEOUS SHEPHERD" FORESEES A DIRE FATE FOR HIS BETRAYER (Mt 26:23,24; Mk 14:20,21)

Mt 26:23 He answered, **"HE WHO DIPS HIS HAND WITH ME IN THE DISH, THE SAME WILL BETRAY ME.** *(could also be referring to the collection plate)*

Mt 26:24 THE SON OF MAN GOES, EVEN AS IT IS WRITTEN OF HIM, BUT WOE TO THAT MAN THROUGH WHOM THE SON OF MAN IS BETRAYED! IT WOULD BE BETTER FOR THAT MAN IF HE HAD NOT BEEN BORN."

677   CURIOSITY PROMPTS PETER TO FIND OUT WHO AMONG THEM COULD COMMIT SUCH TREASON (Jn 13:23-26)

Jn 13:23 One of His disciples, whom Jesus loved *(John the writer)* was at the table, leaning against Jesus' breast.

Jn 13:24 Simon Peter therefore got his attention, and said to him, "Ask who it is of whom He speaks."

Jn 13:25 He, leaning back, as he was, on Jesus' breast, asked Him, "Lord, who is it?"

Jn 13:26 Jesus therefore answered, **"IT IS HE TO WHOM I WILL GIVE THIS PIECE OF BREAD WHEN I HAVE DIPPED IT."** So when He had dipped the piece of bread, He gave it to

Judas, the son of Simon Iscariot.

678   JUDAS MUST RUSH HIS BETRAYAL IF JESUS IS TO BECOME THE "PASSOVER LAMB" (Mt 26:25; Jn 13:27)

Mt 26:25 Judas, who was to betray Him, answered, "It is not me, is it, Rabbi?" He said to him, **"YOU SAID IT."**

Jn 13:27 After he had taken the piece of bread, Satan entered into him. Then Jesus said to him, **"WHAT YOU ARE ABOUT TO DO, DO QUICKLY."**

679   JUDAS TURNS FROM "LOVE'S PURE LIGHT" TO TOTAL DARKNESS TO PERPETRATE HIS SUBVERSION (Jn 13:27-30)

Jn 13:28 Now, no man at the table knew why He said this to him.

Jn 13:29 For some thought, because Judas had the money box, that Jesus said to him, "Buy what things we need for the feast," or that he should give something to the poor.

Jn 13:30 Therefore having received the morsel, he went out immediately. It was night.

> *Joshua 24:15 ...choose you this day whom you will serve...but as for me and my house, we will serve the Lord.*

680   THE PENDING SUFFERINGS OF JESUS WILL BRING GLORY TO BOTH THE SON AND THE FATHER (Jn 13:31,32)

Jn 13:31 When he had gone out, Jesus said, **"NOW THE SON OF MAN WILL BE GLORIFIED, AND GOD WILL ALSO BE GLORIFIED BY HIM.**

Jn 13:32 **IF GOD BE GLORIFIED BY HIM, GOD WILL ALSO GLORIFY THE SON IN HIMSELF. AND HE WILL IMMEDIATELY GLORIFY HIM."**

681   THEIR HOLY COMMUNION IS A PREVIEW OF THE FORTHCOMING SACRIFICE OF THE "HOLY AND JUST ONE" ON CALVARY (Mt 26:26; Mk 14:22; Lk 22:19 1 Cor 11:24)

Lk 22:19 He took bread, and when He had given thanks to His Father, He broke it, (possibly representing a temporary separation of body and soul) and gave it to them, saying,

1 Cor 11:24 ..."**TAKE, EAT. THIS IS MY BODY, WHICH IS BROKEN...**"

Lk 22:19 **...AND GIVEN UP FOR YOU. DO THIS IN MEMORY OF ME."**

1 Cor 12:27 Now you are the body of Christ...

682   *THE "SINLESS JESUS" THEN CONSECRATES HIS BLOOD TO BE GIVEN FOR THE PARDONING OF SINS (Mt 26:27,28; Mk 14:23,24; Lk 22:20; 1 Cor 11:25)*

Mt 26:27 He took the cup, gave thanks, and gave it to them, saying, **"DRINK IT, ALL OF YOU,**

Mt 26:28 FOR THIS IS MY BLOOD OF THE NEW COVENANT *(new agreement)* **WHICH IS POURED OUT FOR MANY, FOR THE FORGIVENESS OF SINS.**

(No longer the Passover of Moses from slavery, but of the new Passover of Jesus, converting from death to eternal life.)

1 Cor 11:25 **...AS OFTEN AS YOU DRINK IT, DO SO IN REMEMBRANCE OF ME.**

Jn 6:53 "unless you eat the flesh of the Son of Man, and drink His blood, you will not have life in you."

Mk 14:23 ...and they all drank of it.

683   *SUCH A COMMEMORATION WILL BE OUR REMEMBRANCE OF HIS DEATH UNTIL HE RETURNS (Mt 26:29; Mk 14:25; 1 Cor 11:26)*

1 Cor 11:26 **"FOR AS OFTEN AS YOU EAT THIS BREAD AND DRINK THIS CUP, YOU PROCLAIM THE LORD'S DEATH UNTIL HE COMES.**

(Jesus will willingly offer Himself, as a "Blood Atonement" to appease and satisfy God for our innumerable offenses.)

Mt 26:29 BUT I TELL YOU THAT I WILL NOT DRINK OF THE FRUIT OF THE VINE FROM NOW ON, UNTIL THAT DAY WHEN I DRINK IT ANEW WITH YOU, IN MY FATHER'S KINGDOM."

684   *WITH JESUS ABOUT TO DEPART FROM THIS WORLD, AN ARGUMENT BREAKS OUT AMONG THE DISCIPLES ABOUT WHO WILL NOW BE CONSIDERED THE GREATEST AMONG THEM (Lk 22:24-27)*

Lk 22:24 There arose also a quarrel among them, as to which of them will now be considered to be greatest.

Lk 22:25 He said to them, "THE KINGS OF THE NATIONS LORD IT OVER THEM. AND THOSE WHO HAVE AUTHORITY OVER THEM ARE CALLED BENEFACTORS. **Lk 22:26** BUT NOT SO WITH YOU. THE ONE WHO IS THE GREATEST AMONG YOU, LET HIM BECOME AS THE YOUNGER *(lesser)* AND THE ONE WHO WANTS TO GOVERN, AS ONE WHO SERVES.

>*Phil 2:3 ...doing nothing through rivalry or through conceit, but in humility, each cosidering others better than himself...*

Lk 22:27 FOR WHO IS THE GREATER, THE ONE WHO SITS AT THE TABLE, OR THE ONE WHO SERVES HIM? IS IT NOT HE WHO SITS AT THE TABLE? BUT I AM AMONG YOU AS ONE WHO SERVES."

>*(Fasting is one of the best ways to attain Christian humility and is a great aid in reducing pride and arrogance.)*

685   *JESUS, OUR "SELF SACRIFICING BROTHER," CALLS US TO AN UNUSUAL KIND OF LOVE (Jn 13:33-35)*

Jn 13:33 "LITTLE CHILDREN, I WILL BE WITH YOU A LITTLE WHILE LONGER. YOU WILL SEEK ME, AND AS I SAID TO THE JEWS, 'WHERE I AM GOING, YOU CANNOT COME,' SO NOW I TELL YOU ALSO.

Jn 13:34 A NEW COMMANDMENT I GIVE TO YOU, THAT YOU LOVE ONE ANOTHER, <u>JUST AS I HAVE LOVED YOU</u>, SO YOU MUST LOVE ONE ANOTHER.

Jn 13:35 BY THIS EVERYONE WILL KNOW THAT YOU ARE MY DISCIPLES, IF YOU HAVE LOVE FOR ONE ANOTHER."

>*Gal 6:2 Bear ye one another's burdens, and so fulfill the law of Christ.*

686   *HIS LOYAL AND TRUSTED FOLLOWERS ARE TO BENEFIT ALONG WITH THEIR "SHARING LORD" (Mt 26:30; Mk 14:30; Lk 22:28-30)*

Lk 22:28 "BUT YOU ARE THOSE WHO HAVE CONTINUED WITH ME IN MY TRIALS.

Lk 22:29 AND I APPOINT UNTO YOU A KINGDOM, EVEN AS MY FATHER BESTOWED ON ME,

Lk 22:30 THAT YOU MAY EAT AND DRINK AT MY TABLE IN MY KINGDOM. YOU WILL SIT ON THRONES, JUDGING THE TWELVE TRIBES OF ISRAEL."

687   JESUS IS TO BE SLAIN ALONE, BUT WILL RISE TO MEET THEM AGAIN (Mt 26:31,32; Mk 14:27,28)

Mt 26:31 Then Jesus said to them, **"ALL OF YOU WILL RUN AWAY FROM ME TONIGHT, FOR IT IS WRITTEN, 'I WILL STRIKE THE SHEPHERD, AND THE SHEEP OF THE FLOCK WILL BE SCATTERED.'** *(Zec 13:7)*

Mt 26:32 BUT AFTER I AM RAISED UP, I WILL GO BEFORE YOU INTO GALILEE."

688   PETER WILL FOLLOW JESUS INTO MARTYRDOM SOMEDAY (Mt 26:33; Mk 14:29; Jn 13:36)

Jn 13:36 Simon Peter said to Him, "Lord, where are You going?" Jesus answered, **"WHERE I AM GOING, YOU CANNOT FOLLOW NOW. BUT YOU WILL FOLLOW AFTERWARDS."**

Mt 26:33 But Peter answered Him, "Even if all the rest deny you, I never will.

689   JESUS, OUR BELOVED "PRAY-ER," WILL KEEP US FROM SATAN'S GRASP (Lk 22:31,32)

Lk 22:31 The Lord said, **"SIMON, SIMON, LISTEN, SATAN HAS ASKED TO HAVE YOU, THAT HE MIGHT SIFT YOU AS WHEAT.**

> *1 Pet 5:8 Be sober; be vigilant; because your adversary the devil, as a roaring lion, walketh about, seeking whom he may devour.*

Lk 22:32 BUT I HAVE PRAYED FOR YOU, THAT YOUR FAITH WOULD NOT FAIL. AND WHEN YOU HAVE RETURNED, STRENGTHEN YOUR BROTHERS."

690   PETER'S BOLDNESS BRINGS FORTH CRIES OF LOYALTY (Mt 26:34,35; Mk 14:30,31; Lk 22:33,34; Jn 13:36-38)

Jn 13:37 Peter said to Him, "Lord, why can I not follow You now? I will lay down my life for You."

Jn 13:38 Jesus answered him, **"WILL YOU LAY DOWN YOUR LIFE FOR ME?**

Mk 14:30 …MOST CERTAINLY I TELL YOU, THAT TODAY, EVEN THIS NIGHT, BEFORE THE ROOSTER CROWS TWICE, YOU WILL DENY ME THREE TIMES."

Mk 14:31 But Peter spoke all the more, "If I must die with You, I will not deny You." And they all said the same thing.

Gal 2:20 I am crucified with Christ; nevertheless I live; yet not I, but Christ liveth in me, and the life which I now live in the flesh I live by the faith of the Son of God, who loved me, and gave Himself for me.

691   EVERY APOSTLE SHOULD HAVE A BIBLE SYMBOLIZING THE SHARP TWO-EDGED SWORD OF THE OLD AND NEW TESTAMENT (Lk 22:35,36)

Lk 22:35 He said to them, **"WHEN I SENT YOU OUT WITHOUT A PURSE, NOR PACK AND SHOES, DID YOU LACK ANYTHING?"** They said, "Nothing."

Lk 22:36 Then He said to them, **"BUT NOW, WHOEVER HAS A MONEY BAG, LET HIM TAKE IT, AND LIKEWISE A BACKPACK. AND WHOEVER DOES NOT HAVE A SWORD MUST SELL HIS COAT AND BUY ONE."**

692   THE BIBLICAL PROPHECY IDENTIFYING JESUS, THE "LOVING KINDNESS," AS A CRIMINAL IS TO COME TRUE (Lk 22:37,38)

Lk 22:37 **"FOR I TELL YOU THAT WHAT IS WRITTEN MUST STILL BE FULFILLED ABOUT ME, 'HE WAS COUNTED WITH THE TRANSGRESSORS.' FOR THAT WHICH CONCERNS ME WILL INDEED BE FULFILLED."** *(Isa 53:12)*

Lk 22:38 They said, "Lord, behold, here are two swords." He said to them, **"THAT IS ENOUGH."**

693   JESUS MAKES YET ANOTHER STAGGERING PROMISE TO HIS FOLLOWERS (Jn 14:1-4)

Jn 14:1 **"DO NOT LET YOUR HEARTS BE TROUBLED. YOU BELIEVE IN GOD, BELIEVE ALSO IN ME.**

Jn 14:2 **IN MY FATHER'S HOUSE ARE MANY MANSIONS. IF IT WERE NOT SO, I WOULD HAVE TOLD YOU. I AM GOING TO PREPARE A PLACE FOR YOU.**

Jn 14:3 **IF I GO AND PREPARE A PLACE FOR YOU, I WILL COME AGAIN, AND WILL RECEIVE YOU UNTO MYSELF, THAT WHERE I AM, YOU MAY BE THERE ALSO.**

Jn 14:4 **WHERE I AM GOING, YOU KNOW, AND YOU KNOW THE WAY."**

694   PURSUE JESUS, "GOD'S ANOINTED," WHO IS THE <u>ONLY WAY</u> TO THAT ETERNAL AND ABUNDANT LIFE (Jn 14:5,6)

Jn 14:5 Thomas said to Him, "Lord, we do not know where You are going. How can we know the way?"

Jn 14:6 Jesus said to him, "<u>I AM</u> "THE WAY," <u>I AM</u> "THE TRUTH," AND <u>I AM</u> "THE LIFE." NO ONE COMES TO THE FATHER, EXCEPT THROUGH ME!"

> *Acts 4:12 ...there is no other name under heaven given among men, whereby we must be saved.*

695   *HE PROVIDES THE SOLUTION FOR ALL WHO HUNGER TO SEE GOD (Jn 14:7-9)*

Jn 14:7 "IF YOU HAD KNOWN ME, YOU WOULD HAVE KNOWN MY FATHER ALSO. FROM NOW ON, YOU KNOW HIM, AND HAVE SEEN HIM."

Jn 14:8 Philip said to Him, "Lord, show us the Father, and that will satisfy us."

Jn 14:9 Jesus said to him, "HAVE I BEEN WITH YOU SUCH A LONG TIME, AND STILL YOU DO NOT KNOW ME, PHILIP? HE WHO HAS SEEN ME HAS SEEN THE FATHER. HOW DO YOU SAY, 'SHOW US THE FATHER?' "

696   *GOD THE FATHER WORKS THROUGH HIS "CHERISHED SON" (Jn 14:10,11)*

Jn 14:10 "DO YOU NOT BELIEVE THAT I AM IN THE FATHER, AND THE FATHER IS IN ME? THE WORDS THAT I TELL YOU, I SPEAK NOT OF MYSELF, BUT ARE FROM THE FATHER WHO LIVES IN ME. IT IS HE WHO DOES THE WORKS.

Jn 14:11 BELIEVE ME THAT I AM IN THE FATHER, AND THE FATHER IS IN ME. OR ELSE BELIEVE ME, BECAUSE OF THE MIRACLES THAT I DO."

697   *THOSE WHO LOVE HIM ALSO HAVE GREAT POWER BY CALLING ON THE NAME OF JESUS (Jn 14:12-15)*

Jn 14:12 "MOST CERTAINLY I TELL YOU, HE WHO BELIEVES IN ME, THE WORKS THAT I DO, HE WILL DO ALSO. AND HE WILL DO EVEN GREATER WORKS THAN THESE, BECAUSE I AM GOING TO MY FATHER. *(because Jesus will be in the presence of Almighty God)*

Jn 14:13 WHATEVER YOU WILL ASK IN MY NAME, THAT WILL I DO, THAT THE FATHER MAY BE GLORIFIED BY HIS SON.

Jn 14:14 IF YOU WILL ASK ANYTHING IN MY NAME, I WILL DO IT.

Jn 14:15 IF YOU LOVE ME, KEEP MY COMMANDMENTS."

698 JESUS, "OUR MEDIATOR," PROMISES TO SEND THE HOLY SPIRIT TO BE WITH US ALWAYS (Jn 14:16,17)

Jn 14:16 "**I WILL PRAY TO THE FATHER, AND HE WILL GIVE YOU ANOTHER COUNSELOR, THAT HE MAY BE WITH YOU FOREVER,**

Jn 14:17 THE SPIRIT OF TRUTH *(Defender, Purifier, Spirit of Wisdom)*, **WHOM THE WORLD CANNOT RECEIVE, FOR IT DOES NOT RECOGNIZE HIM, NEITHER KNOWS HIM. BUT YOU KNOW HIM, FOR HE LIVES WITH YOU, AND WILL BE IN YOU!**" *(at their Pentecost)*

699 OUR "BLESSED ASSURANCE" RISING FROM DEATH WILL CONFIRM OUR OWN ETERNAL LIFE TO COME (Jn 14:18,19)

Jn 14:18 "**I WILL NOT LEAVE YOU ORPHANS. I WILL COME BACK TO YOU.**

Jn 14:19 YET A LITTLE WHILE, AND THE WORLD WILL SEE ME NO MORE. BUT YOU WILL SEE ME. AND BECAUSE I LIVE, YOU WILL LIVE ALSO!"

700 JESUS, THE "JOYFUL PRESENCE," WILL MAKE HIMSELF KNOWN TO ANYONE WHO IS TRULY FAITHFUL TO HIS COMMANDS (Jn 14:20,21)

Jn 14:20 "**IN THAT DAY YOU WILL KNOW THAT I AM IN MY FATHER, AND YOU IN ME, AND I IN YOU.**

Jn 14:21 ONE WHO HAS MY COMMANDMENTS, AND KEEPS THEM, THAT PERSON IS THE ONE WHO LOVES ME. AND THE ONE WHO LOVES ME WILL BE LOVED BY MY FATHER. AND I WILL LOVE HIM, AND WILL REVEAL MYSELF TO HIM."

701 JESUS AND GOD THE FATHER WILL DWELL WITHIN EACH OF HIS FOLLOWERS (Jn 14:22-24)

Jn 14:22 Judas (not Iscariot) said to Him, "Lord, how is it that You are about to reveal Yourself to us, and not to the world?"

Jn 14:23 Jesus answered him, "**IF A MAN LOVES ME, HE WILL KEEP MY WORD. MY FATHER WILL LOVE HIM, AND WE WILL COME TO HIM, AND MAKE OUR HOME WITH HIM.**

Jn 14:24 HE WHO DOES NOT LOVE ME DOES NOT KEEP MY WORDS. THE WORDS WHICH YOU HEAR ARE NOT MINE, BUT THE FATHER'S WHO SENT ME."

702   THE HOLY SPIRIT WILL TEACH AND HELP BELIEVERS TO REMEMBER SPIRITUAL MATTERS (Jn 14:25,26)

Jn 14:25 "I HAVE SAID THESE THINGS TO YOU, WHILE STILL LIVING WITH YOU.

Jn 14:26 BUT THE COUNSELOR, WHICH IS THE HOLY SPIRIT *(Comforter, Teacher, Breath of Life)*, WHOM THE FATHER WILL SEND IN MY NAME, HE WILL TEACH YOU ALL THINGS, AND WILL REMIND YOU OF ALL THAT I SAID TO YOU."

703   JESUS BESTOWS HIS PEACE ON HIS SERVANTS AS HE LONGS TO RETURN TO HIS FATHER (Jn 14:27,28)

Jn 14:27 "PEACE I LEAVE WITH YOU. MY PEACE I GIVE TO YOU. NOT AS THE WORLD GIVES, GIVE I TO YOU. DO NOT LET YOUR HEART BE TROUBLED, NEITHER LET IT BE FEARFUL.

Jn 14:28 YOU HEARD HOW I TOLD YOU, 'I GO AWAY, AND I WILL RETURN TO YOU.' IF YOU LOVED ME, YOU WOULD REJOICE, BECAUSE I SAID I AM GOING TO MY FATHER, FOR MY FATHER IS GREATER THAN I."

704   THE "EVERLASTING HEART" WILL ALWAYS DO WHAT HIS HEAVENLY FATHER WISHES (Jn 14:29-31)

Jn 14:29 "NOW I HAVE TOLD YOU BEFORE IT HAPPENS SO THAT WHEN IT DOES HAPPEN, YOU MAY BELIEVE.

Jn 14:30 I WILL NO LONGER SPEAK MUCH WITH YOU, FOR THE PRINCE OF THIS WORLD IS COMING. HE HAS NO INFLUENCE ON ME.

Jn 14:31 BUT THAT THE WORLD MAY KNOW THAT I LOVE THE FATHER, AND AS THE FATHER HAS COMMANDED ME, EVEN SO I DO..."

705   THEY THEN SING A HYMN AND MOVE AWAY FROM THE UPPER ROOM (Mt 26:30; Mk 14:26; Lk 22:39; Jn 14:31)

Jn 14:31 ..."ARISE, <u>LET US GO FROM HERE!</u>"

Mk 14:26 When they had sung a hymn...

Lk 22:39 He came out, and went, as His custom was, to the Mount of Olives. His disciples also followed Him.

CHAPTER XX

HIS FAREWELL ADDRESS

706 *GOD PURGES US SO THAT WE WILL BECOME EVEN MORE PRODUCTIVE (taken from Jn 15:1-3)*

Jn 15:1 "<u>I AM</u> THE "TRUE VINE," AND MY FATHER IS THE GARDENER.

Jn 15:2 EVERY BRANCH IN ME THAT DOES NOT BEAR FRUIT, HE TAKES AWAY. EVERY BRANCH THAT BEARS FRUIT, HE TRIMS, THAT IT MAY BEAR MORE FRUIT.

Jn 15:3 YOU ARE ALREADY PRUNED CLEAN, BECAUSE OF THE WORD WHICH I HAVE SPOKEN TO YOU."

707 *FOLLOWERS OF JESUS MUST BE TOTALLY DEPENDENT ON THE "ORDAINED SAVIOR" TO BE FRUITFUL (Jn 15:4,5)*

Jn 15:4 "REMAIN *(abide, wait upon, rest)* IN ME, AND I IN YOU. AS THE BRANCH CANNOT BEAR FRUIT BY ITSELF UNLESS IT REMAINS ON THE VINE, SO NEITHER CAN YOU, UNLESS YOU REMAIN IN ME.

Jn 15:5 I AM THE VINE. YOU ARE THE BRANCHES. HE WHO REMAINS IN ME, AND I IN HIM, THE SAME BEARS MUCH FRUIT, FOR APART FROM ME, YOU CAN DO NOTHING."

708 *COMMITTED CHRISTIANS CAN BE BLESSED IN THEIR EFFORTS (Jn 15:6-8)*

Jn 15:6 "IF A MAN DOES NOT REMAIN IN ME, HE IS THROWN OUT AS A BRANCH, AND BECOMES WITHERED. THEY GATHER THESE AND THROW THEM INTO THE FIRE, WHERE THEY ARE BURNED.

Jn 15:7 IF YOU REMAIN IN ME, AND MY WORDS REMAIN IN YOU, YOU WILL ASK WHATEVER YOU DESIRE, AND IT WILL BE DONE FOR YOU.

Jn 15:8 IN THIS IS MY FATHER GLORIFIED, THAT YOU BEAR MUCH FRUIT *(gain* *more souls),* **SO YOU WILL BE MY DISCIPLES."**

709   THE ELECT OF GOD REMAIN IN HIS GRACE BY BEING FAITHFUL TO HIS COMMANDS (Jn 15:9-11)

Jn 15:9 "EVEN AS THE FATHER HAS LOVED ME, I ALSO HAVE LOVED YOU. REMAIN IN MY LOVE.

Jn 15:10 IF YOU KEEP MY COMMANDMENTS YOU WILL REMAIN IN MY LOVE, EVEN AS I HAVE KEPT MY FATHER'S COMMANDMENTS AND REMAIN IN HIS LOVE.

Jn 15:11 I HAVE SPOKEN THESE THINGS TO YOU, THAT MY JOY MAY REMAIN IN YOU, AND THAT YOUR JOY MAY BE RUNNING OVER."

710   JESUS IS THAT "EXCELLENT EXAMPLE" SHOWING US HOW TO LOVE (Jn 15:12-14)

Jn 15:12 "THIS IS MY COMMANDMENT, THAT YOU LOVE ONE ANOTHER, EVEN AS I HAVE LOVED YOU.

1 Jn 4:8 He who does not love, does not know God, for <u>God is love</u>.

Jn 15:13 GREATER LOVE HAS NO ONE THAN THIS, THAT HE LAY DOWN HIS LIFE FOR HIS FRIENDS.

Jn 15:14 YOU ARE MY FRIENDS, IF YOU DO WHATEVER I COMMAND YOU."

711   JESUS INVITES HIS FELLOW LABORERS INTO A CLOSER RELATIONSHIP WITH HIM (Jn 15:15-17)

Jn 15:15 "NO LONGER DO I CALL YOU SERVANTS, FOR THE SERVANT DOES NOT KNOW WHAT HIS LORD DOES. BUT I HAVE CALLED YOU MY FRIENDS, FOR EVERYTHING THAT I HEARD FROM MY FATHER, I HAVE MADE KNOWN TO YOU.

Jn 15:16 YOU DID NOT CHOOSE ME, BUT I CHOSE YOU, AND APPOINTED YOU, THAT YOU SHOULD GO AND BEAR FRUIT. AND THAT YOUR FRUIT SHOULD REMAIN, THAT WHATEVER YOU WILL ASK OF THE FATHER IN MY NAME, HE MAY GIVE IT TO YOU.

Jn 15:17 THESE THINGS I COMMAND YOU, SO THAT YOU WILL LOVE ONE ANOTHER."

712   HATRED IS TO BE EXPECTED IN OUR HOSTILE SURROUNDINGS (Jn 15:18-21)

Jn 15:18 "IF THE WORLD HATES YOU, REMEMBER THAT IT HAS HATED ME BEFORE IT HATED YOU.

Jn 15:19 IF YOU WERE OF THE WORLD, THE WORLD WOULD LOVE YOU AS ITS OWN. BUT BECAUSE YOU ARE NOT OF THE WORLD, SINCE I CHOSE YOU OUT OF THE WORLD, THEREFORE THE WORLD WILL HATE YOU.

Jn 15:20 REMEMBER THE WORD THAT I SAID TO YOU, 'A SERVANT IS NOT GREATER THAN HIS MASTER.' IF THEY PERSECUTED ME, THEY WILL ALSO PERSECUTE YOU. IF THEY KEEP MY WORD, THEY WILL KEEP YOURS ALSO.

Jn 15:21 BUT ALL THESE THINGS WILL THEY DO TO YOU BECAUSE OF MY NAME'S SAKE, BECAUSE THEY DO NOT KNOW HIM WHO SENT ME."

713   PERSECUTORS HAVE NO EXCUSE FOR THEIR HATRED (Jn 15:22-25)

Jn 15:22 "IF I HAD NOT COME AND SPOKEN TO THEM, THEY WOULD NOT HAVE SINNED. BUT NOW THEY HAVE NO EXCUSE FOR THEIR SIN.

Jn 15:23 HE WHO HATES ME, HATES MY FATHER *(the God of Creation)* ALSO.

Jn 15:24 IF I HAD NOT DONE AMONG THEM THE WORKS WHICH NO ONE ELSE DID, THEY WOULD NOT HAVE ANY SIN. BUT NOW HAVE THEY SEEN, AND STILL HATE BOTH ME AND MY FATHER.

Jn 15:25 BUT THIS HAPPENED SO THAT THE WORD MAY BE FULFILLED WHICH WAS WRITTEN IN THEIR LAW THAT, 'THEY HATED ME WITHOUT A CAUSE.'" *(Ps 69:4)*

714   JESUS, THE "LIVING WORD," REPEATS HIS PROMISE TO SEND THE HOLY SPIRIT *(Jn 15:26,27 & 16:1)*

Jn 15:26 "WHEN THE COUNSELOR HAS COME, WHOM I WILL SEND TO YOU FROM THE FATHER, THE SPIRIT OF TRUTH *(Sanctifier, Perfector, Spirit of Knowledge)*, WHO PROCEEDS FROM THE FATHER, HE WILL TESTIFY ABOUT ME.

Jn 15:27 YOU WILL ALSO TESTIFY, BECAUSE YOU HAVE BEEN WITH ME FROM THE BEGINNING.

Jn 16:1 THESE THINGS HAVE I SPOKEN TO YOU, SO THAT YOU WOULD NOT FALL AWAY."

715   BROTHERS IN THE FAITH ARE TO EXPECT PERSECUTIONS BY THOSE WHO DO NOT KNOW BETTER (Jn 16:2-4)

Jn 16:2 "THEY WILL PUT YOU OUT OF THE SYNAGOGUES. YES, THE TIME WILL COME WHEN WHOEVER KILLS YOU WILL THINK THAT HE OFFERS SERVICE TO GOD.

Jn 16:3 THEY WILL DO THESE THINGS BECAUSE THEY HAVE NOT KNOWN THE FATHER, NOR ME.

Jn 16:4 BUT I HAVE TOLD YOU THESE THINGS SO THAT WHEN THE TIME COMES, YOU WILL REMEMBER THAT I TOLD YOU ABOUT THEM. I DID NOT TELL YOU THESE THINGS IN THE BEGINNING, BECAUSE I WAS WITH YOU."

716   HIS LEAVING COMES WITH THE GUARANTEE OF A NEW HELPER (Jn 16:5-7)

Jn 16:5 "BUT NOW I AM GOING TO HIM WHO SENT ME, AND NONE OF YOU ASKS ME, 'WHERE ARE YOU GOING?'

Jn 16:6 BUT BECAUSE I HAVE TOLD YOU THESE THINGS, SORROW HAS FILLED YOUR HEART.

Jn 16:7 NEVERTHELESS, I TELL YOU THE TRUTH, IT IS TO YOUR ADVANTAGE THAT I GO AWAY. FOR IF I DO NOT GO AWAY, THE COUNSELOR *(Indwelling Spirit, Revealer, Encourager)*, WILL NOT COME TO YOU. BUT IF I GO, I WILL SEND HIM TO YOU."

Gal 5:22,23 But the fruit of the Spirit is love, joy, peace, patience, kindness, goodness, faithfullness, gentleness, and self-control…

717   THE COMING MINISTRY OF THE HOLY SPIRIT WILL MAKE IMITATORS OF CHRIST AWARE OF PROPER LIVING (Jn 16:8-12)

Jn 16:8 "WHEN HE HAS COME HE WILL CONVICT THE WORLD ABOUT SIN, ABOUT RIGHTEOUSNESS, AND ABOUT JUDGMENT,

Jn 16:9 ABOUT SIN, BECAUSE THEY REFUSE TO BELIEVE IN ME,

Jn 16:10 ABOUT RIGHTEOUSNESS, BECAUSE I AM GOING TO MY FATHER, AND YOU WILL NOT SEE ME ANY MORE,

Jn 16:11 AND ABOUT JUDGMENT, BECAUSE THE PRINCE OF THIS WORLD *(Satan)* HAS BEEN JUDGED.

Jn 16:12 I HAVE YET MANY THINGS TO TELL YOU, BUT YOU CANNOT BEAR THEM NOW."

718   PEOPLE OF THE LIGHT WILL CONTINUE TO BE ENLIGHTENED BY THE HOLY SPIRIT *(Jn 16:13-15)*

Jn 16:13 "HOWEVER WHEN HE, THE SPIRIT OF TRUTH *(Divine Helper, Fountain of Youth, Presence of God)*, **HAS COME HE WILL GUIDE YOU INTO ALL TRUTH, FOR HE WILL NOT SPEAK OF HIS OWN, BUT WHATEVER HE HEARS, HE WILL SPEAK. AND HE WILL DECLARE TO YOU THINGS THAT ARE COMING.**

Jn 16:14 HE WILL GLORIFY ME, FOR HE WILL TAKE OF WHAT IS MINE, AND WILL DISCLOSE IT TO YOU.

Jn 16:15 ALL THINGS WHATSOEVER THE FATHER HAS ARE MINE, THEREFORE I SAID, THAT HE WILL TAKE OF MINE, AND WILL REVEAL IT TO YOU."

719   JESUS, THE "OASIS OF LOVE," WILL LEAVE THEM, THEN RE-APPEAR *(Jn 16:16-18)*

Jn 16:16 "A LITTLE WHILE, AND YOU WILL NOT SEE ME. AGAIN IN A LITTLE WHILE, AND YOU WILL SEE ME, BECAUSE I GO TO THE FATHER."

Jn 16:17 Some of His disciples therefore said to one another, "What is this that He says to us, 'A little while, and you will not see Me, and again a little while, and you will see Me,' and, 'because I go to the Father?' "

Jn 16:18 They said therefore, "What is this that He says, 'a little while?' We do not know what He is saying."

720   JESUS DESCRIBES THE JOY THEY WILL EXPERIENCE BEYOND HIS CRUCIFIXION *(Jn 16:19-22)*

Jn 16:19 Therefore Jesus perceived what they wanted to ask Him, and He said to them, **"DO YOU INQUIRE AMONG YOURSELVES CONCERNING THIS, THAT I SAID, 'A LITTLE WHILE, AND YOU WILL NOT SEE ME, AND AGAIN A LITTLE WHILE, AND YOU WILL SEE ME?'**

Jn 16:20 MOST CERTAINLY I TELL YOU, THAT YOU WILL WEEP AND LAMENT. BUT THE WORLD WILL REJOICE. YOU WILL BE SORROWFUL, BUT YOUR SORROW WILL BE TURNED INTO JOY.

Jn 16:21 A WOMAN, WHEN SHE GIVES BIRTH, HAS SORROW BECAUSE HER TIME HAS COME. BUT WHEN SHE HAS DELIVERED HER CHILD, SHE DOES NOT REMEMBER THE PAIN ANY MORE, BECAUSE OF THE JOY THAT HER CHILD IS BORN INTO THE WORLD.

Jn 16:22 THEREFORE YOU NOW HAVE SORROW, BUT I WILL SEE YOU AGAIN. AND YOUR HEART WILL REJOICE. AND NO ONE WILL TAKE YOUR JOY AWAY FROM YOU."

721   *A PROPER PETITION TO GOD THE FATHER WILL BRING ANSWERS TO PRAYER (Jn 16:23,24)*

Jn 16:23 "IN THAT DAY YOU WILL ASK ME NO QUESTIONS. MOST CERTAINLY I TELL YOU, WHATEVER YOU MAY ASK OF THE FATHER IN MY NAME, HE WILL GIVE IT TO YOU.

Jn 16:24 UNTIL NOW, YOU HAVE ASKED NOTHING IN MY NAME. ASK, AND YOU WILL RECEIVE, THAT YOUR JOY MAY BE COMPLETE."

722   *JESUS, THE "ETERNAL HEART," GIVES FURTHER PROOFS OF THE FATHER'S INTENSE LOVE (Jn 16:25-28)*

Jn 16:25 "I HAVE SPOKEN THESE THINGS TO YOU IN PARABLES. BUT THE TIME IS COMING WHEN I WILL NO LONGER SPEAK TO YOU IN PARABLES, BUT WILL TELL YOU PLAINLY ABOUT THE FATHER.

Jn 16:26 IN THAT DAY YOU WILL ASK IN MY NAME, AND I DO NOT SAY TO YOU, THAT I WILL PRAY TO THE FATHER FOR YOU,

Jn 16:27 FOR THE FATHER HIMSELF LOVES YOU, BECAUSE YOU HAVE LOVED ME, AND HAVE BELIEVED THAT I CAME FORTH FROM GOD.

Jn 16:28 I CAME FORTH FROM THE FATHER, AND HAVE COME INTO THE WORLD. NOW, I LEAVE THE WORLD, AND WILL GO BACK TO THE FATHER."

723   *THE DISCIPLES NOW UNDERSTAND JESUS BETTER (Jn 16:29-31)*

Jn 16:29 His disciples said to Him, "Behold, now You speak plainly, and speak no figures of speech.

Jn 16:30 Now we know that You know all things. And do not need for anyone to question You. By this we believe that You came forth from God."

Jn 16:31 Jesus answered them, **"DO YOU NOW BELIEVE?"**

724 *JESUS, OUR "PRESCIOUS SAVIOR," SHALL GIVE US THE VICTORY (Jn 16:32,33)*

Jn 16:32 **"BEHOLD, THE TIME IS COMING, YES, AND HAS NOW COME, THAT YOU WILL BE SCATTERED, EVERYONE TO HIS OWN PLACE, AND YOU WILL LEAVE ME BY MYSELF. YET I AM NOT ALONE, BECAUSE THE FATHER IS WITH ME.**

Jn 16:33 **I HAVE TOLD YOU THESE THINGS, THAT IN ME YOU MAY HAVE PEACE. IN THE WORLD YOU WILL HAVE TRIBULATION. BUT BE OF GOOD CHEER. I HAVE OVERCOME THE WORLD!"**

725 *IN HIS PRIESTLY PRAYER HE TEACHES US HOW TO PRAY OPENLY TO GOD OUR FATHER (Jn 17:1-26)*

Jn 17:1 Jesus said these things as He lifted up His eyes to heaven, and said, **"FATHER, THE TIME HAS COME. GLORIFY YOUR SON, THAT YOUR SON MAY ALSO GLORIFY YOU.**

Jn 17:2 **EVEN AS YOU GAVE HIM AUTHORITY OVER ALL FLESH, HE WILL GIVE ETERNAL LIFE TO ALL WHOM YOU HAVE GIVEN HIM.**

Jn 17:3 **THIS IS ETERNAL LIFE, THAT THEY SHOULD KNOW YOU, THE ONLY TRUE GOD, AND HIM WHOM YOU SENT, JESUS CHRIST!**

Jn 17:4 **I HAVE GLORIFIED YOU ON THE EARTH. I HAVE ACCOMPLISHED THE WORK WHICH YOU HAVE GIVEN ME TO DO."**

726 *JESUS, THE "INCARNATE DEITY," REVEALS HIS TOTAL UNITY AND HARMONY WITH THE FATHER (Jn 17:5-8)*

Jn 17:5 **"AND NOW, FATHER, GLORIFY ME IN YOUR OWN SELF WITH THE GLORY WHICH I HAD WITH YOU BEFORE THE WORLD BEGAN.**

Jn 17:6 **I REVEALED YOUR NAME TO THE PEOPLE WHOM YOU HAVE GIVEN ME OUT OF THE WORLD. THEY WERE YOURS, AND YOU HAVE GIVEN THEM TO ME. THEY HAVE OBEYED YOUR WORD.**

Jn 17:7 **NOW THEY KNOW THAT ALL THINGS WHATEVER YOU HAVE GIVEN ME ARE FROM YOU.**

Jn 17:8 **FOR THE WORDS WHICH YOU HAVE GIVEN ME I HAVE GIVEN TO**

THEM. AND THEY HAVE RECEIVED THEM, AND KNOW FOR SURE THAT I CAME FORTH FROM YOU. AND THEY BELIEVE THAT YOU SENT ME."

727   *JESUS, A VERY "PERSONAL GOD," INTERCEDES FOR HIS BELOVED DISCIPLES (Jn 17:9-12)*

Jn 17:9 "I PRAY FOR THEM. I DO NOT PRAY FOR THE WORLD, BUT FOR THOSE WHOM YOU HAVE GIVEN ME, FOR THEY ARE YOURS.

Jn 17:10 ALL THINGS THAT ARE MINE ARE YOURS, AND ALL THAT ARE YOURS ARE MINE, AND I AM GLORIFIED BY THEM.

Jn 17:11 I AM NO MORE IN THE WORLD, BUT THESE ARE IN THE WORLD. I AM COMING TO YOU, HOLY FATHER. KEEP THEM THROUGH YOUR NAME WHICH YOU HAVE GIVEN ME THAT THEY MAY BE ONE, EVEN AS WE ARE ONE.

Jn 17:12 WHILE I WAS WITH THEM IN THE WORLD, I KEPT THEM IN YOUR NAME. THOSE WHOM YOU HAVE GIVEN ME I HAVE KEPT. NOT ONE OF THEM IS LOST, EXCEPT THE SON OF PERDITION *(Judas)*, THAT THE SCRIPTURE MIGHT BE FULFILLED." *(Ps 41:9)*

728   *THE FOLLOWERS OF THE "ROYAL SOVEREIGN," ARE TO BE IN THE WORLD, BUT NOT OF THE WORLD (Jn 17:13-16)*

Jn 17:13 "BUT NOW I COME TO YOU. AND I SAY THESE THINGS WHILE I AM IN THE WORLD, THAT THEY MAY HAVE MY JOY IN THEMSELVES.

Jn 17:14 I HAVE GIVEN THEM YOUR WORD. THE WORLD HATED THEM, BECAUSE THEY ARE NOT OF THE WORLD, EVEN AS I AM NOT OF THE WORLD.

Jn 17:15 I PRAY NOT THAT YOU WOULD TAKE THEM FROM THE WORLD, BUT THAT YOU WOULD KEEP THEM FROM THE EVIL ONE.

Jn 17:16 THEY ARE NOT OF THE WORLD, EVEN AS I AM NOT OF THE WORLD."

729   *JESUS PRAYS FOR THE HOLINESS OF ALL BELIEVERS WHO WOULD FOLLOW THEIR GOSPEL TEACHINGS (Jn 17:17-20)*

Jn 17:17 "SANCTIFY THEM IN YOUR TRUTH. YOUR WORD IS TRUTH.

Jn 17:18 AS YOU SENT ME INTO THE WORLD, EVEN SO I AM SENDING THEM INTO THE WORLD.

Jn 17:19 FOR THEIR SAKES I SANCTIFY MYSELF, THAT THEY THEMSELVES ALSO MAY BE MADE HOLY BY THE TRUTH.

Jn 17:20 NOT FOR THESE ONLY DO I PRAY, BUT FOR THOSE ALSO WHO SHALL COME TO BELIEVE IN ME THROUGH THEIR MESSAGE."

730   JESUS, THE "ABUNDANT LIFE" MAKES A SPECIAL REQUEST FOR CHRISTIAN UNITY (Jn 17:21-23)

Jn 17:21 "MAY THEY ALL BE ONE, EVEN AS YOU, FATHER, ARE IN ME, AND I AM IN YOU, THAT THEY ALSO MAY BE ONE IN US, THAT THE WORLD MAY BELIEVE THAT YOU SENT ME.

Jn 17:22 THE GLORY WHICH YOU HAVE GIVEN ME, I HAVE GIVEN TO THEM, THAT THEY MAY BE ONE, EVEN AS WE ARE ONE.

Jn 17:23 I IN THEM, AND YOU IN ME, THAT THEY MAY BE PERFECTED IN UNITY. AND THAT THE WORLD MAY KNOW THAT YOU SENT ME AND THAT YOU LOVE THEM, EVEN AS YOU LOVE ME."

731   HIS FINAL PRAYER IS THAT GOD'S LOVE WOULD EXTEND TO HIS APOSTLES (Jn 17:24-26)

Jn 17:24 "FATHER, I DESIRE THAT THEY ALSO WHOM YOU HAVE GIVEN ME WILL BE WITH ME WHERE I AM, THAT THEY MAY SEE THE GLORY WHICH YOU HAVE GIVEN ME, FOR YOU LOVED ME BEFORE THE FOUNDATION OF THE WORLD.

Jn 17:25 RIGHTEOUS FATHER, THE WORLD HAS NOT KNOWN YOU, BUT I HAVE KNOWN YOU, AND THESE KNOW THAT YOU SENT ME.

Jn 17:26 I MADE KNOWN TO THEM YOUR NAME, AND WILL DECLARE IT, THAT THE LOVE WITH WHICH YOU LOVED ME MAY BE IN THEM, AND I IN THEM."

(Charles Spurgeon said, "I would rather teach one man to pray, than ten to preach.")

CHAPTER XXI

HIS AGONY AND TRIALS

732   JESUS WILL NOW PUT INTO ACTION AND PERSONALLY LIVE OUT HIS TEACHINGS (taken from Mt 26:36-46; Mk 14:32-42; Lk 22:40-46; Jn 18:1,2)

Jn 18:1   When Jesus had spoken these words, He went out with His disciples over the brook Kidron, where there was a garden, into which He and His disciples entered.

Mt 26:36   Then Jesus came with them to a place called Gethsemane, and said to His disciples, **"SIT HERE, WHILE I GO OVER THERE AND PRAY."**

Jn 18:2   Now Judas, who was to betray Him, also knew the place, for Jesus often met there with His disciples.

733   HE BECOMES TERRIBLY DISTRESSED AS THE HOURS OF HIS UNSPEAKABLE SUFFERING NEARS (Mt 26:37-40; Mk 14:33,34; Lk 22:41)

Mk 14:33   He took with Him Peter, James, and John, and began to be greatly troubled and distressed.

Mt 26:38   Then He said to them, **"MY SOUL IS EXCEEDINGLY SORROWFUL, EVEN TO THE POINT OF DEATH. STAY HERE, AND WATCH WITH ME."**

Mt 26:39   He went forward a little, fell on His face, and prayed, saying, **"ABBA, MY FATHER, IF IT IS POSSIBLE, LET THIS CUP PASS AWAY FROM ME. NEVERTHELESS, NOT MY WILL, BUT THY WILL BE DONE."**

Mt 26:40   He came to the disciples, and found them sleeping, and said to Peter, **"WHAT, COULD YOU NOT WATCH WITH ME <u>FOR ONE HOUR?</u>"**

734   HIS ANGUISH CONTINUES BUT THE DISCIPLES KEEP LETTING HIM DOWN (Mt 26:41,42; Mk 14:40)

Mt 26:42   Again, a second time He went away, and prayed, saying, **"MY FATHER, IF THIS CUP CANNOT PASS AWAY FROM ME UNLESS I DRINK IT, YOUR WILL BE DONE."**

Mk 14:40 Again He returned, and found them sleeping, for their eyes were very heavy, and they did not know how to answer Him.

Mt 26:41 "WATCH AND PRAY, THAT YOU DO NOT ENTER INTO TEMPTATION. THE SPIRIT INDEED IS WILLING, BUT THE FLESH IS WEAK."

735   THE THOUGHT OF THE SEVERITY OF THE ORDEAL HE WILL SUFFER CRUSHES HIM (Mt 26:44; Lk 22:43-45)

Mt 26:44 He left them again, went away, and prayed a third time, saying the same words.

Lk 22:43 An angel from heaven appeared to Him and strengthened Him.

Lk 22:44 Being in agony He prayed more earnestly. His sweat became like great drops of blood falling down on the ground.

Lk 22:45 When He rose up from His prayer, He came to the disciples, and found them sleeping and worn out by their sorrow.

736   RATHER THAN RUN AWAY "DOCILE LAMB" WAITS FOR HIS BETRAYER (Mt 26:45,46; Mk 14:41,42)

Mt 26:45 He came to His disciples, and said to them, "SLEEP ON NOW, AND TAKE YOUR REST...

Mk 14:41 *(after a period of time)*...IT IS ENOUGH *(sleep)*...THE HOUR HAS COME...

Mt 26:46 *(He then wakes them up)*...ARISE...LET US BE GOING...BEHOLD...HE WHO BETRAYS ME IS AT HAND...

Mk 14:41 ...SEE...THE SON OF MAN IS ABOUT TO BE BETRAYED INTO THE HANDS OF EVIL MEN."

737   JUDAS, THE TRAITOR, INSULTS JESUS THE "BENEVOLENT LORD," BY KISSING HIM (Mt 26:47-50; Mk 14:43-46; Lk 22:47,48; Jn 18:3-6)

Mk 14:43 While He was still speaking, Judas, one of the twelve, came. And with him a mob armed with swords and clubs from the chief priests, the scribes, and the elders.

Jn 18:3 Judas then, having taken a band of <u>temple guards</u> and officers from the chief priests and Pharisees *(no Roman soldiers yet)*, came there with lanterns, torches, and weapons.

Mk 14:44 Now he who was to betray Him had given them a sign, saying, "Whomever I will kiss, that is He. Seize Him, and lead Him away firmly."

Mt 26:49 Immediately he came to Jesus, and said, "Hail, Rabbi!" and kissed Him.

Lk 22:48 But Jesus said to him, **"JUDAS, DO YOU BETRAY THE SON OF MAN WITH A KISS?"**

738 THOSE ARRESTING HIM ARE STUNNED THAT JESUS WOULD FREELY OFFER HIMSELF (Mk 14:46; Jn 18:4-6)

Jn 18:4 Jesus therefore, knowing all the things that were going to happen to Him, stepped forward, and said to them, **"WHO ARE YOU LOOKING FOR?"**

Jn 18:5 They answered Him, "Jesus of Nazareth." Jesus said to them, **"I AM HE."** Judas also, who betrayed Him, was standing with them.

Jn 18:6 When therefore He said to them, **"I AM HE,"** they went backward, and fell to the ground.

739 JESUS, "OUR PROTECTOR," STEPS FORWARD TO SPARE HIS DISCIPLES (Mk 14:46; Jn 18:7-9)

Jn 18:7 Again therefore He asked them, **"WHO ARE YOU LOOKING FOR?"** They said, "Jesus of Nazareth."

Jn 18:8 **"I TOLD YOU THAT I AM HE. IF THEREFORE YOU SEEK ME, LET THESE OTHERS GO THEIR WAY."** *(Success in any ministry without successors, means failure.)*

Jn 18:9 That the word might be fulfilled which He spoke, "Of those whom you have given me, I have lost none."

740 HIS DEVOTED FOLLOWERS ARE WILLING TO BATTLE FOR JESUS (Mt 26:51,52; Mk 14:47; Lk 22:49-51; Jn 18:10)

Lk 22:49 When those who were with Him saw what was about to happen, they said to Him, "Lord, shall we strike with the sword?"

Jn 18:10 Simon Peter therefore, having a sword drew it, and struck the high priest's servant and cut off his right ear. The servant's name was Malchus.

Lk 22:51 But Jesus answered, **"STOP! NO MORE OF THIS."** And He touched the ear, and healed him.

Mt 26:52 "ALL THOSE WHO DRAW THE SWORD WILL DIE BY THE SWORD."

741 JESUS, THE "SAVIOR OF THE WORLD," MUST BE SACRIFICED TO FULFILL HOLY SCRIPTURE (Mt 26:53,54; Jn 18:11)

Jn 18:11 Jesus therefore said to Peter, **"PUT THE SWORD INTO ITS HOLDER. THE CUP WHICH THE FATHER HAS GIVEN ME, SHALL I NOT DRINK IT?**

Mt 26:53 OR DO YOU THINK THAT I COULD NOT ASK MY FATHER, AND HE WOULD EVEN NOW SEND ME MORE THAN TWELVE LEGIONS OF ANGELS?

Mt 26:54 HOW THEN WOULD THE SCRIPTURES BE FULFILLED THAT IT MUST BE SO?"

742 EVIL WILL PREVAIL JUST AS SACRED SCRIPTURE SAID IT WOULD (Mt 26:55,56; Mk 14:48,49; Lk 22:52,53)

Lk 22:52 Jesus said to the chief priests, captains of the temple and the elders who had come against Him, **"HAVE YOU COME OUT AS AGAINST A ROBBER, WITH SWORDS AND CLUBS?**

Lk 22:53 WHEN I WAS WITH YOU IN THE TEMPLE DAILY, YOU DID NOT STRETCH OUT YOUR HANDS AGAINST ME. BUT THIS IS YOUR HOUR, WHEN THE POWER OF DARKNESS RULES.

Mk 14:49 THIS IS ALL HAPPENING SO THAT THE MANY SCRIPTURES MIGHT BE FULFILLED."

743 THE DISCIPLES FLEE AS THE "SON OF THE MOST HIGH GOD" IS ARRESTED (Mt 26:56; Mk 14:50-52; Jn 18:12)

Mk 14:50 They all left Him, and fled.

> *Isa 53:6 All we like sheep have gone astray; we have turned every one to his own way; and the Lord hath laid on Him the iniquity of us all.*

Mk 14:51 A certain young man followed Him, having a linen cloth thrown around himself, over his naked body. The men grabbed him,

Mk 14:52 but he left the linen cloth, and fled from them naked.

Jn 18:12 So the commanding officer, and the officers of the Jews, seized Jesus and bound Him.

744   PETER, WHO WAS READY TO DIE WITH JESUS, NOW BEGINS HIS DENIALS (Mt 26:57,58; Mk 14:53,54; Lk 22:54; Jn 18:13-17)

Jn 18:13   They led Him to Annas first, for he was father-in-law to Caiaphas, who was high priest that year.

Jn 18:14   Now it was Caiaphas who advised the Jews that it was in their interest that one man should perish to save all the people.

Jn 18:15   Simon Peter followed Jesus, as did another disciple. Now that disciple *(John)* was known to the high priest, and entered in with Jesus into the court of the high priest.

Jn 18:16   But Peter was standing at the door outside. So the other disciple went and spoke to her who kept the door, and brought in Peter.

Jn 18:17   Then the maid who kept the door said to Peter, "Are you also one of this man's disciples?" He said, "I am not."

745   JESUS STANDS BEFORE CAIAPHAS TO BE QUESTIONED IN A NIGHT TRIAL (Jn 18:18-21)

Jn 18:18   Now the servants and the officers were standing there, having made a fire of coals, for it was cold. They were warming themselves. Peter was with them, standing and warming himself.

Jn 18:19   The high priest therefore asked Jesus about His disciples, and about His teaching.

Jn 18:20   Jesus answered him, **"I SPOKE OPENLY TO THE WORLD. I ALWAYS TAUGHT IN SYNAGOGUES, AND IN THE TEMPLE, WHERE THE JEWS MEET. I SAID NOTHING IN SECRET.**

Jn 18:21   WHY DO YOU ASK ME? ASK THOSE WHO HAVE HEARD ME WHAT I SAID TO THEM. THESE PEOPLE HERE KNOW THE THINGS WHICH I SAID."

746   A SLAP ON THE FACE PROVES NOTHING (Mt 26:59,60; Jn 18:22-24)

Jn 18:22   When He had said this, one of the officers standing by slapped Jesus with his hand, saying, "Do You answer the high priest like that?"

Jn 18:23   Jesus answered him, **"IF I HAVE SPOKEN EVIL, THEN GIVE EVIDENCE OF THAT EVIL. BUT IF NOT, WHY DO YOU STRIKE ME?"**

Jn 18:24   Then Annas sent Him bound to Caiaphas, the high priest.

747   PETER DENIES HE KNOWS JESUS, HIS "INTIMATE FRIEND," AS HE MANEUVERS TO SAVE HIMSELF (Mt 26:69-75; Mk 14:66-72; Lk 22:55-62; Jn 18:25-27)

Mk 14:66 As Peter was in the courtyard below, another maid of the high priest came,

Mk 14:67 and seeing Peter warming himself, she looked straight at him and said, "You were also with the Nazarene, Jesus!"

Mk 14:68 But he denied it, saying, "I neither know, nor understand what you are saying." He went out on the porch, and the rooster crowed.

748   MORE ACCUSATIONS BRINGS A STRONG REJECTION BY PETER (Mt 26:73; Mk 14:69-71; Lk 22:58-60; Jn 18:26)

Mk 14:69 The maid saw him there, and began again to tell those who stood by, "This is one of them."

Mk 14:70 But he again denied it. After a little while again those who stood by said to Peter, "You truly are one of them, for you are a Galilean, and your own speech proves it."

Mt 26:73 Those who stood by came and said to Peter, "Surely you are also one of them, your accent gives you away."

749   A FURTHER DENIAL BY PETER BRINGS THAT LOOK OF LOVE WHICH SENDS HIM FROM THE COURTYARD (Mt 26:74,75; Mk 14:71,72; Lk 22:60-62; Jn 18:27)

Mk 14:71 But he began to curse, and to swear, "I do not know this Man of whom you speak!"

Mk 14:72 The rooster crowed the second time. Peter remembered the word, how Jesus said to him, "Before the rooster crows twice, you will deny Me three times."

Lk 22:61 Then Jesus turned, and looked at Peter. And Peter remembered the Lord's words.

Lk 22:62 He went out, and wept bitterly.

750   JESUS, "LOVE PERSONIFIED," IS MISTREATED BY THOSE WHO GUARD HIM THROUGH THE NIGHT (Lk 22:63-65)

Lk 22:63 The men who held Jesus mocked Him and beat Him.

Lk 22:64 Having blindfolded Him, they struck Him on the face and asked Him, "Prophesy! Who is the one who struck You?"

Lk 6:29 And unto him that smiteth thee on the one cheek offer also the other...

Lk 22:65 They spoke many other things against Him, insulting Him.

751   THE JOINT SANHEDRIN COUNCIL NOW BEGINS THEIR QUESTIONING IN A FORMAL TRIAL (Mt 26:59-61; Mk 14:55-59; Lk 22:66)

Lk 22:66 As soon as it was day, the assembly of the elders of the people was gathered together, both chief priests and scribes, and they led Him into their court chamber.

Mt 26:59 Now the chief priests, the elders, and the whole council sought false testimony against Jesus, that they might put Him to death.

Mt 26:60 And they found none. Even though many false witnesses came forward, they did not agree.

752   OPINIONS DIFFER ABOUT JESUS, THE "UNBLEMISHED LAMB," WHO SPEAKS ONLY TRUTH (Mt 26:59-61; Mk 14:56-59)

Mk 14:56 Many gave false statements against Him, and their testimony did not agree with each other.

Mk 14:57 Some stood up, saying,

Mk 14:58 "We heard Him say, 'I will destroy this temple that is made with hands, and in three days I will build another made without hands.'"

Mk 14:59 Even about this, their testimony did not agree.

753   STILL THE QUESTIONING CONTINUES IN AN EFFORT TO FIND HIM GUILTY (Mt 26:62,63; Mk 14:60-62; Lk 22:67-69)

Mk 14:60 The high priest stood up in the midst, and asked Jesus, "Have You no answer? What is it which these testify against You?"

Mk 14:61 But He stayed quiet, and answered nothing. Again the high priest asked Him, "Are You the Christ, the Son of the Blessed?"

Lk 22:67 "If you are the Christ, tell us." But He said to them, **"IF I TELL YOU, YOU WILL NOT BELIEVE ME.**

Lk 22:68 AND IF I ASK YOU, YOU WILL NOT ANSWER ME, NOR LET ME GO."

*754 JESUS ADMITS TO BEING THE SON OF GOD—AND THUS CONVICTS HIMSELF—
CHOOSING TO DIE TO SAVE US (Mt 26:64; Mk 14:61,62; Lk 22:70)*

Mt 26:63 The high priest answered Him, "I adjure (charge and order) You by the Living God, that You tell us whether You are the Christ, the Son of God."

Lk 22:70 He said to them, **"YOU SAY CORRECTLY, BECAUSE I AM.**

Mk 14:62 AND YOU WILL SEE THE SON OF MAN SITTING AT THE RIGHT HAND OF POWER, AND COMING ON THE CLOUDS OF HEAVEN."

(If you were accused of being a Christian, is there enough evidence to convict you?)

755 AFTER BEING VOTED GUILTY HE IS DISGRACED AND MOCKED FURTHER (Mt 26:65-68; Mk 14:63-65; Lk 22:71)

Mt 26:65 Then the high priest tore his clothing, saying, "He has spoken blasphemy! Why do we need any more witnesses?

Mk 14:64 You have all heard the blasphemy! What do you think?" They all condemned Him to be worthy of death.

Mk 14:65 Some began to spit on Him. They blindfolded Him and began to beat Him with their fists. Even the officers struck Him with the palms of their hands, *(Isa 50:6)*

Mt 26:68 saying, "Prophesy to us, You Christ! Who hit You?"

Isa 52:14 …His visage was so marred, more than any man…

756 THE CHIEF PRIESTS AND ELDERS DELIVER JESUS TO THE ROMAN GOVERNOR (Mt 27:1,2; Mk 15:1; Lk 23:1,2; Jn 18:28-32)

Mt 27:1 Now when morning had come, all the chief priests and the elders of the people took counsel against Jesus to put Him to death. *(Ps 31:13)*

Mt 27:2 They again bound Him, and led Him away, and delivered Him up to Pontius Pilate, the governor.

Jn 18:28 They led Jesus therefore from Caiaphas into the Praetorium. It was early, and they themselves did not enter into the Praetorium, that they might not be defiled, so that they could eat the Passover.

Jn 18:29 Pilate therefore went out to them, and said, "What accusation do you bring against this man?"

757   *THEY REVEAL THEIR DESIRE TO HAVE JESUS EXECUTED (Jn 18:30-32)*

Jn 18:30   They answered him, "If this man was not an evildoer, we would not have delivered Him up to you."

Jn 18:31   Pilate therefore said to them, "Take Him yourselves, and judge Him according to your law." Therefore the Jews said to him, "It is not lawful for us to put anyone to death,"

Jn 18:32   that the word of Jesus might be fulfilled, which He spoke, signifying by what kind of death *(by Roman crucifixion)* He should die.

758   *PONTIUS PILATE STARTS INTERROGATING "THE SACRIFICIAL LAMB" (Mt 27:3-14; Mk 15:2-5; Lk 23:2)*

Mk 15:2   Pilate asked Him, "Are You the King of the Jews?" He answered, "**SO YOU SAY.**"

Mk 15:3   The chief priests accused Him of many things,

Lk 23:2   saying, "We found this Man perverting the nation, forbidding paying taxes to Caesar, and saying that He Himself is Christ, a king."

759   *THE GOVERNOR IS SURPRISED BY JESUS' LACK OF A DEFENSE (Mt 27:12-14; Mk 15:3-5)*

Mt 27:12   When He was accused by the chief priests and elders, He answered nothing.

Mk 15:4   Pilate again asked Him, "Have You no answer? See how many things they testify against You!"

Mk 15:5   But Jesus made no further answer, so that Pilate marveled.

760   *JESUS IS QUESTIONED PRIVATELY AS A PAGAN GOVERNOR'S IGNORANCE OF SPIRITUAL MATTERS IS REVEALED (Lk 23:3,4; Jn 18:33-38)*

Jn 18:33   Pilate therefore entered again into the Praetorium, called Jesus *(away from the elders)*, and said to Him, "Are You the King of the Jews?"

Jn 18:34   Jesus answered him, "**DO YOU SAY THIS ON YOUR OWN, OR DID OTHERS TELL YOU THIS ABOUT ME?**"

Jn 18:35   Pilate answered, "I am not a Jew, am I? Your own nation and the chief priests delivered You to me. What have You done?"

Jn 18:36 Jesus answered, **"MY KINGDOM IS NOT OF THIS WORLD. IF MY KINGDOM WERE OF THIS WORLD, THEN MY SERVANTS WOULD FIGHT THAT I WOULD NOT BE DELIVERED TO THE JEWS. BUT MY KINGDOM IS NOT HERE."**

761 *JESUS, THE VERY "TRUTH," IS NOT RECOGNIZED BY PILATE (Lk 23:4; Jn 18:37,38)*

Jn 18:37 Pilate therefore said to Him, "Are You a king then?" Jesus answered, **"YOU SAY THAT I AM A KING. FOR THIS REASON I HAVE BEEN BORN, AND FOR THIS REASON I HAVE COME INTO THE WORLD, THAT I SHOULD TESTIFY TO THE TRUTH. EVERYONE WHO IS OF THE TRUTH LISTENS TO MY VOICE."**

Jn 18:38 Pilate said to Him, "What is truth?" When he had said this, he went out again to the Jews, and said to them, "I find no basis for a charge against this man."

762 *THE NEWS THAT HE IS A "NAZARENE" FROM GALILEE SENDS HIM TO HEROD ANTIPAS (Lk 23:4-12)*

Lk 23:5 But they insisted, saying, "He stirs up the people, teaching throughout all Judea, beginning from Galilee even to this place."

Lk 23:6 But when Pilate heard Galilee mentioned, he asked if Jesus was a Galilean.

Lk 23:7 When he found out that He was in Herod's jurisdiction, he sent Him to Herod, who was also in Jerusalem during those days.

763 *JESUS, NOT APPEARING IMPRESSIVE, HEROD MAKES FUN OF HIM (Lk 23:8-12)*

Lk 23:8 Now when Herod saw Jesus, he was exceedingly glad, for he had wanted to see Him for a long time, because he had heard many things about Him. He hoped to see some miracle done by Him.

Lk 23:9 He questioned Him with many words, but Jesus gave no answer.

> *Mt 7:6 Do not give that which is holy to dogs, neither throw your pearls before pigs, lest they trample them under their feet, and turn and tear you to pieces.*

Lk 23:10 The chief priests, and the scribes, stood there vehemently accusing Him.

Lk 23:11 Herod with his soldiers humiliated Him, and mocked Him. Dressing Him in a gorgeous robe, he sent Him back to Pilate.

Isa 53:2 ...He hath no form nor comeliness; and when we shall see Him, there is no beauty that we should desire Him.

Lk 23:12 Herod and Pilate became friends with each other that very day, for before that they were enemies.

764   THE LORD JESUS IS BROUGHT BEFORE PILATE A SECOND TIME (Lk 23:13-16)

Lk 23:13 Pilate called together the chief priests and the rulers of the people,

Lk 23:14 and said to them, "You brought this man to me as one who perverts the people, and as you see, I have examined Him before you, and found no basis for a charge against this man concerning those things of which you accuse Him.

Lk 23:15 Neither has Herod, for I sent Jesus to him, and see, nothing worthy of death has been done by Him.

Lk 23:16 I will therefore flog Him and release Him."

765   ONE PRISONER IS TO BE SET FREE EACH YEAR (Mt 27:15,16; Mk 15:6-8; Jn 18:39)

Mt 27:15 Now at the feast, the governor was accustomed to release one prisoner, whom the people desired.

Mt 27:16 They had then a notorious prisoner, called Barabbas,

Mk 15:7 ...bound with those who had made insurrection, men who had committed murder.

Mk 15:8 The crowd, crying aloud, began to ask him to do as he always did for them.

766   TO AVOID THE JEALOUSY OF THE JEWISH AUTHORITIES, PILATE GIVES THE CROWD A CHANCE TO DECIDE (Mt 27:17,18; Mk 15:9-11)

Mt 27:17 When therefore they were gathered together, Pilate said to them, "Whom do you want me to release to you? Barabbas, or Jesus, who is called Christ?"

Mk 15:10 For he perceived that it was out of envy that the chief priests had delivered Him up.

Mk 15:11 But the chief priests stirred up the multitude, that he should release Barabbas to them instead.

767   *THE PEOPLE ARE EASILY INFLUENCED AGAINST THEIR "ONLY MESSIAH"*
(Mt 27:20-22)

Mt 27:20 Now the chief priests and the elders persuaded the people to ask for Barabbas, and execute Jesus.

Mt 27:21 But the governor answered them, "Which of the two do you want me to release to you?" They said, "Barabbas!"

Mt 27:22 Pilate said to them, "What then shall I do with Jesus, who is called Christ?" They all said to him, "Let Him be crucified!"

768   *JESUS, "OUR HEALER," IS THEN BRUTALLY SCOURGED (Jn 19:1)*

Jn 19:1 So Pilate then took Jesus, and had Him flogged. *(In a roman flagellation, the flesh was often torn from the body.)*

> *(Centuries earlier Isaiah wrote that by His stripes <u>we are healed</u>. Isa 53:5*
> *Decades later Peter would write that by His stripes <u>we were healed</u>. 1 Pet 2:24)*

> *(My prayer is often, "Lord Jesus, I would never wish for You to suffer that brutal, agonizing whipping on Your back. But since You already did sustain all of that for me, I do claim Your power for my healing.")*

769   *PILATE IS CAUTIONED BY HIS WIFE NOT TO CONDEMN AN INNOCENT MAN*
(Mt 27:19)

Mt 27:19 While the governor was sitting on the judgment seat, his wife sent word to him, saying, "Have nothing to do with that righteous man, for I have suffered many things this day in a dream because of Him."

770   *HIS BACK IS ON FIRE WITH PAIN AS THE ROMAN SOLDIERS NOW MAKE SPORT OF THEIR "SUFFERING PRISONER" (Mt 27:27-30; Mk 15:16-19; Jn 19:2,3)*

Mk 15:16 The soldiers led Him away within the court, which is the Praetorium. They called together the whole cohort.

Mk 15:17 They clothed Him with the purple robe from Herod...

Mt 27:29 They braided a crown of thorns and put it on His head *(cutting deeply into his scalp)* and *(for a king's scepter)* a reed in His right hand. They knelt down before Him, and mocked Him, saying, "Hail, King of the Jews!"

Isa 50:6 I gave My back to the smiters, and My cheeks to them that plucked off the hair; I hid not My face from shame and spitting.

Mk 15:19 They struck His head with a stick, and spat on Him, and bowing their knees, they mocked Him by paying homage to Him.

771   JESUS, THE "BLAMELESS VICTIM," IS BROUGHT AGAIN BEFORE THE HUGE CROWD (Jn 19:4-6)

Jn 19:4 Then Pilate went out again, and said to them, "Behold, I bring Him out to you, that you may know that I find no basis for a charge against Him."

Jn 19:5 Jesus therefore came out, wearing the crown of thorns and the purple robe. Pilate said to them, "Behold, the Man!" *(Ecce Homo)*

Jn 19:6 When the chief priests and the officers saw Him, they shouted, saying, "Crucify Him! Crucify Him!" Pilate said to them, "Take Him yourselves, and crucify Him, for I find no basis for a charge against Him."

Isa 53:5,7 But He was pierced for our transgressions. He was crushed for our iniquities. The punishment that brought our peace was on Him...He was oppressed, yet when He was afflicted He did not open His mouth. As a lamb that is led to the slaughter, and as a sheep that before its shearers is mute, so He did not open His mouth.

772   PILATE'S AUTHORITY OVER JESUS ACTUALLY COMES FROM GOD (Jn 19:7-11)

Jn 19:7 The Jews answered him, "We have a law, and by our law He ought to die, because He calls Himself the Son of God." *(Lev 24:16)*

Jn 19:8 When therefore Pilate heard this saying, he was even more afraid.

Jn 19:9 He entered into the Praetorium again, and said to Jesus, "Where are you from?" But Jesus gave him no answer.

Jn 19:10 Pilate said to Him, "Are You not going to speak to me? Do You not know that I have power to release You, and have power to crucify You?"

Jn 19:11 Jesus answered, **"YOU WOULD HAVE NO POWER AT ALL OVER ME, UNLESS IT WERE GIVEN TO YOU FROM ABOVE. THEREFORE HE WHO DELIVERED ME TO YOU IS GUILTY OF A GREATER GUILT."**

773 THE ADMINISTRATOR MAKES A LAST ATTEMPT TO SAVE A HARMLESS "HUMAN BEING" (Lk 23:20,21; Jn 19:12,13)

Jn 19:12 At this, Pilate was seeking to set Him free, but the Jews cried out, saying, "If you release this man, you are not Caesar's friend! Everyone who makes himself a king speaks against Caesar!"

Jn 19:13 When Pilate therefore heard these words, he brought Jesus out, and sat down on the judgment seat at a place called the Pavement, but in Hebrew, Gabbatha.

Lk 23:20 Then Pilate spoke to them again, wanting to release Jesus,

Lk 23:21 but they shouted, saying, "Crucify Him! Crucify Him!"

774 THE CHIEF PRIESTS ARE EVEN PREPARED TO SWEAR ALLEGIANCE TO ROME IN ORDER TO HAVE JESUS, THE "MODEL OF HOLINESS," CRUCIFIED (Mt 27:22,23; Mk 15:12-14; Lk 23:22,23; Jn 19:14,15)

Lk 23:22 He said to them the third time, "Why? What evil has this man done? I have found no major crime about Him.

Lk 23:23 But they were firm with loud voices, determined that He should be crucified. Their voices and the voices of the chief priests were winning.

Jn 19:14 Now it was the Preparation Day before the Passover. He said to the Jews, "Behold, your King!"

Jn 19:15 They cried out, "Away with Him! Away with Him! Crucify Him!" Pilate said to them, "Shall I crucify your King?" The chief priests answered, "We have no king but Caesar!"

775 UNABLE TO CONTROL THE BOISTEROUS THRONG, PILATE RELEASES BARABBAS (Mt 27:24-26; Mk 15:15; Lk 23:23-25; Jn 19:16)

Mt 27:24 So when Pilate saw that nothing was being gained, but rather that the disturbance was getting worse, he took water, and washed his hands before the crowd, saying, "I am innocent of the blood of this "Just Man." You see to it yourselves."

Mt 27:25 All the people answered, "May His blood be on us, and on our children!"

Mk 15:15 Pilate, wishing to please the multitude, released Barabbas to them, and handed over Jesus to be crucified.

776 A REBELLIOUS KILLER IS SET FREE ONLY TO HAVE JESUS, THE "PRINCE OF PEACE," CONDEMNED (Lk 23:24,25; Jn 19:16)

Lk 23:24 Pilate decreed that what they asked for should be done.

Lk 23:25 He released him who had been thrown into prison for insurrection and murder, for whom they asked, but he delivered Jesus up to their will.

> *Isa 53:3,4 He was despised, and rejected by men, a man of suffering, and acquainted with grief. He was despised as one from whom men hide their faces, and we esteemed Him not...Surely He has borne our sickness, and carried our suffering, yet we considered Him plagued, struck by God, and afflicted.*

777 JESUS, OUR "SUBSTITUTE SACRIFICE," IS HUMILIATED FURTHER BY CARRYING HIS OWN CROSS THROUGH THE STREETS OF JERUSALEM (Jn 19:17)

Jn 19:17 He went out, bearing His cross...

778 JUDAS WHO TRIED TO BELIEVE WITH HIS MIND AND NOT HIS HEART COMMITS SUICIDE (Mt 27:3-5)

Mt 27:3 Then Judas, who betrayed Him, when he saw that Jesus was condemned, felt remorse, and brought back the thirty pieces of silver to the chief priests and elders,

Mt 27:4 saying, "I have sinned in that I have betrayed innocent blood." But they said, "What is that to us? That matter is yours."

Mt 27:5 He threw down the pieces of silver in the temple, and departed. He went out and hanged himself.

779 BLOOD MONEY IS USED TO BUY A RESTING PLACE FOR FOREIGNERS (Mt 27:6-10)

Mt 27:6 The chief priests took the pieces of silver, and said, "It is not lawful to put them into the treasury, since it is the price of blood."

Mt 27:7 They took counsel, and bought the potter's field with the money, to bury strangers in.

Mt 27:8 Therefore that field is called the "Field of Blood" to this day.

Mt 27:9 Then that which was spoken through Jeremiah the prophet was fulfilled, saying,

"They took the thirty pieces of silver, the price of Him upon whom a price had been set, whom some of the children of Israel did value,

Mt 27:10 and they gave them for the potter's field, as the Lord commanded." *(Zec 11:12,13)*

CHAPTER XXII

HIS CRUCIFIXION AND DEATH

780   A NORTH AFRICAN IS FORCED TO CARRY THE CROSS OF JESUS *(taken from Mt 27:32; Mk 15:21; Lk 23:26)*

Lk 23:26 When they led Him away, they grabbed one Simon of Cyrene, coming from the country, and laid on him the cross, to carry it behind Jesus.

(The Bible does not say that Jesus fell three times. But we can presume that He did after His various difficulties; being awake all night, His agony in Gethsemene, up on His feet through the various trials, with nothing to eat, the severe whipping, then carrying His cross. This may explain why the Roman soldiers made someone carry the cross for Jesus, so as not to lose Him before He got to Calvary.)

781   THEN JESUS, THE "OBEDIENT UNTO DEATH," CONSOLES THOSE WHO WOULD LATER SUFFER GRIEVOUSLY *(Lk 23:27-31)*

Lk 23:27 A great many people followed Him, including women who also mourned and wailed for Him.

Lk 23:28 But Jesus, turning to them, said, **"DAUGHTERS OF JERUSALEM, DO NOT WEEP FOR ME, BUT WEEP FOR YOURSELVES AND FOR YOUR CHILDREN.**

Lk 23:29 FOR BEHOLD, THE DAYS ARE COMING IN WHICH THEY WILL SAY, 'BLESSED ARE THE BARREN, THE WOMBS THAT NEVER BORE, AND THE BREASTS THAT NEVER NURSED.'

Lk 23:30 THEN THEY WILL BEGIN TO SAY TO THE MOUNTAINS, 'FALL ON US!' AND TO THE HILLS, 'COVER US.' *(in an attempt to hide from God's judgment)*

Lk 23:31 FOR IF THEY DO THESE THINGS TO A GREEN *(fruitfull)* **TREE, WHAT WILL BE DONE TO A DRY** *(barren)* **ONE?"**

782   JESUS, WHO BLESSED THE WINE AT THE CANA WEDDING NOW REFUSES THE WINE WHICH WOULD NUMB HIS PAIN *(Mt 27:33,34; Mk 15:22,23; Lk 23:32 ; Jn 19:18)*

Mk 15:22 They brought Him to the place called Golgotha, which is, being interpreted, "The place of the skull."

Lk 23:32 There were also others, two criminals, led with Him to be put to death.

Mk 15:23 They offered Him wine mixed with myrrh to drink, but He did not take it.

783   EVER FORGIVING, JESUS, THE "GIVER OF LIFE," IS FIRMLY NAILED TO THE RUGGED CROSS—THAT EMBLEM OF SUFFERING AND SHAME *(Mk 15:25,28; Lk 23:34)*

Mk 15:25 It was the third hour (9 am), and they crucified Him.

Lk 23:33 ...with the criminals, one on the right and the other on the left.

Mk 15:28 The Scripture was fulfilled, which says, "He was numbered with transgressors."

Lk 23:34 Jesus said, **"FATHER, FORGIVE THEM, FOR THEY DO NOT KNOW WHAT THEY ARE DOING."**

784   WHILE JESUS SUFFERS HORRENDOUS PAIN, HIS EXECUTIONERS DIVIDE HIS GARMENTS AMONG THEMSELVES *(Mt 27:35,36; Mk 15:24; Jn 19:23,24)*

Jn 19:23 Then the soldiers, when they had crucified Jesus, took His clothes and divided them into four parts, one to every soldier, and also the robe. Now the robe was without seam, woven from the top throughout.

Jn 19:24 Then they said to one another, "Let us not tear it, but cast lots to decide whose it will be." So the Scripture was also fulfilled, which says, "They parted My clothes among them. For My robe they cast lots." *(Just as King David was given to prophesy 1,000 years earlier in Ps 22:18)*

Mt 27:36 And they sat and watched Him there.

785   PILATE HOLDS FIRM TO HIS DESCRIPTION OF JESUS *(Mt 27:37; Mk 15:26; Lk 23:38; Jn 19:19-22)*

Jn 19:19 Pilate wrote a title also, and had it put on the cross. There was written, "JESUS OF NAZARETH," the "KING OF THE JEWS."

Jn 19:20 Therefore many of the Jews read this title, for the place where Jesus was crucified was near the city. And it was written in Hebrew, in Latin, and in Greek.

Jn 19:21 The chief priests of the Jews therefore said to Pilate, "Do not write, 'The King of the Jews,' but, 'that He said, I am King of the Jews.'"

Jn 19:22 Pilate answered, "What I have written, I have written."

786   MANY SCOFF AND RIDICULE HIM, BUT JESUS, THE "SUPREME SACRIFICE," REMAINS HANGING ON THE CROSS FOR SIX HOURS *(Mt 27:39-43; Mk 15:39-41)*

Mt 27:39 Those who passed by blasphemed Him, wagging their heads, *(Ps 109:25)*

Mt 27:40 and saying, "You who would destroy the temple, and rebuild it in three days. *(Jesus was referring to His own body, as the temple, and should they destroy Him by crucifying Him, He would arise in three days.)* Save Yourself! If You are the Son of God, come down from the cross!"

Mt 27:41 Likewise the chief priests were also mocking, with the scribes, the Pharisees, and the elders.

> *1 Pet 2:23 Who, when He was insulted, He offered no insult in return; when He suffered, He threatened not; but committed Himself to Him that judgeth righteously.*

787   OUR "BLEEDING SAVIOR" ENDURES ON THE CROSS TO REMOVE OUR SIN-DEBT AND ASSURE OUR SALVATION *(Mt 27:42,43; Mk 15:31,32; Lk 23:35-37)*

Lk 23:35 The people stood watching. The rulers with them also made fun of Him, saying, "He saved others. Let Him save Himself, if this is the Christ. *(Ps 22:7)*

Mt 27:42 ...If He is the King of Israel, let Him come down from the cross now, and we will believe in Him.

Mt 27:43 He trusts in God. Let God deliver Him now, if He loves Him; for He said, 'I am the Son of God.'" *(Ps 22:8)*

Lk 23:36 The soldiers also mocked Him,

> *Ps 22:13,16,17 They gaped upon Me with their mouths...they pierced My hands and My feet...they look and stare at Me.*

Lk 23:37 saying, "If You are the King of the Jews, save Yourself!"

> *Heb 12:2 ...Who for the joy that was set before Him (having you in heaven with Him) endured the Cross, despising the shame...*

788   ETERNAL LIFE IS PROMISED TO A CRIMINAL WHO ACKNOWLEDGES JESUS
(Lk 23:39-43)

Lk 23:39   One of the criminals who was also hanging, insulted Him saying, "If You are the Christ, save Yourself and us!"

Lk 23:40   But the other answered, and rebuking him said, "Do you not fear God, seeing you are under the same condemnation?

Lk 23:41   We hang here justly, for we receive the due reward for our deeds, but this man has done nothing wrong."

Lk 23:42   He said to Jesus, "Lord, remember me when You come into Your Kingdom."

Lk 23:43   Jesus said to him, **"ASSUREDLY, I TELL YOU, TODAY YOU WILL BE WITH ME IN PARADISE."**

789   MARY, THE MOTHER OF JESUS, SEES HER OWN SON HANGING ON THE CROSS, SUFFERING EXCRUCIATING TORTURE *(Jn 19:25-27)*

Jn 19:25   But there standing by the cross of Jesus was His mother, and His mother's sister, and Mary the wife of Clopas, and Mary Magdalene.

   Lk 2:35…also a sword will pierce through your own soul…

Jn 19:26   Therefore when Jesus saw His mother, and the disciple whom He loved standing there, He said to His "mother," **"WOMAN, BEHOLD YOUR SON!"** *(He does not call her mother, because even she must see Jesus as her savior.)*

Jn 19:27   Then He said to the disciple, **"BEHOLD YOUR MOTHER!"** From that hour, the disciple took her to his own home.

790   GOD THE FATHER WHO WAS ALWAYS PLEASED WITH HIS SON, NOW CANNOT LOOK UPON JESUS, THE "SIN-BEARER," WHO CARRIES THE GUILT OF ALL OUR SINS
(Mt 27:45-50; Mk 15:33,35; Lk 23:44-46)

Lk 23:44   It was now about the sixth hour, and darkness came over the whole land until the ninth hour *(noon to 3 P.M.)*.

Lk 23:45   The sun was darkened.

Mt 27:46   About the ninth hour, Jesus cried with a loud voice, saying, **"ELI, ELI, LAMA SABACHTHANI?"** That is, **"MY GOD, MY GOD, WHY HAVE YOU FORSAKEN ME?"**

2 Cor 5:21 For God hath made Him to be sin for us, Who knew no sin, that we might be made the righteousness of God in Him.

Mk 15:35 Some of those who stood by, when they heard it, said, "Behold, He is calling Elijah." *(Ps 22:1 & 22:11)*

791   JESUS, THE ONE AND ONLY "HOLY SACRIFICE" FULFILLS THE PLAN OF REDEMPTION *(Mt 27:48,49; Mk 15:36; Jn 19:28-30)*

Jn 19:28 After this, Jesus, seeing that all things were now finished, that the Scripture might be fulfilled, said, **"I AM THIRSTY."**

Mt 27:48 Immediately one of the soldiers ran, took a sponge, and filled it with vinegar, and put it on a reed, and gave Him a drink. *(Ps 69:21)*

Mt 27:49 The rest said, "Let Him be. Let's see whether Elijah comes to save Him."

Jn 19:30 When Jesus therefore had received the vinegar, He said, **"IT IS FINISHED."** *(namely, to redeem the world by paying the enormous debt for our sins)*

Mk 10:45 For even the Son of Man came not to be ministered unto, but to minister, and to give His life a ransom for many.

792   JESUS, "OBEDIENT UNTO DEATH," EXPRESSES TOTAL FAITH AND RELIANCE ON HIS HEAVENLY FATHER *(Mt 27:50; Mk 15:37; Lk 23:46; Jn 19:28-30)*

Lk 23:46 Jesus, crying with a loud voice, said, **"FATHER, INTO YOUR HANDS I COMMIT MY SPIRIT!"** Having said this, He breathed His last breath.

(A thousand people could choose to die for any of us, and we'd still be guilty of all our sins. Only the sacrificing of the actual Son of the Most High God qualifies to pay the penalty for all our offenses.)

Rom 5:8 But God commends His own love toward us, in that while we were yet sinners, Christ died for us.

793   RELATED EVENTS ACCOMPANYING HIS DEATH CAUSE A CHANGE OF HEART IN MANY OBSERVERS *(Mt 27:51-56; Mk 15:38,41; Lk 23:45-49)*

Mt 27:51 Behold, the veil of the temple was torn in two, from top to bottom. *(Symbolizing that we now have direct access to God.)* The earth quaked and the rocks were split.

Mt 27:52 The tombs were opened, and many bodies of the saints who had fallen asleep were raised,

Mt 27:53 and coming out of the tombs after His resurrection, they entered into the Holy City and appeared to many.

Mt 27:54 Now the centurion, and those who were with him watching Jesus, when they saw the earthquake, and the things that were done, feared exceedingly, saying, "Truly this was the Son of God."

Heb 2:3 How shall we escape if we neglect so great a salvation…

794   *MANY OF HIS FRIENDS ARE ALSO WITNESSES OF HIS CRUCIFIXION (Mt 27:55,56; Mk 15:40,41; Lk 23:48,49)*

Lk 23:49 All His acquaintances, and the women who followed Him from Galilee, stood at a distance, watching these things.

Mt 27:56 Among them was Mary Magdalene, Mary the mother of James and Joses, and the mother of the sons of Zebedee.

Mk 15:40 …and Salome,

Mk 15:41 who, when He was in Galilee, had followed Him, and served Him, and also many other women who came up with Him to Jerusalem.

Lk 23:48 All the multitudes that came together to see this, when they saw the things that were done, returned home beating their breasts.

795   *THE SIDE OF JESUS IS PIERCED FROM WHICH POURS FORTH THE LAST DROP OF HIS "ROYAL BLOOD" (Jn 19:31-34)*

Jn 19:31 Therefore the Jews, because it was the Preparation Day, so that the bodies would not remain on the cross on the Sabbath, for that Sabbath was a high day, asked of Pilate that their legs might be broken *(making it impossible to lift up to keep breathing)*, and that they might be taken down.

Jn 19:32 Therefore the soldiers came, and broke the legs of the first, and of the other who was crucified with Him,

Jn 19:33 but when they came to Jesus, and saw that He was already dead, they did not break His legs.

Jn 19:34 However one of the soldiers pierced His side with a spear, and immediately blood and water came out.

> *1 Jn 3:16 Hereby perceive we the love of God, because He laid down His life for us; and we ought to lay down our lives for the brethren.*

796 MORE OF HOLY SCRIPTURE IS FULFILLED AS PROPHESIED (Jn 19:35-37)

Jn 19:35 He who has seen these things has testified, and his testimony is true. He knows that he tells the truth, that you may believe.

Jn 19:36 For these things happened, that the Scripture might be fulfilled, "A bone of His will not be broken." *(as predicted hundreds of years earlier in Ps 34:20)*

Jn 19:37 Again another Scripture says, "They will look on Him whom they have pierced." *(as foretold in Jewish writings in Zec 12:10)*

797 A MEMBER OF THE SANHEDRIN REQUESTS THE BODY OF JESUS (Mt 27:57,58; Mk 15:42-45; Lk 23:50-53; Jn 19:38,39)

Mk 15:42 When evening had now come, because it was the Preparation Day, that is, the day before the Sabbath *(this indicates Jesus died on a Friday)*,

Jn 19:38 being a disciple of Jesus, but secretly for fear of the Jews,

Mk 15:43 Joseph of Arimathaea, a prominent council member who also himself was looking for the Kingdom of God, came. He boldly went in to Pilate, and asked for Jesus' body.

Mk 15:44 Pilate marveled that He was already dead. And summoning the centurion, he asked him whether He had been dead long.

Mk 15:45 When he found out from the centurion, he granted the body to Joseph.

798 AFTER A CRUEL AND BRUTAL DEATH, THE LIFELESS CORPSE IS PREPARED TO BE ENTOMBED (Mt 27:59-61; Mk 15:46,47; Lk 23:53-56; Jn 19:39-42)

Jn 19:39 Nicodemus, who at first came to Jesus by night, also came bringing a mixture of myrrh and aloes, weighing about a hundred pounds.

Jn 19:40 So they took Jesus' body, and bound it in linen cloths with the spices, as the custom of the Jews is to bury.

Jn 19:41 Now in the place where He was crucified there was a garden. In the garden was a new tomb in which no man had ever yet been laid.

Mt 27:60 They laid Him in Joseph's own new tomb, which he had cut out in the rock. And they rolled a huge stone over the door of the tomb, and departed.

> *Isa 53:12 ...He hath poured out His soul unto death...and He bare the sin of many, and made intercession for the transgressors.*

799   GODLY WOMEN MAKE PREPARATIONS TO GIVE JESUS A PROPER BURIAL (Lk 23:54-56)

Lk 23:54 It was the day of the Preparation, and the Sabbath was drawing near.

Lk 23:55 The women, who had come with Him out of Galilee, followed after, and saw the tomb where His body was laid.

Lk 23:56 They returned, and prepared their own spices and ointments. On the Sabbath they rested according to the commandment.

800   THE JEWISH ELDERS SUCCEED IN SECURING A SENTRY TO GUARD THE TOMB (Mt 27:62-66)

Mt 27:62 Now on the next day, which was the day after the Preparation Day, the chief priests and the Pharisees were gathered together and came to Pilate,

Mt 27:63 saying, "Sir, we remember what that deceiver said while He was still alive, 'On the third day I will rise again.'

Mt 27:64 Command therefore that the tomb be made secure until the third day, lest perhaps His disciples come at night and steal Him away, and tell the people, 'He is risen from the dead,' and the last deception will be worse than the first."

Mt 27:65 Pilate said to them, "You have a guard *(usually four men)*. Go, make it as guarded as you can."

Mt 27:66 So they went and made the tomb secure. And placed a seal on the huge stone.

CHAPTER XXIII

HIS RESURRECTION AND APPEARANCES

801   THE WOMEN GO VISIT THE TOMB ON SUNDAY, THE BEGINNING OF THEIR WORK-WEEK (taken from Mt 28:1; Mk 16:1-3; Lk 24:1; Jn 20:1)

Mk 16:1 When the Sabbath was past, Mary Magdalene, and Mary the mother of James, and Salome, brought spices, that they might come and anoint Him.

Mk 16:2 Very early on the first day of the week *(Sunday)*, they came to the tomb when the sun had risen.

Mk 16:3 They were saying among themselves, "Who will roll away the stone from the door of the tomb for us?"

802   JESUS HAVING ALREADY BEEN RAISED, AN ANGEL NOW OPENS THE BURIAL CHAMBER (Mt 28:2-4)

Mt 28:2 Behold, there was a great earthquake. An angel of the Lord then descended from the sky, and came and rolled away the stone from the door, and sat on it.

Mt 28:3 His appearance was like lightning and his clothing white as snow.

Mt 28:4 For fear of him, the guards shook, and became like dead men.

803   AFTER THE WOMEN ENTER THE EMPTY TOMB, TWO ANGELS GIVE TESTIMONY TO THE RESURRECTION OF THE "CRUCIFIED MESSIAH" (Mt 28:5,6; Mk 16:4-6; Lk 24:2-5)

Mk 16:4 Looking up, the women saw that the stone was rolled back.

Lk 24:3 They entered in, and did not find the Lord Jesus' body.

Lk 24:4 It happened, while they were greatly perplexed about this, two men stood by them in dazzling clothing.

Lk 24:5 Becoming terrified, the women bowed their faces down to the earth. The men said to them, "Why do you seek the living among the dead?

Mk 16:6 Do not be startled. You seek Jesus, the Nazarene, who has been crucified. He has risen. He is not here. Look at the place where they had laid Him!" *(Ps 16:10)*

804   *THE WOMEN ARE INSTRUCTED TO GO TELL THE APOSTLES (Mt 28:7,8; Mk 16:7,8; Lk 24:6-8)*

Lk 24:6 "Remember what He told you when He was still in Galilee,

Lk 24:7 saying that the Son of Man must be delivered up into the hands of sinful men, and be crucified, and on the third day He will rise again."

Lk 24:8 They then remembered His words.

Mk 16:7 "But go, tell His disciples—and Peter, 'He goes before you into Galilee.' There you will see Him, as He said to you."

Mk 16:8 They went out, and fled from the tomb, for trembling and astonishment had come on them. They said nothing to anyone, for they were afraid.

805   *MARY MAGDALENE PROCEEDS ALONE TO TELL A COUPLE OF HIS DISCIPLES (Lk 24:11; Jn 20:2,3)*

Jn 20:2 Nevertheless, Mary Magdalene ran and came to Simon Peter, and to the other disciple *(John)* whom Jesus loved, and said to them, "They have taken away the Lord out of the tomb, and we do not know where they have laid Him!"

Jn 20:3 Therefore Peter and the other disciple went out, and they hurried toward the tomb.

806   *BUT PETER AND JOHN HURRY ONLY TO FIND AN EMPTY GRAVE (Jn 20:4-7)*

Jn 20:4 They both ran together. The other disciple outran Peter, and came to the tomb first.

Jn 20:5 Stooping and looking in, he saw the linen cloths lying there, yet he did not enter in.

Jn 20:6 Then Simon Peter came, following him, and darted into the tomb. He saw the linen cloths lying there,

Jn 20:7 and the wrapping, which had been on His head, not lying with the linen cloths but folded up in a place by itself. *(which Jesus must have done)*

807   THE TWO DO NOT YET COMPREHEND THE LORD RISING FROM THE DEAD
(Jn 20:8-10)

Jn 20:8   So then the other disciple who came first to the tomb also entered in, and he saw and believed.

Jn 20:9   For as yet they did not remember from Scripture, that He must rise from the dead.

Jn 20:10   So the disciples went away again to their own homes.

808   MARY MAGDALENE STAYS BY THE TOMB AND CRIES TEARFULLY FOR HER MISSING JESUS (Jn 20:11-18)

Jn 20:11   But Mary was standing outside at the tomb weeping. So, as she wept, she stooped and looked into the tomb,

Jn 20:12   and she saw two angels in white sitting, one at the head, and one at the feet, where the body of Jesus had lain.

Jn 20:13   They told her, "Woman, why are you weeping?" She said to them, "Because they have taken away my Lord, and I do not know where they have laid Him."

809   SHE BECOMES THE FIRST TO MEET THE "RISEN LORD" (Jn 20:14-18)

Jn 20:14   When she had said this, she turned around and saw Jesus standing but did not know that it was Jesus.

Jn 20:15   Jesus said to her, **"WOMAN, WHY ARE YOU WEEPING? WHO ARE YOU LOOKING FOR?"** She, supposing Him to be the gardener, said to Him, "Sir, if you have carried Him away, tell me where you have laid Him, and I will take Him away."

Jn 20:16   Jesus said to her, **"MARY."** She turned and said to Him, "Rabboni!" which is to say, "Teacher!"

> *Rev 1:17,18 And when I saw Him, I fell at His feet as dead. And He laid His right hand upon me, saying unto me, "Fear not; I am the First and the Last...I am He that liveth, and was dead; and behold, I am alive forevermore, Amen; and have the keys of hell and of death."*

Jn 20:17   Jesus said to her, **"DO NOT HOLD ME, FOR I HAVE NOT YET ASCENDED TO MY FATHER. BUT GO TO MY BROTHERS, AND TELL THEM, 'I AM ASCENDING TO MY FATHER AND YOUR FATHER, TO MY GOD AND YOUR GOD.'"**

810 MARY MAGDALENE GOES TO THE UPPER ROOM TO REPORT TO THE GRIEVING DISCIPLES THAT SHE HAS ACTUALLY SEEN THE "LORD OF LIFE" (Mk 16:9-11; Lk 24:8-12; Jn 20:18)

Mk 16:10 She went and told those who had been with Him, as they mourned and wept.

Jn 20:18 Mary Magdalene told the disciples that she had seen the Lord, and that He had said these things to her.

Mk 16:11 When they heard that He was alive, and had been seen by her, they did not believe her.

811 ALONG THE WAY THE WANDERING, FEARFUL WOMEN MEET THEIR SAVIOR (Mt 28:9,10; Lk 24:9-11)

Mt 28:9 And lo, Jesus met the women on the road saying, **"REJOICE!"** They came and took hold of His feet, and worshiped Him.

Mt 28:10 Then Jesus said to them, **"DO NOT BE AFRAID. GO TELL MY BROTHERS THAT THEY SHOULD GO INTO GALILEE, AND THERE THEY WILL SEE ME."**

Lk 24:9 They returned from the tomb, and told all these things to the eleven, and to all the rest.

Lk 24:11 These words seemed to them to be nonsense, and they did not believe even them.

812 GUARDS REPORT TO THE JEWISH AUTHORITIES AND ARE BRIBED TO LIE (Mt 28:11-15)

Mt 28:11 Some of the guards came into the city, and told the chief priests all the things that had happened.

Mt 28:12 When they were assembled with the elders, and had taken counsel, they gave a large amount of silver to the soldiers,

Mt 28:13 saying, "Say that His disciples came by night, and stole Him away while we slept."

> *1 Cor 1:23,24 But we preach Christ crucified, unto the Jews a stumbling-block, and unto the Greeks foolishness...but unto them that are called, both Jews and Greeks, Christ the POWER OF GOD, and the WISDOM OF GOD.*

813   *AND SO THE DISBELIEVING JEWS MAINTAIN THEIR TRADITION TO THIS DAY (Mt 28:14,15)*

Mt 28:14 "If this comes to the governor's ears, we will persuade him and hold you harmless."

Mt 28:15 So they took the money and did as they were told. This saying was spread abroad among the Jews, and continues until the present time.

> *(The Jewish nation is still waiting for its Messiah after 5,770 years, as though all the many prophecies in the Old Testament about Jesus should be duplicated—in spite of being totally fulfilled two thousand years ago.)*

814   *JESUS MEETS TWO OF HIS FOLLOWERS ON THE ROAD TO EMMAUS (Mk 16:12; Lk 24:13-35)*

Mk 16:12 After these things He was revealed in another manner to two of them, as they walked on their way in the country.

Lk 24:13 The two of them were going that very day to a village named Emmaus, which was seven miles from Jerusalem.

Lk 24:14 They were talking with each other about all of the things which had happened.

Lk 24:15 While they talked and reasoned together, Jesus Himself came near, and walked along side of them.

Lk 24:16 But their eyes were kept from recognizing Him.

Lk 24:17 He said to them, **"WHAT ARE YOU TALKING ABOUT AS YOU WALK, AND ARE SAD?"**

815   *THE NEWS OF THEIR DEAD "LIBERATOR," IS WELL KNOWN TO EVERYONE (Lk 24:18-21)*

Lk 24:18 One of them, named Cleopas, answered Him, "Are you the only stranger in Jerusalem who does not know the things which have happened there, these last few days?"

Lk 24:19 He said to them, **"WHAT THINGS?"** They said to Him, "The things concerning Jesus, the Nazarene, who was a Prophet mighty in deed and word, before God and all the people,

Lk 24:20 and how the chief priests and our rulers delivered Him up to be condemned to death, and had Him crucified.

Lk 24:21 But we were hoping that it was He who would free Israel. Yes, and besides all this, it is now the third day since these things happened." *(The Jews considered any part of a day as a full day.)*

816   *THE MISSING BODY WAS EVEN VERIFIED (Lk 24:22-24)*

Lk 24:22 "Also, certain women of our company surprised us, having arrived early at the tomb.

Lk 24:23 And when they did not find His body, they came saying that they had also seen a vision of angels, who said that He was alive.

Lk 24:24 Some of our people went to the tomb, and found it just like the women had said, but they did not see Him."

817   *JESUS, THE "FULFILLER OF PROPHECY" THEN GIVES THEM A HISTORY LESSON ABOUT THE MANY PREDICTIONS IN THE OLD TESTAMENT OF THE MESSIAH'S SUFFERINGS AND DEATH (Lk 24:25-27)*

Lk 24:25 He said to them, **"O FOOLISH MEN, AND SLOW OF HEART TO BELIEVE ALL THAT THE PROPHETS HAVE SPOKEN!**

Lk 24:26 DID NOT THE CHRIST HAVE TO SUFFER THESE THINGS AND THEN ENTER INTO HIS GLORY?"

Lk 24:27 Beginning from Moses and from all the prophets, He explained to them all the many prophecies concerning Himself.

> *Jn 5:39 Search the scriptures; for in them you think you have eternal life and they are they which testify of Me.*

818   *HE RE-ENACTS THE LORD'S SUPPER WHICH OPENS THEIR EYES TO RECOGNIZING HIM (Lk 24:28-32)*

Lk 24:28 They drew near to the village, where they were going, and He acted like He would go further.

Lk 24:29 They urged Him, saying, "Stay with us, for it is almost evening, and the day is almost over." He went in to stay with them.

Lk 24:30 It happened, that when He had sat down at the table with them, He took the bread and gave thanks. Breaking it, He gave it to them.

Lk 24:31 That is when their eyes were opened, and they recognized Him. Then He vanished out of their sight.

Lk 24:32 They said one to another, "Did not our hearts burn within us, as He spoke to us along the way, when He revealed the Scriptures to us?"

819   *ON THAT RESURRECTION NIGHT, THE DISCIPLES CONTINUE TO EXPRESS THEIR DISBELIEF (Mk 16:13; Lk 24:33-35)*

Lk 24:33 They rose up that very hour, returned to Jerusalem, and found the eleven gathered together, and those who were with them,

Lk 24:34 saying, "The Lord is risen indeed, and has appeared to Simon!"

Lk 24:35 They related the things that happened along the way, and how He was recognized by them in the breaking of the bread.

Mk 16:13 They did not believe them, either.

> *(For those who believe, no explanation is necessary. For those who do not believe, no explanation is possible)*

820   *JESUS, THE "CONQUEROR OVER THE GRAVE," APPEARS TO TEN ASSEMBLED DISCIPLES (Lk 24:36-40; Jn 20:19,20)*

Jn 20:19 When it was evening on that first day of the week, the doors were locked where the disciples were assembled for fear of the Jews. Jesus came and stood in their midst, and said to them, **"PEACE BE UNTO YOU."**

Lk 24:37 But they were terrified and filled with fear, and supposed that they were seeing a ghost.

Lk 24:38 He said to them, **"WHY ARE YOU ALARMED? WHY DO DOUBTS ARISE IN YOUR HEARTS?**

Lk 24:39 SEE <u>MY HANDS</u> *(not my wrists)* **AND MY FEET, THAT IT IS TRULY I. TOUCH ME AND SEE, FOR A SPIRIT DOES NOT HAVE FLESH AND BONES, AS YOU SEE THAT I HAVE."**

Lk 24:40 When He had said this, He showed them His hands, and His feet.

> *Jn 14:19 Yet a little while, and the world seeth me no more; but ye will see me, because I live, ye shall live also!*

821   JESUS THE "DEATH OVERCOMER," BREATHES ON HIS FOLLOWERS TO PASS HIS SPIRIT ON TO THEM (Jn 20:20-23)

Jn 20:21   Jesus therefore said to them again, **"PEACE BE TO YOU. AS THE FATHER HAS SENT ME, EVEN SO I SEND YOU."**

Jn 20:22   When He had said this, <u>He breathed on them</u>, and said to them, **"RECEIVE YE THE HOLY SPIRIT!** *(See Jn 7:39)*

Jn 20:23   **IF YOU FORGIVE ANYONE'S SINS, THEY HAVE BEEN FORGIVEN. BUT IF YOU RETAIN ANYONE'S SINS, THEY ARE RETAINED."**

822   JESUS SCOLDS THEM FOR THEIR LACK OF FAITH BUT THEY ARE EXCITED WITH JOY THAT HE IS ALIVE (Mk 16:14; Lk 24:41-43; Jn 20:20)

Mk 16:14   He rebuked them for their unbelief and hardness of heart, because they did not trust those who had seen Him after He had risen.

Lk 24:41   ...And though they found it hard to believe yet they were full of joy. He said to them, **"DO YOU HAVE ANYTHING HERE TO EAT?"**

Lk 24:42   They gave Him a piece of a broiled fish and some honeycomb.

Lk 24:43   He took it, and ate in front of them.

Jn 20:20   ...The disciples were very glad when they saw the Lord.

823   OUR TRUE "GOD OF THE BIBLE" ELABORATES AGAIN ON SCRIPTURE PROPHECIES ABOUT HIS REDEEMING SUFFERINGS (Lk 24:44-46)

Lk 24:44   He said to them, **"THIS IS WHAT I TOLD YOU, WHILE I WAS STILL WITH YOU, THAT ALL THINGS WHICH ARE FORETOLD IN THE LAW OF MOSES, THE PROPHETS, AND THE PSALMS CONCERNING ME HAD TO BE FULFILLED!"**

Lk 24:45   Then He opened their minds, that they might understand the Scriptures.

Lk 24:46   He said to them, **"THUS IT IS WRITTEN, AND THUS IT WAS NECESSARY FOR CHRIST TO SUFFER AND TO RISE FROM THE DEAD, ON THE THIRD DAY."**

> *1 Cor 15:17 If Christ has not been raised, your faith is vain and you are still in your sins.*

824   DOUBTING THOMAS REFUSES TO BELIEVE THAT JESUS IS ALIVE (Jn 20:24,25)

Jn 20:24 But Thomas, one of the twelve, called Didymus, was not with them when Jesus came.

Jn 20:25 The other disciples therefore said to him, "We have seen the Lord!" But he said to them, "Unless I see <u>in His hands</u> the print of the nails, and put my hand into His side, I will not believe."

825   JESUS, THE "PIERCED MESSIAH," APPEARS A WEEK LATER TO THE ELEVEN DISCIPLES, WITH THOMAS PRESENT (Jn 20:26-29)

Jn 20:26 After eight days His disciples were within, and Thomas was with them. Jesus came again, the doors being locked, and stood in their midst, and said, **"PEACE BE TO YOU."**

Jn 20:27 Then He said to Thomas, **"REACH HERE YOUR FINGER, AND SEE <u>MY HANDS</u>.** *(Because of all His fasting, off and on, He was not that heavy, that the Roman nails had to be driven through his wrists).* **REACH HERE YOUR HAND, AND PUT IT INTO MY SIDE. DO NOT BE UNBELIEVING, BUT BELIEVING."**

Jn 20:28 Thomas answered Him, "My Lord! And my God!"

> *Rom 10:9 ...if thou shalt confess with thy mouth the Lord Jesus, and shalt believe in thine heart that God hath raised Him from the dead, thou shalt be saved.*

Jn 20:29 Jesus said to him, **"BECAUSE YOU HAVE SEEN ME, YOU HAVE BELIEVED. BLESSED ARE THOSE WHO HAVE NOT SEEN ME, AND DO BELIEVE."**

826   HIS SEVENTH APPEARANCE IS TO SEVEN OF THE DISCIPLES FISHING ON LAKE TIBERIAS (Jn 21:1-24)

Jn 21:1 After these things, Jesus revealed Himself again to the disciples at the sea of Tiberias. He made Himself known in this manner;

Jn 21:2 Simon Peter, Thomas, Nathanael of Cana in Galilee, and the sons of Zebedee, and two others of His disciples were together.

Jn 21:3 Simon Peter said to them, "I am going fishing." They told him, "We are also coming with you." They immediately went out, and entered into the boat. That night, they caught nothing.

Jn 21:4 But when day had already come, Jesus stood on the beach, yet the disciples did not know that it was Jesus.

827   JESUS BRINGS ABOUT A SECOND MIRACULOUS CATCH OF FISH, TO ONCE AGAIN REVEAL THE LORD'S PROVIDENCE (Jn 21:5-8)

Jn 21:5   Jesus therefore said to them, **"CHILDREN, HAVE YOU CAUGHT ANYTHING TO EAT?"** They answered Him, "No."

> *Rev. 21:7 He that overcomes shall inherit all things. And I (Jesus) shall be his God, and he will be <u>My son</u>. (As Jesus earnestly followed His Heavenly Father in every respect, we will follow in the footsteps of Jesus. And as He says in this Rev 21:7, we will become His sons, and no longer just His brothers.)*

Jn 21:6   He said to them, **"CAST THE NET ON THE RIGHT SIDE OF THE BOAT, AND YOU WILL FIND SOME."** They cast it and now they were not able to draw it in for the quantity of fish.

Jn 21:7   That disciple therefore whom Jesus loved said to Peter, "It is the Lord!" So when Simon Peter heard that it was the Lord, he wrapped his garment around himself, for he had removed it, and threw himself into the sea.

Jn 21:8   But the other disciples came in the little boat for they were not far from land, about a hundred yards away, dragging the net full of fish.

828   OUR "HOLY KING," PREPARES A MEAL FOR HIS BELOVED FOLLOWERS (Jn 21:9-14)

Jn 21:9   So when they got on the land, they saw a fire of coals there, and fish laid on it, and bread.

Jn 21:10   Jesus said to them, **"BRING SOME OF THE FISH WHICH YOU HAVE JUST CAUGHT."**

Jn 21:11   Simon Peter went up and helped pull the net to land, full of great fish, one hundred fifty-three, and even though there were so many the net did not tear.

Jn 21:12   Jesus said to them, **"COME AND EAT."** None of the disciples dared inquire of Him, "Who are you?" knowing that it was the Lord.

Jn 21:13   Then Jesus came and took the bread, gave it to them, and the fish likewise.

Jn 21:14   This is now the third time that Jesus was revealed to His disciples as a group, after He had risen from the dead.

829 PETER'S THREE DENIALS ARE FORGIVEN BY THREE REQUESTS TO SHEPHERD GOD'S FLOCK (Jn 21:15-17)

Jn 21:15 So when they had eaten their breakfast, Jesus said to Simon Peter, **"SIMON, SON OF JONAH, DO YOU LOVE ME MORE THAN THESE OTHERS DO?"** He said to Him, "Yes, Lord, You know that I love You." Jesus said to him, **"FEED MY LAMBS."**

Jn 21:16 He said to him again a second time, **"SIMON, SON OF JONAH, DO YOU LOVE ME?"** Simon said to Him, "Yes, Lord, You know that I love You dearly." Jesus said to him, **"TEND MY SHEEP."**

Jn 21:17 He said to him the third time, **"SIMON, SON OF JONAH, DO YOU LOVE ME?"** Peter was grieved because He asked him the third time, "Do you love Me?" He said to Him, "Lord, You know everything. You know that I love You." Jesus said to him, **"FEED MY SHEEP."**

830 PETER IS TO FOLLOW THE LORD'S LEADING, EVEN THROUGH THE PORTAL OF DEATH (Jn 21:18,19)

Jn 21:18 **"MOST CERTAINLY I TELL YOU, WHEN YOU WERE YOUNG, YOU DRESSED YOURSELF, AND WALKED WHERE YOU WANTED TO. BUT WHEN YOU ARE OLD, YOU WILL STRETCH OUT YOUR HANDS, AND ANOTHER WILL BIND YOU, AND PULL YOU WHERE YOU DO NOT WANT TO GO."**

Jn 21:19 Now He said this signifying by what kind of death Peter would glorify God. When He had said this, He said to him, **"FOLLOW ME."** *(Jesus on 12 separate occasions said the words, "Follow Me.")*

831 PETER ENQUIRES OF JESUS REGARDING THE APOSTLE JOHN (Jn 21:20-24)

Jn 21:20 Then Peter, turning around, saw a disciple following. This was the disciple whom Jesus loved, the one who had also leaned on Jesus' breast at the supper and had asked, "Lord, who is going to betray You?"

Jn 21:21 Peter seeing him, said to Jesus, "Lord, what about this man?"

Jn 21:22 Jesus said to him, **"IF I DESIRE THAT HE STAY UNTIL I COME, WHAT CONCERN IS THAT TO YOU? YOU JUST FOLLOW ME."**

> *(Being a Christian does not mean going to a certain church, or belonging to a given denomination. Being a Christian means to think, to talk, and to act, as Jesus would, if He were to walk the earth today among us.)*

Jn 21:23 The saying therefore got out among the brothers, that this disciple would not die. Yet

Jesus did not say to him that he would not die, but, **"IF I DESIRE THAT HE STAY UNTIL I COME, WHAT IS THAT TO YOU?"**

832   *"JESUS, ALSO APPEARS TO A NUMBER OF BELIEVERS (1 Cor 15:5-7; Acts 1:3)*

1 Cor 15:6 Then He appeared to over five hundred followers all at once, most of whom remain until now, but some have also fallen asleep.

> *1 Pet 2:9 But ye are a chosen generation, a royal priesthood, a holy nation, a peculiar people, that ye should show forth the praises of Him who hath called you out of darkness into His marvelous light.*

1 Cor 15:7 Then He appeared to James *(His half-brother)*, then to all the apostles,

> *(Jesus made not just one appearance, as shown in just about every "Jesus movie," but He made numerous appearances as revealed in these gospels and epistle letters.)*

Acts 1:3 To these He also showed Himself alive after He suffered, by many convincing proofs, appearing to them over a period of forty days, and speaking about the importance of God's Kingdom.

> *(The Muslims believe that someone else died in His place. The Jews, who were there in great numbers, and who followed Him all the way to the Cross know better. Except that they believe someone stole the body. Both are sincerely wrong as proven by all His many appearances, and the fact that many chose to die than to renounce Him.)*

833   *FOLLOWING HIS COMPLETE SUBMISSION TO HIS FATHER'S WILL, OUR "FOCUS OF GLORY," IS NOW GIVEN DOMINION OVER ABSOLUTELY EVERYTHING (Mt 28:16-18)*

Mt 28:16 The eleven disciples then went into Galilee, to the mountain where Jesus had sent them.

Mt 28:17 When they saw Him, they bowed down to Him, but some were cautious.

Mt 28:18 Jesus came to them and spoke to them, saying, **"ALL POWER HAS BEEN GIVEN TO ME IN HEAVEN AND ON EARTH."**

> *(You and God will always make a majority.)*

834   *SOLDIERS OF THE CROSS ARE TO TELL NO LESS THAN THE ENTIRE WORLD OF GOD'S LOVE AND ACCEPTANCE (Mk 16:15,16)*

Mk 16:15 He said to them, **"YOU GO INTO ALL THE WORLD, AND PREACH THE GOOD NEWS TO ALL MANKIND.** *(Without God you cannot. Without you He will not.)*

Mk 16:16 HE WHO BELIEVES YOU AND IS BAPTIZED WILL BE SAVED, BUT HE WHO DOES NOT BELIEVE YOU WILL BE CONDEMNED."

2 Tim 4:5 But watch thou in all things, endure afflictions, do the work of an evangelist, make full proof of thy ministry.

835   SPECIAL ANOINTINGS ARE GIVEN TO THOSE WHO HAVE FAITH IN JESUS *(Mk 16:17,18)*

Mk 16:17 "THESE SIGNS WILL FOLLOW THOSE WHO BELIEVE. IN MY NAME THEY WILL CAST OUT DEMONS, THEY WILL SPEAK WITH NEW LANGUAGES,

Mk 16:18 THEY WILL TAKE UP SERPENTS. AND EVEN IF THEY DRINK ANY DEADLY THING, IT WILL IN NO WAY HURT THEM. THEY WILL LAY HANDS ON THE SICK, AND THEY WILL RECOVER."

1 Cor 4:20 For the Kingdom of God is not in word, but in power.

836   JESUS THEN GIVES THEM THEIR 'GREAT COMMISSION' *(Mt 28:19,20; Acts 26:18)*

Mt 28:19 "GO, AND MAKE DISCIPLES OF ALL NATIONS, BAPTIZING THEM IN THE NAME OF THE FATHER, AND OF THE SON, AND OF THE HOLY SPIRIT. *(The Holy Trinity)*

Mt 28:20 TEACH THEM TO OBSERVE ALL THINGS THAT I HAVE COMMANDED YOU...

Jer 26:2 "...speak all the words that I command thee to speak...diminish not a word."

Acts 26:18 You are to open their eyes, that they may turn from darkness to light and from the power of Satan to God, that they may receive pardon for their sins, and an inheritance among those who are sanctified, by their faith in Me."

(God will keep building His church with or without you. You can become a big beneficiary in His kingdom, by winning as many souls as possible for the Lord, while you have time.)

837   FORGIVENESS FOR SINS IS AVAILABLE TO ALL PEOPLE, EVERYWHERE *(Lk 24:47-49)*

Lk 24:47 "AND THAT REPENTANCE AND REMISSION OF SINS SHOULD BE PREACHED IN MY NAME, TO ALL THE NATIONS, BEGINNING AT JERUSALEM.

Ps 122:6 Pray for the peace of Jerusalem. They shall prosper that love thee.

Lk 24:48 YOU ARE WITNESSES OF THESE THINGS.

Lk 24:49 AND I WILL SEND FORTH THE PROMISE OF MY FATHER ON YOU. SO WAIT UNTIL YOU ARE FILLED WITH POWER FROM ON HIGH."

(This verse together with Jn 14:23 could have the entire Trinity living within you.)

838   BACK IN JERUSALEM CHRIST-FOLLOWERS ARE TOLD TO EARNESTLY SEEK THE HOLY SPIRIT – UNTIL THEY RECEIVE HIM *(Acts 1:4,5)*

Acts 1:4   Being assembled together with them, He commanded them, **"DO NOT DEPART FROM JERUSALEM, BUT WAIT FOR THE PROMISE OF THE FATHER, WHICH YOU HEARD FROM ME.**

Acts 1:5   **FOR JOHN INDEED BAPTIZED IN WATER, BUT YOU WILL BE BAPTIZED IN THE HOLY SPIRIT** *(Peace of God, Sweet Spirit, Spirit of Holiness)* **NOT MANY DAYS FROM NOW."**

(Once we receive Jesus as our Lord and Savior, His Holy Spirit begins to change us into His likeness.)

839   FROM THE MOUNT OF OLIVES, THE DISCIPLES EXPRESS CONTINUED CONCERN FOR THE RESTORATION OF ISRAEL BUT JESUS AGAIN REFERS TO WHAT IS MORE IMPORTANT *(Mt 28:20; Acts 1:6-8)*

Acts 1:6   Therefore when they had come together, they asked Him, "Lord, will You now restore the kingdom to Israel?"

Acts 1:7   He said to them, **"IT IS NOT FOR YOU TO KNOW THE TIME OR THE SEASON, WHICH THE FATHER HAS DETERMINED BY HIS OWN AUTHORITY.**

Acts 1:8   **BUT YOU WILL RECEIVE POWER WHEN THE HOLY SPIRIT** *(Counselor, Oil of Gladness, Promised Advocate)* **HAS COME UPON YOU. YOU WILL BE WITNESSES ON MY BEHALF IN JERUSALEM, IN ALL JUDEA AND SAMARIA, AND TO THE REMOTEST PARTS OF THE EARTH.**

(That the flames of genuine love in our hearts may spread from where we are, to the world.)

Mt 28:20   ...BEHOLD, I AM WITH YOU ALWAYS, EVEN TO THE END OF THE AGE!"

(Ours is the only religion in the world which can truly say, "God with us.")

840   JESUS, THE "RETURNING KING," IS RAPTURED UP INTO HEAVEN WHERE HE PATIENTLY WAITS FOR YOU (Mk 16:19; Lk 24:50-53; Acts 1:9)

Lk 24:50   And He lifted up His hands, and blessed them.

Lk 24:51   It happened, while He was blessing them, that He departed from them, and was carried up into heaven.

Acts 1:9   As they were looking, a cloud received Him out of their sight.

Mk 16:19   And He sat down at the right hand of Almighty God.

> *1 Pet 3:22 Who is gone into heaven, and is on the right hand of God; angels and authorities and powers being made subject unto Him.*

841   ANGELS TELL THE DISCIPLES THAT THEY WILL SEE JESUS AGAIN (Acts 1:10,11)

Acts 1:10   While they were looking steadfastly into the sky as He went, behold, two men in white clothing stood by them,

Acts 1:11   who said, "You men of Galilee, why do you stand looking into heaven? This same Jesus, who was taken up from you into the sky will come back in much the same way as you saw Him going into heaven."

> *Rev 1:7   Behold, He is coming with the clouds, and every eye will see Him, including those who pierced Him. All the tribes of the earth will mourn over Him.*

842   THE DISCIPLES RETURN, PAYING HOMAGE TO THE "EVER-PRESENT LORD" (Lk 24:52,53; Acts 1:12)

Acts 1:12   Then they returned to Jerusalem <u>from the mountain called Olivet</u>, which is near Jerusalem, a Sabbath day's journey away.

Lk 24:52   They worshiped Him, and returned with great joy.

Lk 24:53   And were continually in the temple, praising and blessing God.

843   THEY JOIN OTHER FOLLOWERS IN FELLOWSHIP AND WORSHIP (Acts 1:13-15)

Acts 1:13   When they had come in, they also went up into the upper room, where they were staying; that is Peter, John, James, Andrew, Philip, Thomas, Bartholomew, Matthew, James the son of Alphaeus, Simon the Zealot, and Judas the son of James.

Acts 1:14 All these with one accord continued steadfastly in prayer and supplication, along with the women, and Mary, the mother of Jesus, and with His brothers.

Acts 1:15 ...and the number was about one hundred and twenty.

844 THE HOLY SPIRIT COMES UPON THE BELIEVERS AS JESUS PROMISED (Acts 2:1-18)

Acts 2:1 Now when the day of Pentecost had come, they were all in one accord, in one place.

Acts 2:2 Suddenly there came from heaven a sound like the rushing of a mighty wind, and it filled the entire house where they were sitting.

Acts 2:3 Tongues like fire appeared, and it sat on each one of them.

Acts 2:4 They were all filled with the Holy Spirit *(All Seeing Spirit, Divine Helper, Spirit of Liberty)*. And began to speak in other languages, as the Spirit gave them the ability to speak.

845 SUCH WAS PROPHESIED CENTURIES EARLIER BY THE PROPHET JOEL THAT THIS WOULD HAPPEN (Acts 2:16-18)

Acts 2:16 But this is what has been spoken through the prophet Joel:

Acts 2:17 'It will come in the last days, says God, that I will pour out My Spirit on all flesh. Your sons and your daughters will prophesy. Your young men will see visions. Your old men will dream dreams. *(Joel 2:28,29)*

Acts 2:18 On My servants and on My handmaidens in those days, I will pour out My Spirit. *(Spirit of the Lord, God Manifested, and Very God)*.

846 BEING BOLD IN THE LORD WILL PRODUCE EVEN MORE BELIEVERS FOR THE KINGDOM (Acts 2:38 to 5:14)

Acts 2:38 Then Peter said unto them, "Repent, and be baptized every one of you in the name of Jesus Christ for the remission of sins, and ye shall receive the gift of the Holy Spirit."

Acts 4:12 ...for there is no other name under heaven given among man, whereby we must be saved.

Acts 4:20 For we cannot but speak the things which we have seen and heard.

Acts 4:33 And with great power gave the apostles witness of the resurrection of the Lord Jesus.

And grace was upon them all.

Acts 5:14 And believers were all the more added to the Lord, multitudes both of men and women.

> *Ps 145:4 One generation shall praise thy works to another, and shall declare mighty acts.*

847   "CHRIST OUR LORD'S" TIMID, WEAK, FAITHLESS, FLAWED FOLLOWERS SOON BECOME LEADERS, HEALERS, TEACHERS, SOUL WINNERS, THROUGH JESUS— AND THE CHURCH IS BORN (Mk 16:20; Acts 5:29,41,42; 6:7)

Acts 5:29 Then Peter and the other disciples answered and said, "We ought to obey God rather than men."

Acts 5:41 (*After being beaten for preaching in the temple*) The disciples departed from the presence of the council, rejoicing that they were counted worthy to suffer shame for Jesus' name.

> (*People have been known to lie, to get out of punishment. But no one would lie about the resurrection of Jesus, only to be punished and some even tortured into martyrdom— if it were not true.*)

Acts 5:42 Nevertheless every day, in the temple and in every house, they never stopped teaching and preaching Jesus, the Christ.

> *1 Cor 2:1,2 When I came to you, brothers. I did not come with excellence of speech or of wisdom, proclaiming to you the testimony of God...for I determined not to know anything among you, except Jesus Christ, and Him crucified.*

Mk 16:20 They went out, and preached everywhere, the Lord working with them, and confirming the Word by the miracles that followed.

> *Gal 6:14 But God forbid that I should glory (in any personal pride), save in the cross of our Lord Jesus Christ...*

848   EVERYONE IS INVITED TO SHARE IN THE HARVEST OF SOULS BY GIVING THAT MESSAGE OF HOPE AND JOY TO OTHERS (Acts 6:7; 13:47; 19:2)

Acts 6:7 The word of God increased. And the number of the disciples multiplied in Jerusalem exceedingly. A great company of the priests were also obedient to the faith.

> *1 Pet 3:15 ...be ready at all times to give a reason for the hope that is in you...*

Ps 107:2 Let the redeemed of the Lord say so…

Mt 5:14 You are the light of world…

Acts 13:47 …I have set thee to be a light to the gentiles, that thou should be salvation to them until the ends of the earth.

Lk 5:4 …Launch out into the deep…

Mt 20:6 …Why do you stand here all day idle?

1 Cor 9:16 …Woe is unto me if I preach not the Gospel.

Lk 19:13 …Occupy till I come.

*(We have only one life to live, t'will soon be past.
Only what's done for Christ will last.)*

Acts 19:2 …Have ye received the Holy Ghost since ye believed?...

Rom 8:9 … if any man have not the Spirit of Christ, he is none of His.

Lk 11:13 … how much more shall your heavenly Father give the Holy Spirit to them that ask Him?

EPILOGUE

Jn 20:30   Therefore Jesus did many other signs in the presence of His disciples, which are not written in this book.

Jn 20:31   But these are written, that you may believe that Jesus is the Christ, the Son of God, and that believing you may have Life, in His name.

Jn 21:24   This is the disciple who certifies these things, and who wrote these things down. And we know that his testimony is true.

Jn 21:25   There are also many other things that Jesus did, which if they would all be written, I suppose that even the world itself would not have room for the books that should be written.

1 Jn 5:13   These things have I written unto you that believe on the name of the Son of God; <u>that ye may know</u> that ye have eternal life, and that ye may believe on the name of the Son of God.

2 Pet 1:16 For we did not follow cunningly devised fables, when we made known to you the power, and coming of our Lord Jesus Christ, because we were eyewitnesses of His majesty.

2 Cor 1:3   Blessed be God, the Father of our Lord Jesus, the Father of Mercies, and the God of All Comfort.

2 Cor 13:14   The grace of the Lord Jesus Christ, and the love of God, and the communion of the Holy Spirit, be with you all.

2 Cor 13:13   All the saints salute you.

1 Thes 5:16   Rejoice evermore.

WHAT NOW?

What you have read may be merely your first meaningful introduction to your Lord and Savior. He loves you and wants the very best for you. He went so far as to suffer and die, that you would be saved and spend all of eternity with Him, in glory.

You may want to read this book over and over again to master its eternal and life-giving principles. You may also wish to distribute copies to your friends.

I have already read the four gospels some 37 times, sometimes as they are given to us, and sometimes harmonized (blended) into a single narrative such as in this format, and even in different translations. It is amazing how I continue to learn something new each time and find myself often asking, "Lord, when did You put that in there?"

For more information on the early Church, you can continue to read the book of Acts, considered to be the fifth gospel, which is the second book that Luke wrote.

Get into a Bible believing church. Reach out to others. If eternity is so vast and everlasting for you, it could be for others, whom you can reach as well.

Practice the presence of God. Pray and talk to Him regularly. Do seek the Holy Spirit daily. Be sure to have your own Bible in a translation you can understand. It will not take long for you to develop a "personal relationship" with Him.

The door of mercy may not be open much longer. You must heed the glorious promises of heaven, and of the fearful warnings of hell. If you are one of those who has not yet accepted the Lord, and wish to do so at this time, just pray the following prayer keeping in mind that without true repentance, there is no forgiveness of sins. Repeat each phrase, with meaning.

Dear Father God... I come to You just as I am... I am very sorry for all my offences... against You... against my fellow man... and even against myself.

I accept the sacrifice You offered... when You sent Your own Son... to carry my cross... to suffer in my place... and to nail all my sins on the cross... I renounce Satan and all his works... I turn away from wrong doing... From now on I have a new Lord... His name is Jesus.

And I thank You Lord Jesus... for having mercy on me... a sinner... I know You will be patient with me... and You will teach me each day... what You want me to know... And because You chose to die for me... I now choose to live for You... Come into my heart.. and live Your life through me.

And do give me more and more... of Your most Holy Spirit... of the Most High God... And thank You... that Your angels and saints... are rejoicing in heaven... over my new start... this day. Amen

PERSONAL OBSERVATIONS

Only Matthew and Luke's Gospels tell us of the birth of Jesus. He is thirty years old when Mark and John begin their Gospels.

Both Mark and John's Gospels are in perfect chronological order. The other two are not entirely in a proper sequence. Nevertheless, the entire contents of all four have been included in this presentation.

As you have read, the Gospel of Matthew brings out the royalty of Jesus, Mark details His service to mankind, Luke highlights His sensitivity to humanity, and John affirms His divine origin.

Matthew, Mark and Luke often cover the same events, and are frequently referred to as the "synoptics." John's Gospel is 93% original, with about 7% overlapping the other three. The feeding of the 5,000 is the first occasion in which all four evangelists write about the same event.

It seems Jesus met the most resistance as He got closer to Jerusalem. He also received the most acceptance as He got further away from Jerusalem.

Jesus shared many theological messages while He walked the earth. But He also gave us numerous examples of kindness in human relationships.

John the Baptist said, "I am not fit to untie His sandals." Yet later Jesus kneels to wash the disciples feet. He blesses the wine at Cana, yet He refuses the wine when they are about to crucify Him, which would have lessened the pain. He feeds the 5,000, but He Himself fasted 40 days without food. The primary Gospel message is one of self-sacrifice—to benefit another.

Also, Jesus was not afraid to come against the money changers, who often took advantage of other people. And He boldly confronted the Pharisees and scribes for their hypocrisy and improper theology.

Is there any significance to Jesus riding into Jerusalem on a borrowed colt of a donkey? To the Passover meal taking place in a borrowed upper room? To His being buried in a borrowed tomb?

Jesus had intense respect for the lowly. He will use you mightily (not just the ordained) when you likewise develop true love and compassion for those who are hurting, or in need.

OVERCOMERS

FROM THE BOOK OF THE REVELATION OF JESUS CHRIST

These are incentives to overcome addictions and bad habits so as to become more Christ-like.

...<u>TO HIM THAT OVERCOMETH</u>, will I give to eat of the Tree of Life which is in the midst of the Paradise of God. Rev 2:7

...<u>HE THAT OVERCOMETH</u>, shall not be hurt by the second death. Rev 2:11

...<u>TO HIM THAT OVERCOMETH</u>, will I give to eat of the hidden manna, and will give him a white stone, and in the stone a new name written, which no man knoweth saving he that receiveth it. Rev 2:26

<u>AND HE THAT OVERCOMETH</u>, and keepeth My works unto the end, to him will I give power over the nations. Rev 2:26

And I will give him the Morning Star! Rev 2:28

<u>HE THAT OVERCOMETH</u>, the same shall be clothed in white raiment, and I will not blot out his name out of the Book of Life, but I will confess his name before My Father and before His angels. Rev 3:5

<u>HE THAT OVERCOMETH</u>, will I make a pillar in the temple of My God, and he shall go no more out. And I will write upon him the name of My God, and the name of the city of my God, which is the new Jerusalem, which cometh down out of heaven from My God, and I will write upon him My New Name. Rev 3:12

<u>TO HIM THAT OVERCOMETH</u>, will I grant to sit with Me on My throne, even as I also overcame, and am set down with My Father on His throne. Rev 3:21

<u>HE THAT OVERCOMETH</u>, shall inherit all things, and I will be his God, and he shall be my son. Rev 21:7

But the fearful, and unbelieving, and the abominable, and the murderers, and whoremongers, and sorcerers, and idolaters, and all liars, shall have their part in the lake which burneth with fire and brimstone—which is the second death. Rev 21:8

DIRECT WORDS OF PRAISE

ALSO FROM THE BOOK OF THE REVELATION

Holy, Holy, Holy, Lord God Almighty, who was, and is and is to come.   Rev 4:8

You are worthy, O Lord, to receive glory and honor, and power, for You have created all things, and for Your pleasure they are and were created.   Rev 4:11

You are worthy to take the book, and to open the seals thereof, for You were slain, and have redeemed us to God by Your blood for every tribe, and tongue, and people, and nation.   Rev 5:9

And have made us unto our God, kings and priests, and we shall reign on the earth.   Rev 5:10

Worthy is the Lamb that was slain to receive power, and riches, and wisdom, and strength, and honor, and glory, and blessing.   Rev 5:12

Blessing, and honor, and glory, and power be unto Him Who sits upon the throne, and to the Lamb for ever and ever.   Rev 5:13

Salvation to our God Who sits upon the throne, and to the Lamb.   Rev 7:10

Blessing, glory, and wisdom, and thanksgiving, and honor, and power and might, be to our God for ever and ever.   Rev 7:12

We give You thanks, O Lord God Almighty, Who is and was, and is to come, because You have taken to Yourself Your great power and have reigned.   Rev 11:17

Great and marvelous are Your works, Lord God Almighty, just and true are Your ways, O King of Saints.   Rev 15:3

Who shall not fear You, O Lord, and glorify Your name? For You alone are Holy. For all nations shall come and worship before You, for Your judgments are made manifest.   Rev 15:4

Alleluia, salvation, and glory, and honor, and power, to the Lord our God.   Rev 19:1

Praise our God, all you His servants, and you that fear Him, both small and great.   Rev 19:5

Alleluia, for the Lord God omnipotent reigns.   Rev 19:6

Let us be glad and rejoice, and give honor to Him, for the marriage of the Lamb is come, and His wife has made herself ready.   Rev 19:7

ABOUT THE AUTHOR

Paul L. LaLiberté was born in January, 1929 in Windsor Ontario, Canada, just across the river from Detroit, Michigan.

He was about 12 years old before he began to speak any appreciable amount of English.

He graduated from Assumption College in 1951 and then emigrated in the U.S. in 1954. Some eight years later he became a U.S. citizen, making his home in Toledo, Ohio for the next 45 years.

In the 1960's he had his name legally changed from Paul Leo LaLiberté to Paul L. Liberty, and currently uses both names interchangeably.

He spent 11 years in aerial photography. This consisted of photographing a close-up of farm homes and buildings from a low altitude, which were then sold to each individual farm owner.

His second successful career came in oil and gas exploration, in which he drilled a number of wells in Appalachia over a period of 10 years in the late 1960's and early 70's.

He accepted the Lord in 1979 at the age of 50. That is when he sold his meager oil and gas production and became a scripture scholar to delve into various Biblical projects, this book being one of them.

From the very beginning some 33 years ago he has worked, off and on, with this merging of the four Gospels, continually improving and perfecting it—this being his ninth "in-house" edition.

He is now 83 years old, in excellent heath, and is very active in the Lord's work.

> "The Lord gave the word: great was the company of those that published it."
> (Psalm 68:11)

You may request

additional copies of this book

for your friends and relatives

by ordering from 866-909-2665, or go to

xulonpress.com

This book is also available through

Amazon, Barnes and Nobles, and Google

Everyone should have their own printed book.

Yes, Brother Paul, I want to do my part to help change lives.

Enclosed is my (tax deductible) gift of $_____

_____ To distribute more of these books

_____ To advance your bibilical research

_____ To help translate this book into other languages

_____ Where most needed

Name _____

Address _____

_____

Email _____

Phone (optional) _____

Mail to:

Peter and Paul Gospel Ministries
P. O. Box 36793
Las Vegas, NV 89133-6793

"The generous soul will be made rich." Pr 11:25

Feel free to photocopy, or cut out this page, to mail in.